SYSTEMATIC THEOLOGY

ROMAN CATHOLIC PERSPECTIVES

Volume II

Francis Schüssler Fiorenza
and
John P. Galvin, Editors

FORTRESS PRESS   Minneapolis

Dedicated to the memory of
John A. Hollar

SYSTEMATIC THEOLOGY
Roman Catholic Perspectives, volume II

Scripture quotations unless otherwise noted are either from the Revised Standard Version of the Bible, copyright © 1946, 1952, and 1971 by the Division of Christian Education of the National Council of Churches, or from the New Revised Standard Version of the Bible, copyright © 1989 by the Division of Christian Education of the National Council of Churches.

Book design and typesetting by ediType
Cover and jacket design by Jim Gerhard

Library of Congress Cataloging-in-Publication Data

Systematic theology : Roman Catholic perspectives / Francis Schüssler
  Fiorenza and John P. Galvin, editors.
    p. cm.
  Includes bibliographical references and indexes.
  ISBN 0-8006-2460-2 (v. 1 : alk. paper)—ISBN
0-8006-2461-0 (v. 2 : alk. paper)
    1. Catholic Church—Doctrines. 2. Theology, Doctrinal.
  I. Fiorenza, Francis Schüssler. II. Galvin, John P., 1944–
  BX1751.2.S888 1991
  230'.2—dc20   91-678
                                                                  CIP

The paper used in this publication meets the minimum requirements of American National Standard for Information Sciences—Permanence of Paper for Printed Library Materials, ANSI Z329.48-1984   ∞™

Manufactured in the U.S.A.   AF 1-2461

95   94   93   92   91   1   2   3   4   5   6   7   8   9   10

CONTENTS

Volume I

Volume II

CONTRIBUTORS

Anne M. Clifford, C.S.J., is Assistant Professor of Theology at Duquesne University. Her publications include "Creation Science: Religion and Science in North American Culture," in William Shea, ed., *The Struggle over the Past: Fundamentalism in the Modern World.*

Regis A. Duffy, O.F.M., is Associate Professor of Theology at the University of Notre Dame. His publications include *Real Presence* (1982), *On Becoming Catholic* (1984), and *The American Emmaus* (1992).

Avery Dulles, S.J., is the Laurence J. McGinley Professor of Religion and Society at Fordham University. He is the author of fifteen books, including *Models of the Church* (1974), *Models of Revelation* (1983), and *The Reshaping of Catholicism* (1988).

Michael A. Fahey, S.J., is Dean and Professor of Ecclesiology and Ecumenism at the Faculty of Theology, St. Michael's College, University of Toronto. His most recent major publication is *Baptism, Eucharist, and Ministry: A Roman Catholic Perspective.*

Francis Schüssler Fiorenza is Charles Chauncey Stillman Professor of Roman Catholic Theological Studies at Harvard University. He is the author of *Foundational Theology: Jesus and the Church* (1984) and over eighty articles in the areas of systematic and foundational theology; he also co-edited and translated Friedrich Schleiermacher's *On the Glaubenslehre* (1981).

John P. Galvin is Associate Professor of Systematic Theology and Chair of the Department of Theology at The Catholic University of America. He has contributed to numerous theological journals, to *A World of Grace: An Introduction to the Themes and Foundations of Karl Rahner's Theology,* and to *The Praxis of Christian Experience: An Introduction to the Theology of Edward Schillebeeckx.*

Roger Haight, S.J., is Professor of Systematic Theology at Weston School of Theology. His latest book is *Dynamics of Theology* (1990).

Monika K. Hellwig is Landegger Distinguished University Professor of Theology at Georgetown University. Among her recent publications are *Jesus, the Compassion of God* and *Gladness Their Escort: Homiletic Reflections for Sundays and Feastdays, Years A, B, and C.*

Elizabeth A. Johnson, C.S.J., is Associate Professor of Theology at The Catholic University of America. She has published numerous journal articles and *Consider Jesus: Waves of Renewal in Christology* (1990).

Catherine Mowry LaCugna is Associate Professor of Theology at the University of Notre Dame. She has published numerous journal articles, and her book, *God for Us: The Trinity and Christian Life,* will be published in 1992.

David N. Power, O.M.I., is Professor in the Department of Theology at The Catholic University of America. His publications include *Worship: Culture and Theology* (1991), *The Sacrifice We Offer: The Tridentine Dogma and Its Reinterpretation* (1987), and *Unsearchable Riches: The Symbolic Nature of Liturgy* (1984).

David Tracy is the Andrew Thomas Greeley and Grace McNichols Greeley Distinguished Service Professor of Catholic Studies at the Divinity School, the University of Chicago; Professor in the Committee on the Analysis of Ideas and Study of Methods; and Professor in the Committee on Social Thought. A member of the American Academy of Arts and Sciences, his most recent works include *Plurality and Ambiguity* and *Paradigm Change in Theology* (with Hans Küng).

ABBREVIATIONS

AG   *Ad Gentes* (Vatican II's Decree on the Church's Missionary Activity)

DF   *Dei Filius* (Vatican I's Constitution on the Catholic Faith)

DS   H. Denzinger and A. Schönmetzer, eds., *Enchiridion Symbolorum*

DV   *Dei Verbum* (Vatican II's Constitution on Divine Revelation)

EM   *Eucharisticum Mysterium* (instruction of the Sacred Congregation of Rites)

GS   *Gaudium et Spes* (Vatican II's Pastoral Constitution on the Church in the Modern World)

LG   *Lumen Gentium* (Vatican II's Constitution on the Church)

NA   *Nostra Aetate* (Vatican II's Declaration on Non-Christian Religions)

PG   *Patrologia Graeca*, ed. J. B. Migne

PL   *Patrologia Latina*, ed. J. B. Migne

SC   *Sacrosanctum Concilium* (Vatican II's Constitution on the Sacred Liturgy)

UR   *Unitatis Redintegratio* (Vatican II's Decree on Ecumenism)

PREFACE

Preceding and following the Second Vatican Council, Roman Catholic theology experienced profound growth and development. These volumes seek to explain the major elements of Roman Catholic theology as it has developed in the wake of Vatican II. They are intended to present postconciliar theology as faithful to the Roman Catholic tradition, influenced by historical and ecumenical studies, open to new philosophical currents, and sensitive to diverse historical and cultural situations.

Planning for these volumes began a few years ago when John A. Hollar of Fortress Press and the editors agreed that a brief exposition of systematic theology from a Roman Catholic perspective would be a useful addition to current theological literature. Karl Rahner's *Foundations of Christian Faith* is an exemplary introduction to major areas of Roman Catholic theology. Yet its philosophical categories often pose a difficult challenge for the student of theology. Moreover, it does not cover several topics important to systematic theology. The need for a less advanced but more comprehensive treatment was obvious. Some classic treatments existed. Yet, preexisting Vatican II, they were somewhat dated. Several excellent catechetical and popular volumes existed. But they often presented the basics of Christian faith without reference to contemporary developments in theological method and categories. We therefore envisioned a collaborative work that would be comprehensive in its coverage, understandable to students, and centered around the current state of the question and the diverse developments in Roman Catholic theology since Vatican II.

In asking individual contributors to offer brief expositions of specific theological treatises, we requested that each contributor keep five specific goals in mind. First, the work was to be rooted in Roman Catholic theology. This goal did not mean that the authors should follow either the manualist deductive method or a one-sided apologetical approach that seeks to prove certain theses. Rather, it meant that individual authors had a double task: to present the teaching of the Roman Catholic church and to discuss significant contemporary Roman Catholic theological reflection. They should integrate into their exposition the relevant Roman Catholic teachings from, for example, Nicaea, Chalcedon, Trent, Vatican I and II, and papal documents, as applicable to the specific topic under discussion. They should make clear what the Roman Catholic teaching is in regard to specific topics. In addition, they should refer to the most significant contemporary theological proposals from leading Roman Catholic theologians (such as, Karl Rahner, Edward Schillebeeckx, Yves Congar, Henri de Lubac, Hans Urs von Balthasar, Joseph Ratzinger, Gustavo Gutiérrez, and others).

The authors, of course, would write from their own specific perspectives as theologians and as Roman Catholics. This goal explains the choice of the title and subtitle. The volumes deal primarily with systematic theology, hence the title; yet in dealing with the specific topics, they represent diverse Roman Catholic theological viewpoints, as the subtitle indicates. We did not intend a handbook of Roman Catholic faith, in the sense that a catechism or a collection of official church doctrines might be. Instead we wanted a work that would explain the diverse theological perspectives within Roman Catholic systematic theology in the post–Vatican II historical situation.

Second, a major impetus to Roman Catholic theology within the twentieth century has come from historical studies. These historical studies have enormously influenced diverse areas of Roman Catholic thought and life. The historical-critical study of the Scriptures has led not only to a much more nuanced understanding of the origins of Christianity, but has also made possible a great degree of ecumenical consensus, as is evident, for example, in the bilateral accords between Roman Catholic and Lutheran scholars about justification, Petrine ministry, and Mary. Historical studies of Christian writers of the ancient church have also influenced liturgical renewal and sacramental practices. Other historical studies have shown that dominant interpretations of Thomas often reflected the rationalistic spirit of the age in which they were written rather than the theology of Thomas. Studies of the Council of Trent and of Vatican I have shown that their decisions were much more nuanced and much more sensitive to historical complexities than scholars had previously thought.

In the light of such influences, the contributors were especially asked to highlight how historical studies have uncovered traditions that have been neglected—traditions that had become, in Karl Rahner's words, "the forgotten truths" of Catholicism. It is the achievement of Vatican II that its renewal of Roman Catholicism took place by means of a genuine struggle to reappropriate the tradition and wisdom of Catholicism.

Third, the contributors should take into account current hermeneutical theories and philosophical reflections. Many modern thinkers, from philosophy, sociology, history, and science, have influenced contemporary Roman Catholic thought. Philosophers such as Kant and Heidegger or Gadamer and Ricoeur have deeply affected contemporary theologians. Phenomenology as well as critical theory, literary theory as well as neopragmatism, have all had their impact. Individual authors will obviously have distinct philosophical and theological perspectives. Consequently, one or two perspectives might dominate in one contribution, whereas other perspectives will influence other contributors. In any event, the contributors were asked to spell out some of these influences in their contributions.

Fourth, contributors were asked to take into account the ecumenical dimension of theology, especially recent consensus and bilateral statements where relevant. They were to explain Roman Catholic theological statements in a way that is sensitive to other Christian churches, especially where the views of other Christians should lead Roman Catholic theologians to be more self-critical. The ecumenical context also requires that Roman Catholic theology not neglect its identity, and so the contributors were asked to make clear, where appropriate, the distinctive Roman Catholic theological position on various topics.

Fifth, the contributors were asked to be attentive to the current emphasis on practice, which has been especially highlighted in recent theologies of liberation. Roman Catholics and all Christians should be sensitive to the social and practical dimensions of their beliefs and reflections. The relation between theory and practice should not be seen simply as a concern of liberation theology in general or Latin American liberation theology in particular. Instead, it affects all aspects of theology. Many readers of the book will be engaged in diverse forms of ministry and come to theology with an ecclesial commitment. Thus the volumes should, where appropriate, address these concerns.

Of course, each contributor has addressed these five tasks in a distinct way. As individual contributors they reflect the diversity of contemporary Roman Catholic theology. Nevertheless, the above goals do provide the parameters for each contribution. Beyond these parameters, the editors did not intend to give the volume a specific theological orientation; nor did they seek to place the contributions within a uniform mold. Realizing that a collection of texts differs from the treatment of a single author and wanting to display the diversity within Roman Catholic theology, we decided that the volumes should follow the classic order of modern theological treatments. We sought to take into account the instructional order of many theological schools, especially in Master of Arts or Master of Divinity programs. Therefore, the order of the various treatises accords with the instructional order in many of these programs. The subject matter of the first volume is usually taught in the first or second year of studies, while the material in the second volume is usually covered in the second or third year.

In addition, it was our intention that the expositions would treat all of the major treatises within systematic theology, though not exhaustively. We did not intend that these two volumes should present the detail that a manual or textbook on an individual subject will provide. The volumes are not textbooks for individual courses in one or another locus. The size of individual treatises prohibits the required comprehensiveness. It is, however, hoped that the volumes serve as a survey and summary of many major topics covered in courses. They can also serve as review volumes for theological students seeking to survey the vast material that they have covered in their systematic theology courses. The volumes can perhaps also serve with some instructional guidance as introductory volumes that can present students with a view of the whole before they delve into the individual treatises. The volumes can also help those who have completed their formal theological education, but now seek some updating into the contemporary theological scene.

The editors wish to thank those who have helped us in various stages of the work's publication. We are especially thankful to J. Michael West of Fortress Press, who guided the manuscript to the final stages of its publication. We are especially grateful to Lucie Ferranti, John Gutierrez, Charles Kletzsch, David Lamberth, Frank Matera, Katherine Messina, and Elizabeth Pritchard for editorial and proofreading assistance.

The volumes are dedicated to the memory of John A. Hollar, the late Editorial Director of Fortress Press. The idea for the work came from discussions with him. Without his inspiration and vision, without his continued support and encouragement at the very early stages, these volumes might not have seen the light of day. He was attracted to the idea that a volume on systematic theology written by Roman Catholic theologians and published by a Lutheran-sponsored press would help make Roman Catholic theology available not only to Roman Catholics but also to a broader Protestant audience. It would also demonstrate to Roman Catholics the ecumenical character of the Fortress Press publishing program. His sudden and unexpected death brought sadness to all. If these volumes contribute to further understanding of Roman Catholic theology among Lutherans and Roman Catholics, it is in no small measure due to the ecumenical vision that he brought to publishing. For this reason, these volumes are dedicated to the memory of Dr. John A. Hollar, our editor and friend.

Francis Schüssler Fiorenza   *John P. Galvin*
Harvard Divinity School   The Catholic University of America

6

CHURCH

6

CHURCH

Michael A. Fahey

THE CONTEMPORARY CONTEXT
OF ECCLESIOLOGY

INTRODUCTION

In presenting a summary account of present-day Roman Catholic teaching on the church, one is faced first with the problem of where to begin. A chronological approach would require beginning with the preaching of Jesus as recorded in the gospel recollections of his public ministry. From there one would follow historically the nascent church's growth during the apostolic era, concentrating on its interaction with civil society and political structures that century-by-century helped to shape the church. Such a chronological approach has its merits. However, the method preferred in this chapter, one also favored by a growing number of theologians reflecting on the reality of church (ecclesiologists), is to begin rather with the church's contemporary context and attitudes. This approach takes stock first of Christians' convictions and feelings today about the church, at least among those members of the international Christian church who have expressed their views. Only after that description would one then retrace retrospectively questions of the origin and historical evolution of the church.

Beginning with a frank description of the present situation could create the impression that a writer is only critical, even disrespectful of sacred traditions, especially if one voices criticism of the church's faults. But critical remarks can also stem from an intense love of the church and can be motivated by a burning desire to see the church respond more effectively to its lofty vocation. In fact, critique of the church, especially when it is temperate and includes a keen awareness of one's own share in the church's faults, can be highly constructive. Critique is not the same as dissent, that activity so feared in some quarters of the church today and frequently judged to be only petulance or unwillingness to accept definitive or official church teachings. Critique may well be a prophetic invitation to the church's fuller self-realization under the power of grace.

This method of beginning study of the church from a contemporary starting point is one used effectively by the French priest and theologian Jean Rigal. His book *L'Église: Obstacle et chemin vers Dieu* (The church as obstacle and path toward God)[1] begins by discussing the church as it is judged by some in today's world: as oppressive, dogmatic, pyramidal, lifeless, and remote from modern realities. Another example of this approach is found in a collaborative work published by several leading German Catholic scholars.[2] Their volume includes an overview of trenchant criticism of the church by the historian Victor Conzemius.[3] Another French theologian, Henri Denis, begins his study of the church with an examination of why there exists such "disaffection" toward the Catholic church today.[4]

Critique has not always been welcomed. When Antonio Rosmini, the nineteenth-century prophet of renewed Catholicism, wrote his *Cinque piaghe della Chiesa* (The five wounds of the church) in 1832 and published it in 1846 on the eve of the election of Pius IX, his reward was to have his work placed on the Index of Forbidden Books in 1849. (It was later removed from the index before his death.) Yet today hardly anyone would dispute the accuracy of his sober account of those five wounds that plagued nineteenth-century Catholicism: the division between people and clergy at public worship; insufficient education of clergy; disunity among bishops; nomination

---

1. Jean Rigal, *L'Église: Obstacle et chemin vers Dieu* (Paris: Cerf, 1983).
2. *Traktat: Kirche*, vol. 3 of W. Kern et al., eds., *Handbuch der Fundamentaltheologie* (Freiburg: Herder, 1986).
3. Ibid., 30–48.
4. Henri Denis, *Chrétiens sans Église* (Paris: Desclée de Brouwer, 1979).

of bishops entrusted to the hands of civil government; restrictions on the church's free use of its own temporal possessions. We know from the diary of John XXIII, the pope who convoked the council of renewal (*aggiornamento*), how impressed he was by the persuasiveness of Rosmini's critique.

The Catholic church, together with other Christian communions, finds its self-understanding primarily from the gospel revelation expressed in the New Testament. For a Christian this is the heart of divine revelation. Yet today's Catholics know they are also ineluctably marked by the aftermath of the Protestant Reformation and the Council of Trent (1545–63), convened to respond to the Reformers' challenge only after many delays. Further, today's Catholics' understanding of church and of its structure is still strongly affected by the decisions of the First Vatican Council (1869–70), long after the immediate problems that it addressed have become remote to present-day consciousness. Also, many modern Catholics read the New Testament and its comments about the church in light of the Second Vatican Council (1962–65). The way that thinking Christians reflect on the church nowadays is also affected by historical consciousness, by awareness of the literary development of the New Testament writings, and by insights born in the upheavals of the two world wars with the resultant dislocations of populations and massive persecutions.

In the creed the church is mentioned in the enumeration of beliefs in the workings of the triune God, who sanctifies and consecrates this community of faith. Because the church is included in the Christian's act of faith, it necessarily possesses a dimension of mystery that can never be totally comprehended. Concentrating on the visible human aspects of the church does not mean denying the fact that it is a human-divine reality or that there is more to church "than meets the eye." Still some of what does meet the eye is disturbing and troubling.

A CHURCH DIVIDED

I begin my reflections on church with its present reality, even though this present situation includes enigmas. The most obvious fact about the Christian church today is that it is divided. Not only are the churches of the East and the West existentially estranged and still living in mutual suspicion of one another after over a millennium, but the churches of the West themselves have been tragically fragmented since the sixteenth century. Emphasizing that is not to seek to impute blame to any particular groups or to deny that the Reformation helped Christians reappropriate their vocation and live more evangelically.

But the fact is that suspicions, anathemas, and de facto or psychological excommunications have separated the Catholic and Protestant worlds for centuries. It is true, especially since the famous 1910 meeting of the Edinburgh Missionary Conference, considered as the starting point for the modern ecumenical movement, that there have been Herculean efforts to heal the separations among Christians that have been and remain a countersign to the preaching of the good news. First among Protestants, then between Orthodox and Protestants, and now between Catholics and other Christians, the modern ecumenical movement has struggled to overcome the ignorance and prejudice that the Christian churches have harbored toward one another. Willingness to cooperate and mutually to explore doctrinal and cultural differences among Christians has been a hallmark of this century, and more dramatically so since the close of the Second Vatican Council.

But unfortunately, after high hopes there is now much disillusionment and self-doubt among Christians, prompting one professional ecumenist to produce what he calls *A Survival Guide for Ecumenically Minded Christians*.[5] The Christian churches are far from overcoming their differences. Christians find a growing hesitancy to progress ecumenically especially at official levels. For example, at official levels there is considerable reluctance to recognize the sacraments of other churches or to permit eucharistic sharing (intercommunion). It can be argued that the differences that exist today among the Christian churches are legitimate variations within acceptable theological, liturgical, or canonical diversity. Yet the decision-makers in the churches seem to move very slowly toward full communion among the churches. Is it only because these barriers take centuries to dismantle? Or is there really an unwillingness to budge when it would mean admitting that one's way is not the only way?

Whereas there is agreement among churches on the importance of confessing the one holy catholic and apostolic church, there are divergences regarding: the divisions of church office into bishop, presbyter, deacon; the role of the bishop as the fullness of ordained ministry and successor to the apostles; the primatial function of the pope; the validity of allowing women access to ordained ministry; theological explanations about sacraments, salvation, and certain moral imperatives. Still on some issues there is growing consensus. One

---

5. Thomas Ryan, *A Survival Guide for Ecumenically Minded Christians* (Collegeville, Minn.: Liturgical Press, 1989).

effort spanning fifty years of research has led theologians within the church to note basic agreement on the sacraments of initiation. *Baptism, Eucharist and Ministry*—a document produced by a broadly based Christian team of theologians, including Roman Catholics, under the direction of the Faith and Order Commission of the World Council of Churches—has been a notable achievement.[6]

Despite the move toward ecumenical exchange, there is still the phenomenon that one specific confessional church will consider itself as "the" church of Christ. Denominationalism remains a fact of life. Among some more sectarian Protestant groups there is an unwillingness to share and interact in the preaching of the Gospels. In other words they are in principle antiecumenical.

New issues such as women's ordination as priests and even as bishops have placed a strain on interchurch dialogue and cooperation. The church of Christ at the visible level is in fact not one. This makes it particularly difficult for a theologian of a specific confession to write about the church in a way that is not sectarian or triumphalistic.

ECCLESIOLOGY AFTER AUSCHWITZ

One of the reasons it has been hard for Christians to talk to one another is that in large measure they have not yet achieved reconciliation with the Jews. Among some Christians a dramatic change has occurred in their perception of Judaism and of Christianity's relationship with the Jews. For them a Christian theology of church is being articulated in light of a slowly but certainly emerging understanding about the relationship of the church with Judaism.[7] A more positive assessment of Judaism has been developing, at least in some quarters, and new thinking has emerged about how Christians and Jews should overcome ancient antipathies. This reassessment follows upon the exposure of the Holocaust in all its horrors and the growing realization at least among some Christians that the Nazi extermination policy was indirectly aided by age-old Christian prejudices and pseudotheological arguments about the guilt of the Jewish people for the death of Jesus, about an imagined cancelation of God's cov-

---

6. *Baptism, Eucharist and Ministry*, Faith and Order Paper No. 111 (Geneva: World Council of Churches, 1982). For a collaborative Roman Catholic evaluation of this document, see Michael Fahey, ed., *Catholic Perspectives on Baptism, Eucharist and Ministry* (Lanham, Md.: University Press of America, 1986).

7. Johannes B. Metz, "Christians and Jews after Auschwitz," in his *The Emergent Church* (New York: Crossroad, 1981), 17–33; see also John T. Pawlikowski, *What Are They Saying about Christian-Jewish Relations?* (New York: Paulist, 1980).

enant with Israel, and about the Jews therefore having ceased to be "the people of God."

A closer critical look at Saint Paul's Letter to the Romans (esp. chaps. 9–11) and the covenantal theology found in the Hebrew Scriptures calls for a corrective in much of homiletic and devotional Christian discourse. The Second Vatican Council's declaration on non-Christian religions—despite its failure to condemn resoundingly every historical form of Christian anti-Semitism, which at times had been present even among certain leaders of the church—rejected in no uncertain terms the charge that Jews were guilty of "deicide" and urged Christians to appreciate better the bonds uniting the two interrelated religions.

Those Christians who have a keen awareness of Christian individual and collective guilt in breeding hateful attitudes toward the Jews and who also recognize their sins of omission especially during the Nazi era are obviously cautious about making grandiose statements about the vocation and role of the church, especially if formulated in exclusivistic terms. It is impossible for Christian ecclesiology to articulate today its self-understanding in total disregard for the perduring vocation of Israel under God's plan of salvation. Christians need to see how their religion has been grafted onto the vine that remains Israel, whose covenant, initiated by God and made with Abraham and his descendants, has not been annulled. That Jesus was a Jew; that he and his disciples were nourished by the spiritual and religious teachings of first-century Judaism; and that Christianity has borrowed much of its Scriptures and spiritual traditions from the Jewish faith—these facts need constant reaffirmation. Exclusivistic affirmations about salvation through the church alone must be rejected. Even provocative New Testament statements about the Jews and the Pharisees, which might be understandable against the background of first-century struggles, need to be contextualized before formulating a balanced ecclesiology.

THE EXPERIENCE OF BEING MARGINALIZED

Another contextual factor that bears upon how one begins to reflect theologically upon the nature of church is the fact that growing numbers of people in the church, speaking primarily but not exclusively from a Roman Catholic perspective, have an acute sense of their own marginalization by those in charge of the church. They see themselves as, practically speaking, irrelevant in the way church leaders establish priorities or shape pastoral strategies.

In North America at least, the most visible group distressed by this insensitivity to their aspirations and convictions is Christian women, especially in the Catholic church.[8] Many women are expressing now more bluntly how they see themselves subtly but effectively ignored or stereotyped by the ecclesiastical establishment. Certainly this is not true of all women, but the wide extent of this fact cannot be ignored. One way for those in charge to try to protect themselves from having to deal with these voices is to categorize these women as "radical feminists" imbued with the questionable values of secularism or consumerist materialism.

That all in the church need to employ inclusive, nonsexist language is a growing and strong expectation, and not only among women. The basic hope is that forgotten dimensions of the Christian revelation about God, salvation, and grace will not be eclipsed. Catholic women want a greater voice in the way that church teaching is formulated; in decision-making about pastoral, liturgical, and educational concerns; in the organization of seminaries; in holding clergy accountable; and in the formation of advisory and regulatory committees and consultations in the Catholic church.

At a 1987 international synod of Roman Catholic bishops on the topic "the role of the laity," Irish Cardinal Tomas O'Fiaich of Armagh, Ireland, noted that the hierarchy of the Catholic church needs to set about "awakening the sleeping giant" that is the laity and noted that "feminism can no longer be considered middle-class madness or an American aberration."[9] Sexism is not a women's issue. It is a concern for men also.

More acute still is the perception that the powerless and oppressed are blithely ignored by those in charge. This perception is growing among the poor and persecuted of this world and among those committed to a preferential option to work for the oppressed. Whether this growing awareness be traced to the many forms of liberation theology that flourish in Latin America, Africa, the Caribbean, and among those discriminated against in affluent nations, or whether this awareness be traced to the experience of base Christian communities or to efforts at inculturation and contextualization of theology, the results are clear: Whoever neglects the insights of the poor, the oppressed, or the victimized does so at the peril of formu-

---

8. See Joan Chittister, *Women, Ministry, and the Church* (New York: Paulist, 1983); Letty M. Russell, *Human Liberation in a Feminist Perspective* (Philadelphia: Westminster Press, 1974). For an insightful rereading of the New Testament from a feminist perspective, see Elisabeth Schüssler Fiorenza, *In Memory of Her* (New York: Crossroad, 1983).

9. *Origins* 17 (Oct. 29, 1987): 361–62.

lating an impoverished ecclesiology. Any ecclesiology insensitive to these matters cannot appropriately understand the special concerns of modern reflection on the church.

A large group of persons perceive themselves as marginalized by both society and church because they are the poor of the world. For them, much of what the Second Vatican Council and papal documents have been saying about the "modern world" rings rather hollow because it does not correspond to their specific experience. Many of these economically disadvantaged people have a profound awareness of God and a Christian faith that perdures even amid injustice. Thus, theologians writing out of the experience of Third World poverty and suffering stress that doing theology must arise out of a prior commitment on behalf of those struggling for freedom. They argue that many in the First World are unaware of how goods from the Third World benefit them at the cost of indirect compliance with an unjust social order. They plead for a renewal in theological methodology that would include a critical analysis of the major structures of oppression. Beyond this they feel that general descriptions of "the church today" exclude their own experience. They expect therefore that more attention will be given to their economic, political, social, cultural, and religious experiences. Their spokespersons reject an abstract conceptualization of God made outside their own historical struggle for liberation. Among these Christians and others too there is an increased awareness about the earth itself as gift of creation, and about the need for ecological, creation-centered reverence. These concerns make new demands on ecclesiology today.

Similar unrest is found among those who suffer from the racism even of churchgoers. The church in some regions and nations can be blamed for subtle (or not so subtle) discriminatory practices that affect, for instance, who is called to ordained ministry, who rises to higher office, and how finances are allocated for projects of particular groups.

BEYOND EUROPE AND NORTH AMERICA

Because so much published material on the theology of church is written in North America and Europe, it is not surprising that people on other continents see North Atlantic Christians as exercising an unhealthy monopoly on how the church is perceived. There is a growing feeling especially among Christians in Africa and Latin America, and to an extent among Asian Christians, that such dominance gives a decidedly false perspective on the nature of the church. These Christians feel that they were evangelized by persons deeply marked by a post-Reformation theology that had little pertinence to their own setting.

One of the recent, notable forums for expressing this frustration has been the Ecumenical Association of Third World Theologians (EATWOT), which was founded in Dar es Salaam, Tanzania, in 1976 and has published a series of ecclesiological studies and consensus statements that are a challenge to the West.[10] After five meetings held among themselves, these Third World theologians invited representatives of the First World to Geneva for the sessions in 1983. Problems were identified such as the imposition of Western anthropology upon people of the Third World and concepts of human nature based on individualism, competition, and struggle for power. Much of this was judged to be neocultural domination in the wake of colonial imperialism among the early missionaries.

CONTEXTUALIZATION

Walbert Bühlmann, a Swiss priest who for many years served the church in sub-Saharan Africa, published in the late 1970s an important work regarding the "coming of the third church" (that is to say the growing importance of churches in the Third World, especially in the southern hemisphere). In his book on "the third church" he indicates that by the year A.D. 2000 Christianity will be distributed in the following way: 58 percent of Christians will be a part of the third church, and 42 percent will be members of the first and second church. According to Bühlmann's definitions, the first church is that which is part of the church "first born" in the Middle East; the second church is that in Europe and North America. Among Roman Catholics the geographical distribution will be more dramatic still: 30 percent of its members will be in North America and Europe; 70 percent will be in Africa, South America, Asia, and Oceania.[11]

10. For the published proceedings of EATWOT see the following: EATWOT 1 (1976, Dar es Salaam): Sergio Torres and Virginia Fabella, eds., *The Emergent Gospel: Theology from the Underside of History* (Maryknoll, N.Y.: Orbis Books, 1978); EATWOT 2 (1977, Accra): Kofi Appiah-Kubi and Sergio Torres, eds., *African Theology En Route* (Maryknoll, N.Y.: Orbis Books, 1979); EATWOT 3 (1979, Sri Lanka): Virginia Fabella, ed., *Asia's Struggle for Full Humanity* (Maryknoll, N.Y.: Orbis Books, 1980); EATWOT 4 (1980, São Paulo): Sergio Torres and John Eagleson, eds., *The Challenge of Basic Christian Communities* (Maryknoll, N.Y.: Orbis Books, 1981); EATWOT 5 (1981, New Delhi): Virginia Fabella and Sergio Torres, eds., *Irruption of the Third World* (Maryknoll, N.Y.: Orbis Books, 1983); EATWOT 6 (1983, Geneva): Virginia Fabella and Sergio Torres, eds., *Doing Theology in a Divided World* (Maryknoll, N.Y.: Orbis Books, 1985).

11. Walbert Bühlmann, *The Coming of the Third Church* (Maryknoll, N.Y.: Orbis Books, 1977). See also his *Forward, Church!* (Slough, Eng.: St. Paul, 1977).

To note another changing contextual situation: In the United States, a large number of Catholics are now Spanish-speaking, having come from the various specific cultures often lumped together as "Hispanic." This growing population is already changing the way that ecclesiology is conceived in North America.

At the same time neoconservatism is another social factor developing worldwide among lay Catholics and Catholic hierarchs.[12] The term *neoconservatism* is used to describe an international, interconfessional mind-set found variously in different continents or churches. In general, Catholic neoconservatives are believers who judge that doctrinal integrity and ecclesiastical structures are being threatened by some in the church who are lessening the solid base of authentic tradition because of misguided enthusiasm and selective emphases or ignorance. Neoconservatives possess an acute, self-confident, but rather nonhistorical sense of tradition. Typically they stress the value of established institutions and possess a wary, cautious outlook on theological pluralism. The pastoral strategy of neoconservatives is to strive assiduously to protect the simple faithful from being disturbed by irresponsible theological speculations. In the Roman Catholic church neoconservatives exhibit concern about changes judged to be undesirable that followed the Second Vatican Council: wider participation of the laity in the liturgy, theological dissent, distinctive assertiveness by national and regional conferences of bishops, decline in vocations to the priesthood and to religious orders. They argue that the church, specifically the hierarchy, has tolerated too much diversity and too much wandering from correct doctrine, especially by theologians. Church life, they argue, has been neglecting spiritual concerns and exaggerating an overly particular inculturation of the gospel. Christian social teaching and praxis have, they feel, in some parts of the world become imbued with Marxist ideology through liberation theology. Furthermore, while official ecumenical dialogues may be desirable, neoconservatives feel that any theological conclusions should not proceed too quickly and all proposals emanating from bilateral conversations should be submitted to appropriate authorities for rigorous scrutiny.

In a book devoted to studying the reasons why the Brazilian liberation theologian Leonardo Boff was for a while silenced by the Vatican Congregation for the Doctrine of the Faith, Harvey Cox, whose roots are in the Baptist church tradition, contrasts two kinds of pastoral strategy in the Roman Catholic church today, one typified

---

12. See *Neoconservatism* (entire issue of *Concilium* 144 [1981]), especially the article on Joseph Ratzinger, 76–83.

in the approach of the Vatican's Congregation for the Doctrine of the Faith under the chairmanship of Cardinal Joseph Ratzinger, the other found in persons such as Boff.[13] Cox argues that Ratzinger favors a "recentering" of the church intellectually and liturgically within its ancient homeland (Europe) and that he is promoting a "restoration" of cultural Christendom in which theological formulations and their philosophical suppositions are clear and distinct. Boff on the other hand is seen to favor "decentering," whereby the gospel takes root in a variety of disparate cultures and flourishes especially among the poor. Powerful forces at recent international bishops' synods and in the Vatican, argues Cox, are now opting for the model of "recentering." Whether this facile distinction is correct or not, and it does seem to have some validity, the fact is that this is how the present-day Catholic church is being marked by a "restoration" strategy.

The papal appointment of the German theologian and cardinal Joseph Ratzinger as prefect of the Congregation for the Doctrine of the Faith has strengthened neoconservative views. Ratzinger shares with neoconservatives a rather pessimistic assessment of Catholicism following the Second Vatican Council, as is clear from his interview published in 1985 under the title *The Ratzinger Report*.[14] Vatican support of the pious association known as Opus Dei—which was founded in 1928 by Msgr. Josémaría Escrivá de Balaguer (1902–75) and was raised by Pope John Paul II to the level of a "personal prelacy," thereby giving it a certain independence from local bishops—is seen as support of neoconservative preferences. Opus Dei, which also has a women's branch and one specifically for priests (The Priestly Society of the Holy Cross), has considerable influence in Vatican circles; even the Vatican's public relations director, Joaquin Navarro-Vals, is a lay member of this organization. The Vatican has also shown support for international conservative lay organizations such as Comunione e Liberazione, a movement acknowledged as an institutional instance of neoconservatism.

One question frequently asked today is why neoconservative Roman Catholics are characteristically so intense and driven in their efforts to protect the church. Why do they possess such self-assuredness in the rightness of their views? The intensity of their efforts is understandable in light of their conviction that the church is gravely threatened even by insiders and that the consequences of neglecting to respond will be a severe decline of Christian values.

---

13. Harvey Cox, *The Silencing of Leonardo Boff* (Oak Park, Ill.: Meyer-Stone, 1988).
14. Joseph Ratzinger, *The Ratzinger Report* (San Francisco: Ignatius, 1985).

Their self-confidence reflects the strict Catholic training and education they received earlier according to a method of teaching that stressed absolutes and unchanging truths.

Neoconservatism differs from the disruptive and radical "traditionalist" movement associated with the dissident archbishop Marcel Lefebvre, who judges that the Second Vatican Council's decisions on religious freedom, collegiality, and ecumenism were capitulations to the secular goals of *liberté, égalité,* and *fraternité.*

DISAFFECTION

Those who follow newspapers and television are well aware of annoyance and dissatisfaction among Catholics in regard to worldwide and diocesan leadership. Many perceive an attempt to promote universalist attitudes in church governance. There is a growing perception that the move toward regional autonomy in the local churches favored at the Second Vatican Council is gradually being replaced by a centralist policy that controls especially through the appointment of bishops and by trying to diminish the theological status of episcopal conferences. The so-called Cologne Declaration, a specific criticism by some European theologians about the procedures now being used to choose bishops, particularly in Europe, is an example of this mood; similar reactions to problems that have developed in South America, especially in Brazil, can also be noted.[15] In earlier days the Swiss theologian Hans Urs von Balthasar described this mood as one of an "anti-Roman affect" on the part of some Catholics.[16]

In some parts of the world Catholics have been disillusioned and shocked by charges of alleged financial and sexual abuse by certain Roman Catholic priests, some of which have been verified as criminal in courts of law. In some places this naturally has led to a distancing from Catholic leadership. It also raises questions about principles of accountability and concerns about the church's orthopraxis.

NEW METHODOLOGY

In recent decades ecclesiology has also been affected by the introduction of the historical-critical method, especially as that method is used for interpreting Scripture, the historical documents of councils, and the development of doctrines. As the fields of theology and

---

15. The Cologne Declaration appeared in the London *Tablet* 243 (February 4, 1989): 140–42; see a similar text from Brazilian theologians entitled "The Church in Rough Water," *Tablet* 243 (July 29, 1989): 882–83.

16. Hans Urs von Balthasar, *Der antirömische Affekt* (Freiburg: Herder, 1974).

ecclesiology become more and more complex, it is not surprising to see that complete treatises on ecclesiology are rarely now composed by individual theologians. Among some of the leading Catholic theologians of this century—Bernard Lonergan, Karl Rahner, Hans Urs von Balthasar, even to a certain extent Yves Congar—no comprehensive ecclesiology has been attempted. Instead we are offered specific reflections on narrowly defined issues of ecclesiology, *quaestiones disputatae*. Attempts at a comprehensive ecclesiology are typically becoming collaborative works.

An alert student of the church will need to practice wise discernment in assessing church situations. Merely because a theologian is under a cloud of suspicion at a particular juncture of time does not mean that he or she has misread the signs of the times or distorted a specific truth relating to the church. If the experience of the Catholic church in the last fifty years can today teach us a special lesson, it is the possibility that here and now there may be insights appropriate to the church that have been neglected in official church teachings. These forgotten truths may be disliked or considered suspect by persons in authority and may be kept alive in only small pockets of the church. Conceivably these insights may one day be heralded even in official teaching as vital signs of the healthy life of the church. This paradox need not surprise those who see the church as a pilgrim people or a sojourning church.

THE ORIGINS AND EARLY DEVELOPMENT OF THE CHURCH

JESUS AND THE CHURCH

Jesus' role in "founding" the church is a central conviction of Christian faith although the event is not specifically cited in prayers such as the Nicene Creed. Catechetical materials used by Catholics commonly stated that Jesus "instituted" the sacraments and by extension the term has come to be applied to the church itself. Jesus is described as having instituted or founded the church during his lifetime. Proof of Jesus' direct intention to found the church has been provided by appeal to the passage in Matthew's Gospel where Jesus confers the keys upon Peter and promises: "On this rock I will build my church" (Matt. 16:18). This New Testament proof-text was further buttressed by citing the words of Jesus' postresurrection appearance to Peter during which the risen Christ, after the triple questioning of Peter ("Simon, son of John, do you love me?"), instructs him to feed and tend his sheep.

Modern exegesis has shown that it may well be possible, indeed is even likely, that the promise of Matthew 16:18 occurred after the resurrection and was retrojected by the gospel writers into the public ministry of Jesus. Historical-critical methodology applied to the genesis of the written form of the gospel accounts argues that certain events presented in the Gospels as occurring before the resurrection may well have been shifted there in light of the writers' firm faith about the deepest identity of Jesus. This way of reading the New Testament has resulted in greater appreciation for the likelihood of the church's foundation in different stages. This perspective not only allows for growth in Jesus' own sense of his mission during his life on earth, but also stresses as crucial, for the founding of the church, the period after the resurrection, as well as the Pentecost experience beginning with the Holy Spirit descending upon the disciples gathered in the Upper Room, an event appropriately called the church's "birthday." From this perspective it is harder to prove that Jesus had a master-plan for structuring his church before his death.[17]

One disadvantage of describing Jesus' intention of founding the church during his preaching in Judea and Galilee is that by placing so much stress on the public life of Jesus as the formative years of the church's foundation one neglects the role of the Holy Spirit during Pentecost and the ensuing years of the apostolic age. Need all the formative factors in the emergence of the church be directly related to the lifetime of Jesus? The fact that certain church ministries were in a state of development during the apostolic period is incontestable. Also it cannot be overlooked that the composition of the New Testament canon was in process over several generations, and the New Testament was only gradually collected into a whole. Both these events were "founding events" of the church under the inspiration of the Holy Spirit.

The care that Jesus took in training the twelve and other disciples as teachers and evangelizers clearly reveals that Jesus intended his message to have a perduring value. It is even likely that he expected his closest followers to learn by heart summaries of his teachings and to memorize instructions such as the Lord's Prayer. The institution of the Last Supper, when Jesus instructs his disciples to "do this in memory of me," implies his wish that this ritual continue on in the midst of his community of disciples.

---

17. On the relationship between Jesus and the church, see Josef Finkenzeller, *Von der Botschaft Jesu zur Kirche Christi: Zweifel, Fragen, Probleme, Antworten* (Munich: Don Bosco, 1974).

Whether Jesus in his humanity understood from the beginning of his public life that his mission was to extend beyond the Jews to include the Gentiles is not altogether clear from the Gospels. Some New Testament scholars conclude that initially Jesus' own understanding of his mission was linked exclusively with Israel, and that only gradually and toward the end of his life, under the influence of grace and through personal discernment, especially after his failure to win more adherents from among the Jews, did he broaden its applicability to include the Gentiles. It is difficult, given the nature of the written Gospels, to know for certain what Jesus thought on such issues.

The central concept of Jesus' preaching in Aramaic is translated in the Gospels composed in the Greek language as: *basileia tou theou* or *basileia ton ouranon*. Volumes have been written about this term, which had a Hebrew substratum and which has commonly been translated into English as "the kingdom of God" or "the kingdom of heaven." The German Catholic exegete Rudolph Schnackenburg stressed in his important monograph on *basileia* that a better translation would be God's "rule" rather than "kingdom" since the notion is not primarily a geographic but a theological one.[18] Recently other English words have been proposed to translate *basileia*: "dominion," "reign," "God's plan for the future," or "special presence."

Commentators on Jesus' use of *basileia* stress the fact that it has a complex, dialectic meaning that describes, depending on the context, different stages of one and the same ongoing religious conviction. In Jesus' preaching, God's *basileia* is neither "already fully present" at the time he is speaking ("realized eschatology") nor wholly absent and still awaiting achievement in the near future ("eschatologism"). Rather God's reign comprehends dimensions partially present and partially future (the "already there" as well as the "not yet"). Jesus prays in the Our Father in regard to God's reign: "[May] thy kingdom come [in a way that has not yet been realized]." But in other sayings he states confidently that because of healings and deeds of wonder worked through him the reign is already present: "If it is by the Spirit of God that I expel demons, then the reign of God has overtaken you" (Matt. 12:28; also Luke 11:20).

---

18. Rudolph Schnackenburg, *God's Rule and Kingdom* (New York: Herder, 1965). For a complementary view by a Protestant scholar, see Norman Perrin, *The Kingdom of God in the Teaching of Jesus* (Philadelphia: Westminster Press, 1963). Also useful here are two works by Daniel J. Harrington, *God's People in Christ: New Testament Perspectives on the Church and Judaism* (Philadelphia: Fortress Press, 1980); and idem, *The Light of All Nations: Essays on the Church in New Testament Research* (Wilmington, Del.: Glazier, 1982).

From a theological viewpoint, one can state that Jesus, by being manifested as Lord in the resurrection, becomes the personification of the kingdom at a decisive moment of its process. Christians believe that the reign of God has entered into a final and decisive stage with the incarnation of God in Christ. This in no way denigrates or marginalizes the covenant with Israel but for Christians adds another dimension that builds upon the first covenant but does not dislodge it.

Another element to be stressed is that this reign or kingdom does not inaugurate for the very first time a special covenantal relationship between God and humanity. Earlier covenants struck with Adam, Noah, Abraham, and Israel still remain in force. What the term *kingdom of God* implies on the lips of Jesus is that at that point in time there began a special, intensified presence of God (which Christians would ultimately describe as the new covenant) that Christians denote as Jesus the Messiah and the incarnate Word of God.

The community that emerged from Jesus' preaching, life, death, and resurrection, the church, cannot be identified purely and simply with God's reign, the *basileia*. The church is rather a privileged locus for the advancement of the rule of God still to be realized. Some modern Catholic writers describe the church as an instrument of God's reign. This formulation is potentially misleading if it suggests that God's reign comes about through our efforts, when clearly it occurs by God's gracious and free intervention. Between the church in the present and the kingdom in the future stands the decision of God that will be made in judgment (see the parable of the net cast into the sea [Matt. 13:47-50] and the parable of the weeds among the wheat [Matt. 13:24-30, 36-43]). The kingdom of God does not depend on our actions but is God's promised eschatological work.

In the earlier half of this century it was not uncommon for Catholic preachers to speak from the pulpit as though the New Testament "kingdom of God" parables were actually descriptions of the Catholic church. Even today, some churches speak as though their particular church were in fact identified with the kingdom, and they do so without any kind of nuancing.

Third World theologians stress that this kingdom of God should not be etherealized into a "purely religious" concept that would imply that the building up of God's reign has nothing to do with the political and social order. This would be totally misleading, just as it would be to argue that God's offer of freedom from slavery and inheritance of a promised land had no political or social implications for Israel.

CHURCH IN THE NEW TESTAMENT

The New Testament term for church, *ekklēsia*, is a word that had appeared already in the Greek translation of the Old Testament (the Septuagint) where it is used about a hundred times to translate the Hebrew word *qahal*, Israel's assembly or congregation under God's call. In the Gospels the word *church* (*ekklēsia*) is not placed on Jesus' lips except in two passages (Matt. 16:18 and 18:17); as noted, these two passages are now generally seen as constructions that the evangelist transposed from their original setting in the postresurrection period of Jesus. Luke does not use the word *ekklēsia* in his Gospel, but the term is frequent in his Book of Acts where it designates first the community in Jerusalem (Acts 5:11), then mission communities (8:1; 14:23), and then both the local community (9:31) and the collective, dispersed church (8:3).

The Roman Catholic church shares with other Christian churches the conviction that a theology of church rooted in the New Testament is formulated not only from the Gospels, especially the sayings of Jesus, but is obviously also based on a number of different canonical writings that emerged from different geographical and religio-cultural contexts. It is a temptation to emphasize one or another of these aspects to the neglect of others. Often this has been done by different church groups in the past, and to a certain extent explains the variant models of church that lie at the base of modern confessional differences. In the New Testament we have diverse aspects held together in creative tension; these tensions are not of themselves signs of fragmentation but of a dynamism whose inner spirit remains one. The whole New Testament is a product of a long maturation process. Paul of Tarsus, arguably the first Christian theologian, played a key role in the formulation of the ecclesiology we associate with the New Testament. His views of church are expressed in his major letters, even though formulating a theoretical account of ecclesiology was not one of his primary pastoral concerns.

It has often been stated as axiomatic in theological summaries of Paul's doctrine of the church that he was at first exclusively concerned with particular churches in specific locations and only later (as in Eph. 5:25 and Col. 1:18) did he or his closest colleagues focus on the transregional church dispersed throughout the Mediterranean basin. In an address delivered in 1981 to the Catholic Theological Society of America, the Catholic exegete Raymond Brown reviewed the data underlying this common assumption and argued the need for much greater nuancing than is usually offered by the conventional wisdom on this matter.[19] It is true, he notes, that Paul in his letters speaks of "the church of the Thessalonians" (1 Thess. 1:1), "the churches of Galatia" (Gal. 1:1), "the church of God which is in Corinth" (1 Cor. 1:1; 2 Cor. 1:1), and "the churches of God which are in Judea" (1 Thess. 2:14). But, Brown argues, there are passages that reveal that Paul also had a wider conception of church. For example, when Paul states in 1 Corinthians 12:28, "God has appointed in the church first apostles, second prophets," it is clear that he is not thinking only of the local church of Corinth. Sometimes too Paul moves quickly from the singular to the plural; in Galatians 1:13 he speaks of having persecuted "the church of God," but in Galatians 1:22 he speaks of not being known by sight "to the churches of Judea which are in Christ." In 1 Corinthians 14:34 Paul says that "the women should keep silence in the churches" but then continues in the next verse to say that "it is shameful for a woman to speak in church." In short there is in Pauline usage no clear progression from the many to the one. The same is also true in other works of the New Testament. The reference in Matthew 16:18 to "my church" covers more than a local church, whereas in Matthew 18:17 the word *church* points specifically to a local community.

Brown finds in Paul's writings the same ambiguity that we find today in using the terms *local* or *particular* relative to church. When Paul speaks of the churches of Galatia or of Asia, he may be referring to a church associated within the specific geographical confines of a political area. But he may also have been thinking of even smaller local churches, namely "house churches," of which there may have been several, especially in larger cities.[20] In a locale such as Antioch or Ephesus about the year A.D. 90, there could conceivably have existed, as Brown notes, a variety of house churches resulting from different Christian missions: one house church of Christian Jews who still adhered to the Mosaic Law and for whom Jesus was Messiah but not divine in origin; one house church of Jewish and Gentile Christians stemming from the mission associated with the Jerusalem apostles and honoring the twelve as founders; another house church from the Pauline mission, consisting mostly of Gentiles who saw themselves free of the Jewish Law; and even a house church of Johannine inspiration, which did not use the title "apostle" but re-

---

19. Reprinted as Raymond Brown, "The New Testament Background for the Emerging Doctrine of 'Local Church'," in his *Biblical Exegesis and Church Doctrine* (New York: Paulist, 1985), 114–34.

20. For further study of the house church, see Robert Banks, *Paul's Idea of Community: The Early Churches in Their Historical Setting* (Grand Rapids, Mich.: Eerdmans, 1980).

garded all as disciples, and regarded Jesus as made present through the Paraclete. It is not clear if any "crossing over" of believers from one house church to another occurred; in some cases a transfer from one to another would have been difficult.

Apparently after a period of some hesitation about which word to use to identify this new community reality, *ekklēsia* became the preferred term for the community that followed Christ. Two other terms used in the formative period might conceivably have been retained to describe the Christian community but in fact were not: "the Way" (*hodos*, from the Hebrew *derek*), as used in Acts 24:14 to describe the church; or again "the communion" (*koinonia*), as used for instance in Acts 2:42.

SPECIFIC NEW TESTAMENT CHURCHES

In recent scholarship there has been special interest in trying to understand the diverse churches or Christian communities that existed shortly after the close of the so-called apostolic age. Raymond Brown identifies (1) three forms of post-Pauline communities with specific characteristics (reflected successively in the pastorals, in Ephesians and Colossians, and in Luke/Acts); (2) two kinds of Johannine communities; (3) a community related to 1 Peter; (4) the Matthean community; (5) a community related to the Epistle of James; and (6) other communities associated with Mark, Hebrews, and Revelation, as well as perhaps with the Didache and 1 Clement. Knowledge of the diversity of the reality called church in the early stages is especially relevant in discussions about the real or imaginary importance of total conformity to one modern church's structures as over against others.

Another focus that has been influential in modern study of local churches has been to identify the large Christian centers associated with cities such as Rome, Ephesus, Jerusalem, and Antioch. A spate of books and ongoing seminars has been the result of this interest.[21] Also there has been a growing appreciation of the complex reality represented by the term *Jewish / Gentile Christianity*—in that form of Christianity Gentiles shared the various different theological emphases of the Jewish Christians who converted them, and much depended on whether the Jewish Christians' original ties had been with Hebrew Judaism or Greek-speaking Judaism. All these com-

---

21. For a cross section of studies on this, see Raymond Brown, *The Community of the Beloved Disciple* (New York: Paulist, 1979); Raymond Brown and John P. Meier, *Antioch and Rome: New Testament Cradles of Catholic Christianity* (New York: Paulist, 1983); Raymond Brown, *The Churches the Apostles Left Behind* (New York: Paulist, 1984).

plexities of the original reality should make a contemporary church very wary of identifying purely and simply its own polity with the ineluctable "will of God." The first-century church was a reality much more complex and diverse than frequently admitted.

The point of all this is to suggest that the claims that individual churches make today about being the only legitimate church are notably exaggerated. In the situation of the dividedness of the church one would have to ask whether it is reasonable for one church to demand that other churches give up much of themselves before they can enter into full communion with it. This is particularly pertinent in regard to churches whose self-identity was shaped not in the West but in the East during the first millennium. If Eastern churches are to be invited today to enter into full communion with the church of Rome, is it correct to require a level of sameness with Rome that never existed even in the first millennium?

Another contemporary academic interest is the social milieu of early Christianity. This is reflected for instance in the work of the American John Gager, who has explored early Christianity in comparison to its religious competitors of the time, such as Mithraism, Judaism, philosophical schools, and Hellenistic religions.[22] Also greater attention is being paid to the religious milieus of classical Mediterranean spiritualities in late antiquity, especially Egyptian and Greco-Roman spiritualities.[23] This interest in the religious environment of the Mediterranean world at the time of the first preaching of Christianity helps us to understand Christianity's particular appeal.

PRE-NICENE CHRISTIANITY

The study of the growth of the early church cannot remain restricted to the New Testament alone. One way to measure the degree of development of church in the first centuries is to follow its growth over several centuries. From the time of the death of Jesus (A.D. 30) to A.D. 337 (the end of the reign of Constantine, the first Roman emperor to become a Christian) is an era of some nine generations (taking a generation to be thirty-three years).[24] During these nine

---

22. See John G. Gager, *Kingdom and Community: The Social World of Early Christianity* (Englewood Cliffs, N.J.: Prentice-Hall, 1975); and the works by Wayne A. Meeks, *The First Urban Christians* (New Haven: Yale University Press, 1983) and his *The Moral World of the First Christians* (Philadelphia: Westminster Press, 1986).

23. See A. H. Armstrong, ed., *Classical Mediterranean Spirituality: Egyptian, Greek, Roman*, World Spirituality 15 (New York: Crossroad, 1986).

24. See Michael Fahey, "Ecclesiae sorores ac fratres: Sibling Communion in the Pre-Nicene Era," *Catholic Theological Society of America, Proceedings* 36 (1981): 15–38, which provides references to the primary sources.

generations the external shape of Christianity solidified and underwent a number of developments that have remained influential even to this day. I have already mentioned the period and genesis of the New Testament texts. During the rest of these three centuries Christianity went through a period of localized, sometimes violent persecutions resulting in the death of many Christians. Toward the end of this age of the martyrs there occurred what is called the Constantinian turning point, brought on in part by the emperor's decision eventually to allow Christianity to become a licit religion in the empire. This tolerance led to notable social changes in the life of the church, especially in the way in which the church hierarchy and the state interacted. Eventually with Constantine's conversion to Christianity and his enrollment as a catechumen, the first of what came to be called ecumenical councils was held. But even in the second and third centuries, church officials were interacting with governmental agencies, and Christianity both in the West and the East assumed certain characteristics adopted from the secular Roman Empire. What happened during the period of nine generations regarding the liturgy, sacramental practices, and growth in monepiscopacy (the practice of having only one *episkopos* or bishop/overseer for each particular church instead of governance by a council of elders) can shed light on the developing shape of church.

Few individuals have the broad knowledge needed to understand the shifting nature of local churches in the second and third centuries. One needs humility and equilibrium to recognize that much of what was written by Catholics and non-Catholics alike about this period in the recent past has been one-sided and apologetical/confessional. In the twentieth century, theologians have recognized that what had been considered in the church an aspect of the *ius divinum* (a feature traceable to God's specific instructions expressed by Christ or by the Holy Spirit to the apostles in the subapostolic period) and what in fact was *ius humanum* (a human or ecclesial decision about an aspect of church) may have been unintentionally blurred. What is needed is careful study to determine what exists in the church because of a specific, divinely formulated "will" expressed formally through revelation and what is the result of human or ecclesial "will," that is an element having its origin in an explicit or implicit decision of the church community.

To understand the interaction of one city church with another (for, in fact, Christianity was at first largely based in cities) it is profitable to refer to some of the historical data. Did these separate, geographically dispersed churches perceive themselves as interrelated into a reality that encompassed the entire Mediterranean? To what extent were the churches united prior to the Council of Nicaea (A.D. 325)? And what means did they use to express their interest in being part of a worldwide church?

The need to identify various strands of Christianity as incompatible with orthodox Christianity—strands such as Gnosticism, Montanism, and Marcionism—led the churches in the second and third centuries to intensify efforts at keeping in touch with one another. Still, each local church was seen as possessing all that was necessary for its functioning as a church. Once evangelized and equipped with supervisors and presiders, once the community had been initiated into the Christian Scriptures and had been taught about the mysteries of baptism and eucharist, such a church associated with a city or part of a city could manage on its own. What needs to be explained about the early church is not how a local, city-based church came to see itself as autonomous, but rather how a local church came to choose various modalities for wider fellowship. For mainline Christian churches being autonomous never meant sterile isolation.

COMMUNION IN PRE-NICENE CHRISTIANITY

Earlier in this century the German scholar Walter Bauer stressed the importance of focusing on a wide spectrum of local or regional churches—including the area around Edessa, Alexandria, Antioch, western Asia Minor, as well as Rome—for understanding how the churches of the East and West developed. Other historians of the early church, such as Ekkart Sauser, have tried to reconstruct what church life must have been like in the East in the Christian communities at Jerusalem, Antioch, Alexandria, Constantinople, Seleucia, and Ctesiphon, and in the West at Lyons, Arles, Carthage, Trier, Barcelona, Ravenna, Milan, and Rome.[25]

It is informative to see how Christian communities after the close of the New Testament period developed in pre-Nicene Christianity and how they promoted ongoing sharing. Although it is not possible to reconstruct the entire period, we do have some useful information about at least six practices used by local churches to foster a sense of solidarity and communion among the disparate communities: (1) prayers for others at eucharistic celebrations and sharing eucharistic bread; (2) installing new bishops by inviting bishops from neighboring churches to consecrate them; (3) convoking regional synods or councils; (4) exchanging and circulating letters; (5) accepting attempts at coordination of the Western churches by the bishop

25. Ekkart Sauser, *Woher kommt Kirche? Ortskirchen der Frühzeit und Kirchenbewusstsein heute* (Frankfurt: J. Knecht, 1978).

of Rome; and (6) submitting to direct interventions by the emperor in the administrative life of the church.

1. Not surprisingly some of the most ardent descriptions of the sense of solidarity among the churches occur in liturgical prayers. By the third generation we have a famous passage from the Didache that may be an even earlier prayer: "As this broken bread was scattered upon the mountains, but was brought together and became one, so let thy Church be gathered together from the ends of the earth, into thy kingdom, for thine is the glory and the power through Jesus Christ for ever" (9:4). In the same document we read a similar prayer: "Remember, Lord, thy Church, to deliver it from all evil and to make it perfect in thy love, and gather it together in its holiness from the four winds to thy kingdom which thou hast prepared for it" (10:5). These are clear signs that the local church had sibling counterparts in other parts of the world. Justin's *First Apology* also records a similar perspective in the context of the eucharistic liturgy: "And on that day which is called after the sun, all who are in the towns and in the country gather together for a communal celebration. And then the memoirs of the Apostles or the writings of the Prophets are read, as long as time permits.... Then prayers in common are said ... for ourselves, for the newly baptized and *for all others wherever they may be.*"[26]

Within the celebration of the eucharist and to a lesser extent perhaps in baptism, there was a powerful dynamism at work leading Christians to perceive themselves as belonging to a people gathered for the purpose of praising and adoring God. There was a sort of supratemporal awareness of community, already adumbrated discreetly in the New Testament, but growing stronger—namely that those who participated locally in a eucharistic celebration were involved in close intersubjective communion with those faithful who by death had gone before the living Christians.

Specific eucharistic practices arose that expressed this awareness of and love for sibling churches. To be in communion with another church or specifically with its bishop/overseer, Christians sent to other churches consecrated bread of communion. Eusebius records this practice in citing a letter from Irenaeus to Victor, the bishop of Rome, concerning an Easter controversy. Irenaeus commented that Roman bishops in earlier times did not allow disagreements about the date for celebrating Easter to interfere with the practice of sending eucharistic bread to other churches as a sign of solidarity.

_____

26. Justin *I Apology* 67; emphasis added.

Another custom related to the eucharist was the practice of sending a fragment of consecrated bread to neighboring churches. The custom seems to be of Roman origin, but it was adopted by bishops in other cities. On feast days, as a sign of union, the bishop would send to priests or to bishops in outlying areas a piece of the communion bread just consecrated; upon arrival the bread would be mixed into the chalice of the receiving church as a sign of oneness. This practice continued until the ninth century and has even left some traces to this day in the Roman liturgy, as in the commingling of the eucharistic bread and wine within the chalice before distribution of communion.

2. It is difficult to date exactly when the practice began of appointing only one bishop (*monos episkopos*) for each Mediterranean city church. But certainly by the fourth generation of Christianity any variant practice that might have existed (such as administering a church by a kind of sanhedrin or council, as seems to have been the original practice in the church of Rome) was replaced by the monepiscopal model. What developed then in the second century was a monarchical concentration of authority for the bishop. Along with that went a certain sacralization of the office of bishop. As we see in a letter of Saint Cyprian of Carthage,[27] the community within a local church was expected to elect its own bishop.

The actual sacramental initiation into the bishop's office was done by laying on of hands by bishops from neighboring churches. Hippolytus of Rome in his *Apostolic Tradition* mentions the requirement of having other bishops present. Shortly before the Council of Nicaea, at a local Council of Arles (A.D. 314), it was specified that there should be seven bishops on hand but "if not seven, one should not dare to ordain with fewer than three bishops." This gave an acute sense of the fact that a local church, though autonomous, needed to be in communion with at least neighboring churches.

But by now there was at work more than simply calling upon neighboring bishops to consecrate episcopal appointees. A network was taking shape that tended to establish an order of importance among the churches: it designated older churches and younger churches. Although it would be premature to speak of patriarchates before A.D. 451, still some churches had greater supervisory roles to perform than did others. Particular prestige came to be associated with certain local or regional churches for a variety of reasons: real or imagined apostolic origins, geographical location, political power, effective leadership, and so on. In this development it seems clear

---

27. Cyprian *Ep.* 67.3.

that the civil system in use among the Romans also influenced the way bishops assumed functions.

3. A third institution in the pre-Nicene church that fostered exchange and coordination among churches was the increased convocation of synods or councils. Councils or synods (the Greek language employs one and the same word for these events: *synodos*) are first mentioned in the second half of the second century when the Christians of Asia conducted a series of open-ended meetings to deal with the problems of Montanism. Synods also multiplied as regional churches tried to iron out difficulties associated with the choice of the date of Easter. These synods were not made up exclusively of *episkopoi*. We know for example from a synod held in A.D. 256 at Carthage concerning a baptismal controversy that "a great many bishops met together in Carthage together with the presbyters and deacons and a considerable part of the people [*plebis*]."[28]

Furthermore the synods exercised only that binding force that individual bishops wished to attach to them. Cyprian makes this clear in a letter in which he summarizes the work of a provincial synod: "No one of us sets himself up as a bishop of bishops, no one of us compels by tyrannical terror any colleague to the necessity of obedience, since every bishop, according to his own right of liberty and power, has his own right to judgment, and can no more be judged by another than he himself can judge another."[29] Most importantly these provincial synods, especially those in the seventh, eighth, and ninth generations of Christianity, created the conditions for what eventually came to be known as an ecumenical council.

4. Another factor that was powerful in establishing contact among the sibling churches was the practice of exchanging letters. Since the time of Saint Paul, Christians had been familiar with this practice. Among Christians letters often contained the views of groups and not merely one individual. Letters could be hortatory and informational. They were hardly all pious or inspirational. They could include angry outbursts, threats, and sarcastic, caustic remarks. What is interesting is not merely the fact they were written in such abundance, but that they were so carefully guarded, copied, and translated when necessary, even filed away for future reference.

---

28. Cyprian *Sententiae Episcoporum*, in *Opera Cypriani* (Hartel 3:435.7).

29. Ibid., 436.3ff. On the role of episcopal synods during the early centuries, see the contribution of Brian E. Daley, "Structures of Charity: Bishops' Gatherings and the See of Rome in the Early Church," in Thomas Reese, ed., *Episcopal Conferences: Historical, Canonical, and Theological Studies* (Washington, D.C.: Georgetown University Press, 1989).

Among the principal forms of letters were the so-called *litterae pacis*, letters conveying absolution for sinners, especially for those who had lapsed at times of persecution; there were *litterae pacis ecclesiasticae*, containing a bishop's permission granted one of the faithful to visit some high dignitary; *litterae festales*, containing information about liturgical calendars and celebrations; *litterae circulares*, encyclicals intended for wide audiences; and the so-called *contessaratio hospitalitatis*, a sort of passport or credit card permitting a visiting Christian to have access to distant Christian communities, a kind of letter of good conduct entitling the bearer to free room and board in a distant church, at least for a short period of time.

5. Another factor that further contributed to contact among churches in the pre-Nicene church, especially in the Western part of the Mediterranean, was the gradual coordination of certain functions by the church of Rome. Rome came to be seen as enjoying a sort of *potentia principalis*, a hegemony of influence over other churches, especially but not exclusively the Western churches. As a local church it was seen to preside in love over other churches. Before the Council of Nicaea there was no juridical formulation about Rome's role, much less talk of jurisdictional primacy or of a kind of universal ministry of its bishop. Still certain factors contributed to increased communion under the initiative of Rome. The church of Rome intervened to reestablish order in the trouble spot of Corinth (see 1 Clement); it exercised a broad pastoral care for those troubled about penitential practices (see the Shepherd of Hermas); a Roman bishop undertook initiatives in regard to certain Eastern churches to settle disputes about the date of Easter; Rome had available a list of episcopal succession and eventually drew ecclesiastical conclusions from that list; a member of the Roman church formulated in the *Apostolic Tradition* appropriate liturgical practices; Rome undertook special acts of charity, notably financial support for other churches.

6. A final element to consider in this survey of factors that fostered communion in the pre-Nicene churches concerns the policies of Emperor Constantine, who reigned from A.D. 306 to 337. Although often guided by more than simple religious motives, still Constantine's policies had enormous repercussions for the future shape of the church. The emperor in his later years was haunted by a vision of coordinated and cooperating local churches. He tried to achieve his goal through his influence and initiatives, and he tried, in fact unsuccessfully, to deal with the Donatists and Arians. He ordered synods to be held in Rome (A.D. 313) and at Arles (314) in search of harmony. For Eusebius, the church historian and writer of lavish encomiums, Emperor Constantine was a "bishop for the outside";

his influence was felt by his sponsorship; his favors toward Christian churches made him a popular benefactor; toward the end of his reign he restored confiscated buildings and made available finances for church buildings, clergy being exempt from certain political duties and from paying taxes. Although it is premature to speak of Caesaro-papism, what Constantine initiated was the prototype to that special mixture of church and state that has dominated so much of church history in East and West.

The growth of cooperation among churches in the period prior to the Council of Nicaea was due to many different factors. Some factors were principally religious, such as the celebration of the eucharist and the sacramental installation of new bishops by neighboring bishops. Some were organizational and social, such as the convocation of synods or letter writing. Others concentrated coordination within one person or one institution, be it the episcopal see of Rome or the imperial court of New Rome. These were outgrowths of the New Testament and, although new solutions, were considered legitimate developments. Of course even within the New Testament there are references to attempts to address the need for the church to adjust to world history.

Based on this quick overview of developments from the New Testament and subapostolic period to the churches of the second and third centuries, two key questions that can be raised are these: Have not today's churches—especially when deciding what is needed for restoring full communion—absolutized specific, contingent developments in historic church orders or in conciliar decisions? And have not they thereby created unnecessary barriers to the restoration of full visible unity among the churches?

THE NATURE OF CHURCH
IN MODERN ROMAN CATHOLIC TEACHING

FROM HIERARCHICAL TO COMMUNITARIAN MODELS

The basic source for the Catholic Christian's understanding of the church remains the preaching of Jesus and the New Testament. Still the community of faith has to continue to strive to articulate its theological understanding of the church under the inspiration of the Holy Spirit and by collective discernment about the signs of the times. In the present section, recognizing that I have leapt over centuries of intervening experiences of church, I will focus on how contemporary Catholic understanding of church has been formulated especially in response to the Second Vatican Council, held between 1962 and 1965. In the following section, I will focus on modern Catholicism's teaching about the responsibilities of the various groups in the church. The Second Vatican Council did not fall out of heaven, but reflected a summing up of much of what had gone before in many theological and pastoral experimentations by those in leadership roles. If the Second Vatican Council was creative in amassing and giving public approbation to collective wisdom gathered from the Catholic and wider Christian community, it was not creative in the sense of producing something out of nothing.

The council accepted aspects of church life that were in danger of being forgotten, even accepting some attitudes and teaching that earlier had been frowned upon by those in authority. At the Second Vatican Council the Catholic church reaffirmed and encouraged much that was alive and healthy inwardly but which had not been enthusiastically supported in Vatican directives or even papal encyclicals.

I propose to give a short account of the Catholic church's self-understanding, taking my lead from the texts of the Second Vatican Council that weave together various currents of ecclesiology that had been under development in the years preceding the council. To a great extent I will concentrate on the Dogmatic Constitution on the Church (*Lumen Gentium* [LG]). But to treat *Lumen Gentium* in complete isolation from other council texts that touch on other aspects of church life would be to produce a lopsided description. *Lumen Gentium* was intended to describe the church's life *ad intra*, that is to say its nature, its relationship to revelation, its inner structures, ministries, and general vocation. But a second far-reaching constitution, the Pastoral Constitution on the Church in the Modern World (*Gaudium et Spes* [hereafter GS]), has much to say about the church in relationship to society. To provide a fuller account of church one would have to analyze other documents that treat specific concerns such as: the vocation of all the baptized, the responsibilities of bishops and presbyters, the relationship of the Catholic church with other Christian churches and with other living faiths, and the imperative of religious freedom. It would be a formidable task to provide a comprehensive synthesis of all the texts of the Second Vatican Council that touch upon the vocation of the church.

Although the church, the community of those called to believe in the triune God, remains faithful to its central affirmations, it needs from generation to generation to examine its relationship to cultural, historical, and political forces. Its institutional structures are attempts to express part of its inner reality. Here changes and shifts are not necessarily for the better. The church is the community that keeps alive the memory of Jesus, but it is also the community that, because of weakness and sin, forgets some dimensions of the message of Christ. Hence it is quite appropriate to refer to the church as a community ever in need of reformation. "The Church, clasping sinners to her bosom, at once holy and always in need of purification, follows constantly the path of penance and renewal" (LG 8).

Theologians attempt to articulate scriptural revelation in terms that facilitate believers' understanding today. Confessional differences emerge more notably in this area. There has not always been a strong sense of the need for ecclesiology. In the West treatises specifically on church were not written until the twelfth century, and for the most part they treated jurisdiction or the relationship of the papacy to governmental leaders.

One theological model for explaining the essence of the church saw the church as a visible society, a perfect society. The model enjoyed widespread support from the time of the Counter Reformation to the first half of the twentieth century. This assertion of the "perfect" character of the society called church was an apologetic attempt to assert the church's independence from the state. That model was weak since it neglected the role of the Holy Spirit, the pneumatological dimension. Bühlmann cites as a typical textbook description of ecclesiology the once widely used work of A. Tanquerey, which uses sixty-four pages to show that Christ founded the church (1) as an infallible authority, (2) as a perfect society, (3) as a hierarchical society, and (4) as a monarchic society.[30] The sources of analogy here were drawn not from biblical sources but from civil society. Such a juridical approach was notably strong in post-Reformation Catholic theology. It neglected the mystical, invisible traits of church life that had been highlighted by medieval believers, including certain Reformers.

Such an extrinsicist, hierarchical approach to ecclesiology is even in certain papal documents. An example is a remark of Pius X in his letter *Vehementer Nos* to the bishops of France (Feb. 11, 1906). Here the pope described the church as "an unequal society" composed of two categories of persons, "the pastors and the flock"; this flock or multitude "has no other duty but to allow itself to be led and to follow its pastors as a docile flock." A widely used distinction at that time was the sharp differentiation between the *ecclesia docens* (the teaching church, understood as the hierarchy) and the *ecclesia discens* (the learning church, those to whom the popes' and bishops' instructions were addressed). The gradual move from that model of ecclesiology

---

30. Bühlmann, *Forward*, 19.

to one of the ones favored at the Second Vatican Council came about in the last hundred years through a variety of causes and influences. One of these was the articulation of a more "spiritual" ecclesiology under the influence of the nineteenth-century German theologian Johann Adam Möhler (1796–1838), whose *Die Einheit in der Kirche oder das Prinzip des Katholizismus* (Unity in the church or the principle of Catholicism), originally published in 1825, did much to promote this change. Other voices emerged in the middle of the twentieth century. One was Yves Congar. His work on ecumenism, especially his pioneering *Chrétiens désunis* (Divided christendom) (1937); his sketch on the mystery of the church, *Esquisses du mystère de l'Église* (The mystery of the church) (1941); and his work on the laity, *Jalons pour une théologie du laïcat* (Lay people in the church) (1953) were all influential. At the same time there was a strong revival in Catholicism of scriptural, patristic, and liturgical studies that led to a closer look at the church of the first several centuries. Important here for ecclesiology was the publication of Lucien Cerfaux: *La théologie de l'Église suivant Saint Paul* (The church in the theology of Saint Paul) (1942).

THE SECOND VATICAN COUNCIL'S DESCRIPTION OF CHURCH

In language strongly marked by biblical allusions, the Second Vatican Council stated in the opening of its main document on the church that just as in the Old Testament the revelation of God's kingdom is made known through symbols, so too in the New Testament the church "is now made known to us in various images" (LG 6). These biblical images are drawn from rural life and include sheep raising, farming, building, family life, marriage, etc. Using scriptural images the church is likened to a sheepfold whose one and necessary door is Christ (John 10:1-10), a cultivated field, the tillage of God, the building of God, the "Jerusalem which is above," "our Mother," or the spouse of the spotless Lamb.

Instead of beginning with a description of the church as perfect society, the first chapter of the Constitution on the Church notes the reflection of the inner life of the triune God in the church itself. Borrowing a phrase from Saint Cyprian of Carthage (d. 258), the council states: "Hence the universal church is seen to be 'a people brought into unity from the unity of the Father, the Son and the Holy Spirit'" (LG 4). This trinitarian dimension stresses the free and mysterious character of God's intervention in the world that was an "utterly gratuitous and mysterious design of his wisdom and goodness" (LG 2). Because of this emphasis on the trinitarian structure, certain Catholics have even come to speak about the church as "icon of the Trinity." The church is structured in its communion according to the image and likeness of the trinitarian communion. The church comes from the Trinity, returns toward the Trinity, and is structured according to its image.[31]

Another basic image adopted by the Second Vatican Council to describe the nature of the church is that of communion (*koinonia*). This notion was inspired by the theological and historical research of several theologians, among whom would have to be listed Hertling and Hamer.[32] The communion or koinonial model for understanding the reality of church overcomes much of the inconveniences of juridical or apologetic notions associated with Catholicism's ecclesiology since the Protestant Reformation.[33] The writings of Yves Congar have had a major impact on the use of the communion model.

The term *communion* is an apt category that has deep roots in human consciousness. *Communion* (or its equivalents, *fellowship* or *participation* or *sharing*) was not originally a specifically religious term, but touched on the intersubjective sharing that we experience with other human beings, through family, marriage, nation, cultural heritage, love. Communion can also extend beyond human beings to communion with living animals, with the cosmos. In religious language there is belief that there can exist a sharing or communion with the transcendent God. In the Hebrew Scriptures, God is described as a loving parent, considerate friend, powerful ruler, but the stress is frequently on the distance between God and the human person. Even the biblical notion of covenant stresses the distance between master and servant. In the New Testament the notion of communion stands in continuity with the basic understanding of human sharing, and of close exchanges between God and the human. What is different is the newness of God's taking on human life in Jesus Christ. For Saint Paul communion became the most intimate union of human beings with God as well as with other human beings made possible through the coming of Jesus Christ.

Saint Paul uses the term *koinonia* to express, along with other images, the mystery of God's love made visible in Jesus Christ. To

---

31. See the work of the Italian Catholic theologian Bruno Forte, in French translation: *L'Église: Icône de la Trinité: Brève ecclésiologie* (Paris: Médiaspaul, 1985), especially p. 33.

32. Ludwig von Hertling, *Communio: Church and Papacy in Early Christianity*, trans. J. Wicks (Chicago: Loyola, 1972) (original German edition appeared in 1943); also Jerome Hamer, *The Church Is a Communion* (New York: Sheed and Ward, 1964).

33. See James Provost, ed., *The Church as Communion* (Washington, D.C.: Catholic University Press, 1978). The original collection appeared first in *The Jurist* 36, nos. 1–2 (1976).

express the presence of Christ through the Holy Spirit in the believer, Saint Paul speaks of *koinonia tou hagiou pneumatos* (communion brought about by the Holy Spirit [2 Cor. 13:13]). Paul's use of the notion of communion may be compared to his image of the body of Christ or to his formulas about living "in Christ" or "with Christ," and it may be compared to Saint John's imagery of the vine and the branches or even John's formulas of reciprocity about the Christian's being or remaining in Christ. The New Testament concept, especially in the writings of Saint Paul, is closely allied to the concept found in Eastern Christianity even today about our gradual "divinization in Christ."

It is true that in Saint Paul the term *communion* is not strictly speaking first and foremost an ecclesial notion. Communion for him reflects a double relationship, one enriching the individual and the other forming ecclesial unity. The Spirit's presence affects first an individual, but this presence is not meant to be an individual possession enjoyed in isolation; communion is rather a gift intended to foster unity within the body of Christ, the church. In Paul the term *communion* implies that Christians partake in Christ by receiving his Spirit and that they enter at the same time a fellowship with each other in possessing different gifts. Sharing one's earthly possessions through financial support, sometimes also called *koinonia* (2 Cor. 9:13; Rom. 15:26; Heb. 13:16), is merely one outward expression of participating in the gift of the Spirit.

The term *communion* is a theological assertion about God's loving kindness shared by those who have been called to faith in Christ. In this sense *communion* does not refer to God's salvific will for all humankind; nor does it refer to the different graces bestowed on persons sanctified by other living faiths or religions separated from Christianity. In the New Testament, *communion* stresses not so much the "horizontal" sharing among Christians but the Christian's "vertical" sharing with God. The term stresses the relationship between God and the believer, but especially the ongoing activity of the Holy Spirit who vivifies the person for life in the church.

In the previous section I enumerated some of the ways that the Christian community expressed ecclesial communion or *koinonia* in the period between the New Testament and the Constantinian era. The basic Pauline term and its equivalency in the Johannine literature were retained and expanded. This is especially true in the writings of Irenaeus of Lyons, who uses the term *koinonia* over eighty times to describe our access to salvation. In his opposition to the false divisions and separations that he saw as introduced into Christianity by Gnosticism, Irenaeus appealed to *koinonia* to describe the communion among humans who share in the Spirit's life. Irenaeus's theological or pneumatological emphasis was rather short-lived, however, since the church of the West came more and more to focus attention upon the institutional aspects of communion rather than upon its source in the Godhead. The term *communion* after Irenaeus was seen, to be sure, as indicating a living relationship between believers and God, but much more stress was placed on the relationship of mutual acceptance between various local churches. This relationship was externalized by various regulations regarding baptism, penitential reconciliation, and eucharistic hospitality. In itself such a shift was quite legitimate and not undesirable. The only danger was that in the development of the concept, some of its original complexity deriving from the biblical texts might be lost sight of.

To the extent that the bishop in the early church assumed more and more responsibility for unifying the church, the regulatory aspects of communion became more marked. In his classic modern study of communion in the early church, the Roman Catholic scholar Ludwig von Hertling described how this word ultimately came to refer to "the bond that united the bishops and the faithful, the bishops among themselves, and the faithful among themselves, a bond that was both effected and at the same time made manifest by eucharistic communion."[34]

The term *koinonia* or *communio* occurs in a citation from Paul used today as a greeting at the beginning of the Roman eucharistic liturgy: "The grace of God our Father, the love of Christ, and the communion [fellowship] of the Holy Spirit..." But it also occurs in the Nicene Creed, the reference being to the *communio sanctorum*. This term can be understood in three ways, all of which are correct: the communion of the Holy Spirit that brings us into communion with other believers; the communion of holy things or realities (taking the antecedent of *sanctorum* to be *sancta*), especially baptism and eucharist; and the communion of the saints (taking the antecedent of *sanctorum* to be *sancti*), or sharing in the fellowship of other believers both living and dead.

I have noted that communion in the New Testament refers primarily to the vertical relationship between believer (as member in a community) and redeeming God. Modern theological usage more commonly employs the term to describe the horizontal or ecclesiological implications of the church's charismatic structure, shared responsibility, and collective accountability. Other terms such as *grace, divinization,* and *sanctification* came to replace *communion* in its

---

34. Hertling, *Communio,* 16.

first sense. Communion has become a highly flexible concept, admitting an indefinite variety of degrees and modalities that are valuable in an age of flux, pluralism, and ecumenism. The concept can refer to (1) communion among churches with identical doctrine and practice (united churches) or (2) communion among divided churches lacking organic unity between each other.

GOD'S PEOPLE IN CHRIST

Chapter 2 of the Second Vatican Council's text on the inner life of the church describes the church as the "new people of God" (LG 9) or the "new Israel." This echoes what is said in the New Testament, especially in Romans 9:25-26, 2 Corinthians 6:14, Titus 2:14, and 1 Peter 2:10: "[You] are now the people of God." Christians need to be careful how they use the title; they need to eliminate possible erroneous conclusions suggesting that Israel has ceased to be the people of God, which would be contrary to the New Testament statements (see Heb. 11:25; Matt. 1:21; Luke 1:68; Rom. 11:1-2). The teaching of the church about Israel's continuing vocation has not always been translated into the church's practice. The church regards itself as the "new people of God" but in a way that does not annul the first covenant given to Israel (Luke 1:72; Acts 3:25; Gal. 3:17). Israel remains God's people (Rom. 9:6); God has not cast off Israel (Rom. 11:1). The vocation of the Jewish people of God is continuous, irrevocable, indestructible; the Jews are and remain God's chosen and beloved people. The new situation of the church does not destroy the old (Rom. 9:3). The Jews remain the people God addressed first. The Second Vatican Council's Declaration on Non-Christian Religions, *Nostra Aetate* (NA), states: "Although the Church is the new people of God, the Jews should not be presented as repudiated or cursed by God, as if such views followed from the Holy Scriptures" (NA 4).

In claiming the title God's new people in Christ, the church also affirms that it is a pilgrim people, constantly in need of forward movement toward holiness. Such is the concern of chapter 7 of *Lumen Gentium*, which is entitled "The Eschatological Nature of the Pilgrim Church and Its Union with the Church in Heaven" (LG 48–51).

CHURCH AS SACRAMENT

Another component of modern Catholic teaching reflected in the Second Vatican Council is the notion that the church itself is a sacrament. The opening section of *Lumen Gentium* states: "The Church, in Christ, is in the nature of sacrament—a sign and instrument, that is, of communion with God and of unity among all human beings" (LG 1). Whereas late medieval Western theology had come to restrict the word *sacrament* to refer to only the seven sacraments, the Second Vatican Council, partly influenced by Catholic theologians from the 1950s, referred to the church in Christ as a kind of sacrament (*veluti sacramentum*).

As Israel and Jesus himself had been visible expressions and signs of God's loving kindness, so now, it was reasoned, the church itself is a sacrament or "mystery." This notion was adumbrated in the nineteenth century in the writings of Möhler and Scheeben and was further developed in the twentieth century by Karl Rahner and Otto Semmelroth, who described the church as the first of all sacraments, a kind of *Ursakrament*. The church was pictured as a sacramental sign, effect, and gift of God. At the heart of the sacramental insight is the conviction that God can and does use the physical, tangible, historical, vocal aspects of human life as "bearers" of divine love. Some have called this use of the material to convey the spiritual a kind of incarnational principle. The modern Dominican theologian Edward Schillebeeckx had also expanded the traditional use of the terminology by describing Christ himself as primordial sacrament, namely "sacrament of humanity's encounter with God."

In saying that the church is a sacrament there is no need whatsoever of creating the impression that sacrament excludes stress on the "Word of God." The popular caricature that describes Catholicism as a Christianity of sacrament and Protestantism as a Christianity of Word is completely misleading. Sacraments are intended to be gospel words expressed in such a way that the words are intensified by ritual gesture. As Saint Augustine remarked in his commentary on John's Gospel, a word is united to a sensible element and becomes a sacrament, or a visible word (*tamquam visibile verbum*).[35]

I do not intend here to expand upon the relationship between the church and the sacraments; that topic is developed in the chapter on sacraments later in this volume. I do wish to point out here that it is clear that the church when celebrating any sacrament, but especially at the memorial of the Lord's Supper, the eucharist, achieves an intensity of its being that is quite central to its self-identity. Sacramental baptism affords a person entry into the community of faith. Marriage and ordination are two sacraments of vocation to life in the church and in society. Through the celebration of the sacraments and

---

35. Augustine *Tract. in Eu Joan.* 80.3 (*Patrologia Latina*, ed. Migne [hereafter PL], 35, 1840).

through the expression of the community's faith, the church realizes one of its very special functions, which is to keep alive the memory of Jesus by worshiping the triune God and giving expression to its hope for the final coming of the kingdom.

THE LOCAL CHURCH AS CHURCH OF CHRIST

One central affirmation of the ecclesiology of the Second Vatican Council is: "This church of Christ is really present [*vere adest*] in all legitimate local congregations of the faithful which, united with their bishops, in the New Testament are also called churches" (LG 26). This emphasis on the local church in Roman Catholic thought is quite close to Eastern Orthodox thought, where this form of ecclesiology goes by the name of eucharistic ecclesiology. In this view, local churches are not considered portions or parts of the church, but the ecclesial body of Christ is present in fullness in each local eucharistic community, realized in a particular place and time. These local churches are the church of Christ only when they live in communion with all the others; otherwise they might run the risk of becoming mere sects.

In the Roman Catholic church there is some ambiguity in the use of the term *local church* since it might refer to the Catholic community within a particular nation, or to the diocesan church under a presiding bishop, or even to the parish or specific eucharistic worshiping community.

CHURCH AS CHARISMATIC COMMUNITY

Another way that the church is described in the perspective of the Second Vatican Council is as a community of charisms. In the Catholic community, as in the Christian community in general except possibly for Pentecostal Christians, there had been a general neglect of the term *charism*. It was almost as though while charisms were important in the early church, the age of charism was dead. In a famous speech at the Second Vatican Council, Cardinal Leo Suenens of Malines-Brussels urged the restoration of the belief in charisms. A charism might be defined as such: A gift or ability conveyed to an individual within the Christian community enabling the person to fulfill a specific service, either over a long period of time or in a relatively short period of time.

In the Decree on the Apostolate of the Laity, the Second Vatican Council noted: "From the reception of these charisms, even the most ordinary ones, there arises for each of the faithful the right and duty of exercising them in the church and in the world for the good of human beings and the development of the church, of exercising them in the freedom of the Holy Spirit who 'breathes where he wills,' and at the same time in communion with his brothers/sisters in Christ and with his bishops especially" (*Apostolicam Actuositatem* 3). Earlier in the text on the church it was noted: "Whether these charisms be very remarkable or more simple and widely diffused, they are to be received with thanksgiving and consolation since they are fitting and useful for the needs of the church" (LG 12). In speaking of the role of priests or presbyters one Vatican II text says: "While testing the spirits to see if they be of God, they [presbyters] must discover with faith, recognize with joy, and foster with diligence the many and varied charismatic gifts of the laity whether these be of a humble or more exalted kind" (*Presbyterorum Ordinis* 9). The same warning is given to bishops: "For they [bishops] know that they themselves were not established by Christ to undertake alone the whole salvific mission of the church to the world, but that it is their exalted office so to be shepherds of the faithful and also to recognize the latter's contributions and charisms that everyone in his or her own way will, with one mind, cooperate in the common task" (LG 30).

Fearing that a vast affirmation of charisms might threaten proper order and authority in the church, the drafters of the Vatican II text on the church inserted a distinction (which is not biblical but has historical relevance) between two different kinds of charisms: The Holy Spirit "bestows upon the church varied hierarchic and charismatic gifts and in this way directs the church and adorns it with his fruits" (LG 4). And in a similar vein: "Among these gifts stands out the grace of the apostles to whose authority the Spirit himself subjects even those who are endowed with charisms" (LG 7).

The Greek word *charisma* or the plural *charismata* is used seventeen times in the New Testament, all (except 1 Peter 4:10) in the Pauline corpus: Romans 1:1; 5:15 (twice); 6:23; 11:29; 12:6; 1 Corinthians 1:7; 7:7; 12:4; 12:9; 12:28; 12:30; 12:31; 2 Corinthians 1:11; 1 Timothy 4:14; 2 Timothy 1:6. For Paul the term is not always a *terminus technicus* since it is a concept in development. In Romans 5:15 it is a variant for the notion of salvation in Christ; in Romans 11:29 it refers to Israel's privilege in the sealing of the covenant, the conferral of the Law, etc. But the classical text is 1 Corinthians 12:4: "Now there are varieties of charisms [*charismaton*], but the same Spirit; and there are varieties of service [*diakonion*], but the same Lord; and there are varieties of working [*energematon*], but it is the same God who inspires them all in every one."

Besides the use of the word *charism(s)* Paul gives in various places in his corpus a list of about eighteen different charisms, some of which are difficult to identify with strict accuracy: apostles, prophets, evangelists, teachers, admonitors, almsgivers, administrators, mercy-workers, those who utter wise statements, those gifted with special faith, healers, miracle workers, discerners of spirits, those with the gift of tongues, interpreters of tongues, and those providing help, counseling, and service.[36]

COLLEGIALITY AND CONCILIARITY/SOBORNICITY OF THE CHURCH

One of the characteristic emphases of the ecclesiology of the Second Vatican Council was its stress that pastoral responsibility for the worldwide church rests not only with the pope but also with all the bishops, especially those who are responsible for one of its dioceses. A new word was introduced into Catholic circles, namely *collegiality*, which refers to the conviction that a bishop, by reason of his episcopal ordination and not specifically by reason of his appointment by the pope, bears responsibility for the church universal. Collegiality is much more specific than the more general term *shared responsibility*, which applies to all the baptized and designates that by reason of baptism and charismatic gifts from the Holy Spirit each believer must be somehow involved in promoting the teaching and life of the Christian faith. Those who planned the Second Vatican Council and partook in its discussions recognized that a somewhat disproportionate emphasis on the role of the pope since the First Vatican Council had clouded the reality of "collegiality," or the ministry of the world's bishops acting as a "college" either at a general synod or by cooperation from their home dioceses.

One of the ways that bishops' cooperative teachings about reading the signs of the times has been expressed since the Second Vatican Council has been through the meetings and publications of the various national episcopal conferences. It is natural to expect that these episcopal conferences sometimes come into conflict or experience tension in relationship to the central offices of the papal administration, the various congregations of the Roman curia. This tension

---

36. The classic study on charisms in Paul and in Vatican II is that of Heinz Schürmann, "Les charismes spirituels," in G. Barauna, ed., *L'Église de Vatican II*, Unam Sanctam 51b (Paris: Cerf, 1967), 2:541–73. The scriptural texts that include partial lists of charisms are: 1 Thess. 5:12; 5:19-22; 1 Cor. 14:1-5; 14:6; 14:26; 14:27-33; 1 Cor. 13:8ff.; 1 Cor. 12:8-10; 12:28-30; 1 Cor. 13:1-3; Rom. 12:6-8; Eph. 4:11. These are largely charisms related to preaching, leadership functions, and charitable deeds.

already existed prior to the Second Vatican Council and some of the more dramatic interventions by bishops at the council related to these conflicts. The Congregation for the Doctrine of the Faith, the chief papal office for supervising the content and manner of official teaching, has suggested that whereas these episcopal conferences have pastoral usefulness they are not properly speaking official teaching organs of the church. Not all agree with this view. In the meantime bishops and theologians alike are studying carefully historical precedents for the modern episcopal conference and showing how in fact they do represent a valuable source of teaching for the church. On the occasion of a working draft on the status of episcopal conferences produced by a Vatican congregation, a number of Catholic bishops and theologians have explored the function and necessity of these national conferences of bishops.[37]

The Eastern churches, especially the Eastern Orthodox churches, continue to stress another profound conviction, that what is crucial to the life of the church is not only collegiality as a complement to papal ministry, but also "conciliarity" or "sobornicity." According to this view, the church is supposed to function as a harmonious symphony of believers who have been gathered in Christ and upon whom the Holy Spirit rests. Conciliarity seeks to fashion ecclesiastical life in a way that will express the church's nature and distinctiveness. Eastern theologians state that the church expresses communion in Christ through its synodal character.

ONE HOLY CATHOLIC AND APOSTOLIC CHURCH

The Niceno-Constantinopolitan Creed—which was formulated in the fourth century at an ecumenical council and has been used since at baptism and other liturgical occasions as one measure of orthodox faith—affirms resoundingly that the Christian community sees itself as "one holy catholic and apostolic." The original meaning of these attributes has not always remained clear; nor has the purpose of these dimensions been properly understood. What is clear is that none of the four attributes was originally intended to be used polemically or apologetically to demonstrate the superiority of one church over another or to imply that one possessed more unity, sanctity, catholicity, or apostolicity.

Just as in other parts of the Christian credo, the assertion of the church as one holy catholic and apostolic is meant to be understood

---

37. See the volume published under the auspices of the Woodstock Theological Center in Washington: Reese, ed., *Episcopal Conferences*, especially my contribution on Eastern synodal life.

eschatologically. By that is meant that these characteristics are associated with the church not to describe purely what visibly exists to the beholder; rather they are part of a prayer of longing and hope that the church may in fact become what it is called to be by reason of its lofty vocation. The attributes are meant to be both affirmations of fact and invitations to hope.

Oneness, holiness, catholicity, and apostolicity are possessed by the church because of the gracious gift of the Holy Spirit that effects these graces through God's mysterious design. But the gifts are clouded and distorted by the presence of sin and willfulness in the members of the church individually and collectively. Hence, just as in the Lord's Prayer we find ourselves obliged to pray "Thy kingdom come," so too in the community of faith do we need to pray: "Thy church become one holy catholic and apostolic." Roman Catholics, especially since the promulgation of the Decree on Ecumenism, have an acute awareness that their church, despite the presence of the one Holy Spirit dwelling within, is not in fact visibly one holy catholic and apostolic. The church is one because of the indwelling of the one Holy Spirit in all the baptized; it is holy because it is set apart by God's graciousness for the reception of a mysterious love of predilection; it is catholic in the original sense of the word, meaning that it is whole and entire, possessing all the parts needed to make it integral; and it is apostolic because it remains in continuity in essentials with the original witnessing of the first-century apostles (and not simply the twelve, but the entire apostolic community of believers in the first generation). Catholics are often inclined to apply these descriptive characteristics only to the worldwide, universal church, yet they are beginning to learn from the Eastern Orthodox churches and others that these characteristics are meant to apply just as truly to the local church.

RESPONSIBILITIES WITHIN THE CHURCH

THE FAITHFUL

One fruitful way to better understand the nature of the church is to reflect on the various responsibilities associated with its members. All members of the church are entrusted by God with specific responsibilities; these may differ but are complementary. The faithful, those who accept God's revelation through belief, are expected to participate in the community's worship of God by joining with

Christ in his heavenly liturgy of adoration and praise. By an active liturgical life turned toward God they learn that faith consists not in a recitation of formulas but in a life imbued with Christian values.

The initial chapter of Vatican II's Dogmatic Constitution on the Church (*Lumen Gentium*) relates the church to the inner life of the triune God. In the discussion of the structure of the constitution there was some difference of opinion at the council as to what should be the next chapter. Some participants argued for a section on the hierarchy. Despite their arguments for that option, the council next took up the church as a whole ("God's People in Christ") rather than the hierarchy. This decision has widely influenced the Catholic church's self-understanding and even affected the structure of the new Code of Canon Law. The primary focus was on what all persons in the church share. Only later, in chapter 4, does *Lumen Gentium* return to a discussion of the specific responsibilities of the *laity*, a term designating "all the faithful except those in holy orders and those who belong to a religious state approved by the church" (LG 31). The emphasis is not on the role of Christians taken as individuals but rather as members of the body of Christ. The faithful find their dignity rooted in the gift of baptism through which even as lay persons they share in the priestly and prophetic office of Christ. The faithful are possessors of numerous charismatic gifts emanating from the Holy Spirit; these are bestowed upon all believers for the building up of the church.

Lumen Gentium gives expression to the conviction that the entire body of the faithful possesses a *sensus fidei*, a supernatural instinct found in Christians that allows them to recognize what is authentic or unauthentic as well as what is central or what peripheral to the Christian faith (LG 12). The entire body of the faithful, it is claimed, cannot err in central matters of belief, which is another way of describing the basic "infallibility" of the church, namely the conviction that the Holy Spirit maintains the church in truth by keeping alive the memory of the identity and significance of Jesus Christ. This religious "sixth sense" has special pertinence in connection with how teachings proposed by pastors or teachers find their "reception" in the church.

Modern ecumenical theology, through an extensive number of theological dialogues in which theologians attempt to go beyond ancient polemics, stresses that a believer can best understand the function of ordained ministry in the church by first gaining an insight into the ministry of Jesus and its continuation in the ministry of all the baptized.[38] One way of speaking that stressed the universal priesthood of all believers, a way of speaking considered rather suspect in post-Reformation Catholicism because it sounded too Lutheran, too Protestant, is in fact affirmed by the council when it notes that the faithful "by virtue of their royal priesthood, participate in the offering of the Eucharist" (LG 10). In a period when the Roman Catholic church in many countries is experiencing a notable decline in the number of persons presenting themselves for ordination, it is important that lay persons not be seen as a poor "substitute" for ordained presbyters. In fact, the faithful are included in participating in the mission of the church. "Each disciple of Christ has the obligation of spreading the faith to the best of his or her ability" (LG 17).

Another task that is applied today to the role of the faithful is co-responsibility or shared decision-making. This may ring hollow in some parts of the church where the faithful, if called upon at all to speak, are not always heard, or where the lay faithful are never asked to participate in crucial decisions, such as the naming of a local bishop.

INSTITUTES OF CONSECRATED LIFE

Another group of persons in the church given special attention in *Lumen Gentium* (chap. 6) constitutes women and men traditionally identified as "religious" or members of religious congregations or orders. According to a new terminology these persons are perhaps best referred to as members of "institutes of consecrated life." The responsibilities of these persons are described both in *Lumen Gentium* and in the Decree on the Appropriate Renewal of Religious Life (*Perfectae Caritatis*). Central to their identity as religious are their public vows or pledges of the evangelical counsels: poverty, chastity, and obedience, promised within the context of a life in community. *Lumen Gentium* describes the powerful sign-value emanating from those persons who wish to mirror Christ in the world (LG 40). Their life style is meant to be a sign of fidelity and dedication to the fulfillment of the spiritual and material needs of the wider human family.

The idea of consecration does not imply separation from the church's mission, a subject I will treat in the next section. Women of these communities have had a significant role in the education and evangelization of generations of young Christians. Also prominent has been the role of communities of brothers. Groups of these

---

38. Several of these consensus statements on ministry are published in *Modern Ecumenical Documents on the Ministry* (London: SPCK, 1975).

men and women see themselves gifted by the Holy Spirit with similar kinds of charisms and for that reason choose to live together in community for the development and nurturing of the charisms conferred upon them for the life of the church.

THE ORDAINED

A third group of persons in the church assigned distinctive sacramental and liturgical responsibilities constitutes the ordained. The Latin texts of the Vatican II documents usually avoid the term *priest* (*sacerdos*), mainly because the New Testament shuns the Greek equivalent word that describes that specific group of ministers in the church. Rather the Latin texts of Vatican II use the term *presbyteros* (its English equivalent is not always used in translations) to refer to those who have been ordained. Most Catholics are probably puzzled by the introduction of this new term that somehow sounds rather "Presbyterian," and in fact this change in terminology has had little impact on usage among English-speaking Catholics. There does however seem to be a gradual preference among some for the term *ordained* rather than the word *priest*. To prevent anyone from drawing too sharp a distinction between ordained and nonordained, the Second Vatican Council did specifically state, referring back to essentialistic rather than scriptural terminology, that "the common priesthood of the faithful and the ministerial or hierarchical priesthood, though they differ in essence and not only in degree, are nonetheless ordered one to another" (LG 10).

The more that the Second Vatican Council's document tries to describe the responsibilities of the presbyter, the more the text becomes removed from Scripture. According to the document, there are two forms of ministry (that of the ordained and the nonordained): "The ministerial priest [*sacerdos*], by the sacred power he possesses, forms and governs the priestly people; he effects the eucharistic sacrifice in the person of Christ, and he offers it to God in the name of all the people" (LG 10). Later in the section on bishops, the task of presbyters is again touched upon. There they are described as "vigilant collaborators with the episcopate, called to assist and serve it, called to serve God's people, and constituted with their bishop one presbyteral college dedicated it is true to a variety of duties." "In each local congregation of the faithful, presbyters, in a way, represent the bishop with whom they are associated in all trust and generosity; in part they take upon themselves his duties and solicitude and fulfill them in their daily labor" (LG 28). If descriptions of the tasks of the ordained presbyter seem rather sparse in *Lumen Gentium* it is in part because two other decrees of the Second Vatican Council treat the role of presbyters: the Decree on the Ministry and Life of Presbyters (*Presbyterorum Ordinis*) and the Decree on the Training of Presbyters (*Optatam Totius*). Still it cannot be denied that the Vatican II texts are more attentive to the bishop's role than to the presbyter's role.

PASTORAL OFFICE

Another distinct group closely connected with the presbyterium is the bishops, who are seen to continue the work of the *episkopoi* in the New Testament. One of the most remarkable consensus statements related to this form of ministry produced in recent decades is a document on the role of the church's concept of *episkopē* ("oversight"); the document was produced by a French-speaking joint Roman Catholic and Reformed Christian commission known as the Group of Les Dombes (a village near the historic monasteries of Cluny and Taizé). Published in 1976, this document, entitled *Le ministère épiscopale* (The episcopal ministry), makes an excellent companion piece to what the Second Vatican Council said about the tasks of the episcopal office.[39]

At the Second Vatican Council the role of bishop was described in two documents: *Lumen Gentium* and *Christus Dominus* (the Decree on the Bishops' Pastoral Office in the Church). These documents include sections on apostolic succession, the sacramentality of the order of bishop, the relation of the college of bishops to its head (the pope), the episcopal authority in the diocese, and finally the governance and teaching authority of the local bishop.

Because of the heavy stress placed on the role of the pope in the previous council, the First Vatican Council, it was important that the Second Vatican Council expatiate on the complementary functions of the bishop and show that the service he undertakes for the community is based not on appointment by the pope but on his sacramental ordination or consecration as a bishop. Thus the document on the church explicitly states that "the fullness of the sacrament of orders is conferred by episcopal consecration.... Episcopal consecration confers, together with the office of sanctifying, the duty also of teaching and pastoring, which, however, of their very nature can be exercised only in hierarchical communion with the head and members of the [episcopal] college" (LG 21).

Historical studies show that those who came to be called *episkopoi* were persons who held responsibilities resulting from a blending of two originally separate functions: each was a successor of the apostles

---

39. An English translation is given in *One in Christ* 14 (1978): 267–88.

(thus having apostolic oversight) and the president of a presbyterium (the single local leader of the community). In appealing to apostolic succession one should not lose sight of the fact that some characteristics possessed by the original apostles are of their very nature unrepeatable and noncommunicable. In the early church a multitude of forms for exercising apostolic responsibilities existed side by side. From these varied and sometimes conflicting sources the office of bishop eventually took shape. Even the notion of apostolic succession had various meanings.

The Second Vatican Council stressed that the triple role of the bishop (teaching, sanctifying, and shepherding) derives directly from sacramental ordination and not from canonical appointment by the pope. The local bishop possesses his right to governance in such a way that his canonical power is "ordinary, proper and immediate." In the administration of his diocese the bishop retains a certain autonomy from national episcopal conferences, from the Roman congregations, and even from the pope himself.

By reason of sacramental consecration into the episcopal college, bishops share in "collegiality," a responsibility for fostering communion among churches throughout the world. Hence the ministry of a bishop, although focused primarily on a local diocese, is not restricted exclusively to his own particular church. The role of bishops in the Catholic church is much more important than in many churches. In a real sense they are seen as in continuity with the role of the apostles in the earliest Christian communities.

The three major functions of the bishop according to Catholic teaching are: teaching, sanctifying, and being a pastor.[40] Catholic teaching also stresses that it is crucial for the maintenance of visible unity at the universal level that there be an exercise of _episkopē_ on a worldwide basis. How this form of more comprehensive pastoral care or _episkopē_ has been and is now realized concretely in ecclesial life must be kept in proper balance between conciliarity and primacy. Could such a service of unity among churches be acceptable within the wider communion of churches beyond Roman Catholicism? What would Catholics and non-Catholics alike wish as the proper maintenance of a primacy that serves unity and diversity among the _koinonia_ of churches?

Some of the language of the Second Vatican Council shows signs of some haste and compromise in the way it treats historical texts and movements relating to the ordained ministry. In its desire to show

---

40. James K. Mallett, ed., _The Ministry of Governance_, With Oars and Sails, 1 (Washington, D.C.: Canon Law Society of America, 1986).

that there is a continuity between New Testament apostles (perhaps without paying sufficient attention to the fact that even in the New Testament the word *apostle* is used with different shades of meaning) and modern-day bishops, the Second Vatican Council states, as though there are no historical problems in this succinct formulation, that: "The apostles were careful to appoint successors in this hierarchically constituted society" (LG 20).

MAGISTERIUM

One perspective on church life that has received close attention in the Roman Catholic church during the last two centuries is that associated with the term *magisterium*. This is a loan-word from Latin that originally designated functions or activities engaged in by a *magister* or teacher, but which nowadays, especially in documents emanating from the pope or Vatican congregations, refers not to the function but to the functionaries, that specific group of persons who are entrusted with the task of overseeing official church teaching. It is a curious fact that a notion that has grown to assume such central importance in an episcopally structured church such as the Roman Catholic church does not have a recognizable equivalent even in the other episcopal communities such as the Orthodox, Anglican, or Lutheran churches.

One would be hard pressed to find any other term in Catholicism that has no obvious counterpart in the Byzantine or Reformed traditions. Hardly any other term at the heart of modern Catholic teaching has been able to maintain its modern usage without being contextualized by reference to its historically original connotation. In the last fifty years or so most Catholics have shown themselves willing to understand the word *magisterium* as referring to a particular group of persons in the church entrusted with the task of providing ecclesiastical teaching that is *magisterium authenticum*, to use the language of the nineteenth and twentieth centuries, including that of the Second Vatican Council. In this case the Latin adjective *authenticum* is often translated (incorrectly) as "authentic" teaching (as opposed to inauthentic?) rather than correctly translated as "authoritative" (in the sense of bearing the force of a teaching that is consistent with the Scriptures).

Crucial to restricting the word *magisterium* to that identifiable group of ecclesiastics entrusted with the task of authoritative teaching is the distinction, again rather recent in the church's history, between the *ecclesia docens* and the *ecclesia discens* (the teaching church [the bishops] and the learning church [the rest of the church, especially the laity]). A number of theologians have recently attempted to show that the distinction between these two parts of the church is not as simple as it seems.[41] But most official modern Catholic documents accept without objection the use of *magisterium* to refer to the pastoral authoritative teaching of the hierarchy as opposed to other forms of teaching, such as that proposed by theologians, prophets, mystics, or the simple faithful. The danger in this now conventional usage is that it is apt to trivialize the complexity of how church teaching is formulated, especially in regard to how the present-day church reads the signs of the times.

The medieval usage of *magisterium* was more nuanced and allowed for serious weight to be given to the teachings of competent church historians, canonists, or theologians who spoke out of their knowledge of the tradition. The insight behind this distinction between the ministry of bishops and of other teachers in the church, such as theologians, an insight that is rather obfuscated by present terminological usage, is that ordained bishops and responsible theologians have distinctive, though complementary, functions in the church. Where they may differ often pertains to prudential judgments about the wisdom of proposing teaching that may be seen as provocative, innovative, or lacking in rigor.

Naturally in the context of this very brief exposition of magisterium, one of the key concepts of papal and episcopal teaching today, it is not possible to give a totally adequate account of the sources and scope of ecclesiastical "magisterium." All that I wish to do is to urge that the notion be carefully contextualized historically and explained in a way that fully accounts for the demands of collegiality, reception of teaching by the faithful, the vocation of learning in the life of the church, and the importance of listening, especially to those through whom the Holy Spirit may be speaking to the church in our time.

PAPAL PRIMACY

The Catholic church has strongly expressed the conviction that there must be a form of primatial authority exercised in the church. The function of papal primacy may have changed notably since the invention of new methods of communication and travel. The pope's function is seen to be in continuity with the role of Peter among the rest of the twelve in the New Testament. Peter's role was as a

---

41. See, for instance, Ladislas Orsy, *The Church Learning and Teaching* (Wilmington, Del.: Glazier, 1987), as well as the volume by Francis A. Sullivan, *Magisterium: Teaching Authority in the Catholic Church* (New York: Paulist, 1983).

missionary, as one who first received the promise of the keys (Matt. 16:18).

To understand the central importance that the primacy of the pope has assumed in the Catholic church it is important to look back at the nineteenth-century general council, the First Vatican Council (1869–70). Because it is more remote from our times and its preoccupations are less obvious to us today, some historical background is necessary. The Second Vatican Council, which was more interested in focusing its energies on the role of bishops, decided not to reformulate earlier descriptions of papal primacy and infallibility. One can be a loyal Catholic theologian and still regret that the Second Vatican Council did not sufficiently nuance what the First Vatican Council had stated about the papacy.

Roger Aubert, whose special area of competence is the First Vatican Council, has clearly established through his research that those bishops at the First Vatican Council who hoped for the most comprehensive statement of papal infallibility (the maximalist position) were roundly rejected.[42] However, some of the popular commentaries in England and in other parts of the English-speaking world exaggerated what the First Vatican Council had stated about papal infallibility. These exaggerations were in part based on a famous two-hundred-page pastoral letter on papal infallibility circulated by the English cardinal Henry Edward Manning. This letter, published shortly after the council and written from an unabashedly maximalistic perspective, was intended to be a kind of commentary on the doctrine; it exercised an enormous impact on teaching in seminaries in England and other seminaries using the English language, which may help to explain why there were different perceptions about papal infallibility among bishops from the English-speaking world and other countries (such as Germany and France) at the beginning of the Second Vatican Council. Some of the subsequent theological explanations of what the First Vatican Council is purported to have stated may also have been at the root of that maximalizing tendency that predicates infallible status to many of the pope's utterances. The more moderate positions of John Henry Cardinal Newman were not generally as well known in the nineteenth century as those of Cardinal Manning.

One astute explanation of what the First Vatican Council had said came from some twenty-three German bishops who had attended the council and who in December 1874 responded in a newspaper article to a dispatch from Chancellor Bismark; this dispatch argued that

---

42. See Roger Aubert, *Vatican I* (Paris: Orante, 1964).

the council had effectively nullified the power of the bishops. These German bishops reasoned that in the mind of the council the pope clearly did not have unlimited powers, that he remained subject to divine law and to Christ's intentions for his church. Nor are the bishops simply instruments of the pope, bereft of personal responsibility. The notion that the pope is an absolute monarch, they argued, is a wholly false interpretation of the dogma of infallibility. On March 4, 1875, in an apostolic letter to the German episcopate, Pope Pius IX praised the interpretation of the German bishops and wrote: "Your declaration is an expression of that true Catholic doctrine which is at once the teaching of the Vatican Council and of the Holy See."[43]

What did the First Vatican Council say? The circumstances under which that council began were not the most auspicious, when on December 8, 1869, 660 prelates assembled in Rome. There was reason to think that the council might be brought to a halt if the military forces seeking Italian unification (the *risorgimento*) were to overrun the remaining papal territory. Such fears of invasion proved grounded, and less that a year after the opening ceremony, on September 20, 1870, Rome was occupied by troops who laid claim to the city as the capital of the new Italy.

The accomplishments of the First Vatican Council were very limited and restricted because of the constraints of time. Two lengthy drafts on "The Church," the first prepared by the Roman theologians Perrone and Cardoni, and the second developed by Kleutgen, were never discussed in any detail, much less ratified, because of the rush of time at the council. In ecclesiology proper, all that was promulgated was the Dogmatic Constitution *Pastor Aeternus* (voted upon July 18, 1870), which describes basically only the function of the papacy in the church. Still its preamble sets the doctrine regarding the institution, perpetuity, and nature of Petrine primacy in the context of preserving the unity of the bishops "in order that the episcopate itself might be one and undivided, and in order that the entire multitude of believers might be maintained in unity of faith and of communion by means of the close union of the bishops one with another" (Denzinger-Schönmetzer, *Enchiridion Symbolorum* [hereafter DS], 3051). The necessity for expounding the doctrine of papal primacy is attributed to contemporary threats to the security of the Catholic church: "With daily increasing hatred the forces of hell are rising on all sides against this divinely established foundation to overthrow the church, if possible" (see DS 3052). However dubious

---

43. For an English translation of the text of the German bishops, see F. Donald Logan, "The 1875 Statement of the German Bishops on Episcopal Powers," *Jurist* 21 (1961): 285–95.

its necessity and however inopportune its definition, the text of the First Vatican Council did in fact try to situate the Petrine function in the context of serving the unity of faith and charity. According to the text, the twofold unity of faith and of communion ("charity" earlier in the text) was said to be maintained by the bishops as a whole. Far from being a "juridical" perspective, the primacy of the pope was located in the context of an episcopate that serves unity of faith and of charity/communion.

After the introductory section to *Pastor Aeternus* there follow four chapters, each devoted to a central theme: (1) the institution of the apostolic primacy in Peter; (2) the perpetuity of the primacy of Peter in the Roman pontiff; (3) the power and nature of the primacy of the Roman pontiff; and (4) the infallible teaching power of the Roman pontiff. For the purposes of this exposition I will not dwell on the first two chapters. As insufficient and naive as was the use of the scriptural texts (Matt. 16 and John 21), the claim in chapter 1 that in the New Testament Peter did have a leading role among the apostles would not be challenged by the consensus of biblical scholars today.[44] What is problematic in chapter 1 is the claim that this "primacy" is one not only of "honor" but also of "jurisdiction."

In chapter 2 it is stated that "what was instituted in blessed Peter for the constant protection and unceasing good of the church must, by the will of the same Founder, remain continually in the church" (DS 3056). The objections of other churches, such as the Eastern Orthodox church, to teaching about the papacy, if I understand correctly, have been not so much that in some sense the bishop of Rome inherited Petrine functions, but rather that too many functions have been bestowed on him.

Chapter 3 contains five lengthy paragraphs and concludes with a canon or anathema. To begin with that concluding canon is helpful since it succinctly summarizes the entire chapter. The canon anathematizes those who dare to deny that the pope enjoys "full and supreme power of jurisdiction over the whole church not only in matters pertaining to faith and morals, but also in matters pertaining to the discipline and government of the church throughout the entire world" (DS 3064). It anathematizes those who deny that he possesses "the full plenitude of this supreme power" or that this power is "ordinary and immediate over all churches and over each individual church, over all shepherds and all the faithful." The terminology used here requires some clarification. "Power" in this context

---

44. See Raymond Brown, Karl P. Donfried, et al., eds., *Peter in the New Testament* (New York: Paulist, 1974).

(*potestas* or *exousia*) refers to the holder's rightful freedom to act, the authority that he has been granted, and not his having the power to impose his will on others by force or by intimidation. But *potestas* in the sense of "right" easily becomes confused with *potestas* in the sense of "might." The phrase *potestas jurisdictionis seu regiminis* had become standard since the early Middle Ages to describe the governing aspect of the pastoral care in the church. Unfortunately the gospel figure of the shepherd came to be focused on jurisdiction.

To say that papal jurisdiction is "ordinary" does not mean that it is likely to be used ordinarily, habitually, on a day-to-day basis. On the contrary it requires extraordinary circumstances for this "ordinary" authority to come into play. It means simply that the authority belongs to the holder, in this case the pope, *ex officio*, i.e., as part of his papal office and is not delegated to him (for example by a general council) or conceded to him (for instance, on the initiative of some bishop or local church). To say that his jurisdiction is "immediate" is to say that the pope is not obliged to work through intermediary authorities; access to him is direct, and his intervention need not be channeled through the local bishop or the local civil powers or whatever. These somewhat abstract "rights" begin to make better sense when one reads the rest of the chapter and reconstructs the kinds of situations being envisaged.

The burden of the first paragraph of chapter 3 is that "full power was given to him [the pope] in blessed Peter, by Jesus Christ, to rule, feed and govern the universal church" (see DS 3059). This means the pope is given a universal pastoral care, an ecumenical shepherding function, that remains, so far, remarkably vague and undefined, for all the document's grandiloquence.

The second paragraph of chapter 3 continues by stating that the power of jurisdiction is ordinary, immediate, and "truly episcopal." The addition of the term *truly episcopal* has led some persons to think that the only *truly* episcopal authority is that of the pope, and that consequently bishops are merely his delegates. This was in no way the intention of the formulation, as is clear from the acta of the First Vatican Council. "Truly episcopal" was included because some "Gallicans" were suspected of calling the pope's ordinary authority "primatial," as opposed to "truly episcopal," thereby wishing to limit it to emergencies and very rare circumstances. The First Vatican Council saw the pope as a symbolic center even when nothing is going wrong. The third paragraph of chapter 3 of *Pastor Aeternus* continues on a theme touched on in the preface to the constitution, stating that "this power of the supreme pontiff is far from obstructing the ordinary and immediate power of episcopal jurisdiction by which individual bishops, placed by the Holy Spirit and successors of the apostles, feed and rule as true shepherds the individual flocks assigned to them" (DS 3061).

The fourth paragraph (DS 3062) rejects the opinions of "those who hold that communication between the pope and the bishops and their flocks can lawfully be impeded; or who make this communication subject to the will of the secular power, so as to maintain that whatever is done by the Apostolic See, or by its authority, for the government of the church, cannot have force or value unless it be confirmed by the assent of the secular power." Behind this text of course was the memory of Pius VI's and Pius VII's humiliation by Emperor Napoleon Bonaparte.

The fifth and final paragraph in the third chapter on papal jurisdiction (DS 3063) states that the pope is the tribunal of last appeal for the faithful. While not laying down the limits within which papal jurisdiction may function in any detail, the instances referred to clearly indicate that its purpose is to maintain the rights and liberties of the local church and its bishop, while also enabling any who feel badly treated by the local leadership to appeal to a higher judgment.

In the fourth and final chapter of *Pastor Aeternus* it is stated that "that infallibility with which the divine Redeemer willed His church to be endowed in defining a doctrine concerning faith or morals" may, in certain circumstances, enable the bishop of Rome, in his capacity as successor of Saint Peter, to define a doctrine to be held by the universal church. What the church has as a permanent endowment, the successor of Saint Peter may on occasion have available to him, enabling him to so act.

The three councils that the text cites (Constantinople IV [869–70], Lyons II [1274] and Florence [1438–39]) are not received as ecumenical councils by other churches. It is well to note that in 1974, for the anniversary celebration of Lyons II, Pope Paul VI took special pains to refer to that council as "the sixth of the general synods of the West." Whether that initiative opens the way for Catholics to regard Trent and the First Vatican Council as "general synods of the West," rather than ecumenical councils in the full sense of the term, and what effect that would have on the status of their decrees, is another matter. Despite what is commonly supposed in popular Roman Catholic listings of ecumenical councils, there is no definitive official list and the numbering system dates back only to Saint Robert Bellarmine.

The functioning of the pastoral office of the pope is described in some detail: "The bishops of the entire world, sometimes individually, sometimes assembled in synods, have followed the long-standing custom of the churches and the form of the ancient rule by referring to this Apostolic See dangerous situations, particularly those that have risen in matters of faith." The context of action by the pope is thus always envisaged in terms of his being approached by other bishops who find themselves unable to deal with some dissension or heresy. The text concludes with the assertion:

> When the Roman Pontiff speaks *ex cathedra*, that is, when in the discharge of his office as shepherd and teacher of all Christians, and by virtue of his supreme apostolic authority, he defines that a doctrine concerning faith and morals must be held by the whole church, he possesses through the divine assistance promised to him in blessed Peter that infallibility with which the divine Redeemer willed His church to be endowed in defining a doctrine concerning faith or morals; and therefore such definitions of the Roman Pontiff are irreformable of themselves, not from the consent of the church [*ex sese non autem ex consensu Ecclesiae irreformabiles*].

It is well to clear up misunderstanding about the meaning of this last phrase. Readers cannot be blamed if they assume that these words mean that papal judgments may be issued independently of other bishops and of the church, and that such judgments are never open to revision in any sense. A number of historical studies based on the acta of the First Vatican Council appeared in the years immediately preceding the Second Vatican Council so that the 1962–65 council could officially clarify the misleading terminology by stating in *Lumen Gentium*:

> His definitions are rightly said to be irreformable by their very nature and not by reason of the assent of the Church, inasmuch as they were made with the assistance of the Holy Spirit promised to him in the person of blessed Peter himself; and as a consequence they are in no way in need of the approval of others, and do not admit of appeal to any other tribunal. For in such a case the Roman Pontiff does not utter a pronouncement as a private person, but rather does he expound and defend the teaching of the Catholic faith as the supreme teacher of the universal Church, in whom the Church's charism of infallibility is present in a singular way [LG 25].

In stating that such decisions are "irreformable" the First Vatican Council did not mean that they could never be improved, clarified, expanded, developed, or placed in a new perspective so that in a sense they might be called "revised." The intention was to state that episcopal or conciliar validation or confirmation was superfluous. The specific terminology regarding the consent of the church was a direct reference to the Fourth Gallican Article of 1682, which stated that the pope's judgment in doctrinal controversies is irreformable only when covered by the subsequent consent of the church (*nec tamen irreformabile esse judicium nisi Ecclesiae consensus acceserit*). Some readers of the documents of the First Vatican Council mistakenly translate the term *consensus* as though it means prior consultation, as though the pope can reach conclusions without prior consultation of the church. In fact prior consultation is presupposed. What is excluded by the term *consensus* is rather the idea of subsequent approval. It is because a papal infallible judgment articulates the *consensus Ecclesiae* in the real and deep sense that it requires no *consensus Ecclesiae* in the merely juridical or formal sense.

Many questions remain. To admit that the pope on occasion might be called upon to make such a prophetic judgment is not to specify the circumstances in which it might happen. Nor is it to say that an ecumenical council might not equally well make such a judgment. (In fact, historically, the councils have de facto been the means of dogmatic clarifications needed to settle the trinitarian and christological controversies.)

It is true that the Second Vatican Council repeated much of the language and statements of the First Vatican Council and that there seems to be little further nuancing on an issue that has vexed other Christian churches since 1870. But in the way that the Second Vatican Council balanced the papal prerogatives with a fuller statement of the responsibilities of the episcopacy, and in the way that it describes the *sensus fidelium* of the entire people of God, there is some movement toward refining the earlier teaching.

Alois Grillmeier comments on the key passage in paragraph 25 of *Lumen Gentium* by noting that: "In the mind of the faithful, as in that of the magisterium, the gift of infallibility had been too one-sidedly concentrated on the office, and even on a papal primacy which was considered in isolation from the episcopate as a whole. This could only lead to passivity and indifference with regard to responsibility for the word of God."[45]

Stating that the consensus of the entire people of God is infallible does not solve the complex questions that follow from that. How is the truth implicitly present in the mind or tradition of the faithful in fact discovered? Is it enough that the laity throughout the world take for granted that a particular doctrine is true without having

---

45. See Herbert Vorgrimler, ed., *Commentary on the Documents of Vatican II* (New York: Herder, 1967), 1:164–65.

seriously examined it? Thirty years ago, for instance, the vast majority of Catholics believed that unbaptized infants went to limbo, and they believed in the intrinsic evil of artificial contraception in marriage. Few believe these doctrines today. Is it that, placed in a new perspective, the truth that these doctrines expressed can now be better said by denying them? If that is the case, our faith in the undeceivable and undeceiving *sensus fidei* in the people of God must allow for radical changes of direction.

The primary perspective within which the apostolic primacy in Saint Peter was envisaged and presented at the First Vatican Council is that of the papacy's being "the abiding principle of this twofold unity [of faith and communion] and its visible foundation." This description is repeated again in *Lumen Gentium* 23. But this primacy of the papacy leaves room for a principle of unity that is other than "perpetual" (such as the eucharist that is frequently repeated but is not a continuous celebration), and it leaves room for an invisible foundation of this unity, namely, the presence of the Holy Spirit at work in the church. The papacy is not the *only*, or even the most important and fundamental, principle of unity of faith and communion.

The real stumbling block to the reunification of the Roman Catholic and other churches lies less in the actual verbal formulation of the Roman doctrines in the last two general councils and more in the real or de facto exercise of the papal functions, marked as they are at times by an excessively Romanizing tendency, by a sometimes rigid selection process for the appointment of bishops, and by an isolation from the convictions of its own believers and even more so from the insights of non-Catholic Christian saints and scholars. I share the judgment of the distinguished theologian and church historian from the Pontifical Oriental Institute in Rome, Wilhelm de Vries, that it is regrettable that the Second Vatican Council lacked the resoluteness to reformulate in a more satisfactory way many of the obscure expressions of the First Vatican Council. For instance, the First Vatican Council did not indicate the limitations to papal primacy, and so one might conclude that none exists. Clearly, however, the *plenitudo potestatis* has its limits in the will of Christ's institution of the church. Perhaps the fact that the Second Vatican Council did not give non-Catholic observers voice to raise questions from the floor of the council meant that clarification could not come from that setting, but could come initially only from bilateral consensus statements.

EVANGELIZATION AND
OTHER CHURCH TASKS

This section addresses the frequently asked question: What exactly are the church's tasks? There are the obvious answers: keeping alive the memory of Jesus and his significance; preaching the gospel within the Christian community; organizing and celebrating public worship and joining in the heavenly liturgy presided over by Christ himself; and teaching the faithful how to praise God in prayer. But there are also other tasks that relate to the church's mission to the world. The church is called upon, in the words of the Second Vatican Council, to read the "signs of the time" (GS 4) in order to understand the church's context in the world. Although the Pastoral Constitution on the Church in the Modern World spoke of humanity's "joys and sorrows," some have felt that the perspective of the text was too optimistic, too mesmerized by the progress of technology, and not sufficiently imbued with a solid "theology of the cross." At any rate, in the 1985 international synod of bishops that tried to assess the Second Vatican Council's impact over the intervening twenty years, it was noted that the signs of the times had become more grim, with an increase in hunger, oppression, injustice, war, sufferings, terrorism, and other forms of violence. Perhaps, it was suggested, the new challenge for the church was to show how human history of suffering and salvation history are closely intertwined and can be understood only in light of the paschal mystery. Another issue touched upon in the 1985 synod was inculturation. According to this organizing principle, the church, because of its present understanding of diversity and unity and in order to communicate its message more appropriately, commits itself to draw from every culture all that possesses positive value in the communication of God's revelation in Christ. Inculturation tries to facilitate an intimate enrichment of authentic, cultural values through their integration in Christianity. This requires a process of discernment that demands prayerful reflection and contemplation to communicate the gospel.

THE CHURCH'S MISSION

No understanding of the nature of the church is complete without a comprehension of its mission.[46] What is the function of the church toward that large segment of humanity that has been untouched

---

46. See *The Church as Mission* (entire issue of *The Jurist* 39, nos. 1–2 [1979]). Also Francis Schüssler Fiorenza, *Foundational Theology: Jesus and the Church* (New York: Crossroad, 1984), esp. chaps. 7 and 8.

by Christian revelation? Besides the call to worship and adoration, what is it that Christians are asked to do? The concept of mission is fraught with many possible misunderstandings, not the least of which is a potential confusion between mission and proselytism.

The original Christian concept of mission reflected in the New Testament employed a specific metaphor, which was inspired largely by John's Gospel, to express how God's love had reached out toward the created universe, especially the universe of humankind.[47] In the Fourth Gospel, Jesus refers with reverence to "the Father who sent me." Jesus also speaks about a second, interconnected mission or sending of the Paraclete whose role would be to continue and perfect the work begun by Jesus Christ. The term *mission* described in pictorial language God's redemptive concern for the human community; the preexisting Word of God was perceived as having been sent to put on humanity, to "dwell amongst us," and to fulfill a salvific mission that would eventually be complemented by the Holy Spirit.

As medieval theology would reason, these divine "missions" were expressions of the inner-trinitarian processions thrust outward toward humanity. In its strictest sense, therefore, missionary theology is theology about the work of the three persons of the triune God as they communicate grace toward human beings. If the present-day church chooses to retain the word *mission* for what the community is called upon by God to undertake, then it is important to remember that the church participates in a mission rather than performs a mission. Mission is better understood by its origin than by its objective.

It was quite late in the history of the church, even after the medieval synthesis of Thomas Aquinas, that theologians began to speak of the "mission of the church." At first, influenced by the Western canonists, there was a gradual introduction of the idea of a *missio canonica* to describe the church's authoritative commissioning of clerics to preach the gospel. But even as late as the manualist Catholic theologians of the nineteenth and early twentieth centuries, one finds hardly any mention of the "mission" of the church. The only indirect reference is mention of the church's end (*finis*) or purpose. This perspective is reflected in the language of the First Vatican Council's decree *Pastor Aeternus* (1870), which describes the church's finality as acting "so that Christ might render lasting the saving work of redemption" (DS 3050).

---

47. Michael A. Fahey, "The Mission of the Church: To Divinize or to Humanize?" *Catholic Theological Society of America, Proceedings* 31 (1976): 51–69. See also Karl Rahner, "The Church's Commission to Bring Salvation and the Humanization of the World," in his *Theological Investigations* (New York: Seabury, 1976), 14:295–313.

However, it is true that even John's Gospel twice cites sayings of Jesus to members of the nascent church about "sending." At the Last Supper, Jesus is said to "send" the disciples gathered for the paschal meal in the Upper Room: "As you [Father] have sent me into the world, so I have sent them into the world" (John 17:18). And then in the postresurrection appearance in the same location Jesus says: "As the Father has sent me, so I send you" (John 20:21). In popular piety these sayings from John are connected with the various "go" commands of Jesus ("Go into the whole world . . . ") as found in Mark 16:15 and Matthew 28:19. Can these sayings that were originally addressed to the eleven be extended to each and every member of the church so that mission is part of every Christian's mandate? The answer is doubtlessly yes, but it is important to distinguish between the mission of the triune God, the all-embracing power of salvation at work wherever the reign of God is in effect, and the mission of the church, obviously a modest participation within that broader process.

For four or five decades now in the Catholic church some theologians, including even the drafters of texts at the Second Vatican Council, have become hesitant about using the word *mission* to explain the church's activities in the world. One reads rather about the church's task, role, concern, function, presence, need to witness, challenge, mediation, and responsibility, concepts that are related to the general notion of the church's mission. The participants at the Second Vatican Council chose to describe the church from a double perspective: the church's internal life (*ad intra*) and its external life (*ad extra*). But at the council, rather than appealing to the church's *missio*, they spoke of its *munus* instead: *de munere ecclesiae in mundo hujus temporis*. This Latin term is usually translated into English as *task* (perhaps the plural form, *tasks*, would have been better) and sometimes as *role(s)*, reflecting the various responsibilities that the church is called upon to shoulder. The decision at the Second Vatican Council to use the word *task(s)* rather than *mission* had the advantage of removing an exaggerated parallel between the trinitarian missions and ecclesial mission. Also the church's "tasks" are much more comprehensive than the specific responsibility exercised by those formally involved in preaching the gospel to believers and to potential believers.

EVANGELIZATION

Among its own family the Christian community celebrates a common vision of God through its preaching and sacramental worship. This vision can grow dim or seem unimportant to individuals or could even conceivably become partly distorted by inadequate instruction. Hence, even within the church, the Christian vision needs to be rekindled, refined, made more attractive, more central to the life of individual Christians or regional or national churches. The church needs to give much more thought to how it can keep ever fresh and attractive the gospel message, especially when the level of preaching is so pitifully poor among many ordained men, and when the quality and quantity of instructional and devotional literature are so problematic. Neglect of "distant" Catholics by the institutional structures of the church should be a major concern today. The more distant from church those people become who by family ties or national origins once tended to identify themselves as Catholic Christians, the more does what is preached to them parallel the message to the non-evangelized.

Besides the church's preaching to its own inner family members, the community called church is expected to share its vision with the wider human family. This outreach is the task of evangelization exercised according to different styles and approaches. This evangelization needs to be undertaken within the context of a hierarchy of truths that reaffirms God's universal salvific will and the possibility that for many (even the majority?) a religious or even a humanistic tradition that is not Christian will be the source of holiness. Hence evangelization undertaken out of love for the sacredness of Christianity, a sense of commissioning by God, and the simple desire to share a precious value in one's life must be done in a way that is respectful of the intrinsic value of other religions, and the human person's freedom of conscience.

My point is that even after formal evangelization has been practiced (and clearly this will not always be successful) or even before evangelization is begun (postponed temporarily, for instance, until one feels better equipped to understand the potential recipients' value systems and cultural setting), Christians are expected to do other things besides "preaching the gospel" in the strictest sense of the phrase. Formulated in other words, the question is: What, apart from direct evangelization (telling the gospel story), is the Christian community expected to "do" in the world? Christians should be careful not to have an exaggerated sense of their own importance, and they should not be so self-congratulatory that they fail to recognize that others who are neither Christian nor religious have more acute insights and more sensitive moral commitments for improving the human condition than some Christian leaders. I am speaking on the level of theoretical possibility, not stating that this is always or even frequently being done with zest and creativity.

In their relationship to the world (taken here as meaning specifically the non–Christ-confessing community) the Christian communities are expected to exercise functions that can be described as integrational, prophetic, and eschatological.

Integrational

Christian communities have the ability to exercise an "integrational" role vis-à-vis those who do not share their religious creed by asserting the basic unity of the order of creation and the order of redemption. This means that becoming more fully human and becoming more fully sanctified have a common finality since the gospel satisfies and fulfills the most profound needs of humankind. Christians can be conscious collaborators with God in the functions of creating, redeeming, and glorifying the world through Christ. What the Christian "knows" is that humanity has been raised to a new level of dignity through God's personal communication with the world through Christ. Because of language barriers, geographical isolation, cultural prejudices, human frailty, etc., none of this may be recognized by those before whom this is being proclaimed. Classical theology stated that the gift of faith is unmerited and that in the inscrutable designs of God not all receive the gift of faith during their lifetime (though they may very well be slated eventually to enter into glory with God). Every individual sin, especially those sins that directly abuse others, and every corporate sin or scandal associated with the community called church, makes the possibility of responding to Christian revelation more difficult.

Prophetic

Christian communities have the ability to exercise a prophetic role in the world. The communities inspired by faith in Christ are called upon to express disdain for every form of evil, injustice, and abuse of power. Obviously this does not imply that Christians have special insights into the concrete proposals that must be made to correct social evils. Christians' specific suggestions will be only as good as the expertise and competence of individuals skilled in politics, economics, or psychology. The word *prophetic* is not meant to suggest purely denunciatory discourse. Ecclesial communities can also mobilize energy behind positive, beneficial initiatives begun in non-Christian communities. By acting as a leaven in the world, in family, professional, social, cultural, and political life, the Christian communities can mobilize forces that are creative; this is one step beyond pure denunciation of injustices and abuse.

Eschatological

Since redemption remains an ongoing, unfinished process dependent both on God's grace and human response in freedom, a response often weakened by sinfulness, the full appropriation of salvation is incomplete even in the church. Christian communities are expected to reflect the truth that our true home is in God, that we are called to a "beatific vision." As explained by modern theologians, such as Jürgen Moltmann in his *Theology of Hope*, Christianity's function is carried out not within the horizon of expectation provided by the social role that society concedes to the church but within its own particular horizon of eschatological expectation of the coming reign of God, of future righteousness, and of future peace and freedom.[48]

This eschatological perspective emphasizes that the social aims of Christian communities are not merely progress, movement toward affluence, and elimination of struggle. Christianity, because of its understanding of the transitional character of this world, stresses the radical ambiguity of human activity. The centrality of the cross and the paradox of life emerging from death that marks the Christian vision of life as well as its paschal dimension can prevent the new humanity in Christ from subjecting the gospel to political reductionism.

The Pastoral Constitution on the Church in the Modern World (*Gaudium et Spes*) touches on a number of aspects of the church's responsibilities to the world that had never been treated in a conciliar text. The document recognizes that the church has "a feeling of deep solidarity with the human race and its history" and that "the joy and hope, the grief and anguish of persons of our time, especially of those who are poor or afflicted in any way, are the joy and hope, the grief and anguish of the followers of Christ as well" (GS 1). The church offers to cooperate unreservedly with the rest of humankind in fostering a sense of family ties within humanity.

This pastoral constitution tries to analyze the modern situation of humanity, its successes and its failures. It first treats the theoretical framework. Part 1, entitled "The Church and the Human Vocation" (nos. 11–45), treats specifically these themes: (1) the dignity

---

48. Jürgen Moltmann, *Theology of Hope: On the Ground and the Implications of a Christian Eschatology*, trans. J. W. Leitch (New York: Harper and Row, 1967).

of the human person (12–22); (2) the human community (23–32); (3) human activity in the universe (33–39); and (4) the role of the church in the modern world (40–45). Part 2, "Some Problems of Special Urgency" (46–93), treats marriage and family, culture, economic and social life, politics, and finally peace.

A study of numbers 40–45, which address the church's role in the modern world, may help elucidate Catholic teaching on the tasks of the church. At first the perspective is simply that of *Lumen Gentium*, namely that the church is a visible organization and a spiritual community. But the document continues by saying, much as is done in the writings of Karl Rahner, that the church can contribute greatly to humanizing humankind and its history through each of the church's members and its community as a whole.

In a display of humility that one might judge uncharacteristic, the participants of the Second Vatican Council, in regard to the aim of humanizing the world, admit that the Catholic church "values what other Christian churches and ecclesial communities have contributed and are contributing cooperatively to the realization of this aim" (GS 40). The council even states that the Catholic community is convinced that it can receive considerable help from the world in preparing the ground for the gospel, both from individuals and from society as a whole by means of the talents and activity found in the world.

Perhaps these sections of *Gaudium et Spes* have not received as close attention as some other texts. There is stress on the need for exchange, on the church's need to listen to the experts in the world. "It is the task of the whole people of God, particularly of its bishops and theologians, to listen to and distinguish the many voices of our times and to interpret them in the light of the divine Word" (GS 44). It even adds, echoing an idea of Justin Martyr, that "the church itself also recognizes that it has benefited and is still benefiting from the opposition of its enemies and persecutors" (GS 44).

Much of what is said here is traceable to the efforts of some European theologians who in the 1940s and 1950s developed a "theology of earthly realities," especially the Belgian Catholic theologian Gustave Thils.[49] The biblical teaching of this interrelatedness of church and world was given a strong christological basis. Cooperating with the modern world is helping to complete the journey that has as its goal "to unite all things in him [Christ], things in heaven and things on earth" (Eph. 1:10).

---

49. Gustave Thils, *Théologie des réalités terrestres. I: Préludes* (Paris: De Brouwer, 1946).

It is arguable that many church leaders do not in fact follow these remarks about the need to learn from the world, especially when they hastily condemn certain biomedical or medical procedures they may not always completely understand. One example of broad consultation among a specific hierarchy that respected the need of this listening was the preparatory work of the U.S. Catholic Conference of Bishops in formulating two recent pastoral letters (i.e., those on peace and on the American economy). Not only was a broad spectrum of informed opinions consulted but texts were even prepared in drafts with serious requests for reactions and comments before final promulgation. By consulting experts even outside of the ecclesial community, an important doctrine was being communicated. This was the recognition that the task of humanizing the world can in no way be the exclusive work of the church as institution and social organization.

Following the Second Vatican Council the Catholic church has become more aware of its responsibilities in the service of the poor, the oppressed, and the outcast. In this "preferential option" (which is not intended to be exclusive) special attention is given to Jesus' sayings in the Gospels about how the poor are blessed (Matt. 5:3; Luke 6:20) and to Jesus Christ's wish to become poor for us (2 Cor. 8:9). The Catholic church has come to stress too that besides material poverty lack of liberty and of spiritual goods in some way may be considered forms of poverty. Hence the church is more willing to denounce prophetically every form of poverty and oppression and to promote the inalienable rights of the human person.

THE CHURCH'S CALL TO HOLINESS

Another dimension of modern Catholic teaching about the church is treated in two sections of *Lumen Gentium*. One section, in chapter 5, explores "The Call of the Whole Church to Holiness"; a second complementary section treats "The Eschatological Nature of the Pilgrim Church and Its Union with the Heavenly Church." These perspectives may also be considered part of the mission of the church, a call to sanctity of life. Catholics have left themselves open to criticism in the past in the way that they seem to exult in "good works" without being careful to stress that even the remote desire to practice some particular virtuous act is itself the result of divine grace and goodness. Catholics have a very distinctive way of relating to the saints in glory that they share fully with the Eastern Orthodox and to an extent with Anglicans. Some of the prayers of petition that Catholics formulate to the saints, especially to Mary the mother of Jesus, seem to other Christians somewhat odd because they appear to avoid direct invocation of Christ the Savior. The use of relics, now happily reduced in Catholic practice, and the celebration of saints' feast days even when it clouds the church's liturgical calendar, are rather unique to Catholic devotional life and are looked upon by other Christians with a high degree of suspicion and cautious reception.

UNANSWERED ECCLESIOLOGICAL QUESTIONS FOR FUTURE RESOLUTION

A venerable practice of Western theology since the time of the Middle Ages has been holding open debates on various *quaestiones disputatae*. These are not matters of definitive dogma, but are doctrinal issues where there is not complete unanimity, issues that bear on important aspects of the church's corporate self-identity and are of more than mere academic interest.

In this section I shall address four issues of this type. They are these: (1) the binding force of the general councils held in the West in the second millennium, from the ninth council (Lateran I [1123]) to the twenty-first (Vatican II [1962–65]), with special attention given to the Council of Trent (1545–63) and Vatican I (1869–70), which have had such an impact on Roman Catholic life even to these days; (2) eucharistic sharing or hospitality (intercommunion) between believers in the Roman Catholic church and in other Christian churches not now in full communion; (3) recognition of the ordinations of persons commissioned within other Christian churches, especially of women ordained to the presbyterate or to the episcopate; and (4) new ways of exercising papal primacy in the context of the worldwide network of churches.

ECUMENICAL COUNCILS

In the second millennium, the Western church in general and then— after the Reformation—the Roman Catholic church held a series of councils that have given a particular stamp to life among large segments of the Christian community. Some Roman Catholics are now beginning to note that in fact there is no list numbering the ecumenical councils that has been imposed with dogmatic authority. True, Rome refers to certain councils held in the West (e.g., Trent, Vatican I, Vatican II) with a specific number and with the description "ecumenical." But this attribution is not a dogmatic pronouncement and reflects simply a common enumeration of the ecumenical councils traceable to the relatively late work of Robert Bellarmine in his *De Controversiis* (1586).

In recent times, under the leadership of Pope Paul VI, an important initiative of the See of Rome took place that has unfortunately largely gone unnoticed. Paul VI expressed the conviction that in fact there are two sorts of councils in the patrimony of the West, the early ecumenical councils of the undivided church and then the later general synods of the West. In an important letter dated October 5, 1974, and addressed to Cardinal Willebrands on the occasion of the seventh centenary of Lyons II (1274), the pope wrote: "This Council of Lyons counted as the sixth of the general synods held in the West."[50] This terminology of "general synods" suggests that Catholic teaching is willing to accept the notion of varying levels of councils, what Yves Congar has called a hierarchy or relative order of importance among councils and synods (*hierarchia conciliorum*). If this distinction were widely accepted then the anathemas pronounced against those who did not accept the canons of these general synods would seem to be softened or eliminated. This would have considerable import in the event of other churches reestablishing full communion with the See of Rome.

The questions raised in this connection are extremely interesting. Does this not imply then that the Church of Rome would at least in principle be willing to accept the notion of full communion with certain churches that would however not be required to assent to the dogmatic status of certain teachings adopted by Rome at general synods? This would give much wider scope to the possibilities of other churches being associated with Rome. It would not in any way imply that members of the Roman Catholic church could ignore or neglect these teachings, but they would be seen as attempts of their own church to explain a profound truth of revelation, which might be understood by other Christians in a different way, and even with different terminology.

SHARED EUCHARISTIC HOSPITALITY

Another matter of some disputation even among Catholic theologians and church leaders today is the appropriateness of divided Christians celebrating together and sharing in the eucharist, occa-

---

50. French text in *Documentation Catholique* 72 (1975): 63–67. See also Yves Congar, "Church Structures and Councils in the Relations of East and West," *One in Christ* 11 (1975): 224–65; Francis Dvornik, "Which Councils Are Ecumenical?" *Journal of Ecumenical Studies* 3 (1966): 314–28.

sionally or regularly, and that on the basis not of a spontaneous personal decision but rather on the basis of expectation of eventual official approval.[51] Many theologians prefer to use the expressions *eucharistic sharing* or *eucharistic hospitality* rather than *intercommunion*, a word that is ambiguous if one thinks of the *koinonia* or *communio* that already exists among different Christians on the basis of their baptism in the same Holy Spirit.

In its decree on ecumenism, the Second Vatican Council wrote of "the wonderful sacrament of the Eucharist by which the unity of the church is both signified and brought about" (*Unitatis Redintegratio* 2). The official position of the Catholic church on eucharistic sharing, a position expressed at the council and in subsequent guidelines, is that this sharing should normally take place only when it signifies an already existing unity. Shared eucharist, the Catholic church argues, should not take place indiscriminately as a means of achieving unity. The precondition would be doctrinal unity and not only that unity in Christ already present through baptism. But these guidelines are not permanently fixed. In fact, the official bilateral and multilateral ecumenical dialogues that have followed the council have made it clear that in very many cases what divides churches on eucharistic or sacramental teaching is not related to the core of belief, that is to the dogmatic heart of faith, but centers rather on theological elaborations of that faith, elaborations that may properly allow for different emphases.

What would be the implications of such a shift in discipline within the Roman Catholic church? One closely related issue of course would be the need to recognize unequivocally the genuine character of ordinations in churches that do not understand apostolic succession in the same way as do Catholics and that practice ordinations without the presiding function of a bishop.

RECOGNITION OF ORDINATIONS

For the sake of its future self-understanding, the Catholic church needs to turn its attention to the recognition of ministries in Anglican and Protestant churches along the lines of its already stated recognition of orders in the Eastern Orthodox and Ancient Oriental churches. For purposes of discussion I will limit discussion for the moment to the Anglican communion. As is widely known, the Anglican communion has in principle always recognized the orders of Roman

---

51. See "Eucharistic Sharing (Intercommunion)," in *New Catholic Encyclopedia*, vol. 17, *Supplement: Change in the Church* (Washington, D.C.: Publishers Guild, 1979), 215–17, with full bibliography.

Catholic priests or presbyters. For complex historical and theological reasons the Church of Rome has not recognized orders in the Anglican communion as "validly conferred." In part this was due to the way that Rome perceived the Church of England's understanding of the sacrificial nature of the Mass and the finality associated with ordination rites in the sixteenth century. In 1896, after a long study by a papal committee on this question, Pope Leo XIII (who disagreed with the conclusions of the majority of the committee he had appointed to study this matter) published a bull, *Apostolicae Curae*, on Anglican orders; the document concluded that in fact Anglican orders were "absolutely null and thoroughly void."

Based on the intense ecumenical investigations of the Anglican/Roman Catholic International Commission, culminating in the publication of its *Final Report*, it seems possible to assert that in fact the differences regarding both eucharist and ordination are not dogmatically divisive issues. Rather it seems that these differences are based on theologically diverse but complementary insights that are not necessarily exclusive.[52] Were the authorities in the Roman church to become convinced of this, it would conceivably be possible to change that church's previous assessment of this matter.

How this would apply to other Christian churches—both those that have formally retained the episcopal structures of church polity that Catholics find so imperative and those "free churches" that allow *episkopē* to be expressed in other ways besides "bishops"—remains a central issue that will need much further study.

The matter becomes all the more complicated today by the fact that some of those ordained as priests in churches of the Anglican communion have been women, and in at least two instances, women ordained as bishops. The Roman Catholic church (as the Eastern Orthodox church) does not recognize the possibility of a woman being ordained, and has expressed this view in a document published by the Congregation for the Doctrine of the Faith entitled *Inter Insigniores* (Declaration on the Question of the Admission of Women to the Ministerial Priesthood), published on January 27, 1977. While the declaration intends to be authoritative in some sense and in fact argues in favor of maintaining the present position, theological discussion of the question continues within the Roman Catholic community. The present official teaching—especially reasons given about the impossibility of a woman being a proper *repraesentatio Christi*—has not found full "reception" among Catholic theologians.

---

52. Anglican-Roman Catholic International Commission, *The Final Report* (London: SPCK, 1982).

PAPAL MINISTRY

Another controverted question that will need to be discussed both within the Catholic community and among other Christian churches is whether it would be possible to reformulate the ministerial role of the bishop of Rome, the pope, in such a way that what Catholics see to be his primatial service of unity may become acceptable to other Christians outside the boundaries of the Roman Catholic church. This is an issue about which there are many different perspectives stemming from the specific polity of a historical church or the distinctive theological emphases of a Christian community. Because of this diversity of perspectives, resolution of this issue will be slow and will be achieved only step by step. In the process, not only will one segment of the church be enriched but the entire *corpus Christianorum* will come to understand more profoundly the mystery of the church.

FOR FURTHER READING

NEW TESTAMENT STUDIES

Congar, Yves. *The Mystery of the Church.* Baltimore: Helicon, 1960.

A characteristically insightful work on the biblical origins of the church by the acknowledged doyen of Catholic ecclesiology.

Congar, Yves. *The Mystery of the Temple.* Westminster, Md.: Newman, 1962.

An equally fruitful study that stresses the importance of the Holy Spirit for understanding church.

Cwiekowski, Frederick J. *The Beginnings of the Church.* New York: Paulist, 1988.

A study that traces the recent shifts in how scholars understand the first three generations of church life.

Dunn, James D. G. *Unity and Diversity in the New Testament: An Inquiry into the Character of Earliest Christianity.* Philadelphia: Westminster Press, 1977.

Written by a Protestant, this work provides a solid account of complementary biblical theologies of the church.

Meeks, Wayne A. *The First Urban Christians.* New Haven: Yale University Press, 1983. Idem. *The Moral World of the First Christians.* Philadelphia: Westminster Press, 1986.

Taken together, these two volumes enrich enormously our understanding of the cultural and social context of various local Christian
communities in New Testament times.

Minear, Paul S. *Images of the Church in the New Testament*. Philadelphia:
Westminster Press, 1960.

A definitive study of all the metaphors and similes used by the New
Testament writers to describe the reality called church.

Theissen, Gerd. *The Social Setting of Pauline Christianity*. Philadelphia: Fortress Press, 1982.

A major study of the sociological context of the communities associated
with Saint Paul's churches.

GENERAL STUDIES

Dulles, Avery. *Models of the Church*. New York: Doubleday, 1974.

Since 1965 probably the most influential English-language study of
Catholic ecclesiological paradigms.

Duquoc, Christian. *Provisional Churches: An Essay in Ecumenical Ecclesiology*.
London: SCM, 1986.

The book stresses the importance of local "provisional" churches for
ecclesial self-understanding and for ecumenical progress.

Forte, Bruno. *L'Église: Icône de la Trinité*. Paris: Médiaspaul, 1985.

A French translation from Italian, this book is by a Catholic ecclesiologist who is well versed in the eucharistic ecclesiology and pneumatology
of the Eastern churches.

Hillman, Eugene. *The Church as Mission*. New York: Herder and Herder,
1965.

Although this book was published in 1965, it is still remarkably insightful about the task of evangelization. The writer lived in East Africa for
many years, working with the Masai in particular.

Jay, Eric. *The Church: Its Changing Image through Twenty Centuries*. Atlanta:
John Knox, 1980.

Ecumenically sensitive, the book gives a remarkably comprehensive
overview of the history of ecclesiology.

Kasper, Walter. *Theology and Church*. New York: Crossroad, 1989.

This collection of essays offers a stimulating cross section of Kasper's
major studies on church.

Lauret, B., and F. Refoulé, eds. *Initiation à la pratique de la théologie*. Vol 3. Paris: Cerf, 1983.

Part of a five-volume study on systematic theology, this particular volume contains the treatise on ecclesiology. It contains a matchless treatment by one of Yves Congar's protégés, Hervé Legrand, on the theology of "local church."

Rigal, Jean. *L'Église: Obstacle et chemin vers Dieu*. Paris: Cerf, 1983.

A thoughtful and honest look at the ways in which sinfulness in the church hinders the full flowering of the gospel.

Sullivan, Francis. *The Church We Believe In: One, Holy, Catholic and Apostolic*. New York: Paulist, 1988.

The work of an American Catholic ecclesiologist whose writings are steeped in tradition but attentive to contemporary issues.

STUDIES ON VATICAN II AND ITS IMPACT

Alberigo, Giuseppe, ed. *Les Églises après Vatican II*. Paris: Beauchesne, 1981.

Unfortunately this work has never been translated into English. It contains the speeches of a number of major contemporary ecclesiologists given at an international colloquium held in Bologna, Italy, in the late 1970s on central aspects of the doctrine of church.

Alberigo, Giuseppe, et al., eds. *The Reception of Vatican II*. Washington, D.C.: Catholic University of America, 1987.

An international team of Catholic scholars evaluate the developments in ecclesiology twenty years after the close of the council.

Hastings, Adrian. *Modern Catholicism: Vatican II and After*. New York: Oxford University Press, 1991.

British and North American Catholics collaborated on this magisterial assessment.

Latourelle, René, ed. *Vatican II: Assessment and Perspectives, Twenty-Five Years After (1962–87)*. 3 vols. New York: Paulist, 1988–89.

Produced by professors of the Gregorian University Consortium in Rome, this major work (published in several European languages) discusses how the Second Vatican Council affected Catholic theology. Though uneven in quality, some essays on church are well done.

Reese, Thomas J., ed. *Episcopal Conferences: Historical, Canonical, and Theological Studies*. Washington, D.C.: Georgetown University Press, 1989.

One of the first studies by a North American Catholic to explore the many-faceted aspects of episcopal collegiality, especially as expressed in national conferences of bishops.

STUDIES ON MAGISTERIUM

O'Donovan, Leo, ed. *Cooperation between Theologians and the Ecclesiastical Magisterium*. Washington, D.C.: Canon Law Society of America and Catholic Theological Society of America, 1982.

Two of the leading Catholic professional societies in America collaborated for several years to prepare these background papers and recommendations aimed at effectively resolving tensions between bishops and theologians on doctrinal matters.

Orsy, Ladislas. *The Church Learning and Teaching*. Wilmington, Del.: Glazier, 1987.

A popular but very well informed treatment of the teaching office of bishops and the role of other church teachers. Useful in contextualizing notions such as dissent in the church.

Sullivan, Francis A. *Magisterium: Teaching Authority in the Catholic Church*. New York: Paulist, 1983.

A well-informed and balanced systematic treatment of how ecclesiastical magisterium is currently understood in the Catholic tradition.

STUDIES ON THE PAPACY

Granfield, Patrick. *The Papacy in Transition*. New York: Doubleday, 1980. Idem. *The Limits of the Papacy*. New York: Crossroad, 1987.

These twin volumes on the papal ministry are historically informed and ecumenically sensitive.

McCord, Peter J., ed. *A Pope for All Christians?* New York: Paulist, 1976.

Orthodox, Anglican, and Protestant theologians in the United States discuss whether the office of pope could ever be acceptable in their churches. All but one give a qualified yes.

Tillard, Jean Marie. *The Bishop of Rome*. London: SPCK, 1983.

The author, a Catholic ecclesiologist, has been very active in dialoguing with Orthodox and Anglican Christians. His thoughtful volume, originally written in French, contains historical data and helpful proposals for a renewal of papal ministry in the church.

7

SIN AND GRACE

7

SIN AND GRACE

Roger Haight

INTRODUCTION

The doctrines of sin and grace define an anthropology, a Christian conception of human existence. Whenever revelation of God occurs, human existence appears in a new light, for God's disclosure always also reveals the human as standing before God. The doctrines of sin and grace, then, unfold the core of Christian self-understanding. They deal with the mystery of human existence in relation to the God revealed in Jesus Christ.

A concise account of these doctrines can be put forward only under severe limitations, and these should be stated at the very outset. First, what follows will be a constructive systematic theology of sin and grace; it is not historical. A thorough appreciation of the language of sin and grace demands a survey of the history of these doctrines because of the many developments and changes in understanding that have occurred in different periods. Knowledge of this history is presupposed and only schematically represented. At the same time this systematic interpretation of the doctrines will draw on classical sources from the history of theology and doctrine.

Second, this systematic theology of sin and grace enters into dialogue with the tradition of the Reformation. The analysis will always seek to preserve the theological insights and values of that tradition even while they are drawn into the overall framework of a Roman Catholic imagination.

Third, the perspective governing this theology of sin and grace may be called liberationist, since some form of a theology of liberation alone can respond to the problems we face. But at the same time this synthesis will be attentive to the concerns of other theologies, and the classical issues underlying the doctrines of sin and grace will be integrated into the development.

Fourth, a short treatise on the theology of sin and grace that also seeks in some measure to be adequate to the many issues involved in these doctrines cannot fail to appear schematic. Arguments must be curtailed, full explanations foreshortened. For example, we must presuppose the historical and exegetical study of biblical sources, the historical conditions that led Augustine to his understanding of sin and grace, and the intentions behind the Roman Catholic formulations of these doctrines at the Council of Trent. The goal of this account is to portray the theological logic underlying these doctrines in a way that makes them credible today.

Finally, this theological analysis of the doctrines of sin and grace does not pretend to be *the* Roman Catholic account. Roman Catholicism shares in the pluralism that currently characterizes all Christian theology. These doctrines, then, are Roman Catholic, but as in the case of all constructive theology, what follows can only be considered a particular account of them.

METHOD

A systematic understanding of any doctrine consists in a methodical unfolding of its meaning and an attempt to display its truth. The doctrines of sin and grace make up part of the tradition of the self-understanding of the Christian community from its beginning. These teachings lie embedded in the founding Scriptures and the history of the church's confessional witness. Thus these categories may be considered as simply given; the notions of sin and grace are intrinsic parts of Christian language and belief. But what do they mean? Do they indeed correspond to and accurately describe human existence as it is experienced today by Christians and others?

These questions, which arise automatically in any reflective consideration of any doctrine, define the overall method employed here. The general logic of that method may be stated concisely in the following way: Given these doctrines of the church as they appear in its foundational sources and classical symbols, an effort will be made, first, to make sense out of the doctrines and, second, to show how they illumine the actual situation of human existence. The truth of these doctrines, then, will appear in the measure in which they actually disclose our human existence in a mediated but self-evident way.

This general logic can be specified in the following series of steps: First, the analysis begins with a preliminary anthropology. This description of human existence as it is experienced today serves as an a priori of the investigation of sin and grace. On the one hand, this can represent only a particular interpretation of our common situation. But on the other hand, this description is not closed, but meant to open up the mystery that human existence is to questions that demand some kind of response.

Second, the questions arising out of common human experience today will be addressed to the traditional symbols of sin and grace. In this procedure, then, the doctrines of sin and grace will be interpreted in such a way that they will shed light on the human existence that embodies these questions. The doctrines of sin and grace will appear intelligible in the measure in which the questions to which they respond genuinely represent our situation, the doctrines themselves appear coherent, and they open up human freedom to meaningful action in the world. The interpretation will be faithful and authentic in the measure in which it is open to the symbols of the past and allows them to shape our understanding.

From beginning to end, the method employed here is dialogical and interpretative. The point is not to represent the historical understanding of the doctrines of sin and grace at any point in the past of the church, although this is where one must begin. It is rather to draw that meaning forward into our own context to shed light on human existence today.

DIVISION

The method involved in this systematic account of the doctrines of sin and grace yields the following division of the material: The first part will contain a preliminary anthropology that will show that human existence must be considered from both an individual and a social perspective. These two levels of human existence account for a twofold perspective on both sin and grace. The second and third parts will then deal with sin from these perspectives. And the fourth and fifth parts will treat the symbol of grace from the same two perspectives. This short treatise will conclude in the sixth part with an account of the relevance of these doctrines for spirituality. No doctrine has a greater bearing on Christian life than the doctrine of grace in response to sin, death, and ultimate human destiny.

A PRELIMINARY ANTHROPOLOGY

The following characterization of human existence will be no more than preliminary. It seeks to state in descriptive terms the essence of the way the human phenomenon appears in common experience. What are the profound junctures at which human existence today becomes a question to itself?

Human existence may be characterized as freedom. In such a definition, however, the term *freedom* should be understood both substantively and analogously. Ordinarily *freedom* points to a quality of human existence. In this case, however, the term indicates what human existence *is* in distinction from other creatures. Human existence is freedom. The definition of human existence as freedom enables one to transcend the alternatives of substance and process philosophy, for existential freedom always is the act of becoming. But the term is analogous as well, for the freedom that constitutes the human manifests itself on a large variety of different levels.

On the most fundamental level freedom may be understood as synonymous with the human spirit; the human spirit is freedom, a freedom that always in some measure transcends the determinations of matter. The elemental freedom that constitutes the human appears everywhere in human action: in self-consciousness itself, in thinking, in synthetic understanding, in weighing options, in deciding, in acting this way as opposed to that. The human spirit is spirit by being freedom: the freedom of the spirit to transcend physical necessity by bending back on itself in reflection, to stand outside itself by a consciousness of its own consciousness, and to choose against an impulse to do otherwise. Thus freedom reveals itself in the individual psychologically as the self, and corporately it manifests itself in the culture with which human beings inform nature. If the category of freedom is neither exaggerated nor minimized, but allowed to refer to the inner core of the spiritual existence that constitutes humanity, then human existence may be defined as freedom.

Human freedom is constituted at a variety of distinct but inseparable levels that one might call dimensions of human being. For example, human freedom bears an essential relationship to the external world. It is intrinsically related to matter, to the physical world of nature and the environment; human existence is in continuity with other forms of life. One cannot understand human freedom simply as standing over against the worlds studied by the sciences; freedom unfolds within them. An understanding of human existence, even theologically, should include analogous correlations with the world and other forms of life. Another dimension is temporal-historical; human freedom at any given time is intrinsically related to and constituted by a solidarity with and responsibility to the past and the future. These dimensions will not receive the explicit attention they deserve, but remain implicit in the analysis that follows.

Two dimensions bear a special importance for understanding human existence today, namely the individual and the social dimensions of freedom. The individual dimension of human freedom appears readily enough to immediate self-consciousness. Existential-ism has thoroughly analyzed the presence to and responsibility for oneself that constitute the individual's freedom. In the West, the in-violability of personal autonomy hardly needs an apology; in North American culture various forms of individualism are accepted im-plicitly as dogma. By contrast, the social constitution of human freedom is not self-evident and needs to be demonstrated to ordinary consciousness.

That human beings are not totally autonomous subjects can be shown from many points of view. Human freedom begins at birth when human beings are in a state of total dependence on their envi-ronment, and freedom matures over a long period of time in which individuals gain their personal identity within the second womb of society. Society provides each person's language, which largely me-diates the very power to think; culture provides a set of values that largely determine the concrete things that people hold dear. Psycho-logically one's objective image of the self is derived from interaction with other selves. Fundamental moral dispositions and the conscience by which people judge and are judged are partly fashioned within us by those outside us.[1] The social environment that is internalized in the becoming of each individual cannot be considered a function of any single person's freedom. Objective patterns of interdependence are prior to any individual freedom and mold it in some measure. On the social level, then, human existence or freedom cannot be considered a collection of individual freedoms. Corporate and social existence enjoys a certain autonomy relative to each individual, and all individual freedoms are drawn up into this shaping solidarity.

These two dimensions of human existence unfold in a reciprocal, dynamic, and tensive relationship. On the one hand, each individ-ual enjoys an inner autonomy that appears in self-consciousness as personal responsibility. But on the other hand, the self is always inescapably a responding self.[2] Individual freedom is always fash-ioned by interaction with the material world and the social world of behaviors and meanings that shape the self. The self is a social self. Viewed from the other direction, human freedom is a corpo-rate and solidaristic phenomenon; individuals come into being and are sustained only within the relationships that help to define the very self of each one. After one has granted the dimension of the personal-individual constitution of human freedom and responsibil-

---

1. H. Richard Niebuhr, *The Responsible Self: An Essay in Christian Moral Philosophy* (New York: Harper and Row, 1963), 69–79.

2. The notion of the human person as a responding self, taken from H. Richard Niebuhr, implies that the self is intrinsically and essentially social.

ity, one must also emphasize the social constitution and responsibility of human freedom.

On both levels the modern experience of freedom indicates a power of creativity. The meaning and exercise of freedom extend well beyond a capacity to consider options and choose among several objects. Freedom makes new reality come into being; it creates, not in the theological sense "out of nothing," but out of the subjectivity of freedom itself and the raw material of the environment. Freedom fashions genuine novelty, what did not exist before. Thus, both personally and in the solidarity of corporate existence human freedom continually refashions the world and in so doing re-creates itself. This modern *prise de conscience* of the awesome power and creativity of human freedom gives a new dimension to the patristic image of human existence as the image of God.

The shadow side of the capacity of human freedom for creativity consists in its power to destroy. Exhilaration at freedom's potential creativity cannot evade a sober analysis of what it has actually wrought. On the individual level of personal history, a lifetime of striving often ends in failure or success at the expense of others. It seems a law of life. On the social level, enormous advances in science and technology have been turned into more effective instruments of human oppression and death. The statistical or quantitative increase of the human population of our planet is more than matched by an increase of human suffering. The sheer amount of poverty, hunger, lack of medicine, and early death of so many demonstrates that the actuality of human freedom cannot be conceived as simple creativity. The dark side of human freedom, its capacity for perversity, its aggressive self-seeking, its passive lack of concerned reaction, does not allow an easy optimistic anthropology. If this appears too strong a judgment, it is only because each person is all too able to make an accommodation, to define a small world for the self that is tolerably acceptable.

This hasty phenomenology of human existence as a praxis of freedom across time yields a fundamental experience of contrast that must structure all understanding of the human. On the one hand, human freedom appears to be a transcendent and creative power that constructs new reality and meaning in history. On the other hand, that very creativity appears fatally flawed. What ought to be is not; what should be is negated at every turn. The two experiences reinforce and augment each other; evil appears more pervasive against the background of the ideals that human freedom projects, the dreams dreamed and the values hoped for. And against the background of the chaos of human history, every little breakthrough of self-transcending love fuels new efforts of creative energy in hope.

Many questions arise out of this experience of duality and contrast. But two are especially crucial in our time for a Christian understanding of the nature of human existence. Both of them arise out of the context of the relation of human freedom to God, which has been explored in other doctrines, especially creation and christology.

The doctrine of creation reveals that human existence has been constituted by God, who sustains it in its semiautonomous freedom. By "semiautonomous" I mean the autonomous creativity enjoyed by human beings within the larger context of being absolutely dependent on God for existence itself. Beyond this, Jesus Christ is the disclosure of God's salvation, God's initial and final benevolence in regard to human beings. In this context the experience of the radical duality in human existence generates a first line of questioning relative to the status of human freedom before God. The first set of questions are these: Given the experience of semiautonomous human freedom and its dual propensity for creativity and self-destruction, how does human existence stand now before God and relate to God? How does God relate to it? Concretely, what is the character of the ongoing, saving dialogue between God and human existence across time? Within the context of the doctrine of creation and God's salvation revealed in Jesus, these questions concern the way God's salvation is played out concretely in actual historical existence.

A second line of questioning is equally important for any final understanding of human existence. One must suppose that in creating human existence as freedom, God had a purpose for that freedom. The question of the destiny and purpose of human freedom is inescapable; it necessarily arises, and one cannot avoid answering it at least implicitly by the logic of one's action. Moreover it is crucial in our time to recognize the two distinct aspects of the question, the one regarding freedom's ultimate destiny, the other concerning the purpose of human freedom within this world and history. For while the question of final destiny has long been given attention in the history of theology, the question of the purpose of human freedom in this world takes on an entirely new aspect in a historically conscious age. What is the inner reason for each person's creative freedom in the world? What are the intention and will of the creator who bestows meaning and purpose on the collective exercise of human freedom *in this world*? This question is new today because it arises out of the new experience of the creativity of human freedom within the context of historical consciousness. Yet it is this purposiveness that is most threatened today. The diversity of responses to this issue, both theoretical and lived, amounts to a confusing chaos. And the massive human suffering witnessed in the world today throws the very meaningfulness of the history of this world into doubt. What is the Christian conception of the purpose of human freedom in history?

The two sets of questions proposed here find their Christian answer in the doctrines of sin and grace. These questions also help to illumine these doctrines by providing a way of interpreting their meaning relative to secular existence in the world and history. In addition, this preliminary anthropology provides a way for structuring an approach to the doctrines of sin and grace. On the one hand, because of the two distinct but inseparable dimensions of human freedom, both sin and grace must be explored on both the individual and social level, for sin and grace qualify the whole history of human freedom. Individually and socially, both of the symbols sin and grace disclose real transcendental dimensions of human existence as such and the concrete historical working out of these dimensions. On the other hand, the realities of sin and grace must be understood within the context of the purpose of human existence in this world and its final destiny. The following account, then, will deal with sin and then grace, first on the personal and then on the social level of our corporate existence, and always within the context of the questions of God's interaction with human existence in history and the purpose of human freedom.

SIN AS A DIMENSION
OF INDIVIDUAL EXISTENCE

INTRODUCTION

The subject of this discussion is the sinful condition of human existence as distinct from sinful acts. Unless explicitly stated to the contrary, the word *sin* refers to what has traditionally been called original sin. The term *original sin* has had simultaneously two interrelated referents: the originating sin at the dawn of human existence, often called the fall, and the damaging effects of that sin resulting in a sinful condition of the whole race. These two aspects will be merged together in this account. The recognition of this sinful condition is a matter of faith. The doctrine of sin depends on some form of revelation. Despite the obvious moral evil massively displayed in human history, only a revelation of some other possibility can unveil the fact that this is not what human existence could or should be.

The more obvious perception would depict human existence in continuity with the animal realm where survival through competition, power, and violence is natural. Sin and grace then are simultaneously revealed, and each is perceptible only in the light of the other. An experience of grace thus enters into the account of sin; and sin will be the horizon for describing the experience of grace.[3] From the outset one should understand that the doctrine of sin can be understood only in the context of an experience of standing before God.

It follows that on its deepest level the doctrine of sin is a doctrine of human freedom. In the end, it says, the moral evil in the world is not due to either God or nature, but it emerges out of human freedom. Paradoxically, the bondage that the doctrine of sin points to is a bondage of spiritual freedom to itself.

The term *sin*, representing what has been called original sin, is used analogously. What is being described is not personal sin but a "condition" of freedom prior to its actual exercise. If one is to retain a doctrine of sin, one must link it to freedom itself. Sin to really be sin and yet not personal sin must be a quality, structure, and dynamic process of freedom itself.

Before turning to the sources for the doctrine of sin, a consideration of the state of the question in Catholic theology is in order.

RECENT CATHOLIC THEOLOGY OF SIN

Current Roman Catholic theology of original sin is undergoing a radical transition and is marked by considerable pluralism. The reason for the many different theologies of sin is not difficult to pinpoint. The latest, most official teaching of the Catholic church stems from the Council of Trent and is a reexpression of the doctrine formulated in the time of Augustine, largely through the influence of Augustine himself. But that early fifth-century expression of doctrine clashes with current conceptions of the world: our knowledge of the age of the planet; our sense of the evolution of the species; our growing knowledge of our continuity with other forms of life; our psychological views of the destructiveness of guilt; our attempts to formulate a more positive view of matter, the human body, sexuality, and emotion; the inadmissibility of guilt without responsibility. Truly, the doctrine of original sin in its received form does not appear credible.

The theological reinterpretation of the doctrine of sin has progressed mainly on three fronts over the last forty years. The first

---

3. Because of this mutuality of sin and grace the account of sin that follows will be incomplete in itself and must be understood in relation to the theology of grace.

has run parallel with the renewal of biblical studies. The historical-critical method has allowed exegetes to understand Scripture in its own terms. It has enabled theologians to get behind the doctrinal framework and see the degree to which later doctrine exceeds the scriptural witness. Indeed, in many respects the Scriptures provide little support for some details of the developed doctrine.[4]

Second, patristic scholarship and the study of Augustine provide insight into why and how Augustine came to his formulation of the doctrine of sin. In effect, this critical, historical work relativizes Augustine's theology and the particular formulation of the doctrine that resulted from it. By displaying Augustine's teaching as a function of his time and experience this historical work opens up further the possibility of reinterpreting the doctrine of Trent that is so dependent upon it.[5]

Third, current systematic theology displays a host of different constructive reinterpretations of the doctrine that attempt to make it intelligible.[6] In one form or another all of these constructive, speculative theologies proceed by a method of correlation. Such a method brings the received doctrine into dialogue with current theological conceptions of human existence that are themselves informed by scientific and philosophical thought. The following examples are representative of some of the current theologies of original sin.

In the theology of Piet Schoonenberg the distinctiveness of original sin is correlated with the sin of the world. The concept of the sin of the world is drawn from Scripture and points to the accumulation of sin in history that in turn constitutes the situation into which everyone is born. The notion of "situation" is key here: "Situation may be defined as 'the totality of the circumstances in which somebody or something stands at a certain moment, the totality of circumstances prevailing in a certain domain.'"[7] Thus the situation

---

4. For example, A. M. Dubarle, *The Biblical Doctrine of Original Sin*, trans. E. M. Stewart (London: Geoffrey Chapmam, 1964); Herbert Haag, *Is Original Sin in Scripture?* trans. Dorothy Thompson (New York: Sheed and Ward, 1969); Kevin Condon, "The Biblical Doctrine of Original Sin," *Irish Theological Quarterly* 34 (1967): 20–36.

5. See Henri Rondet, *Original Sin: The Patristic and Theological Background*, trans. Cajetan Finegan (Shannon, Ire.: Ecclesia Press, 1972).

6. A number of works survey recent developments in the systematic theology of original sin: William Hamilton, "New Thinking on Original Sin," in *Herder Correspondence* 4 (1967): 135–41; James L. Connor, "Original Sin: Contemporary Approaches," *Theological Studies* 29 (1968): 215–40; George Vandervelde, *Original Sin: Two Major Trends in Contemporary Roman Catholic Reinterpretation* (Washington, D.C.: University Press of America, 1981); Brian McDermott, "The Theology of Original Sin: Recent Developments," *Theological Studies* 38 (1977): 478–512; Christian Duquoc, "New Approaches to Original Sin," *Cross Currents* 28 (1978): 189–200.

7. Piet Schoonenberg, *Man and Sin: A Theological View*, trans. Joseph Donceel (Notre Dame, Ind.: University of Notre Dame Press, 1965), 104–5.

of sin is prior to the exercising of freedom of each one and intrinsically enters into human freedom to determine the direction of the
commitment and decisions of all individuals. Schoonenberg believes
that all the assertions of Trent can be preserved by reinterpreting
them within the framework of the sin of the world.[8]

A considerable amount of reflection has been devoted to the
doctrine of sin within the context of an evolutionary view of the
emergence of human freedom. Paradise is not a state at the beginning of the human race, but a utopic symbol of the goal of human
existence. Moreover an evolutionary framework postulates elements
of analogous continuity between human existence and the physical
and organic world out of which it arose. Thus, for example, Juan
Luis Segundo sees analogies in human existence of a tension between
two fundamental evolutionary forces, entropy and negentropy. In
human freedom these are represented by the pull of spontaneous,
routine, mechanistic, and unfree behavior over against the liberating, creative energy of grace that urges loving and humanizing acts
of freedom. Sin, then, is part of a permanent structure of human existence always in tension with grace.[9] It is not that God the creator
willed sin; sin is still a function of freedom; but there is a deep tensive structure in human existence that leads to sin and is analogous
in all of reality. The price of a really creative human freedom is a
situation in which actual sinning remains an ongoing fact.

Some theologians deny the existence of original sin as a distinct
reality in itself, that is, as distinguishable from personal sin. What
the doctrine really signifies is the profound entrapment of human
freedom in a tendency to sin. And this is manifested, as it were, in
the "fact" that all human beings sin. The point of the doctrine of
original sin is simply that all are sinners and depend absolutely on
God's power of grace for the salvific exercise of freedom.[10]

Many of the insights of the recent theology of sin are drawn
together in the reinterpretation of Stephen J. Duffy.[11] The distinctiveness of his essay lies in the method underlying it. Duffy is less
interested in a systematic accounting for all the elements of the

---

8. Ibid., 177–91.

9. See Juan Luis Segundo, *Evolution and Guilt*, trans. John Drury (Maryknoll,
N.Y.: Orbis Books, 1974); idem, *An Evolutionary Approach to Jesus of Nazareth*,
trans. John Drury (Maryknoll, N.Y.: Orbis Books, 1988). See also McDermott, "The
Theology of Original Sin," 496–502.

10. See Alfred Vanneste, *The Dogma of Original Sin*, trans. Edward P. Callens
(Brussels: Vander, 1971). See also McDermott, "The Theology of Original Sin,"
493–96.

11. Stephen J. Duffy, "Our Hearts of Darkness: Original Sin Revisited," *Theological
Studies* 49 (1988): 597–622.

received doctrine, and more interested in examining what it reveals about ourselves. His method is hermeneutical. He reviews the Adamic myth, Paul, and Augustine with a view to uncovering the dark side of human existence that they open up to our self-awareness. He then weaves together insights from a variety of contemporary authors to explore several dimensions of the sin that works its way in us. In short, the analysis is descriptive of an anthropology of sin.

The treatment of sin and grace that follows employs a similar hermeneutical method. The focus of attention is human life; the goal is to illumine human existence under the light of the traditional doctrinal symbols of sin and grace. In this way the doctrines themselves are reinterpreted. The result will be an analytic, descriptive account of the meaning of these doctrines for Christian life and spirituality. This analytic description of sin unfolds on two levels, the individual and social. These correspond to a need for both transcendental and historical methods of analysis. Neither is complete in itself; the complexity of sin demands that both of these dimensions always be understood together. I begin with the sources of the doctrine.

THE SYMBOLIC SOURCES OF THE DOCTRINE

An account of the doctrine of sin should begin with the data of Christian witness to the experience of it, with the sources of the doctrine and its traditional symbols. The term *symbol* refers to any concept, word, event, thing, person, or literary expression that mediates an experience of transcendent reality. As a modern equivalent of the analogy of faith, the religious symbol shares in the reality it mediates to consciousness. But a religious symbol does not represent or correspond to the transcendent mystery it points to in the same direct manner that concepts represent the objects of our knowledge of this world. Rather than a weak mode of understanding doctrinal expressions of faith, symbols should be understood as expanding the horizon of human perception toward an encounter with reality not available to merely conceptual knowledge. The original symbols that are the source of a doctrine and provide the first expression of it are fundamental to its interpretation.

One of the principal sources of the doctrine of sin is the classical biblical story of a first pair of human beings, originally at peace with God and completely integrated within themselves, with each other, and within their environment. But through outside temptation they rebelled and disobeyed God, in the wake of which came a history of sin (Gen. 3ff.). This story is a narrative and mythic symbol. It deals with human existence by depicting it in a primeval or mythic time, after creation but, as it were, prior to actual history.[12] It thus preserves deep experiences about the nature of human existence, a subject to which I shall return in dealing with how it should be interpreted. But the single most important conclusion of Catholic biblical studies relative to original sin consists in breaking down the misinterpretation of the story of Adam and Eve and their "fall" as a descriptive historical account, and breaking it open as an interpretation of ourselves.

A pastoral note may be helpful in the use of the category of myth. There is no common definition of myth because myths can be studied and analyzed from many different points of view. A myth may be understood as a traditional story that represents the deep truths about the world, nature, and human existence. The story of Adam and Eve is also etiological; it represents the "origins" of sin as if it were an "explanation" of the present situation of sin in the world. Transcendent mystery is depicted in anthropomorphic forms. But the term *myth* will be received differently by different audiences. For example, young people may have grown up believing that the story of Adam and Eve is a literal historical account of the origins of the human race. Particular attention, therefore, is needed to explain and mediate an understanding of this biblical symbol.[13]

The second major biblical source of the doctrine of sin is found in Paul. In his Letter to the Romans Paul personifies sin as a power or force in world history and in the human person that keeps human freedom in bondage. The self is divided: "For I do not do the good I want, but the evil I do not want is what I do. Now if I do what I do not want, it is no longer I that do it, but sin which dwells within me" (Rom. 7:19-20). The power of sin, a universal force in the world, resides in each one of us.

In Romans 5:12-21 Paul gives an extended contrast between Christ and Adam. Adam is taken as a real person, the progenitor of the race. The point of the comparison is to show that, whereas the powers of sin and death originated with Adam, the righteousness and eternal life caused through Christ abound even more. In

---

12. "The narrative explains human existence in its essential elements as something which came about in primeval time, and indeed the created state in contrast to the state of humanity limited by death, suffering and sin. It is a misunderstanding of the narrative as a whole to explain it as a succession of historical or quasi-historical incidents" (Claus Westermann, *Genesis 1–11: A Commentary*, trans. John J. Scullion [London: SPCK, 1984], 276). Westermann provides a full commentary summing up current exegetical opinion on the narrative of Genesis 2–3.

13. See John L. McKenzie, "Aspects of Old Testament Thought," in R. E. Brown, J. A. Fitzmyer, and R. E. Murphy, eds., *The New Jerome Biblical Commentary* (Englewood Cliffs, N.J.: Prentice Hall, 1990), 1288b–90a. On religious symbols and how they communicate see Roger Haight, *Dynamics of Theology* (Mahwah, N.J.: Paulist Press, 1990), chaps. 7 and 8.

the course of this comparison, however, Paul indicates that the sin of Adam is the cause of the universal condition of sinfulness and of spiritual and bodily death. Since the narrative in Genesis is etiological, that is, a projected explanation of the present condition of humankind, Adam is depicted as affecting that situation, which is then compounded by a history of actual personal sinning. Paul, however, does not explain this causality by inheritance. Although the later doctrine of an original sin in which all participated by inheritance was read back into this passage of Paul, it is agreed today that it cannot be found there. The intention of Paul is to assert that all are sinners and share in a situation that is universal from the beginning. But rather than providing a developed doctrine of original sin, the emphasis of the entire passage is on Christ as Savior.[14]

More than any other single source, Augustine is responsible for developing the doctrine of sin as it is known in the Western tradition. Augustine's basic position on' sin and grace was in place before he encountered the doctrine of Pelagius and his followers in 411. The Pelagians had a more optimistic view of human nature and of the power of human freedom than Augustine, and thus a very different notion of grace. For example, part of God's grace is God's commands, and, if God commands, it must be presupposed that human freedom can obey. For Augustine all possibility of salvation originated not with human freedom but with God's grace; even the impulse toward God was impelled by the love of God that "has been poured into our hearts through the Holy Spirit which has been given to us" (Rom. 5:5). The completely prevenient or initiating quality of grace, passively received without any merit, is supremely illustrated in Augustine's doctrine of original sin.[15]

It is often pointed out that Augustine's Latin text of Scripture led him to interpret Romans 5:12 as saying that all humankind sinned in Adam. All human beings were sinners in the progenitor's sin insofar as all emerged from him as sinners, propagated sinful along the line by inherited sinful flesh. But far more deeply than exegesis ran Augustine's fundamental conviction, the central point to which he always returns: If all are not sinners, then Christ is not the Savior of all. But this conviction was indeed radical; it knew no exceptions; it applied even to infants. The practice of infant baptism was already

---

14. See Joseph A. Fitzmyer, "The Letter to the Romans," in *The New Jerome Biblical Commentary*, 844b–47a, for a concise but thorough commentary on this passage. See also Fitzmyer, "Pauline Theology," in ibid., 1402a–3a. For a survey of the notion of sin in the Bible as a whole, see Stanislas Lyonnet, *Sin, Redemption, and Sacrifice: A Biblical and Patristic Study* (Rome: Biblical Institute Press, 1970), 1–57.

15. Jaroslav Pelikan, *The Christian Tradition*, vol. 1, *The Emergence of the Catholic Tradition (100–600)* (Chicago: University of Chicago Press, 1971), 302.

in place, a baptism that was for the remission of sins. And other Latin theologians had already linked infant baptism to an objective sinful condition. For Augustine, then, the conviction of the absolute necessity of God's salvific grace through Christ was confirmed by infant baptism, which entailed an inherited sin. Thus the doctrine of original sin appears as the dramatic extreme of Augustine's theology of grace.

The Pelagians were the occasion for Augustine's doctrine of original sin becoming the doctrine of the church. At the Synod of Carthage held in 418 to take up the teachings of the Pelagians, the doctrine of an original sin inherited from Adam was affirmed (Denzinger-Schönmetzer, *Enchiridion Symbolorum* [hereafter DS], 222–30). But the issues of human nature, freedom, grace, and original sin lingered on and had to be taken up again a century later. In 529, at the Synod of Orange, the essential Augustinian theology was reaffirmed (DS 370–97). These canons and decrees from Carthage and Orange became the substance of the church's doctrine and their content was reaffirmed at Trent.

In the Roman Catholic tradition, the Council of Trent contains the fullest doctrinal teaching on original sin. It is put forward in its Decree on Original Sin of 1546 (DS 1510–16). But it is not substantially new doctrine; for the most part it repeats the teachings of Carthage and Orange, which stem from Augustine's interpretation of the doctrine. The major assertions of the Council of Trent, which are a *reprise* of fifth-century doctrine, are the following: Adam (and Eve), the first parents, sinned, and thus lost the original holiness and justice in which they were created, and incurred God's wrath and the punishment of death. The consequences of this one sin were subsequently transmitted to all human beings by propagation, not by imitation; all human beings are born into a state of sin and guilt, a state of spiritual death, which the salvation of Christ alone, mediated by baptism, can remit. In reaction to Luther, the council also taught that although concupiscence, which stems from sin, remains after baptism, it is not properly sin in itself.[16]

This history of the doctrine of sin is not smooth or continuous; it contains a sharp break. That break begins to show itself in late Jewish literature where Adam is presented as a real human being. This understanding continues through Paul to its climax with the doctrine

---

16. The Council of Trent, Decree on Original Sin (1546), in J. Neuner and J. Dupuis, eds., *The Christian Faith in the Doctrinal Documents of the Catholic Church* (Westminster, Md.: Christian Classics, 1975), 129–32.

of original sin in Augustine.[17] But the break goes much deeper than this interpretation; what has occurred by the time of Augustine is a passage from a symbolic understanding of the story of Adam and Eve to a false claim of theoretical or rational knowledge.[18] In other words, the primal symbols of faith stimulated theological reflection and the desire to understand in more conceptual ways, and based on that the faith experience contained in the foundational symbols was changed into beliefs conceived as knowledge. This was hardened into doctrines that seem to convey religious truth in historical terms or propositions that seem to describe reality directly if not literally and univocally. The result is that the doctrine of Trent seems at several points to be contradicted either by the descriptions of human origins by science or by current religious sensibility. For example, what does it mean to say that a newly born is sinful and guilty?

This split between the traditional doctrine and current under-standing of reality has resulted in the large number of essays and books that reinterpret the Tridentine doctrine of sin.[19] A study of these reinterpretations and of reinterpretations of Augustine could yield a typology of a variety of different types or models for under-standing the doctrine of original sin.[20] In various ways the different current models exemplify attempts to preserve the inner truth of the doctrine, while at the same time transcending but not bypass-ing the formulas of the Council of Trent, and to reconcile it with contemporary conceptions of the origins of human existence.

Another way of interpreting the doctrine of original sin would be to explicitly employ a hermeneutical method of correlation, a method that in some respects is implicitly operative in all recent the-ology of original sin. A brief outline of what this entails will explain how the sources of the doctrine come to bear on our understanding of sin today. Such a method involves going back to the primal sym-bols through which the doctrine was first mediated in the Jewish and Christian traditions. The historical-critical approach to Scripture has uncovered the symbolic quality of the Genesis account of Adam and

17. See Westermann, *Genesis 1–11*, 275–77. See also Fitzmyer, "Pauline Theol-ogy," 1402a–b.

18. See Paul Ricoeur, " 'Original Sin': A Study in Meaning," in his *The Conflict of Interpretations: Essays in Hermeneutics*, ed. Don Ihde (Evanston, Ill.: Northwestern University Press, 1974), 269–86. For the same point, made in terms of the philosophy of language, see Gabriel Daly, "Theological Models in the Doctrine of Original Sin," *Heythrop Journal* 3 (1972): 121–24.

19. For a list of some of these essays and books, see above, note 6.

20. Gabriel Daly, "Theological Models," 121–42, sees the main problem of the doctrine of original sin stemming from a literal use of language. He considers rein-terpretations of the doctrine in terms of other models than the "genetic model" of Augustine.

Eve. The first premise in such a method requires that the symbolic nature of this account be respected.

This premise raises an issue that is crucial for the theological interpretation of the doctrine of original sin. The language of Augustine, the early councils, and especially the Council of Trent does not appear to be symbolic language, and may not have been considered such by their authors, at least not in those terms. Rather it is clear that their assertions unfolded within a historical framework. In other words, the language presupposes Adam and Eve as historical persons; this is the context of the thought. But doctrinal language generally, insofar as it deals with God and the mystery of human existence before God, entails the symbolic language of faith. And this is even more clearly the case insofar as the language of Trent actually reflects the imaginative symbolic framework of an etiological story or narrative. Thus the Tridentine doctrine of original sin is really symbolic; it shares in the same character of the story of Genesis upon which it depends. Thus it is to be understood and interpreted in the same way as one would interpret the myth of Adam and Eve. And, inversely, by unfolding the symbolic significance of the narrative of the fall, one is at the same time reaching the deepest intentionality of the doctrinal tradition as well.

An intentional analysis of the primal myth of the sin of Adam and Eve will reveal the deep themes concerning human existence that are embedded in it.[21] Beneath the story lies the experience of sin and guilt; this penitential experience forms the context in which it was composed, and the experience that it expresses and interprets. By analyzing the structure and dynamics of the story, one can uncover that experience, not in merely psychological terms, but precisely in the terms of the symbols themselves. For example, the story indicates that human existence is fallen, not from a past state, but from its essential potentiality and what it is designed by God to be. Human existence is not what it should be when viewed in the light of God's single creative and salvational intention. Worse, this condition includes a certain propensity to sin. This experience is universalized;

---

21. "On the one hand, it must be said that the concept [of original sin] refers back to the myth, and the myth refers back to the penitential experience of ancient Israel and the Church. Intentional analysis goes from pseudo-rationality to pseudo-history, and from pseudo-history to ecclesiastical *lived experience*. But the path that must be taken [in interpretation] is the opposite one: myth is not only pseudo-history, it is a revealing. As such, it unearths a dimension of experience which otherwise would have remained without expression and which would have aborted precisely as lived experience" (Ricoeur, " 'Original Sin': A Study in Meaning," 285). For a more general discussion of the method employed here, see Haight, *Dynamics of Theology*, chaps. 9 and 10.

sin is a universal condition affecting all human beings, both as individuals and as groups. The externalization of temptation reflects the universal tendency of human beings to find excuses; and the deceit of the serpent thematizes the illusion of unlimited human freedom and autonomy. The condition of sin is "objective" in the sense of being prior to the exercise of our human freedom, prior to conscious responsibility; human beings do not simply participate in sin, they discover it as a power that is there already. And this situation is not from God, for God's creation, complete before the symbolic first sin, is good; sin thus emerges out of freedom itself.[22]

But the interpretation of the doctrine of sin does not end with a consideration of the sources. These themes must be brought forward and made to interpret human existence today. In other words, this symbolic doctrine must be, as it were, applied and used to understand ourselves. The doctrine must be expressed in more reflective, universal, but still symbolic, theological language. The story of Adam and Eve is the story of human existence itself. It points to a drama that transpires in every person, in society, and in the interaction between the individual and the social dimension of the human. The story accurately portrays point by point the concupiscence, temptation, and sin of all human beings personally and collectively. Its narrative represents a pattern of behavior that is reenacted in every age.[23]

It is important to grasp the reasons that underlie this doctrine of sin. What is the need for such a doctrine, and why have Christians always insisted upon it? Besides the fact that the doctrine of sin truthfully portrays human existence, the necessity of the doctrine can be recognized in the fundamental questions to which it responds. The question underlying the Adamic story is basic in the light of the doctrine of creation: What is the source of moral evil in the world? The doctrine is central for understanding God and human existence in relation to God's creation. The biblical doctrine is that what God creates is good. The doctrine of sin maintains that its origin is not God; the source of sin is human existence itself.

In the Christian tradition another reason for the doctrine was added to the rationale found in the Jewish writings. The doctrine of sin underscores the universal need for God's salvation revealed in Jesus Christ. Thus Paul's contrast between Adam and Christ. The doctrine of sin may be seen as a negative way of asserting the universal relevance of the event of salvation in Jesus Christ. The fi-

---

22. See Paul Ricoeur, *The Symbolism of Evil*, trans. Emerson Buchanan (Boston: Beacon Press, 1969), 232–60, and "'Original Sin': A Study in Meaning."

23. Langdon Gilkey, *Message and Existence: An Introduction to Christian Theology* (New York: The Seabury Press, 1979), 135–39.

nal argument of Augustine against Pelagius is always that, if human beings do not need grace, then Christ came in vain.

While both of these traditional logics remain valid today, there is a new exigency for the doctrine of sin that is more pointedly anthropological. The doctrine accurately portrays human existence as it is, that is, as both sinful and free. The present context for understanding this doctrine, however, is quite different from that of Augustine and Trent in two ways. First, unlike Augustine Christians today do not live in a world marked by an elitist striving for Pelagian self-perfection; rather their world is marked by a complacent acceptance of the world as it is and an acceptance of sin as if it were not sin but merely "the way things are."[24] Sin then must be highlighted as a misuse of human freedom, and grace as the power to resist it. Second, and theologically, grace and sin cannot be reified; they should be understood, not in objective and quasi-physical categories, but in the personal, dialogical terms of God's self-communication to human freedom and the sinful reaction of freedom to that grace. In this context sin will appear as a resistant structure within the emergence of freedom itself.

In sum, given the traditional testimony to the experience of the sinfulness of humankind, the task of theology is to provide a descriptive analysis of human existence that both makes sense of the doctrine and at the same time allows it to shed light on actual existence, on the understanding of individual and collective history. I turn now to that descriptive analysis.

CONCUPISCENCE AND TEMPTATION

Concupiscence has traditionally been understood as an effect of sin, a concomitant of the condition of sinfulness. I begin the analysis of sin with concupiscence because it is most prominent in human experience.[25]

The freedom that is human existence is not unmixed; there is no pure freedom. Human existence is limited, qualified, and determined by physical nature, the physiological, biological, psychological, temperamental, and emotional structures that help constitute the one single and whole person. Each individual person is both free and unfree, free and determined.

---

24. Gabriel Daly, "Original Sin," in J. Komonchak, M. Collins, and D. Lane, eds., *The New Dictionary of Theology* (Wilmington, Del.: Michael Glazier, 1987), 730.

25. This analysis of the dynamics of concupiscence and the "prior sin" is dependent on Karl Rahner, "The Theological Concept of Concupiscentia," in *Theological Investigations* (Baltimore: Helicon Press, 1964), 1:347–82, and Reinhold Niebuhr, *The Nature and Destiny of Man* (New York: Charles Scribner's Sons, 1964), 1:179–86.

As a result human life unfolds within a fundamental tension of forces that have a bearing on the actual being of each one. For on the one hand, freedom is oriented to posit or dispose the self completely, fully, and without reserve in being before God. But on the other hand, because of the resistance to freedom that stems from the spontaneous and determining desires or impulses of nature, it is impossible to commit the self completely and fully. On a first and fundamental level, then, concupiscence refers to the sheer resistance of the whole of an individual to the freedom of self-actualizations for good or for evil. Concupiscence in this sense is not an evil; it is simply the finite condition and actual situation of human existence.[26]

Because the intrinsic finality of human freedom is toward a self-disposition in trust, faith, and love relative to God and according to God's will, the tension between freedom and unfreedom or determination becomes temptation. On the one hand, the infinite reach of freedom tends toward absolute existence, which can be guaranteed only by God; but on the other hand, the finite, limited, and determined aspects of human nature make it subject to the laws of diminishment and ultimate death. This tension creates a fundamental existential anxiety in and of human being itself, which may or may not come to psychological awareness, but which is always operative within human freedom.[27] This anxiety is ambiguous, both positive and negative at the same time. On the one hand, anxiety is the condition for the possibility of human creativity and achievement; on the other hand, it is a temptation to posit the self in being now against the threat of nonbeing or being-unto-death by proclaiming the self a fully autonomous center of being. This anxiety about being is so deep that motivational analysis cannot sort out the ambiguity in the exercise of human freedom. Because freedom cannot fully commit or determine the self in being, because it always suffers the threat of nonbeing, it is always tempted and in some measure seeks to secure itself in being on its own terms.

This initial approach to sin in descriptive analytic terms corresponds to Paul's dramatic and classic description of the divided self already cited; that description continues as follows: "For I delight in

---

26. Surely concupiscence may be *experienced* as negative with respect to the revealed final destiny of human existence as union with God. See Rahner, "The Theological Concept of Concupiscentia," 375–76. But in itself concupiscence is simply the entailment of the finite structure of existence as freedom in tension with nature.

27. This anxiety is a transcendental or universal structure of human existence. But it unfolds concretely and historically in a different way in each person. For example, anxiety about one's being will undoubtedly manifest itself in a distinctive way among the poor who have no job, little to eat, and no access to medical service. See Gregory Baum, *Theology and Society* (New York: Paulist Press, 1987), 263.

the law of God, in my inmost self, but I see in my members another law at war with the law of my mind and making me captive to the law of sin which dwells in my members. Wretched man that I am!" (Rom. 7:22-24).

SIN

Adam, it was said, is the symbol for every person and for the collectivity. The story of Adam and Eve is also the symbol for the emergence of freedom in history. In order to understand the significance of these symbols, therefore, one must understand the sinful condition of human existence as a process, a historical drama in each person and, as we shall see, in society; that drama characterizes human existence in its very unfolding as freedom. On the level of the individual, the imagination should be focused equally both on the emergence of freedom from infant potentiality to its flowering in responsibility and on the exercise of freedom in every moment of conscious adult life. The dynamics of sin can be understood through the elements that are involved in it.

The point of departure for the emergence of sin is the coming into existence of human freedom that lacks an appropriation of God's self-communication in grace. But grace should not be understood primarily in objective terms, because foundationally grace is the personal self-presence of God to human beings in love. Therefore, the objective condition of not being able to respond to God's grace because of a lack of responsibility should not be considered as sin in any sense. One obviously cannot respond to grace at the beginning of human life. Freedom begins as a potentiality that is meant to grow into responsibility and actual response to God's grace.

This condition of coming into existence without an appropriation of God's grace is complexified by the dynamics of concupiscence and temptation. In the beginning human freedom exists as a mere virtuality that must emerge within the determinisms of nature that also constitute each person. Indeed the historical process of that emergence depends on these determinisms and can never overcome them.

Within this complex structure and not apart from it the sinful condition of human existence appears within the emerging exercise of freedom itself. The permanent threat of nonbeing involved in the condition of finitude, the resistance of nature to the full disposition of the self before God, and the positive temptation to posit the self in being autonomously, qualify every human act. Every human exercise of freedom is in danger of becoming an autonomous assertion of the self, and in that measure a failure of total trust, complete faith, and absolute self-disposition before God, who alone can secure human existence in being. This is not to be construed as formal, conscious, and intentional sin; it is an existential condition that is actualized in an emergent exercise of freedom.

Sin is both a structure prior to the exercise of freedom and one that is actualized by freedom itself. For the inherent lack of openness, faith, and love, the measure of failure in fully appropriating God's grace or even rejecting it, retains the status of "prior sin," the prior reason for this or that sinful action. Paradoxically, this emergent condition is both prior to the concrete exercise of freedom, not chronologically but as the deep structure out of which freedom operates, and yet it becomes actualized only with the exercise of freedom itself. Paradoxical too is the fact that the actualization of this structure, resulting in actual sins, is both inevitable and free. Sin cannot be considered necessary or caused by God's creation because, emerging with the exercise of freedom, especially within the context of God's ever-present offer of grace, human beings could act in a totally self-transcending trust in God as the security of their being.[28] And yet they don't, and personal sinning is a universal phenomenon.[29]

But there is more to it than a lack of an adequate response to God. Out of the structure of temptation and prior to particular personal sins one finds a certain propensity to sin, an aversion to God and God's will for human self-transcendence, an active resistance to God. As Piet Smulders expresses it: "In the heart of human beings lies a kind of will not to love God; anterior to personal choice, it encompasses and fetters that choice."[30] This is what Augustine called the curvature of the self in upon the self, resulting in a kind of tendency away from God in the direction of self, and drawing all things into the self as means to end.[31]

---

28. Reinhold Niebuhr, *The Nature and Destiny of Man*, 1:183.

29. This of course is not an empirical judgment. It stems from the correspondence of the scriptural and doctrinal witness with the inner experience of repentance and remorse of the sinner. See Reinhold Niebuhr, *The Nature and Destiny of Man*, 1:255–60. Sin can be recognized only by the sinner. But the transcendental analysis of this experience reveals a structure in which all participate. Inevitability then is not necessity, because sin is a function of freedom. The notion of inevitability remains paradoxical and cannot be fully understood. It points to a *historical* rather than a metaphysically necessary condition of estrangement, and this will be developed further on the social level of human existence.

30. Piet Smulders, *The Design of Teilhard de Chardin: An Essay in Theological Reflection*, trans. Arthur Gibson (Westminster, Md.: Newman Press, 1967), 176.

31. From this analysis it is clear that baptism, as the Christian community's mediating sacrament of grace and faith in the name of Jesus, bears a direct relationship to the condition of the lack of grace and the lack of faith in the emergent freedom

In sum, sin on the individual level may be described as a structure and a process of human freedom that begins with a lack of an appropriation of God's grace but then qualifies every moment of a human being's existence in this world. This structure leads through concupiscence and temptation to the prior sin, that is, some measure of a lack of openness and surrender in self-actualization before God and according to God's will, and, more aggressively, a propensity against God and for the self. Sin emerges as a fallen condition only when it is actualized through human freedom. But at the same time it is not identical with any personal sin; it is a structured dynamic process of unfaith, a lack of trust and love that is prior to and underlies every personal sin.[32]

This description of the sinful condition of human existence does not remove the ultimate mystery involved here. One cannot fully understand the propensity to evil that this sin generates as distinct from the structure of human existence itself, which comes from the hands of God.[33] Some reflections, however, are helpful in considering this mystery. In fact God has chosen to create human existence through an evolutionary process, and now human history lies open to the future as a function of human freedom. The God who creates human freedom respects the creative autonomy that God established. So serious is this freedom that it contains the possibility of a rejection of God's own address in love together with the responsibility and power for true creativity within God's love.[34]

Finally, one must consider the nature of the personal sins that arise out of this emergent structure of sin. Sin itself can exist only in human freedom, in the spiritual dimension of human existence. But the roots of sin reach back into the polar tension between spirit and nature that structures human freedom. Thus personal sins may be

---

even of a child. He or she is initiated into the explicit community of grace and faith. This will become clearer in the discussion of the social dimensions of sin and grace.

32. It is crucial to see that sin is both a structure and a dynamic process. If sin were not a process culminating in inherent attitudes prior to any actual sin, it could not itself be called "sin." The tradition supplies many defining names for this prior sin: pride, unfaith, idolatry, disobedience, rebellion, egocentrism, and so on. All of them bring out particular aspects of sin. Perhaps the most central is an egocentric autonomy that can manifest itself both actively and passively, as aggressivity and escape from freedom and responsibility.

33. In other words, the problem, not of sin but of the propensity to sin that seems to emerge out of the very structure of human existence, is similar to the problem of evil and suffering generally in the world; it is insoluble and transcendentally mysterious.

34. If one conceives of history as involving a genuine dialogue between God and human beings in such a way that human beings are real dialogue partners in freedom, then the possibility and even the temptation to reject God's free initiative can be coherently encompassed in this worldview.

characterized according to the predominance of the one or the other pole in the dynamic structure of existence.[35] Such a description, however, remains abstract and simply points to two extreme possibilities on a continuous spectrum. On the one hand, the freedom and autonomy of the human spirit spawn aggressive and domineering acts of egocentrism and pride. All the power, creativity, generativity, and potential for achievement by human freedom become autonomous self-assertion over against what is other: other persons, society, the world, and even God. These are the active sins of aggression. But on the other hand, the intrinsic link of the human spirit to the determinisms of nature also spawns what may be called sins of passivity or omission. Still rooted in the dynamism of spirit, here freedom negates itself, refuses to act, tries to escape the responsibility and potentiality intrinsic to freedom itself. Often active sins are regarded as the more typical and destructive. But since the structure of anxiety is also the basis for creativity, when the sins of passivity or omission are viewed against the horizon of God's grace, and on the assumption that God has assigned a purpose for human freedom within this world, they appear as an abdication of responsibility that is equally serious and ravaging.[36] This will become more apparent within the context of the social dimension of sin.

THE SOCIAL DIMENSION OF SIN

Any reduction of sin to its personal dimension and dynamics trivializes its power in the world. The history of the theology of sin has not been wrong in conceiving sin as a kingdom of evil or personifying it as a cosmic agent that holds human existence in bondage. An adequate analysis of sin cannot remain on the level of the personal dynamics of each individual and at the same time do justice to the awesome hold that sin has on human existence. The analysis of the social dimension of sin is thus not simply "added on" to the previous understanding as some complementary reflection. Rather sin *is* social as well as individual, and what follows could well be the point of departure for understanding sin in itself.

---

35. Reinhold Niebuhr, *The Nature and Destiny of Man*, 1:186–203, 228–40.

36. See Juan Luis Segundo, *The Humanist Christology of Paul*, trans. John Drury (Maryknoll, N.Y.: Orbis Books, 1986), 177. The theme of passivity, omission, and failure to assume the responsibility of love underlies all of Segundo's work on sin and grace. The analysis here also takes into account feminist critiques of an overly masculine depiction of sin in the tradition.

The idea of the social is used loosely to designate any and every form of routinized behavior of groups. It refers to constant relationships and patterns of actions that human beings have with one another and with the world. Thus society or the social denotes any form of institutionalized behavior or the systems that govern and are implicit in such behavior. A society or institution, however, is not an entity with an autonomous existence, for societies do not exist apart from the subjects that make them up. Yet the routinized or formalized patterns of behavior can be spoken of in objective terms, as the social sciences suggest.

Few people would deny the existence of moral evil in human history. If one steps back and views history generally, it can be seen as a process of sin, guilt, and consequent suffering from which no one is exempt. Viewed especially from the point of view of the victims, it would not be too strong to say that human history consists in human beings preying on others. Momentary peace, harmony, and community, usually experienced within definable groups, are the wonderful exceptions that prove the rule. But one cannot rest with this abstract and impressionistic statement. Because human existence is essentially social, human egocentrism, competitiveness, hostility, aggression, and lack of concern are always mediated through concrete organized structures of behavior and institutions.[37] The issue, then, is to show how and in what measure social evil in history is not only objective evil, but is really sin as distinguished from evil, that is, a function of human freedom. How is this sin constitutive of the human freedom of every person prior to the actual exercise of his or her freedom? How is social sin not personal sin or actual sinning but an existential propensity toward it?

THE OBJECTIVITY OF SIN AND
THE SOCIAL CONSTITUTION OF HUMAN EXISTENCE

From one point of view social institutions and structures seem to be objective. They are in some degree invariant relationships or patterns of behavior. Language is governed by grammar and standard usage, society by law, culture by sets of values and ideals established

---

37. This description of social sin consists in a historical and social analysis. Very often what is called "the sin of the world" in current theologies of sin is the product of a transcendental imagination that is abstract and general. By translating this abstract notion into the concrete and historical analyses of social sin from liberation and political theologies, one arrives at a more historical and realistic view of sin. See Patrick Kerans, *Sinful Social Structures* (New York: Paulist Press, 1974). Because of restrictions on space, what is lacking in the account of social sin here is an adequate historical phenomenology of sin.

in tradition, corporations by constitutions, by-laws, and custom. This objectivity is precisely that which allows social "entities" to be studied in a disciplined manner. This objectivity appears most clearly in relation to each individual, for society and its institutions exist prior to the freedom of any single person. Human beings are born into society, and they voluntarily join a whole host of pre-established institutions.

Social arrangements are meant to enhance human freedom. The organization and regularization of patterned behavior should and to some extent always do release freedom through memory, habit, and instinctive routine to grapple with new issues. But institutions also limit and determine behavior. Moreover they invariably involve oppressive elements. All institutions that enhance the freedom of some always exclude or repress in some measure the freedom of others. The larger groups and organizations become, the less they possess an inner self-identity or autonomously conscious and reflective center, the more they become the projected and glorified self of the individual members, and the more corporate self-transcendence is impeded.[38] The identity of every group is defined by its boundaries over against other groups. Generally speaking, for one must speak generally about social institutions, individuals do not transcend the limits of the institutions that govern their lives; rather social structures set them over against those in other groups. One is inclined to be loyal to one's family, tribe, cast, corporation, professional guild, economic class, regional society, race, nation, sex—right or wrong.

The objective structures that define social institutions are internalized by those born into them or joined to them. Thus either by the necessity of birth or by choice through voluntary association the ideas, values, and patterned relationships between people help to constitute each individual in the group. The most dramatic example of this is the already cited phenomenon of language, where one's very power to think, and hence judge, evaluate, and decide, is in some measure determined by the learned system of speech with all the social and cultural biases and prejudices it carries. This objective determination of human beings does not remain an external influence; it is certainly not merely a question of imitation and *learning* from example. The influence of the multiple levels of society enters into the personhood of each individual as a "second nature." Thus every individual *is* social or socially constituted in being. This accounts for the infectious quality of the sin of the world

---

38. Reinhold Niebuhr, *Moral Man and Immoral Society* (New York: Charles Scribner's Sons, 1960), xii, xxiv, 35, 73–75, 83–93.

and its contagion.[39] All human beings are in some way tainted by the negativities of the social institutions they inherit or join. In terms of the previous analysis of sin on the individual level, one must speak of social concupiscence and temptation. The social determinants of every human being, generally speaking, cannot be controlled. From one point of view they are internalized as part of the self; from another point of view one acts within them. Thus their positivities and negativities channel human freedom and determine human behavior. The positive and negative impulses of these levels of the second nature of each person, this social concupiscence, become temptation. The aggressive aspects of institutions enhance the power of the group, and hence individual autonomy, power, and dominance, over other people in other groups. They also tempt negatively, because it is very difficult for individuals to transcend the institutions that nurture them and assume a responsibility against their evil effects. Thus social structures are also temptations to escape from freedom by sins of omission. In sum the social determinisms of the institutions that make up the second nature of human existence amount to a concupiscence and temptation that are often stronger than the impulses of one's individual nature.

THE SUBJECTIVITY OF SOCIETY AND THE PHENOMENON OF SOCIAL GUILT

While from one point of view society and its institutions appear to be objective, from another they must be considered subjective. This is easily demonstrated by their changeability and pluralism. Social institutions gradually change over time and become quite different from what they were. And at any given time the differences in the way even the most fundamental structures of human living unfold in various cultures show their relativity. No institutions, not even those governing sexual behavior, eating, or communicating, are sheerly the product of nature; every human institution is cultural, a product of human freedom and creativity.

Social institutions, then, are grounded in human freedom. Born out of creative human response to the world and others, they are carried along by a human freedom that continually internalizes these patterns of meaning and behavior. From this point of view, then, one passes from the sphere of objective evil to that of sin. The destructive aspects of social institutions are more than objective evils

---

39. Schoonenberg, _Man and Sin_, 98–123; idem, "The Sin of the World," in _Sacramentum Mundi_ (New York: Herder and Herder, 1969), 5:90–91.

that are contrary to the will of God; they are also sin because they are produced and sustained by human freedom. This sin, however, is not personal sin; it is not necessarily formal sin in the sense of being deliberate; it is precisely social sin. As distinct from personal sin or actual sinning this social sin is an integral part of what has traditionally been called original sin.

The sinful aspect of social involvement can be drawn out by a consideration of the phenomenon of social guilt, not guilt for society of the past of which one was not a part, but responsibility for the present and future sin of society. This is a very delicate issue because people rarely admit to guilt even in their individual lives, and this guilt is so difficult to measure that it tends to escape evaluation. Thus one should be clear at the outset about certain qualifications. First and foremost social guilt is not individual guilt, but precisely an analogous reality that is social. The sameness and difference that constitute this analogy are crucial. We do not control society in the same way we control ourselves. Yet at the same time we participate in society and contribute to its functioning. As prior to individual guilt, social guilt is part of the complex of prior sin. Second, it is impossible to quantify this social guilt because it exists on so many different levels and in so many different degrees. Within the framework of these qualifications, however, social guilt remains inescapable.

This becomes clear from the fact that no one can escape participation in social structures and institutions that inevitably do harm to some people. By their action within these institutions, prior to the immediate object of any particular action, all participants in some measure help perpetuate the social institutions in which they live. Individuals and groups can react against various aspects of social sin; human freedom can transcend society at any given point and become countercultural. But no one can escape all the aspects of one's social existence and participation. Even an attempt to escape from society and its structures can be an escape from the social responsibility that allows them to continue.

But there are variables in responsibility and guilt that can be located along the axes of knowledge and power. Some elements of society are more responsible than others for society itself and for all institutions. On the one hand, people are not explicitly responsible for what is unknown or beyond the sphere or capacity of their freedom. But on the other hand, some measure of knowledge and power is inherent in freedom itself, so that social guilt may vary from the merely virtual to the conscious and explicit. Often social situations appear as genuine entrapments; they entail dilemmas from which no course of action emerges that will not cause damage to whole groups of people. At this point one begins to experience the all-encompassing power of sin and one's own and society's inability to escape it.

In the end, however, apart from these distinctions, the final demonstration of social sin and guilt is experiential, and it stems from the ontology of human solidarity. All are part of the concrete human condition. One cannot regard a social tragedy with indifference by saying "it does not concern me." The strongest testimony to social sin and guilt is conscience, which is at the same time a consciousness of solidarity with others and implicitly a standing before God.

THE PRIOR SITUATION OF SIN AND
THE PURPOSE OF HUMAN FREEDOM

The Christian doctrine of sin is intrinsically paradoxical, for it teaches that a universal condition of a propensity to sin, prior to the exercise of freedom, is part of freedom itself and affects every exercise of freedom. It states that human existence is fallen in such a way that sin, which is a function of freedom, is omnipresent. A gentler way of expressing this characterizes every and all exercise of freedom as ambiguous. But this fails to express the power, contagion, and aggressive force behind moral evil in history and in the individual self.

The power of sin in the world is simply inescapable. Sin is the condition prior to the exercise of personal freedom, constituted by the native structure of each individual and by a socially inherited second nature. It is sin inasmuch as these structures are appropriated and ratified through a lack of hope, faith, and love. This entails in some measure an assertion of the self or an escape from freedom over against others and implicitly God, who alone can guarantee security in being. On the one hand, sin is simple: It is the emergence within human freedom of false autonomy and egocentrism over against other human beings and God. On the other hand, it is complex, for it is fed by multiple factors, transcendentally on the individual level and historically on the social level. Sin is an aggressive power within each person's freedom that cumulatively projects itself out into history, or a recessive negation of freedom that fails to be responsible for the self and the world in response to grace. It is also a concrete historical sphere, region, or environment that enters into and influences each person's freedom. Both of these dimensions are necessary factors in its description: Social sin cannot be explained without the individual dimension; the sheer power of sin and its hold on the race cannot be explained without the social dimension. Thus sin is both outside individual human freedom and within it, both "objective" and subjective at the same time. It inescapably qualifies all human behavior, every exercise of freedom.

The inescapability of sin provides a first negative answer to the questions arising out of a preliminary anthropology. First, what is the status of human existence before God? In straightforward language, human existence is sinful. No human being can measure the self against its transcendent ideals and say "I am what I should be," any more than any Christian can stand before God and confess personal holiness. No society or collectivity, no institution or group, can claim to measure up to what it should or could be. Thus insofar as human existence is freedom, it is also both "objectively" and freely sinful.

The second question concerns the purpose of human freedom. The issue of its final destiny will be resolved in a consideration of grace as the kingdom of God. But relative to the purpose of human freedom within this world, the inescapability of sin provides a preliminary negative answer. There is no escape from sin in this world. One should not interpret the transcendence of human freedom as an escapist drive to live above the sphere of limits, determinants, concupiscence, and temptation. Rather, within this world the purpose for freedom is the struggle against sin. Though sin is inescapable, it can be resisted and its power and effects minimized within the self and in history. But a more positive indication that this is the intrinsic God-given purpose of human freedom lies in the doctrine of grace.

GRACE ON THE INDIVIDUAL LEVEL
OF HUMAN EXISTENCE

INTRODUCTION

Speaking generally the notion of God's grace refers to God's goodness, graciousness, and benevolence toward human beings. Grace is God's love for human existence. But this grace is always understood against the background of a human dilemma. In relation to human sinfulness God's grace appears as mercy and forgiveness. Against the background of human finitude and death, God's love appears as a power unto ultimate salvation in eternal life.[40] The history of

---

40. In Protestant theology grace tends to be understood against the background of the horizon of sin; Catholic theology tends to define grace in response to the finitude of human nature and death, although it does not neglect the problem of sin. There seems to be no compelling reason to consider these two frameworks in exclusion of one another; they can be combined.

the theology of grace yields no single systematic understanding of the term. Moreover the same history deals with a whole host of different questions, all of which cannot be subsumed into this account.

The theology of grace that follows rests on the following premises: First, it aims at a systematic theology by drawing the diverse notions of grace into a single consistent language. Second, grace is understood against the background of both sin and the finitude of human existence leading to death. Third, in defining God's salvation from sin and death, the theology of grace provides the Christian response to the fundamental questions that run parallel to those underlying the theology of sin. They concern the way God relates to human beings in their sinful existence leading to death; how consequently human beings stand before the God who approaches them in grace; the character of the ongoing dialogue between God and human existence; the very purpose of human freedom in history.

The fundamental character of these questions that underlie the whole history of the theology of grace should not be underestimated. So basic are these issues that the theological anthropology developed in response to them casts its interpretation on the understanding of Christianity as a whole.[41] The theology of grace interprets the concrete appropriated meaning of God's salvation revealed in Jesus Christ.

Before examining the sources and analysis of this doctrine, however, I turn to a review of the state of the question in Catholic theology today.

CATHOLIC THEOLOGY OF GRACE TODAY

The theology of grace contained in Catholic manuals before the Second Vatican Council consisted in a highly technical treatise that was divided into the specific topics of actual and sanctifying grace. It employed a variety of distinctions of various aspects of what was called grace, these distinctions having developed over the centuries in response to different problematic issues.[42] The treatise bore little relation to everyday Christian experience. Even the precise subject matter, what was being studied and its significance relative to the substance of Christian faith, was not self-evident.

---

41. It is not surprising, therefore, that the fundamental theological issue underlying the Reformation concerned grace. The differences between Catholic and Protestant understandings of grace lead to basic differences in anthropology and spirituality that color their whole interpretation of Christianity and that are still operative today.

42. Quentin Quesnell, "Grace," in Komonchak, Collins, and Lane, eds., *The New Dictionary of Theology*, 437, 442–44.

The doctrine of grace as an explicitly distinct topic or area of reflection was most decisively determined for Western theology by Augustine. For him the notion of God's grace, as God's agency of human salvation, contained a central datum for the whole Christian vision. In his fight with Pelagianism Augustine insisted that God alone saves through the grace mediated by Christ. By firmly positing the absolute priority and gratuity of grace over against sin and human impotency for our own salvation, Augustine laid the groundwork for a fundamental Christian conception of human existence. But his theology also opened up many areas of mystery that pervade the ongoing relationship between God and human life, such as a precise understanding of what "grace" is, the relationship between grace and human freedom, and the balance between God's providence and the unfolding of human history.

In the twentieth century no Catholic theologian has done more than Karl Rahner to restore the theology of grace to its position close to the center of Christian thought. The renewal of the theology of grace began on a foundational level with modernism, and a number of modernist theologians anticipated some of Rahner's conclusions. Other theologians contributed to the questioning of the theology of the manuals by historical studies of Aquinas and the medieval tradition.[43] But it was Rahner who most effectively transformed the theology of grace in Catholic theology. His theology, or at least many of the conclusions of this thought, are almost presupposed in the theology of grace today. Some of the force of Rahner's theology of grace, especially when viewed in contrast to the Neo-Scholasticism to which he was reacting, will help define the state of the question today. One can see four reversals at work in his reinterpretation of grace.[44]

First, since the time of Aquinas the term *grace* designated primarily, although not exclusively, "created grace," a habit or quality of the human soul infused by God. Concomitantly with this sanctifying grace, God, who is "uncreated grace," was present to and

---

43. For example, Henri Bouillard, *Conversion et grâce chez S. Thomas d'Aquin* (Paris: Aubier, Éditions Montaigne, 1944); Bernard Lonergan, *Grace and Freedom: Operative Grace in the Thought of St. Thomas Aquinas,* ed. Patout Burns (New York: Herder and Herder, 1970); Henri de Lubac, *Surnaturel: Études historiques* (Paris: Aubier, 1946).

44. See Karl Rahner, "Some Implications of the Scholastic Concept of Uncreated Grace," in *Theological Investigations,* 1:319–46; idem, "Concerning the Relationship between Nature and Grace," in ibid., 297–317; idem, "Nature and Grace," *Theological Investigations* (Baltimore: Helicon Press, 1966), 4:165–88; idem, *Foundations of Christian Faith: An Introduction to the Idea of Christianity,* trans. William V. Dych (New York: The Seabury Press, 1978).

dwelt in the human person. Rahner simply reverses this relationship between created and uncreated grace. Grace is first and foremost God's self-communication and presence to human existence. This simple shift completely reorients one's thinking about grace and opens up the possibility of interpersonal categories to analyze it.

Second, in response to the implied extrinsicism of Neo-Scholastic theology, Rahner defines the offer of grace as constitutive of the actual condition of human existence. The supernaturality of grace does not mean that it comes to a purely self-enclosed human nature as an alien, arbitrary, and merely additional factor of the human condition. Rather, God's presence as an offer of salvation is part of the historical condition of a human existence whose salvation God wills from the beginning.

Third, against the implication that grace is scarce, then, or that there is no salvific grace outside the Christian sphere, Rahner argues theologically to the universality of grace on the basis of the universality of God's saving will. The implication of this position is dramatic: It means that the whole sphere of human life, even in its most secular aspects, is potentially "graced." The position breaks down barriers separating the church and the world and unveils to Christian vision a kingdom of grace beyond the church.

Fourth, against the widespread Neo-Scholastic position that grace cannot be experienced, because it is supernatural, Rahner holds that people do experience grace. This is a qualified view, however, since grace is still not known directly or distinctly as grace but in and through experiences of genuine self-transcendence. But at the same time this conclusion opens the theology of grace to phenomenological and narrative methods of analyzing grace in and through experience.

With these theological moves Rahner has returned the theology of grace to a consideration of the very nature of salvation and how it is experienced in human existence. In some ways Rahner's theology of grace is transitional; he broke open the narrow objectivist treatise on grace and reconceived it in foundational anthropological terms. Yet to a large extent the current Catholic theology of grace, even when it moves beyond Rahner, is dependent on him.

The movement beyond Rahner has occurred in several areas. One clear instance of this development lies in the explicit context of ecumenical theology. In an early work Hans Küng succeeded in bringing much closer together the teaching of the Council of Trent on justification and the widely respected Neo-Reformation theology of Karl Barth.[45] The work of the Lutheran-Catholic dialogue on the theme of grace charts many areas of agreement while respecting differences of language, theme, and accent.[46]

The significance of the theology of grace has also been expanded by liberation theology. Building implicitly on conclusions shared by Karl Rahner, liberation theology stresses grace as a liberating force in public, social life. It offers a conception of the Christian life of discipleship as participation with Christ in the mediation of grace to society and the building up of social grace.[47]

The concept and theology of grace have also been deepened by a return to biblical sources. Reaching back especially into the New Testament for the foundations of a theology of grace, which of course are prior to Augustine's formulation of the issues, Edward Schillebeeckx has opened up the rich pluralism of the symbolism of grace. By merging the theological notion of grace with the very experience of salvation that is expressed in so many different ways by early church communities, Schillebeeckx has again demonstrated the centrality of this concept.[48]

Finally, there are efforts to relate the technical theology of grace more closely to Christian life within the church. Using the category of grace in a more diffuse and generic sense, and relating it to the experience of God mediated through Jesus and the church, Brian McDermott draws out the significance of the recent theology of grace for everyday Christian experience.[49]

In the interpretation of the theology of grace presented here the framework of Rahner's theology is foundational. In the light of a preliminary anthropology that raises questions and provides a

45. Hans Küng, *Justification: The Doctrine of Karl Barth and a Catholic Reflection* (New York: Thomas Nelson and Sons, 1964).

46. See H. G. Anderson, T. A. Murphy, and J. A. Burgess, eds., *Justification by Faith: Lutherans and Catholics in Dialogue VII* (Minneapolis: Augsburg Publishing House, 1985).

47. See especially the work of Juan Luis Segundo as represented in *Grace and the Human Condition*, trans. John Drury (Maryknoll, N.Y.: Orbis Books, 1973), and *The Humanist Christology of Paul*; see also Leonardo Boff, *Liberating Grace*, trans. John Drury (Maryknoll, N.Y.: Orbis Books, 1979). The liberation theology of grace has had an influence on the theology of the church's center. For example, it is clear that the Congregation for the Doctrine of the Faith's *Instruction on Christian Freedom and Liberation* (Vatican City: 1986) deals with human freedom as merely one aspect of human life, much as, for example, one might address the themes of work or sexuality. But if freedom is considered as the central constitutive factor that distinguishes human existence, thereby encapsulating an integral anthropology, the significance of this instruction is enhanced far beyond the intentions of its authors.

48. See Edward Schillebeeckx, *Christ: The Experience of Jesus as Lord*, trans. John Bowden (New York: Seabury Press, 1980).

49. See Brian McDermott, *What Are They Saying about the Grace of Christ?* (New York: Paulist Press, 1984).

hermeneutical standpoint, this initial concept of grace will be developed along the lines of liberation theology, but in dialogue with the landmarks of the history of the theology of grace.

THE SOURCES FOR A THEOLOGY OF GRACE

The Jewish-Christian Scriptures as a whole are depictions of God's grace. God is gracious, and God's grace is God's salvation, and human salvation from God in all its aspects is grace. This substance of the Scriptures, this grace, is approached from every imaginable viewpoint throughout the whole of the Bible. An integral approach to grace in the Scriptures can never be reduced to a word-study of the Greek and Hebrew terms associated with "grace" or to any particular concept. Most fundamentally the term *grace* applies to God as God acts for human salvation. And Scripture is a record of the Jewish and Christian experiences of God's grace in myriad different ways. The Scriptures contain innumerable images and symbols characterizing the way God deals graciously with the world and human existence.

But a systematic account of grace must contain a center of gravity, a symbolic and conceptual focus. This account of grace focuses on the notion of God as love and the outpouring of this love on humankind. In the Jewish tradition God is depicted as the God of steadfast and faithful love. In the New Testament, in John, God *is* love. Jesus is the manifestation of that love of God; Jesus is grace. The risen Christ is grace. Grace is God as Spirit poured out anew through Jesus and dwelling in human hearts (Rom. 5:5). Often the risen Christ and God as Spirit are scarcely distinct.[50]

The effect of grace is salvation, and what that salvation consists in is itself depicted in many different way. The Christian undergoes a spiritual rebirth, becomes a child of God, or is adopted by God. The Christian receives the gift of the Spirit and experiences God as Spirit in his or her life. One is formed in the image of Christ and is impelled to follow Jesus. All of this unfolds within a tension between an "already now" and the "ultimate future." Grace now leads to fulfillment and eternal life.[51]

---

50. Schillebeeckx, *Christ*, 463–68.

51. Ibid., 468–77. Schillebeeckx goes on to describe the many different ways in which the New Testament literature characterizes the salvation or liberation that is effected by the grace mediated by Christ. How are we saved? What are we saved from? What are we saved for? Salvation is from death; it is freedom and redemption from slavery to sin; it is reconciliation with God; it is peace with God through satisfaction. Redemption is an expiation through a sin offering; it is forgiveness of sins; it is justification and sanctification. Salvation is accomplished through Jesus' intercession. Human beings are freed for love in the community, for renewal of the world, from the demonic powers, and for life in its fullness (ibid., 477–514).

In the Scriptures there is no single symbolic conception of grace or the salvation it brings. Rather there is a pluralism of different and, on the level of symbolic representation, irreducible images. Yet, as Schillebeeckx notes, "A fundamentally identical experience underlies the various interpretations to be found throughout the New Testament: all its writings bear witness to the experience of salvation in Jesus from God."[52] This experience is captured by the symbol of God as Spirit being poured out anew in the world through the mediation of Jesus. This symbol will become the central focus for this account of grace.

Among the most prominent and consistent images in both the Jewish writings and the New Testament is the Spirit of God. For Israel the Spirit of God is God; like the wind, the unseen but sensible presence, power, and force of God work in the world. God's Spirit is spontaneous; it comes and goes. Never static, never possessed, uncontrolled, God's Spirit effects what it will in the world but remains transcendent. God's Spirit gives life to human beings; its absence is death. God's Spirit inspires; it moves great figures "to deeds above their known capacity and habits of behavior—deeds of delivering Israel from its enemies."[53]

In the New Testament the Spirit of God is the same God as Spirit from the Jewish tradition specified now through Jesus who is seen as Messiah; hence the Spirit is poured out on human beings in a new way. In Paul, for example, the Spirit represents "the indwelling of God in Christian experience."[54] The Spirit of God within is the source of faith, hope, and love; the Spirit within inspires and frees one from external law; it frees from sin, from immoral conduct; it assists in prayer; it enlightens the mind to make one aware of one's relation to God. In his Letter to the Romans Paul follows up his classic account of the divided self, torn apart by concupiscence, temptation, and sin, with a description of how God's Spirit within the human spirit overcomes this sin and death. In a systematic summary of the work of the Spirit, John Calvin argues that God's Spirit is the internal working of God that accounts for

---

52. Ibid., 463.

53. John L. McKenzie, "Aspects of Old Testament Thought," in R. Brown, J. Fitzmyer, and R. Murphy, eds., *Jerome Biblical Commentary* (Englewood Cliffs, N.J.: Prentice Hall, 1968), 742.

54. Joseph A. Fitzmyer, "Pauline Theology," in *Jerome Biblical Commentary* (1968), 814. See also Schillebeeckx's survey (in *Christ*, 463ff.) for the consistency with which the Spirit of God recurs as the symbol of grace and salvation in the New Testament.

the appropriation into human life of God as God is revealed in Christ.[55]

A DEFINITION OF GRACE

Can the diffuse idea of God's love for humankind manifested as Spirit be formulated in more specific theological language? The following definition of grace consists in an attempt to be faithful to the scriptural symbol of God as Spirit at the same time that it adopts the theological framework of Karl Rahner.[56] The method underlying this move is similar to the one used in the understanding of sin. Although Karl Rahner is not ordinarily considered a biblical or evangelical theologian, his conception of grace can be understood in terms of a method of hermeneutical correlation. Beneath the multiple biblical symbols for salvation lies the experience of God as Spirit in the community. That experience is also had today, so that the experience expressed in the biblical symbol can be drawn forward and restated in more reflective, intellectual symbols and a generalized theological concept of grace.

In Rahner's theology grace may be considered the sum and substance of the whole Christian message. Grace is salvation. If one were to ask in what salvation ultimately consists, the New Testament as a whole would yield the answer that salvation is participation in God's own life. Human existence is called in the end to personal communion with God, but in such a way that, even now in this world, God communicates God's self to human beings. Grace then is God's personal communication of God's own self to human beings.[57]

This first definition of grace can be seen as theologically synonymous with the scriptural symbol of God as Spirit. In other words the two symbols refer or point to materially the same thing. Thus

---

55. John Calvin, *Institutes of the Christian Religion*, ed. John T. McNeill, trans. Ford Lewis Battles (Philadelphia: The Westminster Press, 1960), bk. III, chap. 1 (pp. 537–42).

56. This systematic move to identify grace and God's Spirit entails both a loss and a gain. On the one hand, it does not reproduce the richly differentiated accounts of grace in Scripture or of such tradition-defining theological figures as Augustine, Aquinas, Luther, and Calvin. See, for example, the extensive retrievals of the notion of grace in Paul, Augustine, and Aquinas in a trinitarian key by Jean-Marc Laporte, *Patience and Power: Grace for the First World* (New York: Paulist, 1988). On the other hand, the very diffuseness of the concept of grace in the tradition often undermines an appreciation of the precise meaning of the doctrine and its place in systematic theology. What is needed today is a retrieval of developed doctrines in their most fundamental forms. This will be successful insofar as it does not distort but releases the same Christian experience of grace that is expressed in the differentiated language of the tradition.

57. Rahner, *Foundations of Christian Faith*, 116–26.

the presence of God's Spirit can be interpreted theologically to mean God's self-communication to human beings, or God's personal presence to and influence on human subjects. Inversely, this self-communication of God to human beings can be referred to and in turn be interpreted in relation to the meaning and function of God's Spirit in Scripture. Grace, then, quite simply refers to God. But God is understood here as God at work outside of God's self, so to speak, and immanently present within human subjects as an offer of personal encounter. By extension, grace includes the influence that God's Spirit has upon human beings and the effects it has when accepted. Grace is God's Spirit, which is God's personal communication of God's own self in love. This is what is revealed in and through Jesus of Nazareth; this is the message of salvation in the New Testament.[58]

Intrinsic to this concept of grace is the total and absolute gratuity in every respect that makes grace grace, and that is uncompromised in the whole history of the theology of grace. The very logic of a personal communication of God's own self indicates that this self-giving or opening up to human beings in personal love is totally free; it emerges out of God's inner freedom and cannot be other than gratuitous, unowned, unmerited, prior to any value or claim that might be construed as human deserving. No love that is authentic love, that is self-transcending giving over of the self to another, can be claimed or forced, and this applies absolutely to God. Thus even prior to the unworthiness caused by sin, God's impulse to communicate with human existence is absolutely gratuitous with the full literal force of absoluteness. All merit in any strict sense of the term is totally ruled out because, quite simply, to admit this in any degree distorts the very notion of grace and salvation. In the simple formula of Augustine, grace would not be grace.

This conception of grace should be projected into the broadest possible cosmological framework. What is revealed in the event of Jesus and mediated to us through the New Testament is the very nature of God and not an arbitrary decision on God's part. This means that although completely gratuitous, grace describes God's nature. This is the way God relates to human existence absolutely and universally. Grace describes the universal attitude and relation

58. The phrases "the Spirit of God," "God's Spirit," and "God as Spirit" are used in a theocentric framework that envisages God as Spirit at work in all of history. In the Christian community the Spirit of God is revealed and identified by Jesus. In terms of trinitarian theology, the stress is put on the doctrine that the Spirit is not less or other than God.

of God to all human beings always. In this supralapsarian framework, that is, a view that regards things prior to any notion of a fall, God's gracious and salvific intent precedes creation; God creates human beings because God intends an interpersonal dialogue with creatures who can respond. This dialogue is genuine; God engages a human freedom that is so other than God and so free that through sin it can refuse God's offer of grace. But grace is intrinsic to the very purpose of creation; grace is not "added on" as an "afterthought" to "repair" a human history run afoul. God's saving self-communication is absolutely gratuitous and yet an intrinsic and "objective" sphere or context of human existence itself. It is the milieu into which every human being is born.[59]

The universal dialogue of God's Spirit with human beings is not merely a theoretical construct but concrete and historical. Because human freedom is tied to matter, the only way human beings and God can interrelate is through the world and history, in concrete moments through the actual conditions and circumstances of each human life. It follows that for every human being the place, the medium, and the point of historical contact with God's love consist in those things that make up the ordinary conditions of everyday living. The ordinary place of encountering God's grace is the historical world. Granted, God's presence as Spirit and offer of love is within each one always. In the light of revelation one cannot imagine God's presence to human beings by creative power except as including God's gracious personal love. But God's love is meant to be appropriated by a personal response mediated through the concrete situation of each person. Thus on the one hand, concrete history unfolds within a sphere or region of God's salvific love, present to each one, in such a way that all human beings, from the beginning of their existence, live in the condition of God being personally present to them in an offer of love. But on the other hand, God's Spirit calls for response. Thus the concrete events of history become the media

---

59. Karl Rahner, "The Order of Redemption within the Order of Creation," in *The Christian Commitment*, trans. Cecily Hastings (New York: Sheed and Ward, 1963), 38–74. The existential but not individualistic interpretation of the fall, of course, rules out a chronological interpretation of the meaning of *supralapsarian*. But the point is still valid, namely, that salvation through grace is conceived as the purpose of God's creation, that there can be no separation between the spheres of creation and redemption, or nature and grace, and that human freedom emerges from the beginning, in each instance, into a region of the offer of God's personal love to which it is invited to respond. Despite the primacy of salvation to creation one should, I believe, still maintain with Rahner the Augustinian tradition of double gratuity, that is, the gratuity of salvation over and above creation, in order to protect the gratuity of grace and the semiautonomous character of human freedom. The controlling metaphor is history as God dialoguing out of freedom with genuine human freedom.

of the actual dialogue between human beings and God present and at work through them.[60]

This vision corresponds to the biblical symbolism that from the beginning God's Spirit hovers over all creation, giving it form and life, and offering it salvation (Gen. 1:1-2). It remains now to unfold the theological testimony regarding the effects of this grace and how it supports human existence over against sin and death.

THE EFFECTS OF GRACE

The effects of God's Spirit within human existence testified to by Scripture are too many to list. But the history of the theology of grace dwells on certain dominant effects, and each one of these, from different points of view, could be considered central to the Christian life. The following four effects of grace, liberation from sin, liberation to love, active cooperation of God with human freedom, and participation in God's life, are presented in terms of the thought of theologians who focused on each of these aspects and offered important analytic descriptions of them.

Liberation from Sin

Viewed in Luther's terms, God's grace, by accepting the sinner as sinner through forgiving and re-creating grace, is justifying. The first effect of grace in human existence is liberation from sin.[61]

Luther conceives of grace and salvation not in terms of God's Spirit, although the Spirit has a role in leading one to faith, but in terms of God's Word who is ultimately Jesus Christ. Following Paul, he sees all human beings as fallen and inextricably caught in the web of sin. No amount of external works can release the inner bondage of sin and guilt one must experience standing before the holiness of God. The only escape from sin can come from another,

---

60. Rahner, *Foundations of Christian Faith*, 138–52.

61. A historically developmental account of the effects of grace is broken here on the basis of a systematic concern. The prevenient character of grace is also stressed by Augustine, who is the first theologian of grace in the Western tradition. But Luther is even more anti-Pelagian than Augustine, if such is possible. And God's initiating grace and salvation have to be the logical points of departure in considering the effects of grace. A classic statement of Luther's view of the working of grace in contrast to works is "The Freedom of the Christian," in *Luther's Works*, vol. 31, *Career of the Reformer*, ed. Harold J. Grimm (Philadelphia: Muhlenberg Press, 1957), 1:327–77. See also *Luther's Works*, vol. 26, *Lectures on Galatians, 1535*, ed. and trans. Jaroslav Pelikan (St. Louis: Concordia Publishing House, 1963). For a summary of Luther's concept of grace as justification, see Paul Althaus, *The Theology of Martin Luther*, trans. Robert C. Schultz (Philadelphia: Fortress Press, 1966), 201–73.

outside the self, who is the realization of God's promise of acceptance and forgiveness. Christ, by taking sin upon himself, and by a cosmic victory over the personified power of sin itself, is himself the grace of God, God's promise of forgiveness, acceptance, and re-creating love of human beings. This grace is mediated by faith, a personal clinging to God in Christ, in such a way that human existence is transformed by a mystical union in which the person of faith takes on and is re-created by the qualities of Christ with whom one is united, even as Christ absorbs human sinfulness and guilt.

Through a shift in language it is possible to retain significant features of Luther's account within a vision that conceives salvation in terms of God as Spirit. Such a move is encouraged by the already arrived at conclusion that the dynamics of grace operate universally and thus outside a historical or explicit encounter with Jesus. The main point to be expanded concerns the way grace liberates from sin.

One of the major contributions of Luther consists in his return to scriptural language and his presentation of the dynamics of grace in the personalist categories of faith. Faith is not mere belief or assent to objective truth, but a total surrender of self, a clinging, that in this sense includes hope and love of God. Thus the release from sin must be understood as occurring within the context of an interpersonal relationship between God and each human being. But this personal offer of God's forgiving love is precisely given universally by God as Spirit. Human existence itself "objectively" unfolds within the context of God's loving and forgiving presence that reaches human consciousness implicitly in every human decision as a call to faith and as an opportunity for self-transcending hope and love.[62]

The release from sin that Luther describes is forgiveness; it is not a negation of past sinfulness, which is impossible, or an escape from fallenness.[63] Human existence is constituted in a condition of concupiscence and temptation to which it freely yet invariably succumbs. The liberating effect of grace lies precisely in God's acceptance of human beings as they are. Grace means that God is the lover of every single human being, infinitely and as if there were no other, with a love that makes each person infinitely valuable despite sin.

---

62. Rahner, *Foundations of Christian Faith*, 129–33.

63. In the objective ontological categories of Aquinas it was possible to say, after the pattern of an ontological change in substance, that one is either in grace or not. A person either does or does not possess sanctifying grace. See Roger Haight, *The Experience and Language of Grace* (New York: Paulist Press, 1979), 71–72. When the framework for understanding grace is interpersonal communication and response, one can think of degrees of intensity of communication and union with God. One can also speak of a person as simultaneously a sinner and justified.

This liberation from sin is thus profoundly ontological, and when it reaches into consciousness in any form, but particularly in its explicit mediation through Jesus, its psychological power can be total. Human existence, sinful though it be, is freed, released, liberated from the burden of sin, especially of the impossible, frustrating, and crushing illusion of trying to prove one's worth before God. Forgiving mercy is the very name of God. It is hard to imagine other effects of grace becoming operative without this prior and primary liberation. The sacraments of baptism and penance are symbolic mediations of this specific aspect of God's forgiving and universally available self-presence as Spirit.

Before moving to the second effect of grace, we must consider briefly the Roman Catholic response to Luther's view of salvation as justification by grace through faith. Without attempting to determine the precise thought of the individual Reformers, the Council of Trent (1545–63) sought to articulate Catholic teaching on the disputed issues. Its Decree on Justification, adopted in 1547 after seven months of discussion, is the Catholic church's most complete official statement on the doctrine of grace. Trent did not seek to provide an exhaustive account of the topics it addressed; in addition, aware of diversity among Catholic theologians on such topics as justification, it refrained from passing judgment on matters controverted within Catholicism. Only the chief points of its teaching relevant to Luther's theology of grace will be summarized here.

Trent identifies faith as the "beginning of human salvation, the basis and root of all justification, without which it is impossible to please God" (DS 1532; see Heb. 11:6). It teaches that grace effects an internal transformation of the sinner, so that we are not merely considered just but become just (DS 1529). Faith, hope, and love are conferred with justification (DS 1530), but, if separated from hope and love, faith "neither unites perfectly with Christ nor makes one a living member of his body" (DS 1531). In keeping with this distinction, Trent holds that the grace of justification is lost by every mortal sin, even if faith is not lost (DS 1544, 1577). Finally, the council presents a dialectical description of the life of Christians. Aware of Christ's promise that one who gives even a cup of cold water to one of his little ones will not lack a reward (Matt. 10:42), Christians are nonetheless to confide and glory only in the Lord, not in themselves. Since we all offend in many ways (see James 3:2), we should keep before our eyes God's severity and justice as well as mercy and goodness. Even if conscious of no fault, we should be unwilling to judge ourselves, for each human life will ultimately be subjected, not to any human judgment, but to the judgment of God (DS 1548–49).[64]

The reasons for the differences between Lutheran and Roman Catholic theologies of grace, most evident in the varying usages of the central term *faith*, lie below the surface within fundamentally different paradigms of interpretation. The theological tradition from Augustine to Aquinas sees grace working in and transforming human freedom. In Luther, human freedom is minimized to leave complete room for the total priority and gratuity of God's gracious forgiveness. Grace is identified as Christ and God's Word, and faith's passivity means that human justification is always the justice of another, Christ, with whom the Christian is united. In contrast to this, a constant underlying theme in Trent's Decree on Justification, while granting the priority and gratuity of grace, deals with human responsibility and freedom. The differences of conception that this underlying concern produces are reflected in the decree, especially in its canons.

Many of these differences between the Lutheran and Catholic languages of grace still persist today. Yet they may not be "church-dividing," since so much of what is essential to the doctrine of grace is held in common. In other words, while these two languages of grace cannot quite be reconciled, they appear to fall within the range of legitimate theological pluralism.[65] It will be clear from the emphasis on human freedom and responsibility in what follows that the account of grace given here represents the language of grace behind the doctrine of Trent, even though it is open to the basic themes of Luther's theology.

Liberation to Love

Viewed in terms of Augustine, God's prior grace liberates human existence from the bondage of egoism and opens up freedom by an im-

---

64. For the Latin text and an English translation see DS 1520–83 and Neuner and Dupuis, eds., *The Christian Faith*, 519–35. For analyses of Trent's teaching see José Martín-Palma, *Gnadenlehre: Von der Reformation bis zur Gegenwart*, Handbuch der Dogmengeschichte III, 5b (Freiburg: Herder, 1980), 48–66; and Piet Fransen, "Dogmengeschichtliche Entfaltung der Gnadenlehre," in *Mysterium Salutis* (Einsiedeln: Benziger, 1973), 4/2:712–27.

65. See Anderson, Murphy, and Burgess, eds., *Justification by Faith: Lutherans and Catholics in Dialogue VII*, esp. the Common Statement, 13–74.

pulse to love, pushing or drawing freedom toward self-transcending values and, through faith, toward God.[66]

In Augustine one finds an understanding of grace predominantly, but not exclusively, in terms of God's Spirit. We have already seen Augustine's instinctive and total reaction against any Pelagian hint of self-reliance for salvation. Like Luther, Augustine views grace against the background of sinful human nature, but not outside a teleological context that implies a life of sanctification leading to salvation as victory over death. Augustine understood human existence in a Neo-Platonic framework as having come forth from God by creation and tending to return to God as creation's final resting place. In terms of spatial imagery, human existence is meant to rise through finite truths and goods to the supreme Truth and Goodness of absolute Being. But human existence is fallen. Augustine was overwhelmed by the dynamics of concupiscence, temptation, and sin, which have already been analyzed. Human existence for Augustine is freedom, and this freedom is clearly manifested in the power of free choice. But on another level this freedom is held in bondage. The captivity of concupiscence, the sheer weight or gravity of materiality and sensuality, complexified by the entanglement of ingrained habit and custom, is one thing. But the real mystery lies in the way human spirit or freedom, which is precisely other than matter, is a prisoner to itself. Human freedom, which can command the body to act, cannot command or will itself out of itself in self-transcending love.[67] Without the prior impulse that must implant even the desire for self-transcending values or objects, human freedom is incapable of the love that constitutes real freedom, namely, actuating the self beyond the self. In this framework, then, grace is God's Spirit expanding freedom, opening it up, in a desire and impulse of love.

Augustine's position on grace, that no authentic love exists in the world apart from the impulse of God's Spirit, may seem difficult to accept from an objective and detached point of view. To appreciate it, two things are required. First of all, one must ask the right question. Today people agonize over the question of why there is evil in the world. But Augustine also asked *how* there could be goodness and love in the world: "From what source is there in people the love of God and of one's neighbor?"[68] Second, Augustine's response to the question can be understood as correct only from within the

---

66. Several of Augustine's treatises against Pelagius and on grace can be found in *Basic Writings of Saint Augustine*, vol. 1, ed. Whitney J. Oates (New York: Random House, 1948).

67. Augustine *Confessions* bk. 8, chap. 9, in *Basic Writings*, 1:122.

68. Augustine "On Grace and Free Will" chap. 33, in *Basic Writings*, 1:763.

context of religious experience itself. Referring to a foundational experience, Augustine responded to his own question by another question he appropriated from Paul: "What hast thou that thou didst not receive?" (1 Cor. 4:7).[69] Augustine realized that, in the religious context of standing before God, Jesus' parable of the Pharisee and the publican provides the only answer possible.

God as Spirit, then, expands the horizon of freedom and opens up human creativity to values beyond the self, implicitly in the direction of God and divine values. At this point one can see a mutual complementarity in the understanding of the effects of grace in the systems of Augustine and Rahner. On the one hand, in the light of Rahner's and the Second Vatican Council's theology, one should reverse the Augustinian presupposition that grace, because it is absolutely gratuitous, is also rare in human history. If love abounds in the world, it is because all human existence unfolds within the context of God's love that impels human freedom toward self-transcendence. On the other hand, Rahner's whole system is strictly Augustinian, for it presupposes that any act of self-transcendence must also be an effect of God's grace.

Cooperative Grace

Augustine distinguished and defined cooperative grace in relation to operative grace in the following way: "God operates, therefore, without us, in order that we may will [love]; but when we will [love], and so will [love] that we may act, God co-operates with us."[70] Augustine saw this distinction as a way of protecting free choice while still affirming the role of grace. But while the distinction is sound, Augustine's cosmic doctrine of double predestination finally undermines his conception of personal freedom. Otherwise God does not have a free dialogue partner in history.

In the twelfth century Bernard of Clairvaux also took up the concept of cooperative grace as a way of dealing with the problem of the determinism of grace versus freedom. But in Bernard free choice under the influence of grace appears as little more than consent, an "allowing" or "going along with." Freedom is a weak concept suggesting at best pliability, a mere choice that allows the self to be moved.[71] Like Augustine, Bernard cannot have been expected to

---

69. Augustine "On the Spirit and the Letter" chap. 57, in _Basic Writings_, 1:509.

70. Augustine "On Grace and Free Will" chap. 33, in _Basic Writings_, 1:761.

71. Bernard of Clairvaux _On Grace and Free Choice_, in _Treatises III: On Grace and Free Choice_, trans. Daniel O'Donovan (Kalamazoo, Mich.: Cistercian Publications, 1977), nos. 46–47 (pp. 105–6).

accommodate the modern experience of freedom. Human beings to-day experience freedom as much more than mere choice or consent. Human freedom is commitment to values that results in creativity or destruction. In either case human freedom is a power to produce what is new. The question, then, is whether Bernard's reflection on cooperative grace can sustain both the absolute primacy of grace in all salutary actions of human freedom and the modern experience of freedom's initiating creativity.

Three reflections help to soften the paradox involved in coop-erative grace, although the relationship between grace and human freedom remains mysterious. The first is the principle of Aquinas that God always acts upon creatures according to their nature, and since freedom is of the nature of human existence, God acts within and not against that freedom.[72] Thus one cannot conceive of human freedom as a merely passive instrumental cause of the activity and ef-fects stemming from God's presence within a human subject, because the instrument in this case is the free power and self-initiating en-ergy of human freedom. The personalist context for understanding the dynamics of grace completely transcends images of mechanical force, power, or coercion.

Second, insofar as grace is genuinely cooperative, the initiatives of grace and human freedom should not be seen in competitive terms. Very often this tacit presupposition underlies the dichotomous alter-native that concessions to either God or human freedom somehow undermine the real initiative of the other. Granted that the sinful as-pect of human action is precisely in competition with God, that which is sustained by grace need not be. As Luther said, works performed out of faith give glory to God.[73]

Third, the power of grace and of human freedom should never be conceived as operating on the same level. God is God, human beings are creatures operating on the level of finite history. A distinction of levels allows one to grant the power and efficacy of freedom on the overt level of conscious action in the world, while at the same time allowing one to insist on the presence of God's influence within the ontic depths of the sheer existence and animation of this particular exercise of freedom.

With these qualifications, the formula of Bernard takes on new meaning:

---

72. Thomas Aquinas *Summa Theologiae* I-II, q. 113, a. 3, in *The Gospel of Grace*, ed. and trans. Cornelius Ernst (Oxford: Blackfriars, 1972), 30:170–71.

73. Luther, "The Freedom of the Christian," 353.

[Grace] so co-operates with free choice, however, that only in the first case [thinking] does it go a step ahead of it; in the others [willing and doing], it accompanies it. Indeed, the whole aim in taking the step ahead is that from then on it may co-operate with it. What was begun by grace alone, is completed by grace and free choice together, in such a way that they contribute to each new achievement not singly but jointly; not by turns, but simultaneously. It is not as if grace did one half the work and free choice the other; but each does the whole work, according to its own peculiar contribution. Grace does the whole work, and so does free choice—with this one qualification: that whereas the whole is done *in* free choice, so the whole is done *of* grace.[74]

The remnant of Bernard's weak concept of freedom is contained in the underscored prepositions. It would be more accurate to say the whole work is done *by* freedom and *by* grace. For this is the paradox: The *whole* of the salutary exercise of human freedom is both a work of God's grace and of human freedom. On one level God sustains human freedom in being by creation, while God's presence and influence of love inform its self-transcending character. On another level, what is done in this world on the level of history is manifestly the creation of human freedom. Thus the whole of salvific action is performed by human freedom wholly sustained by grace. This view of cooperative grace is radically anti-Pelagian and respects the absolute gratuity of salvation in every respect. Yet it supports the semiautonomous character of human freedom.

Participation in God's Life

A fourth effect of God's personal self-communication as Spirit is a bestowal on human existence of a participation in God's own personal life, already in this world, but destined toward completion in eternal life. Another way of expressing this bestowal anthropologically would be in terms of the transformation of human existence that this participation entails.

This sanctifying and divinizing effect of grace is more typical of Greek than Latin theology, but it has been a standard feature in Catholic thought on grace since the medieval synthesis. In Aquinas, the primary referent of the term *grace* is a new and infused supernatural quality of the human soul. This habitual grace raises up human nature to a new supernatural level of participating in the divine life of God. In Rahner's system, however, infused created grace becomes

---

74. Bernard of Clairvaux *On Grace and Free Choice* 47 (p. 106).

the effect of God's personal self-communication to the human person. Since Catholic theology frequently and mistakenly has denied that Luther too affirmed this effect of grace, it might be fitting to describe it in his personalist terms, which are coherent with those of Rahner, while at the same time shifting Luther's Christ-mysticism into a framework of Spirit-mysticism.

Luther gives two metaphors that illustrate the transformation through participation in divine life that is effected by grace. "Just as the heated iron glows like fire because of the union of fire with it, so the Word imparts its qualities to the soul."[75] This metaphor displays in physical terms the total transformation of the human person through a "transfer of qualities" effected by union. In other words, the human person, with God's life within, takes on divine qualities—it is sanctified, but in and through the presence of God's life.

More dramatically, because Luther relies on a more interpersonal account of the dynamics of love, he describes the same process in terms of a divine bridegroom marrying a "poor, wretched harlot."[76] The dynamics of the transformation occur in this instance through creative or re-creative love. The sheer personal love and personal self-communication of the divine lover raises up and reconstitutes the beloved on a new level of being. This is not simply a communication that makes the beloved feel better. Rather in the case of God's real self-communication in the love that is God's Spirit, human existence is reconstituted as God's own.

These then are the four principal effects of grace, and they respond directly to the existential structure of sin and the personal sins it spawns. Grace is God's Spirit that is itself God's personal self-communication offered to every human being. But God being present to a human being is also a force and a new power within human freedom. This is not to be conceived mechanically as a physical or determining causal agent. The whole logic of grace must be conceived in terms of a dialogue between two freedoms. Within human subjectivity the personal presence, love, concern, and influence of a personal God are immanently at work. In the unfolding of freedom from mere potentiality into responsibility, one should not expect responses completely lacking in openness and basic trust, or every measure of faith and love. Where sin abounds, grace abounds even more. Whatever the measure of hope, faith, and love, it is a product of the impulse of, and drawing out by, God's own loving

---

75. Luther, "The Freedom of the Christian," 349.
76. Ibid., 351–52.

presence.[77] The tension between sin and grace cannot always be measured in the absolute terms of No or Yes; it is not always a question of either sin or grace. For sin and grace and their appropriation involve subjectivity, the personal responses of freedom in existential dialogue. It is hard to imagine either an absolute No or Yes to God in a finite condition filled with ignorance and concupiscence that impede an absolute self-disposition of self, even though one cannot rule out these potentialities of freedom for acceptance and refusal.

In the following section it will be shown how these effects of God's Spirit reach out into the social and historical spheres and respond to the issues of social sin and death by promising the final meaningfulness of human freedom.

THE SOCIAL DIMENSION OF GRACE

If in dealing with sin one cannot ignore its social dimension, it follows that there must also be a social dimension to grace. As in the case of sin, to reduce the intentionality and power of God's Spirit of love in the world to its manifestations in the behavior of individuals would trivialize its significance. To appreciate the significance of social grace, however, requires an appreciation of historical consciousness and the shift that has occurred in regard to the context for thinking about grace. This may be introduced by a consideration of the groundwork of the theology of grace of Thomas Aquinas and the need to reappropriate it in a new historical and eschatological framework.

FROM TELEOLOGY TO ESCHATOLOGY

The theology of grace of Aquinas is often characterized as static and mechanical. In fact, however, it is not, and this can be shown by looking at its foundations. Two fundamental conceptions work together to supply the groundwork that supports a dynamic conception of the working of grace.[78]

The first is teleology. The whole of Aquinas's theology of grace is governed by teleology, which means a logic or rationale that de-

---

77. As in the case of sin, the final "proof" of the role of God's grace in self-transcending human action is experiential. It cannot be demonstrated objectively, but only "recognized" after the fact as due to a power within one. Thus Paul exclaimed: "I live, yet not I, but Christ lives in me" (Gal. 2:20).

78. The dynamic quality of Aquinas's theology has been retrieved in metapsychological terms by Jean-Marc Laporte, *Patience and Power*, 194–257. But the dynamism of his theology is rooted in its metaphysical and ontological framework.

termines the intelligibility of being or a being by its *telos* or purpose and goal. All beings exist for a purpose or goal to which they are oriented. Since there is a correspondence of proportionality between the kind of being any being possesses and its purpose, one can understand a particular form of being in relation to its goal, and, inversely, one can discern its goal by the kind of being it is.

The second concept is that of nature. In one respect the nature of a being is that which makes it the kind of being it is. From this logical point of view nature denotes the essence of what a being is. But in Aquinas nature also determines how a being acts, for nature is a principle of operation and action. As the principle of activity, informed by its proper powers and faculties, a nature governs the kind of actions performed by a being, and as the source of action it generates behavior typical of its kind of being. In a teleological framework, natures correspond to their goal or final end and purpose, and thus elicit actions that tend toward this goal.

In the confluence of these two conceptions one can see the fundamental rationale of Aquinas's theology of grace. For revelation discloses that human existence is called to a supernatural goal of personal union with God, one that exceeds the power and the activity of human nature in itself. Grace, as a supernatural quality of the human soul, in effect creates a new and supernatural nature with concomitant new powers of faith, hope, and love that enable a raised human nature to become the source of a supernatural kind of activity corresponding to a supernatural goal.[79] In all of this it is important that one see the dynamic action-oriented logic of this conception, for it has become one of the hallmarks of the Catholic theology of grace. Human existence reaches its final goal of divine salvation through action, action played out in the world but at the same time filled with a supernatural or divine potency and power that overcome the "natural" limits of its finitude.

From today's perspective the weakness in this teleological conception can be appreciated on the basis of certain aspects of historical consciousness. Historical consciousness refers to the contemporary sense of being in history, the awareness that human beings have emerged out of a long and distant past and are moving toward an unknown future in this world. It also involves an expanded horizon of consciousness, a product of modernity, by which people are aware of the multiple histories of other peoples and their own interrelatedness with them and interdependence upon them. History implies

79. Aquinas *Summa Theologiae* I-II, q. 109, a. 2; q. 110, aa. 1–4, in *The Gospel of Grace*, 30:72–77, 108–23.

change, and the relativity and contextuality of all human values and ideas.

But two characteristics in particular of current historical consciousness have a direct bearing on Thomistic teleology. The first is the realization that the social and cultural structures of history were not given with nature, but were created out of and by human freedom. In other words, the journey of human existence to its end does not lead through naturally given and unchanging structures but through structures and forms that are themselves changing because they are the creations of human beings themselves. Classical culture and the teleology of Aquinas could not have done justice to this current appreciation of things.

Second, this new awareness brings with it a new concern that focuses attention on the meaningfulness and direction of human creativity *within history*. It is not enough to so focus on the end or goal of human existence that actual historical conditions be seen as the mere means to attain it. There must be some intrinsic meaning to historical existence itself, to the corporate project of human creativity. Some intrinsic continuity should connect the activity on the grand social level and its final goal. Although this is not necessarily the case, in fact the teleological conception tended to so focus on the end that it minimized the intrinsic value of the means themselves. And although human nature is by definition a generic concept, it often operated individualistically; each human being was called upon through grace to behave in such a way as to save his or her own soul.

Given our historical consciousness and concern for the meaning of human history, the theology of grace should reappropriate Aquinas's Aristotelian metaphysical perspective of teleology into a biblical eschatological framework. This is in fact what has occurred in Catholic theology of grace. In systematic terms, however, it is not so much a negation of the Thomistic theology of grace as a reinterpretation and retrieval.

Eschatology refers to a theory or understanding of the eschaton or end-time. It deals not only with end in the sense of *finis* or end-point, but also with the goal of human existence. Thus it is structurally analogous to teleology. But biblical eschatology was not fashioned within the framework of analytically defined principles of being. Rather it was constructed as a theory of history, and sought to define the corporate direction in which the people of God was heading. Eschatology is metaphysical and it too deals with being, but that which determines the end-time is God, the source of all being and the ruler of history. The eschaton will be determined by God's will and power. But this end-time is not totally discontinuous with the history of Israel or the world. They are connected; history is leading there; and "signs of the times" indicate that God's final establishment of what is to be in the end is not totally disconnected with God's rule within history.

Implicitly and sometimes explicitly the Roman Catholic theology of grace is being reinterpreted within an eschatological framework. This does not mean retreating from a medieval mode of thought to an even more culturally distant one. For the biblical eschatological perspective too is being refashioned by current post-Enlightenment conceptions and concerns. As a reinterpretation of Aquinas this means that while changing his thought one seeks at the same time to be faithful to elements that are fundamental to it. In this case one should continue to regard human existence dynamically as a principle of action in the world and heading for its goal. But within the framework of eschatology three things are added as explicit foci of attention. First, the *telos* of human existence is not translated into the individual or private concern of each one for his or her own destiny. Rather the question of the direction of human history is raised for human existence socially, not merely as a particular social group or nation, but as a race. Second, the question of both the goal and the end (*finis*) of history is merged with the question of the purposiveness of human creative action within history itself here and now. Third, within this new context the question of the purpose of human freedom takes on a new meaning when compared with the theology of Aquinas. Over and above the metaphysical meaning that is realized in each person, the purpose of human freedom also takes on meaning in socio-historical terms. Eschatology opens up the question of the use of human freedom corporately in history. In short, the question of grace also concerns human society here and now and into the future. This leads to the question of social grace.

THE SOCIAL DIMENSION OF GRACE

One cannot avoid speaking about social grace today for two reasons. The first is negative; there has never before been such an awareness of social evil, which is not simply objective evil but sin. The great sin that bears down on individuals and corporately on human existence as a whole is social. If grace is understood only and exclusively on the individual level, then it leaves this world in its socio-historical forms to sin. Positively, since human existence is social, one must ask the question of the relationship of grace to social existence. What is the impact of grace on society? If by analogy with personal sin one can speak of social sin, there must also be a correlatively analogous reality of social grace. The question then concerns the way one should define, explain, and talk about this grace.

The idea of social grace, like the recognition of grace generally, can be conceived only against the background of sin and death. On the individual level, sin and grace are revealed together. Sin appears as sin against the background of grace as that which should not be; and grace appears against the background of sin as God's movement within human existence that overcomes a "natural" but free propensity to sin. So too on the macro or social level of sin. However one explains the phenomenon of social sin, the contrary to it will appear as social grace. One may define social grace, then, as the institutionalization and objectification of the dynamics of grace originating in personal-individual freedom.

There are many examples of social grace; one should not imagine that social grace is rare. Any group, institution, organization, or society may be considered social grace insofar as it is concerned with human life and enhances the common good. From a Christian point of view the tendency is to describe the church as the prime example of social grace. Objectively it is an institution that serves as the sacrament of God's grace after the pattern of the revelation of God in Jesus. But other institutions may also serve the same function anonymously in the social sphere.

Given the parallelism just mentioned, the analysis of what social grace is will follow the pattern found in the analytic description of social sin. On the one hand, social grace accounts for just and life-giving institutions because it is within human beings, and human institutions are subjective; on the other hand, social grace is embedded in objective social institutions in the sense that they objectively mediate God's grace when they impel self-transcending concern for others.

Human beings create social institutions; they are not given with nature. When one finds just institutions, organizations that are dedicated to the nurture and care of human life not only of their members but also of those whom the institutions affect, it may be assumed that they derive from the wills of people who are concerned about others. Institutions dedicated to the enhancement of the common good stem from self-transcending freedom that is actively concerned with equality and the protection of life. This is the subjective side of social grace.

But institutions are also objective relative to the freedom of any individual; they are prior to and become the internalized context for the exercise of any particular person's freedom. They appear in every sphere and phase of life helping to form that second nature that in turn shapes ideas, values, and concrete modes of behavior. When the influence of these structures urges self-transcendence in the service of other human beings, the institutions in question may be considered objective channels of God's grace.

Finally, it is important to realize exactly what one is talking about in the discussion of social institutions. There is no such thing as an institution that is purely sinful or a pure social grace. Of course some social movements may spring to mind that appear to be the very archetype of a social sin or grace. But generally both of these antithetical concepts, social sin and social grace, are heuristic. They are questioning categories that shed a particular light on certain aspects of social constructions and allow one to perceive them in a certain way. These categories raise questions and provide a perspective and a tool for regarding social institutions in a theological way. They enable a critical theological examination of the just and unjust aspects of every social institution.

SOCIAL GRACE AND THE PURPOSE OF HUMAN FREEDOM

We come now to the question of the purpose of human freedom that was raised in the preliminary anthropology, then negatively relative to sin, and again in the discussion of eschatology. Since God has created human existence as freedom with the potentially creative and destructive power that we experience today, what is the intrinsic raison d'être written by God into that freedom? The question is directed first of all to the immediate purpose of freedom, to its exercise in this world. Another way of asking this question would be in terms of the direction in which the effects of grace lead.[80]

The analysis of social grace leads to the conclusion that the purpose of human freedom in this world under the influence of grace is the creation of graced social structures. This position can be made persuasive from two points of view, the one from the present looking forward into the future, the other from the perspective of eschatology.

---

80. From one point of view this is not a new question in theology, for the pre-Enlightenment churches did have a body of social teachings. But when one considers practical spirituality and theological conceptions of the Christian life, the tendency was to so focus on final salvation that the issue of the use of freedom in this world did not receive the attention that the present cultural context demands. There are of course exceptions to this in some of the Anabaptist movements. And John Calvin, with his doctrine of sanctification and his theology of the Christian life in this world, including the principle of stewardship, stands out in this regard. See *Institutes of the Christian Religion*, bk. III, chap. 10 (pp. 719–25).

The purpose of human freedom in this world can be understood as the direction in which the effects of grace lead. The forgiveness of sin and opening up of freedom in self-transcending love; cooperative grace and the participation in God's life that gives human freedom a capacity for creativity that it does not have on its own—all these lead to the classical Christian virtue of love of neighbor. But in the light of a new appreciation of the social constitution of human existence, and of interdependence and solidarity in social existence, love of neighbor cannot be reduced to interpersonal relationships; it must also be understood in social terms. Participation in the formation of emancipatory social structures is a necessary form of love of neighbor.

Our actual situation today is one in which the massive amount of social suffering calls the very meaningfulness of our corporate history into question. But that meaningfulness that human beings long for is not simply there in history as an objective given to be discovered. It is a possibility that must be created by human freedom through the power of grace. In other words, God's grace calls upon and impels human beings to establish the meaningfulness of history in the open future.

More specifically the movement of grace in human freedom has a double direction. The first is to resist social evil and sin. Negatively, the purpose of human existence as freedom in this world is not to escape social sin, but to resist it. Within history the dynamism of God's Spirit moves human freedom against sin; militancy in the Christian life counteracts sin by fighting against it. Positively, the movement of grace is toward the construction of social institutions of grace in every sphere of human life. No area of institutionally structured human life is alien to the influence of graced freedom patterned on the life of Jesus.

THE ESCHATOLOGY OF GRACE

The second perspective that yields a conclusion about the purpose of human freedom comes from eschatology. One cannot avoid the eschatological question of the end of history. In response to this issue of the goal of history the Christian has only the one answer contained in the symbol "the kingdom of God." No other symbol was more important for the teaching of Jesus than the kingdom of God; it formed a center of gravity for his whole message and for all the activity of his life.

It is of course difficult to determine exactly what Jesus meant by the kingdom of God. Not only is it a religious symbol about something transcendent and eschatological, but also Jesus' teaching about it in parable and figure of speech does not yield a precise conceptual formula. But even if one could determine exactly what Jesus meant by the kingdom of God, its meaning would still have to be interpreted anew to be intelligible to twentieth-century culture. And from this perspective the symbol means with surety at least this: The kingdom of God is God's rule, an order of reality according to God's will, "on earth as it is in heaven" (Matt. 6:10).[81] The kingdom of God implies an order of justice, of peace and harmony among people—for the kingdom of God is made up of people—who all give glory to God by being in accord with God's will in the final order of things.

The kingdom of God is an eschatological symbol. But it has a bearing on human history. On the one hand, the New Testament testifies to the breaking in of God's kingdom in a new way with Jesus, and on the other hand, it would make little sense to exempt history from the intention of the will of its creator. The kingdom of God, then, as God's will, God's values, God's intention for historical existence, also applies to history. As in teleology, so too in eschatology: The end of history illumines what history should be like at any given time. The view that the purpose of human freedom is found in its dedication to social grace is not imposed upon the idea of the kingdom of God but is a faithful interpretation of its intrinsic meaning today.

But the continuity between history and the end-time under the symbol of the kingdom of God reaches further. The eschatological question is the question of the ultimate meaningfulness of human existence as freedom in history. From this perspective, it follows that for human life to be ultimately meaningful, it must actually contribute to that eschatological reality that Jesus called the kingdom of God.

Several considerations lead to this conclusion. The first is the reasonable inference that if the exercise of human freedom does not have a bearing on and enter into the construction of final reality, it is then finally and ultimately meaningless. In other words, the only way that one can affirm the meaningfulness of the creativity of human freedom in history is to affirm that it contributes to the ultimate and final condition of reality itself.[82] Second, it is also reasonable to think that this accords with the intention of God, who created in

---

81. E. P. Sanders concludes "that *we know perfectly well what [Jesus] meant in general terms [by the kingdom of God]: the ruling power of God*" (*Jesus and Judaism* [Philadelphia: Fortress Press, 1985], 127).

82. As Segundo puts it, "The values to which Jesus of Nazareth bore concrete testimony in his message and life can be realized only if the 'I' of each person has

God's image the creative and world-fashioning freedom of human existence. It would seem to frustrate the creative intention of God if the positive achievement of human freedom were in the end worthless, made no difference, and counted for nothing. Third, Catholic theology of grace has always maintained a continuity between the operation of grace in this world and final union with God.[83] It is not unreasonable to extend this continuity to cooperative grace. This means that what is accomplished by human freedom in grace, the works and achievements of human freedom done in love, is constitutive of the ultimate reality of the end-time.[84] Finally, in current interpretations of the theological significance of the resurrection of Jesus, many theologians see the resurrection as God's ratification and validation of Jesus and his message. Extending this view, faith in the resurrection of the life and actions of Jesus becomes a witness to and hope in this eschatology. He is the "first-born of many," the one whose whole life and praxis of love have been raised up and preserved in a salvation paradigmatic for all.

In sum, the theology of grace, in tension with the theology of sin, proposes an anthropology of creative human freedom and action. It was said earlier that, in this view of God's grace, the intention of God for salvation was prior to that of creation itself, so that prior to all sin God's offer of personal love and self-communication provides the actual context of all human existence or freedom. God's Spirit is the symbol expressing this constant personal presence to and dialogue with human freedom. The effects of this grace are the accepting and forgiving of sinful human existence and the opening up of human freedom in self-transcending love. But this means that, when viewed from a new historically conscious perspective, new creation appears to be the intention prior to grace, and grace is *for* new creation.[85] In other words, the purpose of grace and human freedom together is the struggle against sin and the fashioning of ever-new history in love. What is done in free-

---

the power to accomplish a project that is both personal and definitive" (*The Humanist Christology of Paul*, 133).

83. Rahner, "Some Implications of the Scholastic Concept of Uncreated Grace," 319–46.

84. Segundo, *The Humanist Christology of Paul*, 123–25, 157. Segundo also adds that God in the end-time will not make up what is not accomplished by human freedom in love. It should be noted that, although Segundo works within a framework of evolution, this does not imply a theory of moral progress or the view that love accumulates in history. On the level of empirical history, the effects of sin are more manifest than the effects of grace. Segundo is thus not subject to the critique leveled against nineteenth-century liberal theology.

85. Frances Stefano, "The Absolute Value of Human Action in the Theology of Juan Luis Segundo," Ph.D. thesis (Toronto: St. Michael's College, 1988), 335.

dom informed and sustained by grace will be transformed into the permanent, definitive, and ultimate reality of the kingdom of God.[86]

SIN, GRACE, AND SPIRITUALITY

The point of theology is to open up an understanding of God, the world, history, and human existence in such a way that it provides a vision for human living. Just as all knowledge is for human life and action, so too the value of theology lies in the way of life it opens up to Christian imagination and freedom. No area has more direct bearing on Christian life than Christian anthropology. Insofar as they are anthropological, the doctrines of sin and grace contain the fundamental principles of Christian spirituality.

THE MEANING OF SPIRITUALITY

The term *spirituality* refers to the way human beings, individuals, and groups lead their lives considered from the point of view of union with God. Spirituality in this sense can be considered on a number of different levels. On the existential level spirituality is constituted by the actual way any given person leads his or her life. The point here reaches deeper than the superficial notion of life style. Spirituality refers to the way people *lead* their lives; it includes the deepest purpose toward which a life is directed and the values and goals that underlie motivation. Spirituality is thus a general anthropological category; all persons have some form of spirituality insofar as they consciously direct their lives. Christian spirituality refers to the way Christians actually live. But on an abstract, reflective, and cognitive level spirituality refers to the theory of how human life should be led. Here the meaning of spirituality approaches the meaning of theology insofar as theology has bearing on Christian life.[87]

The point of this concrete, existential, and historical definition of spirituality lies in the problems it seeks to overcome. First of all, as a common anthropological category spirituality places the Christian way of life in dialogue with other human conceptions of life. Second, the definition is inclusive of all the dimensions of Christian life. By

---

86. Segundo, *The Humanist Christology of Paul*, 157. For Segundo, what is not done in love will not survive.

87. One may also refer to different schools of spirituality surrounding specific historical conceptions of the Christian life. Spirituality may also refer to a discipline that studies the literature of various aspects and forms of the Christian life.

not identifying one aspect of Christian life, such as prayer or sacramental worship, with the whole of Christian spirituality, it does not evacuate the full range of human behavior of spiritual value. Thus, third, the definition is integrative. It seeks to bind together the many dichotomies, between the spiritual and material, sacred and profane, eternal and temporal, supernatural and natural, that have marked Christian life. In sum, this conception sees all aspects of human life as sacred because, suffused with the offer of God's Spirit, all human action can mediate response to God's grace.

Although the object of spirituality is actual human living, its formal and defining perspective lies in the question of life's conformity with the ultimate reason of things. What is the ultimate truth of human existence? Thus the question of union with God is the fundamental issue or formality that defines the subject matter of spirituality. How is human life united with God? Or what is it in Christian life that unites people to God?

The subject matter of spirituality may be thought of in terms of action, where action is understood in a comprehensive way to include the whole of human existence.[88] Although logically distinct, the notions of human freedom and action are intimately related. Human existence is freedom, but it is always freedom in action. The point of using the term *action* is to highlight the dynamic nature of human existence. Thus spirituality most generally may be looked upon simply as human action.

By helping to define a Christian anthropology, the doctrines of sin and grace relate directly to Christian spirituality. The theology of sin and grace functions as second-level or reflective spirituality. By responding to the questions of how human existence stands before God; of how God relates to human beings; of how human existence should respond to God, other human beings, and history; and finally of the purpose of human freedom in this world, this theology provides the fundamental theological framework for understanding how concrete Christian life should unfold.

GOD'S PURPOSE OF HUMAN FREEDOM AND ACTION

From the theology of sin and grace it appears that the purpose of freedom and action in this world is, on the one hand, to resist sin; on the other hand, it is to love and serve the neighbor both on the

---

88. This broad concept of human action, which makes it synonymous with existential human existence itself, is drawn from Maurice Blondel, *Action (1893): Essay on a Critique of Life and a Science of Practice*, trans. Oliva Blanchette (Notre Dame, Ind.: University of Notre Dame Press, 1984).

individual level of personal relationships and socially through the mediation of social structures. This flows from the recognition of sin and the nature and effects of grace.

On the most fundamental level the doctrines of sin and grace refer to the structural condition of human existence. The prior sin, the fallen condition of human existence, describes the existential situation of human freedom as such. This sin cannot be escaped; sin lies within human freedom as a dynamic structure and process, and human freedom exists in it as in an "objective" sphere. So too God's permanent, universal, yet gratuitous offer of personal self-communication constitutes another sphere or region for the unfolding of human action, on both the individual and social levels. This divine milieu of God as Spirit or grace tends in the opposite direction of sin; it is God's energy for the freeing of freedom from the imprisonment of sin and its effects, both individually and socially.

The dynamic nature of human existence as freedom in action, combined with the permanent situation of sin and grace, implies that the purpose of human freedom in this world is to resist sin. Only the end of human life will provide a resting place from this struggle. But this implies that the fundamental logic of human freedom and action lies not in escape from this world, not in a religious society separated from this world, and not in a mere passing of time waiting for the end. Human life is not merely a "test" or a "prelude" to the real life of eternity.[89] Rather the fundamental theme of Christian spirituality is responsibility, the assumption of the God-given purpose and intentionality of human freedom to establish the works of love in the world in contrast to the effects of sin and final death.

This dynamic and activist understanding of Christian anthropology and spirituality should not obscure the tensions out of which it unfolds. Sin and grace are in constant tension, and there is always both a passive and an active dimension to human life understood in Christian terms. Human beings are in bondage, captive to, and imprisoned by sin, even as God's Spirit is a power, force, and energy within human existence drawing human existence out in a freedom that transcends these bonds. One can understand the active, responsible, self-transcending exercise of freedom in love only against the background of our release from the anxiety for our own being through basic trust and faith in God.

What is important for the dynamics of sin and grace in today's world is the recognition of their social dimension. At no time in his-

89. Juan Luis Segundo, *The Christ of the Ignatian Exercises*, trans. John Drury (Maryknoll, N.Y.: Orbis Books, 1987), 41–124, passim.

tory has historical consciousness made human beings more aware of the significance and power of this dimension of life. The movement of grace is not merely a power to resist sin in one's individual life. In fact the strongest bonds of sin in individual lives are mediated by social concupiscence, temptation, and sin. Thus inversely, the dynamic teleology of grace, reinterpreted in an eschatological framework, leads human freedom in a socio-historical direction to the exercise of responsibility in resisting social sin. The overriding purpose of human freedom in this world, and the direction in which God's grace impels it, is toward the construction of social grace in history. Sin will be resisted in one's individual life in the very dedication to that immediate goal.

UNION WITH GOD

What makes human action spirituality is the way it binds human existence to God and God's grace. What makes Christian anthropology a study of spirituality is the way it explains how union with God is effected in this world through the exercise of human freedom. Is it by faith? Works? Worship? Retired contemplation?

An anthropology of sin and grace that is set within the context of human freedom implies that the only way one can be united with God is through responsive human action. But since action is such a general category, does this formula not raise the question of which particular actions forge this union with God? Such an approach to the problem cannot avoid reintroducing dichotomies into the Christian life.

One is finally united with God by the whole of one's life and action and not by any single kind of action. All of one's actions in every sphere, and the whole history of one's actions up to the present, constitute and carry one's fundamental option. The sum total of one's action defines the form of one's basic trust, faith, and love. All individual actions—including those commonly associated with the domain of spirituality, such as sacramental and liturgical worship, retreat and prayer—are concrete and more or less conscious mediations of God's grace that merely feed into the generalized action where union with God or rejection of God is finally effected. All human actions performed out of self-transcending love mediate union with God.

The ability of action to actualize union with God can be understood on three levels. First, by defining a person's fundamental option, action effects a union of wills. One is united with God by doing God's will. Such a union with God is possible without being aware of it.

Second, on a conscious level of awareness of God, action mediates a possessive knowledge.[90] Through action one does not merely know *about* God and God's will in a kind of objective knowledge in which subject and object are separated. Through action God is appropriated by the connatural knowledge that can be mediated only by doing God's will. Human action, a taking up and acting on the basis of that which is known theoretically, makes the doctrine of grace a principle of one's behavior. In this qualitatively different kind of knowledge mediated by action the distance and separation between the object of faith and the believer are overcome. One possesses because one is possessed by the Spirit of God.

Third, through action one is ontically united with God through the response to grace that becomes cooperative grace. This is participation in God's life, though not in a static way that overlooks the dynamic quality of human existence as a principle of action. Rather this participation in God's life implies new capacity, energy, empowerment, and coaction within the power of God's Spirit.

The crucial point in the spirituality of sin and grace, however, turns on the recognition that action for social grace and justice in this world is of itself genuine spiritual activity that unites one to God. This is not an addition to or the consequence of Christian spirituality that is somehow defined as complete in other terms. Action in the world and history that resists social sin and is engaged in the construction of social grace out of love *is* Christian spirituality. Of itself, by the power of grace, it unites one to God.

RESURRECTION HOPE

Finally, intrinsic to Christian spirituality, as the depth dimension that sustains the whole of it, is Christian hope. This is an openness to the future that trusts in God's power of creation and gratuitous love despite the destructiveness of time that leads to death. The life of Jesus together with faith in his resurrection enter intrinsically into and constitute this hope. But this hope is not a mere wish and desire for survival. In Christian anthropology this hope bends back and gives meaning to history itself and the exercise of human freedom in creative action. Christian hope, then, is a fundamental trust that human freedom and action count, and that both individual freedom and history are meaningful because in the end what is done in love supported by God's grace will constitute the kingdom of God.

---

90. Blondel, *Action*, 434.

FOR FURTHER READING

Augustine. *Basic Writings of Saint Augustine*. Ed. Whitney J. Oates. New York: Random House, 1948.

Contains several of Augustine's anti-Pelagian writings that formulated the fundamental categories of the theology of grace for the Western tradition.

Duffy, Stephen J. "Our Hearts of Darkness: Original Sin Revisited." *Theological Studies* 49 (1988): 597–622.

A well-written interpretation of the doctrine that takes account of its genesis and combines several levels of understanding from other contemporary authors.

Haight, Roger. *The Experience and Language of Grace*. New York: Paulist Press, 1979.

An accessible historical treatment of the theology of grace in terms of important theological landmarks followed by a constructive liberationist interpretation.

McDermott, Brian O. "The Theology of Original Sin: Recent Developments." *Theological Studies* 38 (1977): 478–512.

A clearly written survey of a variety of post–Vatican II interpretations of the doctrine.

Rahner, Karl. *Foundations of Christian Faith: An Introduction to the Idea of Christianity*. Trans. William V. Dych. New York: The Seabury Press, 1978.

Contains the basic elements of Rahner's theology of grace, which has been the main influence on the Roman Catholic systematic interpretation in the post–Vatican II period.

Ricoeur, Paul. *The Symbolism of Evil*. Trans. Emerson Buchanan. Boston: Beacon Press, 1969.

An authoritative investigation and analysis of various levels of the symbolism of evil. It may serve as a background for the more direct and methodological study of the doctrine in Ricoeur's " 'Original Sin': A Study in Meaning," in his *The Conflict of Interpretations: Essays in Hermeneutics*, ed. Don Ihde (Evanston, Ill.: Northwestern University Press, 1974).

Rondet, Henri. *The Grace of Christ: A Brief History of the Theology of Grace*. Westminster, Md.: Newman Press, 1966.

An informative history of the theology of grace.

Rondet, Henri. *Original Sin: The Patristic and Theological Background.* Trans. Cajetan Finegan. Shannon, Ire.: Ecclesia Press, 1972.

Essays on the early history of the doctrine of original sin.

Schillebeeckx, Edward. *Christ: The Experience of Jesus as Lord.* Trans. John Bowden. New York: Seabury Press, 1980.

Contains a masterful synopsis of the theme of grace in the New Testament terms of salvation.

Schoonenberg, Piet. *Man and Sin: A Theological View.* Trans. Joseph Donceel. Notre Dame, Ind.: University of Notre Dame Press, 1965.

An early Catholic effort at interpreting the doctrine of original sin in historical and social terms; important for its independent grounding of liberationist understandings of sin and grace.

Thomas Aquinas. *Summa Theologiae.* Vol. 30, *The Gospel of Grace.* Ed. and trans. Cornelius Ernst. Oxford: Blackfriars, 1972.

The classic statement of the medieval interpretation of the theology of grace in Aristotelian categories that remained authoritative for the Roman Catholic church up to the Second Vatican Council.

8

SAINTS AND MARY

8

SAINTS AND MARY

Elizabeth A. Johnson

Like threads woven into a rich tapestry, key themes in theology converge in Christian reflection on saints as a whole and on that one special saint, Mary of Nazareth. The theology of God is involved, for God alone is the Holy One; the saints, or holy ones, from the Latin *sanctus*, which means holy, are recipients of the gift of divine holiness and, like signs or sacraments, reveal the face of God to the world. Christology and pneumatology are also implicated, since Jesus Christ is the redeemer through whose life, death, and resurrection the Holy Spirit is poured out in a saving way upon the world. Led by the Spirit of Christ, the lives of holy people assume a christic pattern as each follows the path of discipleship. The saints are furthermore those members of the pilgrim church who have died. Since death cannot break their bond with Jesus Christ in the Spirit, they are still members of the community of God's people, and therefore are a subject of ecclesiology. Themes of Christian anthropology are woven in, since sin and grace come to concrete expression in these people who are definitively redeemed sinners. Finally, this topic involves eschatology, or doctrine about the final fulfillment of all creatures in God, for the saints personify such fulfillment, being signs of hope that God's promises are to be trusted. Thus, a theology of the saints including Mary is a microcosm of broader themes of Christian theology.

This theological thumbnail sketch, however, does not do justice to all elements of the subject: to multiple meanings of the term *saints;* to the colorful history of the development of devotion and doctrine; to the existential situation among present-day believers with regard to the saints and the special saint, Mary. Since this is clearly one area where the priority of praxis has held sway, with doctrine being led by piety and practice, discussion of these aspects is a necessary prolegomenon for a contemporary theology of the saints and Mary.

BACKGROUND

MEANING OF THE TERM *SAINTS*

Who are the saints? The term covers a wide gamut and includes biblical, popular, theological, canonical, and liturgical meanings. Most ancient is the key meaning in the Scriptures, where saints are considered to be all the holy people of God, with emphasis on those who are living. The Hebrew Scriptures see holiness as a mark of the people of Israel, liberated from bondage and chosen for covenant: "For you are a people holy to the Lord your God" (Deut. 7:6). Early Jewish Christians transferred this insight to the living members of their own community. Paul, for example, frequently opens his letters with designations such as: "To all God's beloved in Rome, who are called to be saints" (Rom. 1:7); "To all the saints in Christ Jesus who are at Philippi" (Phil. 1:1). Saints or the *hagioi* (the Greek term) are all the people who form the holy community elected by God. While sinners, they are yet redeemed in Christ, and their lives reflect this in their faith and the quality of their ethical behavior.[1]

Under the impact of the persecution of Christians, the term began to expand to include Christian believers who had "fallen asleep" and were regarded as already with Jesus Christ in glory. Already in the late New Testament the victorious dead were referred to as saints; for example, when Babylon falls those in heaven are exhorted, "Rejoice over her, O heaven, O saints and apostles and prophets, for God has given judgment for you against her!" (Rev. 18:20). In time the term excluded the living altogether, saints being spoken of almost exclusively as those people who had lived a Christian life, had died, and were now enjoying their destiny with Jesus Christ in glory. Between them and the living existed a communion (*communio sanctorum*), as the final Western version of the Apostles Creed confesses. To this day the reference to saints as those in glory continues to be the usual Catholic popular and theological denotation of the term. There is growing awareness that these saints cannot be restricted to members of the Roman Catholic community, or even to Christians alone. According to the Scriptures, Abraham, Sarah, and other significant Jewish women and men are in the number of the holy ones (Heb. 11:1—12:2). Furthermore, in ways known only to God, saving grace reaches to all people of good will who are trying to live according to the light of their conscience, guiding them toward fulfillment in God.[2]

For the first thousand years of the church's history, precisely *who* among deceased believers were to be honored in a special way was decided more or less spontaneously by the people and their bishops in different locales. In the tenth century, bishops in council at the Lateran involved the pope officially in this decision for the first time. Papal participation grew to the point where by the thirteenth century naming new official saints was restricted to the papacy. The process is

---

1. "*Ágios*," in G. Kittel, ed., *Theological Dictionary of the New Testament* (Grand Rapids, Mich.: Eerdmans, 1964), 1:88–115.

2. See Vatican II, Dogmatic Constitution on the Church (*Lumen Gentium* [hereafter LG]) 16; and Decree on the Church's Missionary Activity (*Ad Gentes* [hereafter AG]) 7. The documents of Vatican II are in Walter Abbott, ed., *The Documents of Vatican II* (New York: America Press, 1966).

now a complex one governed by canon law and subsidiary decrees.[3] The meaning of the term *saints* in this perspective is thus canonical and juridical. Saints are those deceased believers who have been canonized, or inscribed on the list or canon of officially recognized holy ones.

Throughout the year on certain days, the church in its official prayer celebrates the memory of certain saints, some officially canonized, some not. (None of the apostles was ever officially canonized; nor was Mary.) The relative importance attached to this liturgical remembering is signified by the rank assigned to the feast, from solemnity to optional memorial. Mary is the saint most often commemorated. The calendar also includes celebrations for other noteworthy women and men throughout the ages, culminating with the Feast of All Saints. In this context, saints are those remembered either generically or by name in the church's liturgy.[4]

In this chapter, the term *saints* is used predominantly in the popular and theological sense indicated above, that is, as referring to all those who have died and are with God in Christ. This meaning encompasses those who have been canonized, but is broader in scope. While all people of good will are potentially included, the focus here is on the Christian dead.

HISTORICAL DEVELOPMENT

In the Scriptures, dead holy people who were believed to be with God were honored if at all through a recollection of their names or deeds. This remembrance led either to praise of God who had given them the victory of faith, or to exhortation of believers to lead similarly worthy lives. A key example of the latter approach is found in the Epistle to the Hebrews where, after recounting the stories of faith of Abraham, Sarah, and numerous others, the author concludes:

> Therefore, since we are surrounded by so great a cloud of witnesses, let us also lay aside every weight, and sin which clings so closely, and let us run with perseverance the race that is set before us, looking to Jesus the pioneer and perfecter of our faith [Heb 12:1].

---

3. The 1983 Code of Canon Law dropped the section on beatification and canonization previously carried in the 1917 code, noting that henceforth the process would be guided by separate pontifical norms. See James Coriden, et al., eds., *The Code of Canon Law: Text and Commentary* (New York: Paulist, 1985), c. 1403. For the history, consult Michael Perham, *The Communion of Saints* (London: SPCK, 1980); David Farmer, *The Oxford Dictionary of Saints* (Oxford: Clarendon Press, 1978), ix–xxiii.

4. A.G. Martimort, ed., *The Church at Prayer*, vol. 4, *The Liturgy and Time* (Collegeville, Minn.: Liturgical Press, 1986), 108–50.

The lives of holy forebears were of significance for present living, inspiring those who remembered them to praise God and to lead worthy lives themselves. The Scriptures, however, while remembering the story of Mary and other significant persons, present no evidence for practices that later became characteristic of their veneration.

The rise of such devotional practices began in the postapostolic age of Roman persecution, when some people gave the ultimate witness to Christ—they gave their very lives. Condemned, tortured, bloodied, and executed, martyrs were perceived by other Christians as entering in a graphic way into the dying of Jesus, and so into his rising. They were icons of Jesus Christ, awesome signs of the victory of his power in the face of the evil of this world. Christians loved these martyrs and found ways to express their esteem. Small shrines were built near their graves, which became places of pilgrimage and prayer. On the yearly anniversary of their death, which, unlike pagan custom, was considered the day of their true birth, night-long vigil would be kept at their graves culminating at dawn in a eucharist and common meal. Even after the passing of the generation that knew a martyr personally, the memory continued to be cherished. The spirit of this veneration was at first one of *koinonia*, with living disciples loving these sisters and brothers who had given such witness.

The martyrs did not replace Christ but formed one community with all those who followed Christ. This was verbalized for the first time by the church at Smyrna in the second century. One of the members of that church—responding to the charge that the community was inclined to abandon Christ in order to worship their beloved martyred bishop, Polycarp—wrote:

> They did not know that we could neither forsake the Christ who suffered to save those who are saved in the whole world, nor worship anyone else. For we worship him since he is the Son of God; but the martyrs we love as disciples and imitators of the Lord, and worthily because of their matchless affection for their own king and teacher. May we, too, become their comrades and fellow disciples.[5]

At its best, veneration of the martyrs was penetrated by this lively sense of community between the living and the dead, or between

5. *Martyrdom of Polycarp* 17.2–3, in *Early Christian Fathers*, ed. Cyril Richardson (New York: Macmillan, 1970), 156. For background, see H. Delehaye, *Les origines du culte des martyrs* (Brussels: Bureaux de la Société des Bollandistes, 1912); Josef Jungmann, "The Veneration of the Martyrs," in *The Early Liturgy to the Time of Gregory the Great*, trans. Francis Brunner (Notre Dame, Ind.: University of Notre Dame Press, 1959), 175–87; W. Frend, *Martyrdom and Persecution in the Early Church: A Study of a Conflict from the Maccabees to Donatus* (Garden City, N.Y.: Doubleday, 1967).

those still struggling and those who had been victorious, all one in Christ. As Augustine preached on the feast of the young women martyrs Perpetua and Felicity:

> Let it not seem a small thing to us that we are members of the same body as these.... We marvel at them, they have compassion on us. We rejoice for them, they pray for us.... Yet do we all serve one Lord, follow one master, attend one king. We are joined to one head, journey to one Jerusalem, follow after one love, embrace one unity.[6]

Once the age of Roman persecution ceased and martyrdom was no longer a prevalent element of the church, other holy women and men whose lives had given witness in the church were also venerated.[7] The Christian cloud of witnesses grew to include confessors who had been tortured for the faith but not killed; ascetics, especially those who lived a life of celibacy; wise teachers and prudent church leaders; and those who cared for the poor. Mary of Nazareth was also honored because of her faith and discipleship in her relationship as mother of Jesus Christ.

Recent studies have shown how significant the political, social, economic, and religious world of late antiquity was for shaping new forms of veneration of these saints.[8] Modeled on the Roman system of patronage, a system developed whereby saints came to be thought of as heavenly patrons of individuals, communities, or certain undertakings, so that prayers to them for their intercession before God or even their direct aid became common. Saints likewise became direct mediators of the presence of the "holy." Not only their graves but their very bodies were holy. Building churches over or near their graves, moving their bodies into more distinguished settings, and distributing pieces of their bodies or belongings as relics resulted. Saints were also considered a locus of the breakthrough of divine power and, in contact with their holy place or relics, blessings such as cures, exorcisms, and other miracles were prayed for and experienced.

---

6. Augustine *Sermo* CCLXXX.6 (in *Patrologia Latina*, ed. Migne [hereafter PL], 38:1283–84).

7. P. Séjourné, "Saints (culte des)," in *Dictionnaire de théologie catholique* (Paris: Librarie Letouzey et Ané, 1939), 14/1:870–978. For development of the cult of Mary, see Walter Burghardt, "Mary in Western Patristic Thought," in Juniper Carol, ed., *Mariology* (Milwaukee: Bruce, 1955), 1:109–55, and idem, "Mary in Eastern Patristic Thought," in ibid., 2:88–153; also Hilda Graef, *Mary: A History of Doctrine and Devotion*, 2 vols. (1963; reprint, Westminster, Md.: Christian Classics, 1985).

8. For studies using the approach of social history, see Peter Brown, *The Cult of the Saints: Its Rise and Function in Latin Christianity* (London: SCM Press, 1981); Stephen Wilson, ed., *Saints and Their Cults: Studies in Religious Sociology, Folklore and History* (Cambridge: Cambridge University Press, 1983), with annotated bibliography, pp. 309–417.

In the case of Mary, patronage, presence, and power coalesced in a uniquely effective way as veneration utilized elements from the Mediterranean cult of the Great Mother.[9] As a missionary strategy, images, titles, prayers, and roles of the goddess were attributed to Mary, being "baptized" into a Christian framework, although this "baptism" was not always thoroughly successful in popular piety. In a direct outcome of the controversy over the unity of natures in Christ, the Council of Ephesus in 431 legitimated the title *Theotokos* or God-bearer for Mary, reasoning that if Jesus Christ is in truth the Word incarnate, then she who bore him can be called the Mother of God (DS 251).[10] During these centuries, belief in Mary's bodily virginity developed to include not only the scripturally attested virginal conception of Jesus but also her virginity during his birth and forever after (virginity *ante partum, in partu, post partum*), a belief given official status through an anathema of the Lateran Council of 649 (DS 503).

By the end of the early Christian centuries in both East and West it was clear that while all the redeemed were one in Christ, particular saints, including Mary, besides being comrades in the following of Jesus and a cloud of witnesses for the encouragement of faith, were now also powerful patrons and intercessors. In the context of this growing popular cult of the saints, increasingly expressed in the use of icons, and in the context of strong criticism of these practices, the last ecumenical council to occur before the split between East and West made clear the distinction between honoring God and honoring the saints. In 787 the Second Council of Nicaea noted that God alone is worshiped and adored (*latria*), while to the saints simple respect and veneration are given (*dulia*) (DS 601).

In medieval times, all of the above characteristics of devotion to the saints blossomed with a profusion that is impossible to codify. On the one hand, the church in its public liturgy soberly honored the memory of those whose lives had given splendid and striking witness to Christ. God was praised for them, their example was held up to be followed, and the *koinonia* of believers was strengthened as the church prayed in their company. On the other hand, uncounted thousands of local saints were honored in popular piety,

---

9. Jean Daniélou, "Le culte marial et le paganisme," in Hubert du Manoir, ed., *Maria: Études sur la Sainte Vierge* (Paris: Beauchesne, 1949), 159–81; R. E. Witt, *Isis in the Greco-Roman World* (Ithaca, N.Y.: Cornell University Press, 1971), 269–81.

10. References to official church teaching are taken from J. Neuner and J. Dupuis, eds., *The Christian Faith in the Doctrinal Documents of the Catholic Church* (New York: Alba House, 1981). The notation DS followed by an Arabic numeral indicates the 1962 Denzinger-Schönmetzer collection of doctrinal documents (entitled *Enchiridion Symbolorum*) as translated in Neuner-Dupuis.

some of them even legendary. Credulity and superstition abounded, as evidenced by zeal for collecting relics, use of auguries and incantations, innumerable reports of miracles, superheated hagiography, and the divorce of piety from ethics. Mary, Mother of Jesus, Mother of God, assumed a magnified role in piety as beautiful virgin, merciful mother, and powerful queen of heaven and earth who could command even her Son.[11] Conviction grew that she was connected with mercy for the unfortunate sinner in the face of the severe justice of Christ. All of this occurred within a complex cultural context where the Latin liturgy and Scholastic theology became ever more remote from ordinary people's experience, and where daily life was hard and dangerous. There was felt to be a need for human mediators who were closer to little people and unworthy sinners than was the magnificent Savior and just Judge, Jesus Christ.

In spite of some efforts of bishops and theologians to curb abuses, these did continue, becoming part of the late medieval distortion of the gospel criticized by the Reformers in the sixteenth century. The theological leaders of the Reformation did not turn against the saints or Mary in themselves. Luther, for example, wrote movingly of the community of saints, and penned a commentary on the Magnificat in which Mary is described as a woman of faith and the foremost example of the grace of God. The historic "Apology of the Augsburg Confession" makes clear that for Lutherans there remains a proper veneration of the saints expressed in thanking God for them, letting faith be strengthened by them, and imitating their example where appropriate.[12] But what the Reformers forbid is invocation, or calling upon the saints for their prayers and favors. Not only is there no scriptural warrant for this practice, but it dangerously detracts from Christ as the sole mediator between the human race and God. The Council of Trent, on the other hand, declared that it was "good and useful" to thank God for the saints as well as to invoke them, and gave regulatory authority over the cult of the saints to bishops in order to correct abuses.[13]

---

11. Jaroslav Pelikan, *The Growth of Medieval Theology* (Chicago: University of Chicago Press, 1978), 158–84; Heiko Oberman, *The Harvest of Medieval Theology* (Cambridge: Harvard University Press, 1963), 281–322; Elizabeth Johnson, "Marian Devotion in the Western Church," in Jill Raitt, ed., *Christian Spirituality: High Middle Ages and Reformation* (New York: Crossroad, 1987), 392–414.

12. Martin Luther, "The Large Catechism," in *The Book of Concord*, ed. Theodore Tappert (Philadelphia: Fortress Press, 1959), 415–19; and his "Commentary on the Magnificat," in *Luther's Works*, ed. Jaroslav Pelikan (St. Louis: Concordia Pub., 1953), 21:295–355. Luther, "Apology of the Augsburg Confession," XXI:4–16 (in *The Book of Concord*, 229–30).

13. DS 1821–23. Full text in *Canons and Decrees of the Council of Trent*, trans. H.J. Schroeder (St. Louis: Herder, 1941), 214–17.

Succeeding polemic centuries saw these two divergent paths intensify as the Reformation tradition developed a case of amnesia about the saints and Mary, while in response Catholic piety and doctrine concentrated more fixedly upon them. Protestants tended to fulfill Luther's prophecy that when the saints were no longer thought to be able to give us benefits, they would be left to rest unmolested in their graves.[14] Catholics meanwhile, with egregious abuses held in check, continued to venerate the saints through old and new practices. By the nineteenth century attention was turned in a particular way to Mary. Two Marian dogmas were papally defined. The dogma of the immaculate conception (defined in 1854) declared that from the first instant of her conception, by the grace of God and the merits of Jesus Christ, Mary was preserved free from original sin (DS 2803); the dogma of the assumption (defined in 1950) declared that after her life on earth Mary was assumed body and soul into the glory of heaven (DS 3903). Piety and theology kept pace with these official developments. New "true" devotions were advocated, apparitions occurred, new places of pilgrimage attracted millions (Lourdes, Fatima), a theology of Mary as mediatrix of grace and even co-redemptrix was developed.

Such was the situation on the eve of the Second Vatican Council: centuries of silence and high suspicion of the veneration of the saints on the Reformation side, and overluxuriant growth of devotion on the Catholic side. Fueled by genuine ecumenical concern as well as by the biblical, patristic, and liturgical renewals already underway, the Second Vatican Council produced the first extended systematic theological teaching on the saints and Mary ever given by a council. Incorporating this teaching into its constitution on the church and bearing out its insight in the practical norms of the constitution on the liturgy, the council set a new, more ecumenically promising direction for subsequent Catholic theology and practice.

EXISTENTIAL SITUATION

Analysis of Catholic pastoral practice since the council also sheds light on present theologizing. As might be expected in a world church, the situation is multifaceted. There has been a noticeable diminishment of private veneration of the saints among numerous people in the countries of the North Atlantic. This may well be a direct result of the biblical, eucharistic, christocentric spirituality to which the council gave impetus. With access to God in Christ

---

14. Luther, *Smalkald Articles*, pt. II:II, 28 (in *The Book of Concord*, 297).

through Word and sacrament, there is no longer such great need for approachable intercessors. Again, the phenomenon in all likelihood also arises from the climate of thought of secular culture wherein the analogy between heaven and earth has broken down. People experience that those who die have truly disappeared from this world; they are no longer accessible to the living in any direct fashion, as was possible to imagine in a previous age. Karl Rahner's analysis roots this situation most profoundly in the contemporary Western experience of God. God is eclipsed, hidden, silent, experienced as utterly incomprehensible and remote even if known as the holy mystery who is ineffably near. People today feel this with a new and radical keenness because

> the world has become so inescapably vast and at the same time so profane and also because, not surprisingly, God does not appear as one factor "along with" others which are given in the everyday experience of this world. God is, to a large extent, experienced as the silent mystery. . . . Into this silent, unfathomable and ineffable mystery the dead disappear. They depart. They no longer make themselves felt. They cease any further to belong to the world of our experience.[15]

If this is the Western experience even with known loved ones who have died, it is not surprising that saints of the past seem inaccessible and that their veneration has diminished.

In other regions, however, the situation is decidedly different. In Latin America, Eastern Europe, and the Mediterranean countries veneration flourishes, sometimes related to national aspirations but more often as the expression of a national character that is warmhearted and affectionate. The church in Africa is drawing on the genius of the African tradition with its sense of the vital relationship between the living and the "living dead," a sense of the unseen presence of ancestors as foundational for the whole social fabric including ethical values.[16] The ancient cult of ancestors is being adapted into veneration of the saints, with several Christian corrections: Only God is powerful, so ancestors can do no harm; and Christ rather than family blood ties is the foundation for relation with the living dead. With these provisos, new forms of veneration of the saints are developing. These in turn may contribute to the worldwide church's

15. Karl Rahner, "Why and How Can We Venerate the Saints?" in *Theological Investigations* (New York: Herder and Herder, 1971), 8:7. See also Rahner, "The Life of the Dead," in *Theological Investigations* (New York: Seabury, 1974), 4:347–54.

16. John Mbiti, *New Testament Eschatology in an African Background* (Oxford: University Press, 1971); Edward Fasholé-Luke, "Ancestor Veneration and the Communion of Saints," in M. Glasswell and E. Fasholé-Luke, eds., *New Testament Christianity for Africa and the World* (London: SPCK, 1974), 209–21.

sense of itself as a communion, too often depreciated in the West by unrestrained individualism. The situation is, then, complex, with the experience of believers in different cultures reflecting basic mentalities of their time and place. Within this diversity, basic aspects of a contemporary theology of the saints and Mary are being shaped.

ECUMENICAL TURNING POINT: SECOND VATICAN COUNCIL

PERSPECTIVES

The fundamental vision and concrete affirmations of the Second Vatican Council are of pivotal importance for subsequent theology of the saints including Mary. After fierce dispute over its placement, teaching about Mary was folded into the Dogmatic Constitution on the Church (LG) rather than issued as a separate document. Likewise incorporated was a less contentious document on the saints. This constitution's teaching stresses central christological, ecclesiological, and eschatological themes without which reflection on Mary and the saints tends toward distortion.[17] The very structural design of this document provides a hermeneutical clue for a theology of the saints and Mary. The constitution's first chapter, "The Mystery of the Church," opens with the unequivocal proclamation that "Christ is the light of all nations" (LG 1). In the radiance of this light the church itself is brightened and, by proclaiming the gospel to every creature, helps to shed on all people the light of Christ. This, then, is the foundational relationship that constitutes the very essence of the church: Christ the sole Redeemer, and the church as the assembly of all those who believe in him and witness him to the world.

Subsequent chapters then consider aspects of this church among its living members: the whole church as the pilgrim people of God (chap. 2); the various functions of episcopacy and clergy (chap. 3); the role of the laity (chap. 4); the call of the whole church to holiness (chap. 5); and the life of religious who live this out in a special way (chap. 6). But the reality of the church is not exhausted in these aspects, in those who are still alive at any given moment. Some of its members have already arrived in the promised future. They are still

---

17. For commentaries on the constitution see Otto Semmelroth's article in Herbert Vorgrimler, ed., *Commentary on the Documents of Vatican II* (New York: Herder and Herder, 1967), 1:280–96; Donal Flanagan's article in Kevin McNamara, ed., *Vatican II: The Constitution on the Church* (Chicago: Franciscan Herald Press, 1968), 317–56; Anne Carr, "Mary in the Mystery of the Church: Vatican Council II," in Carol F. Jegen, ed., *Mary according to Women* (Kansas City: Leaven Press, 1985), 5–32.

united with the pilgrim church, for the bonds that join believers to Christ in the Spirit are so strong that not even death can break them. One does not leave the church by dying. Therefore, the constitution goes on in its penultimate chapter (chap. 7) to turn its attention to the faithful dead, those "friends and fellow heirs of Jesus Christ" (LG 50) with whom the living form one community. This it does in tandem with reflection on the eschatological nature of the pilgrim church, to which these definitively redeemed persons give concrete expression. Within this context of those believers who are now forever with God, the final chapter (chap. 8) discusses the role of the Blessed Virgin Mary, faith-filled Mother of Jesus Christ and preeminent member of the church. Thus, the precise placement of the saints and Mary in this constitution reveals a theological order of relationship basic to the subject.

SAINTS

The doctrinal content of these chapters is likewise important. The chapter on the saints, entitled "The Eschatological Nature of the Pilgrim Church and Her Union with the Heavenly Church," considers the church's promised future when all people and the cosmos itself will be brought to *shalom* in Christ. Until the coming of that new heaven and new earth where justice dwells, the church on earth groans in travail on its way through history. But some of its members are already being gathered up in the great harvest. Between them and living disciples there is a genuine community. In an age of individualism, the constitution thought it important to clarify both the fact and the foundation of this *koinonia*. This lies in the truth that "in various ways and degrees we all partake in the same love for God and neighbor, and all sing the same hymn of glory to our God. For all who belong to Christ, having his Spirit, form one church and cleave together in him" (LG 49).

This is not a new belief. Historically, the church from its beginning centuries has understood that the apostles and martyrs as well as Mary and other holy people are united in Christ with those still alive, and has therefore venerated their memory in special ways (LG 50). While not claiming detailed knowledge about the condition of the saints, the church believes they are definitively united with Christ. In this relationship they contribute to the upbuilding of the church on earth through their holiness and their prayer offered in and with him. The benefits that accrue to the living by remembering the saints are many. Our faith is inspired by theirs; our path is made more sure by their example; the communion of the whole church is strengthened. The right response of living disciples is to love these friends of Christ, to thank God for them, to imitate them in their following of Christ, to invoke their intercession (which means to ask them to pray for us), and to praise God in their company especially during the eucharistic liturgy. In the vision of the constitution, each one of these actions terminates through Christ in God, who is wonderful in the saints (2 Thess. 1:10).

Concerned that veneration of the saints has not always hewn to a rightly ordered christocentric/theocentric pattern, the constitution calls for hard work to correct abuses that have crept in, and to restore the veneration of the saints to ample praise of God in Christ. Significantly, it exhorts: "Let the faithful be taught, therefore, that the authentic cult of the saints consists not so much in the multiplying of external acts, but rather in the intensity of our active love" (LG 51). Provided it is understood in the more adequate light of faith, communion with those in heaven serves but to enrich our worship and service of God through Christ in the Spirit.

The Constitution on the Sacred Liturgy (*Sacrosanctum Concilium* [SC]) translates these exhortations into concrete directives. Saints' feasts proclaim the achievement of Christ's paschal mystery in the saints and set an example before us. Consequently, feasts of Christ take precedence over those of the saints; the number of universal feasts of the saints is to be pruned; private devotions should be harmonized with the liturgy that far surpasses any of them (SC 102–11, 13). To sum up, the council developed a theology of the saints that is centered in Christ, based on the vital community of all disciples in the one Spirit, and evocative of the hope of future *shalom*. In essence, "Just as Christian communion among wayfarers brings us closer to Christ, so our companionship with the saints joins us to Christ, from whom as from their fountain and head issue every grace and the life of God's people itself " (LG 50).

MARY

It is within this context of the whole church together, living and dead, centered in Christ, that the constitution's final chapter (chap. 8) turns to one special saint, Mary. Entitling the chapter "The Role of the Blessed Virgin Mary, Mother of God, in the Mystery of Christ and the Church," the council does not intend to present a complete doctrine about this woman, but rather to highlight her role in both the mystery of Christ and the church. The key to interpretation here is the dual relationship in which Mary is perceived. If certain trends of the nineteenth- and twentieth-century Marian era had tended to imagine Mary in privileged and splendid isolation, the council makes clear that she is related firmly and in differing ways to Christ and the church. She is that preeminent and singular member of the church whose destiny it was to hear the Word of God and become the Mother of the Son of God. Indeed, while she is redeemed in a special way, she is at the same time a daughter of Adam and, as such, one with all human beings in the need for salvation (LG 53). Christ and church form the grid on which is sketched out her significance.

Mary and Christ

By means of a running commentary on scriptural texts woven together in a harmonious narrative, *Lumen Gentium* tells the story of Mary's life in relation to the gospel events of the life of Jesus.[18] What is emphasized throughout the story is both her maternity by means of which the Redeemer entered the world, and her faith that led her to respond creatively to the call of God in different situations. The dynamism of her life is seen to lie in the way she advanced in her "pilgrimage of faith" (LG 58), all the way to the cross. She is blessed because she hears the Word of God and acts upon it (Luke 11:28). This same dynamism led her into the midst of the community of the first disciples as they awaited the outpouring of the Spirit. Ultimately it led her into the glory of Christ. The reality of her life, then, is intertwined with the great events of the coming of salvation.

Mary and the Church

Recovering the patristic theme of Mary as a model or *typos* of the church, the constitution reflects on the ways in which Mary shines forth to the whole community as an exemplar of integral faith, firm hope, and sincere charity. As the constitution on the liturgy phrased the same insight, in Mary the church "holds up and admires the most excellent fruit of the redemption, and joyfully contemplates, as in a faultless model, that which she herself wholly desires and hopes to be" (SC 103). Since preconciliar development had given so much attention to the question of Mary as mediatrix of grace, special attention is paid within the Christ/church framework to Mary's mediation. The constitution repeatedly confesses that we have but one mediator, Christ Jesus, who gave himself as a ransom for all. Risen

---

18. Subsequent biblical scholarship has used a more critical methodology on the Marian texts; see Raymond Brown, Karl Donfried, et al., eds., *Mary in the New Testament* (Philadelphia: Fortress Press; and New York: Paulist, 1978).

in the Spirit, he continues to be the one mediator, living to make intercession for those trying to draw near (Heb. 7:25). The power of Christ's mediatorship shows itself by drawing all believers into his mediating prayer, so that they pray for one another. This Catholic understanding of the participatory nature of Christ's sole mediation does not overshadow Christ but rather shows his effectiveness. This key claim is illuminated by means of a nest of examples that show the Catholic analogical imagination at work. There is only one priest of the new covenant, Jesus Christ, but this priesthood is shared in different ways by all the people of God (the royal priesthood) and by ordained ministers. Again, God alone is good, but this goodness is shared in different ways with all creatures who exist. In a similar way, only Jesus Christ is mediator, but this mediation gives rise to "a manifold cooperation which is but a sharing in this unique source" (LG 62). The mediation of the saints, and in this case of Mary, in no way obscures the unique mediation of Christ, but reveals its effectiveness as they participate in his prayer for the world. With the heart of a mother, Mary continuously prays for those who are still on the way and beset with difficulties. For this reason she is called upon in the church (not *by* the church, as the original text had said) under many titles such as Auxiliatrix and Mediatrix. The latter title is not given dogmatic status, as some had wished, but is contextualized in piety. In no way does any of this mean that the creature Mary could be classed with the incarnate Word. Rather, Christ is at the center, believers have immediate union with him, and all are empowered by him in the Spirit.

Finally, the chapter gives attention to the special reverence with which believers should venerate Mary's memory. Differing essentially from the adoration due to God alone, this veneration has taken diverse forms in various cultures and should be encouraged. But theologians and preachers are earnestly exhorted to avoid the opposite excesses of both false exaggeration and narrow-mindedness. With ecumenical sensitivity, all members of the church are encouraged to remember that

> true devotion consists neither in fruitless and passing emotion, nor in a certain vain credulity. Rather, it proceeds from true faith, by which we are led to know the excellence of the Mother of God, and are moved to a filial love toward our mother and to the imitation of her virtues [LG 67].

The constitution ends by circling round to the eschatological theme with which it began its treatment of the saints and Mary. In glory with Christ, Mary is an image of the church as it will be in the age to come; as such, she is a sign of hope and comfort for the pilgrim people of God.

The theology of the saints and Mary developed and taught by the Second Vatican Council is integrated with major insights of Christian faith. Rooted in Scripture and the patristic tradition, it is christological, ecclesial, and eschatological in perspective, and ecumenical in tone. Mary in the midst of the community of saints in heaven; the saints as friends of God sharing community of life with the pilgrim people of God on earth; and the whole church itself reflecting the light of Christ as the moon does that of the sun—such is the vision of the Second Vatican Council.

PARADIGM SHIFT

With the council's emphasis on community among believers, a basic shift has occurred in the way saints and the living are seen to interrelate. In the centuries after Trent, although people approached saints with the correct intuition that all believers in Jesus Christ are meant to be of help to one another, there was heavy and continued stress on personal neediness. Sinners were exceedingly conscious of the long distance still to be traveled before they were safely home. With a kind of naive realism it was pictured that the saints, closer in their own experience to the human struggle than was God, could obtain material benefits and spiritual help from the almighty God, though no clear theological explanation of this was ever given. The saints including Mary were thought to be mediators in the sense that they came between Jesus Christ and believers, even while being subordinated to him. It may be simplistic to sum up a complex history in a single model, but there is truth in the notion that from the sixteenth to the twentieth centuries, in the context of a strongly juridical experience of church, veneration of the saints took the predominant form of a patron-petitioner model. A needy living person was dependent on a powerful heavenly intercessor.

The effect of conciliar teaching has been to shift the basic model to one of communion and solidarity. We are all working, loving, and praying together in this community called church; all are companions in Christ. As early Christian writers described it, saints are comrades, fellow disciples, pilgrims with us who follow after the one love. To continue with the spatial metaphor, the saints are not situated *between* Jesus Christ and believers, but are *with* their sisters and brothers in the one people of God. It is not distance from Jesus Christ, or fear of his judgment, or a sense of his cold disinterest, or need for grace given only in small portions, or any other such motivation sometimes found in the patron-petitioner model that impels honoring of the saints. Rather, we take great gratitude and delight in honoring this cloud of witnesses because we share with them a common humanity, a common struggle, and a common faith. This is not to say that there is no difference between pilgrims on earth and saints now blessedly with God in heaven. But it is to emphasize that in the light of salvation by God in Jesus Christ, the relationship between all of the redeemed is fundamentally mutual and collegial.

SUBSEQUENT THEOLOGICAL OPTIONS

Coherent with the pluralism now existing in Catholic theology, several different approaches to the saints and Mary are discernible. Working with categories of philosophical anthropology, one option highlights the universal significance of the saints as indispensable signs of grace and ecclesial examples of holiness. Karl Rahner, for example, integrates the saints into his fundamental theology of grace, describing them as manifestations of the charismatic dimension of the church. They are concrete persons in whom the grace of God has become victorious in this world in such a way that others can actually recognize it.[19] The church's proclamation of their holiness is a function of its own identity as holy church, a witness to the gift of the saving power of God who not only makes the church holy in its sacraments or other institutional aspects, but in an unpredictable way in its people. Since the grace of God does not work in a vacuum but in the midst of history, saints are also significant for the community because in response to the impulse of the Spirit they took risks and were successful in shaping new styles of holiness suitable for particular ages. As both redeemed sinners themselves and creative models of holiness for others, they are a vital part of the history of grace in the world. In a particular way Mary carries out this vocation of the saint: She is full of grace, and archetype of redeemed humanity as a hearer of the word par excellence.[20] In God's favor to her and the pattern of her faith-filled life, the mystery of victorious grace is

---

19. In addition to the works cited in note 16, see Rahner, "The Church of the Saints," in *Theological Investigations* (Baltimore: Helicon, 1967), 3:91–104; idem, "One Mediator and Many Mediations," in *Theological Investigations* (New York: Seabury, n.d.), 9:169–84; idem, "All Saints," in *Theological Investigations*, 8:24–29; see also *The von Balthasar Reader*, ed. Medard Kehl and Werner Löser, trans. Robert Daly and Fred Lawrence (New York: Crossroad, 1982), 376–407.

20. Rahner, *Mary, Mother of the Lord*, trans. W. J. O'Hara (New York: Herder and Herder, 1963); Otto Semmelroth, *Mary: Archetype of the Church*, trans. M. von Eroes and J. Devlin (New York: Sheed and Ward, 1963); Max Thurian, *Mary, Mother of the Lord, Figure of the Church*, trans. N. Cryer (London: Faith Press, 1963).

made uniquely manifest to the people called church who are similarly called through grace to ultimate glory. In this anthropological approach, the meaning of the saints and Mary receives ultimate definition from the perspective of eschatology. God's victorious grace has already won in them, as pledge of divine fidelity and promise of the future for all: "We hope because there are saints."[21]

The turn to praxis-oriented theologies takes this spiritual, academic reflection on the saints in new directions. Whether in European political theology or liberation theology in its Latin American or feminist forms, the practical, critical significance of the saints in the midst of suffering and oppression comes to the fore. The categories of memory, narrative, and solidarity developed by J. B. Metz for his practical fundamental theology, while not yet fleshed out in a full-blown approach to the saints and Mary, provide a strong intellectual base for such a construction by political theologians.[22] The act of remembering our solidarity with the dead, both known and unknown, and telling their stories of victory and defeat has the power to unleash action on behalf of justice. This is as true for the religious community of the church as for civil society.

In a more direct way Latin American liberation theologians are reclaiming saints as partners in the struggle against the people's oppression. Critical of the present roster of canonized and liturgically celebrated saints, the majority of whom are white Europeans of upper- and middle-class standing and thus unrepresentative of the poor on the underside of history, liberation theologians search for new models of holiness among those in the ancient and recent past who have struggled for justice. Leonardo Boff, for example, uses the liberation stance as a hermeneutic with which to reread the significance of Francis of Assisi, finding in his story powerful witness to God's love for the poor and the need to speak truth to power on their behalf.[23] Taking poignant note of the new generation of martyrs being created on his continent, Boff furthermore argues the need for political saints today as revelatory of the grace of God in the midst of conflict.[24] In this perspective, Mary in particular is retrieved as a her-

---

21. Rahner, "All Saints," 29.

22. Johannes Baptist Metz, *Faith in History and Society*, trans. Davis Smith (New York: Seabury, 1980).

23. Leonardo Boff, *Saint Francis: A Model for Human Liberation*, trans. John Diercksmeier (New York: Crossroad, 1982).

24. Leonardo Boff, "The Need for Political Saints," *Cross Currents* 30 (1980–81): 369–76. See J. B. Metz and E. Schillebeeckx, eds., *Martyrdom Today* (entire issue of *Concilium* 163 [New York: Seabury, 1983]); C. Duquoc and C. Floristan, eds., *Models of Holiness* (entire issue of *Concilium* 129 [New York: Seabury, 1979]); Lawrence Cunningham, *The Catholic Heritage* (New York: Crossroad, 1983).

ald of liberation, singing the song of the justice of the coming reign of God (the Magnificat [Luke 1:46-55]).[25] The poor have rediscovered her solidarity with them as a village woman, a poor woman of the people, a member of a people oppressed by an occupying force, a refugee woman fleeing with her newborn child from the wrath of a murderous ruler, a bereaved mother of a victim of unjust execution. This solidarity carries political significance, for it is to *this* kind of woman that God has done great things. Her veneration aids and abets the realization of the dignity of all those thought to be nonpersons. While there is as yet no fully developed liberation theology of the saints and Mary, directions taken so far indicate that such a theology entails revaluation of popular religion, recognition of holy men and women who emerge within local communities, and reclamation of the liberating impulse present but repressed in inherited understandings.

With its focus on the experience of women and analysis of prevailing patriarchal relationships of male domination and female subordination, feminist theology likewise critically recovers liberative dimensions of our relation to the saints and Mary. The saints honored in the church to date have been predominantly male: On the present liturgical calendar 73 percent of the saints celebrated are men, 27 percent women, if one counts Mary once; of the saints canonized in this century to the end of Paul VI's pontificate, 79 percent have been clergy, 21 percent lay, of whom an even smaller percentage are women.[26] This official silence about the history of women's holiness and creative religious initiatives is no accident, but a socio-political function of the androcentric worldview that takes the humanity of men to be paradigmatic and normative. One task is to retrieve the hidden history of holy women and to present it free of stereotypical distortions of the feminine, providing impetus for mature adult personhood for women as well as men. Thus with the key of feminist hermeneutics, Elisabeth Schüssler Fiorenza unlocks the New Testa-

---

25. Leonardo Boff, "Mary, Prophetic Woman of Liberation," in his *The Maternal Face of God: The Feminine and Its Religious Expressions*, trans. Robert Barr and John Diercksmeier (San Francisco: Harper and Row, 1987), 188–203; Virgil Elizondo, "Our Lady of Guadalupe as a Cultural Symbol: The Power of the Powerless," in H. Schmidt and D. Power, eds., *Liturgy and Cultural Religious Traditions* (entire issue of *Concilium* 102 [New York: Seabury, 1977], 25–33); Ernesto Cardenal, *The Gospel in Solentiname*, trans. D. Walsh (Maryknoll, N.Y.: Orbis Books, 1978), 1:25–32; Ivone Gebara and Maria Clara Bingemer, *Mary: Mother of God, Mother of the Poor*, trans. Phillip Berryman (Maryknoll, N.Y.: Orbis Books, 1989).

26. Statistics in Shawn Madigan, "Models of Holiness Derived from the Saints of Universal Significance in the Roman Calendar: Exposition and Theological Critique" (Ph.D. diss., Catholic University of America, 1984); and Pierre Delooz, *Sociologie et canonisations* (The Hague: M. Nijhoff, 1969).

ment to reveal the myriads of women who were active and influential in the ministry of Jesus and the founding of the church, shedding unique light on the leadership of Mary Magdalene, no repentant sinner at all.[27] Using the saint's own writings Joann Wolski Conn shatters the image of the sweet, pliable Thérèse of Lisieux to find a mature young woman of independent thought and originality.[28] The power of these rediscoveries is creatively communicated in feminist liturgies of remembrance and litanies of the saints.[29] In this perspective, the traditional image of Mary as a passive, sexless, subordinate minor and the use of this image as model for women are criticized, while Mary is retrieved precisely as a woman, strong, resourceful, suffering, our sister in faith and the feminine face of the church.[30] As with Latin American liberation theology, what is sought in these reconstructive efforts is theology in aid of a more just society, in this case with emphasis on the inclusion of women.

A THEOLOGICAL SYNTHESIS

One point where these diverse theological options meet today on common ground is concern for the well-being of persons in the social/political as well as the individual sphere. Whether it be explicitly political, liberation, or feminist theology, or more classic theology attuned now to human rights, justice, and peace, a turn to praxis has occurred and has made a significant impact on the understanding of classical doctrines. These are being interpreted to yield their critical and productive force that challenges believers to become genuine disciples, following the suffering, liberating Messiah of God on a path that will inevitably bring them into the struggle for the good of all human beings. To express the faith in the light of this consciousness, new conceptual tools are brought into play. Predominant among

---

27. Elisabeth Schüssler Fiorenza, *In Memory of Her: A Feminist Theological Reconstruction of Christian Origins* (New York: Crossroad, 1983).
28. Joann Wolski Conn, "Therese of Lisieux from a Feminist Perspective," in J. W. Conn, ed., *Women's Spirituality: Resources for Christian Development* (New York: Paulist, 1986), 317–25.
29. Rosemary Radford Ruether, *Women-Church: Theology and Practice* (San Francisco: Harper and Row, 1985), 141–43, 224–28, and bibliography.
30. Rosemary Radford Ruether, *Mary, the Feminine Face of the Church* (Philadelphia: Westminster Press, 1977). For critique and reappropriation of the Marian tradition, see idem, "Mariology as Symbolic Ecclesiology: Repression or Liberation?" in her *Sexism and God-Talk: Toward a Feminist Theology* (Boston: Beacon, 1983), 139–58; Marina Warner, *Alone of All Her Sex: The Myth and Cult of the Virgin Mary* (New York: Knopf, 1976); Carol F. Jegen, *Mary according to Women*.

these are the categories of solidarity, memory, and narrative.[31] These are not decorative notions brought in to adorn the Christian proclamation that can be better understood by more abstract thought processes. Rather, they are basic categories of human historical consciousness that are important to doing the truth in love in the midst of a conflictual world. What theology classically expressed in the doctrine of the communion of saints receives new intelligibility in these categories.

CATEGORIES

Solidarity

In a foundational sense it has always been realized that the cosmos and human existence within it have an intercommunicative character. Biologically, psychologically, culturally, politically, economically, and socially, who one is and what one does are affected in essential respects by others. In turn, one's own person and deeds have inescapable impact on those nearest, and ultimately on all. No one is or can be a solitary player. For better or worse, everyone depends on everyone else.

This social structure of human existence is not eradicated, but is respected by the advent of God's saving mercy. The people formed by the Spirit of Jesus Christ likewise have an intercommunicative character by virtue of which they affect each other for better or worse. If one suffers, all suffer together; if one is honored, all rejoice (1 Cor. 12:26). Christian piety and reflection have extended this state of affairs among the living also to the dead. It is a fundamental Christian hope that just as the death of Jesus had no ultimate power to separate him from God, so too communion with God through Christ extends beyond death. Life in the Spirit is so strong that death cannot break it: "Whether we live or whether we die, we are the Lord's" (Rom. 14:8). The courage of hope affirms that God saves those who are faithful, and does not let one get lost. In and beyond death they abide in a living community with God and thereby with all others in a completely new way. While we have no image or concept of what

---

31. In addition to Metz and Schillebeeckx, eds., *Martyrdom Today*, for solidarity see Matthew Lamb, *Solidarity with Victims* (New York: Crossroad, 1982); Helmut Peukert, *Science, Action, and Fundamental Theology*, trans. J. Bohman (Cambridge: MIT Press, 1984). On memory and narrative, see Stephen Crites, "The Narrative Quality of Experience," *Journal of the American Academy of Religion* 39 (1971): 291–311; David Tracy, *The Analogical Imagination* (New York: Crossroad, 1981), 275–81, 307–9; Gary Comstock, "Two Types of Narrative Theology," *Journal of the American Academy of Religion* 55 (1987): 687–717.

this may be like, death being impenetrable, we believe such persons are the beginning of the eschatological community of the redeemed. They remain a part of God's people, forming one *koinonia* with the living. The solidarity of the church thus extends not only to the community gathered here, not only across space to believers living on different continents, but also across time to disciples of all ages.

As shaped by contemporary usage, however, solidarity signifies more than these generic relationships of human and Christian interdependence. It connotes as well a vital union of interests in a group, a genuine community of desires, expectations, and goals, usually in the face of opposition. Besides common feeling for people like ourselves it involves partnership with those unlike ourselves, particularly with those in need, perhaps causing us loss. When used in theology of the saints and Mary, this category signifies a vital community in God between the living and the dead in the face of the powers of evil. In a particular way it evokes alliance with the victims of history, those who have been defeated and overcome. The living do not go on as if these persons are unimportant but witness to their lasting value before God. Solidarity is thus a category of help, support, and challenge by means of which the dead are affirmed as having a future and the living are strengthened to struggle to advance the unfinished agenda of justice. It brings critical, productive power to the conciliar community model of Mary and the saints.

Narrative Remembrance

The dead who are in God, the saints, are no longer accessible to human reach as they were during their historical time. As is the case with Jesus himself, they have entered into the inner sanctum behind the veil (Heb. 6:19). They have become part of the eschatological mystery that, although it anchors human beings in hope, escapes human comprehension: "eye has not seen, nor ear heard..." (1 Cor. 2:9). In spite of the persistence of human imagination that with a kind of naive realism pictures saints and prayer to saints on models of human transactions on earth, their situation is only analogous to what living human beings experience, more unlike than like ordinary human existence and interchange. For this reason, solidarity with the saints is activated primarily through narrative memory, an anamnesis that makes present the effectiveness of their lives.

Narrative remembrance is not understood here in a nostalgic sense that bathes the past in a transfiguring light; nor is it perceived as having a reconciling function, bringing the challenge of the past into harmony with the misery of the present. Rather, telling the story of the sufferings and victories of the past serves to break the stranglehold of what is currently held to be plausible and calls the present into question. By lifting up unfulfilled promises it galvanizes unquenchable hope that new possibilities can be realized now, at last. By remembering a future that is still outstanding it paves the way to protest and resistance, startling those who are despondent into movement. The future is opened up in a new way by the surplus of meaning carried in the act of remembering, that incalculable visitation from the past that energizes persons.

At the heart of Christian faith is the *memoria passionis, mortis, et resurrectionis Jesu Christi*, a very definite narrative of concrete suffering, injustice, violence, and death, and of God's victory through that, a victory that grounds the promise of future freedom for all. This is *the* dangerous memory that guides the church's life. Remembering Jesus as the crucified one, now alive, brings into view all those who have followed his way. As noted repeatedly in the liturgy and in conciliar documents, the church "venerates the memory" of the saints and Mary, an action that leads to the praise of God and both evokes the challenge of their lives and enkindles hope among wayfarers (LG 50; SC 8, 104).[32] Their stories are interwoven with those of Jesus Christ.

When focused on saints whose names are known, narrative remembrance evokes praise of God, healthy pride, humor, warning, a host of useful encouragements. Each one lived discipleship of Jesus in a different way, responding to circumstances and the needs of their time according to their own brokenness and their own God-given insight and gifts. In spite of their sinfulness and personal quirks, there is not one in whom the elements of suffering in Christ and goodness toward others do not shine through. Telling their stories can galvanize faith. In the stories of Christian leaders of church or state who acted with compassion and justice, the power of present oppressors is judged. Remembrance of committed people who were publicly ridiculed and executed lifts up the memory of all whom the world has scorned but God has loved. And so on. Solidarity with these saints warms, challenges, and cheers believers along their own way in the present moment of history.

There is also a host of forgotten dead whose stories cannot be told because they are not known. These multitudes of unknown people, the true "anonymous Christians" whose love has effected what good there is in the world, are the majority of the saints. They are

---

32. Besides the conciliar documents, see the actual liturgical texts, such as the solemn blessing of the liturgy for the Feast of All Saints.

remembered officially on the Feast of All Saints, the most inclusive feast on the liturgical calendar. Among these unnamed millions who rest in unvisited graves are also those who were literally victims, those who like Jesus have been unjustly destroyed in history. Their remembrance on the Feast of All Saints is subversive. Proclaiming the livingness of the dead in God alerts tyrants to their impotence: They do not have the last word. Thus narrative remembrance of the saints and Mary presses for the transformation of personal and social/political life, as consciousness of pain suffered and freedom gained coupled with the eschatological surplus hidden in the history of the cross and resurrection works out in a practical way.

After a season of forgetting, the categories of solidarity, narrative, and memory drawn from the wellsprings of Scripture and liturgy are being pressed again into the service of Christian theology of the saints and Mary. Based on vital solidarity, the narrative remembrance of Jesus and with him of his friends both known and unknown articulates and mediates the experience of saving grace in the midst of the disasters of history. Inevitably critical of the banality of evil, this theology orients believers to praxis, to action on behalf of the reign of God in the face of a godless world. Protest, resistance, celebration, and hope in God who raises the dead become a way of life for the church, that community that cherishes and publicly witnesses to the dangerous memory of Jesus as God's presence and activity in this world.

Within this context of the solidarity of the church centered in Jesus Christ, remembrance of Mary and the saints serves important ecclesial functions. Saints are embodiments of the victory of God's grace (their eschatological function); models of diverse ways of discipleship (their exemplary function); manifestations of the presence of God (their sacramental function); and companions with the living in the worship of God (their liturgical function).[33] These are the main ways in which narrative remembrance in solidarity with the saints both results from and gives sparks to the praxis of the reign of God.

FUNCTIONS

Eschatological

The saints are those in whom the historical dialectic between sin and grace has been finally resolved in favor of grace. They struggled

---

33. These functions are synthesized from LG, chapters 5, 7, and 8. See Paul Molinari, *Saints: Their Place in the Church*, trans. Dominic Maruca (New York: Sheed and Ward, 1965); "Saints," in Karl Rahner, ed., *Sacramentum Mundi* (New York: Herder and Herder, 1968), 5:394–405.

along the path of living faith, bearing witness to love in the midst of their own brokenness. Now God has won in the blessed humanity of these persons, the beginning of the harvest. They personalize the future toward which the pilgrim church is traveling, beaming a signal of hope in a difficult world. So vital is this function of embodying the victory of God's grace that if there were no more new saints it would seriously call into question basic Christian doctrines, such as the sanctifying power of the Holy Spirit and the promise of future glory.[34]

The victory of God's grace is signaled in a particular way in the remembrance of Mary, the foremost example of the unmerited grace of God (Luther) and the first of the redeemed in Christ (Rahner). The dogmas of Mary's freedom from original sin (immaculate conception, which in positive terms signifies her original gracing) and of her eschatological victory in Christ (assumption) find vital interpretation within this framework. The former celebrates God's victories over the powers and principalities of this world as this woman comes into existence: In her very being through the mercy of God the grip of the Evil One is broken. The latter dogma recognizes God's creation of the new heaven and the new earth, inaugurated in the resurrection of Jesus, as coming to further fruition in this woman. In her very person she participates in the new life promised to the human race through the cross. Both dogmas take very seriously that life and death are a struggle; that the forces of evil are enormous; that only by the power of God can anyone ultimately prevail. Each recognizes the critical distance that history still has to travel before salvation is complete, at the same time that each revitalizes hope in the ongoing power of God, working through human persons such as this woman and overcoming the forces of evil. The dogmas are remembered as prophecy in the face of the untold history of suffering.

Exemplary

The saints' exemplary function results from the happy circumstance that redeeming grace can be lived out in a countless diversity of ways, giving rise to different "bright patterns of holiness" (LG 41). Particular saints have exercised a paradigmatic role in showing concretely how certain circumstances are to be met in the name of the gospel. Some have even pioneered new paths of discipleship, taking successful risks with living the gospel amid changing circumstances.

—————————————

34. The thesis of Patrick Sherry, *Spirit, Saints, Immortality* (Albany: State University of New York Press, 1984).

Their exemplarity results from their attractiveness to others who are moved to join them on the same path: "A saint is a person so grasped by a religious vision that it becomes central to his or her life in a way that radically changes the person and leads others to glimpse the value of that vision."[35] These historical persons of creativity who lived in the spirit and praxis of the Beatitudes (Matt. 5:1-12, gospel for the Feast of All Saints) serve to challenge the church to conversion from sin and apathy.

Mary's pattern of discipleship gives a particularly striking witness to the church. Biblical and theological scholarship as well as recent magisterial documents highlight discipleship as key to Mary's meaning. Paul VI describes Mary as a strong woman who experienced poverty and suffering, flight and exile. In the midst of these troubles she consistently gave active and responsible consent to the call of God, made courageous choices, and worked to strengthen the faith of others. Far from being repellently pious, she did not hesitate to proclaim that God vindicates the oppressed. She is proposed as an example to be imitated not because of the socio-economic circumstances of her life but because of her own active discipleship:

> She is held up as an example for the way in which, in her own particular life, she fully and responsibly accepted God's will (see Lk 2:38), because she heard the Word of God and acted on it, and because charity and a spirit of service were the driving force of her actions. She is worthy of imitation because she was the first and most perfect of Christ's disciples.[36]

Similarly, Mary's faith receives emphasis at the hands of John Paul II. Her faith presses the pilgrim church toward its own greater fidelity to Christ; her praise of God moves the church toward a preferential option for the poor in the spirit of her Magnificat.[37] In every retrieval Mary's exemplarity, as well as that of other saints, turns present disciples more faithfully toward the following of Christ.

Sacramental

In Jesus Christ first of all, and then in the saints who reflect his light like facets of a diamond, the presence of God whom no one has seen

---

35. Lawrence Cunningham, _The Meaning of Saints_ (San Francisco: Harper and Row, 1980), 65; this book is an excellent discussion of the exemplary function of the saints.

36. Paul VI, _Marialis Cultus_, translated as "Devotion to the Blessed Virgin Mary," in _The Pope Speaks_ 19 (1974/75): 49–87; no. 35.

37. John Paul II, _Redemptoris Mater_, in _Origins_ 16 (April 9, 1987): 35–37; nos. 12–19.

is made manifest. This sacramental function is rooted in the *imago Dei* doctrine, particularly as it developed in the early Christian East. If the glory of God is the human being fully alive, then in the saints God's glory shines through in most attractive, even poignant ways. In the poetic words of the Second Vatican Council, in the lives of those who shared our humanity and yet were transformed into successful images of Christ, God vividly manifests to us the divine presence and even the divine face, speaks a word to us, and gives us a sign of the kingdom to which we are powerfully drawn surrounded as we are by such a great cloud of witnesses (LG 51). Saints are a sign of God's presence, a symbol of the Holy One, a living parable. Through their lives God sends a message to the world, communicating something that helps unfold the covenant (Pius XI).[38] Through their love, living evidence of God is revealed to all people. This function is receiving increasing scrutiny in the case of Mary, who is interpreted as presenting, within a patriarchal tradition, the maternal face of God to the world.[39]

Liturgical

When the church assembles for public liturgy, explicit commemoration of Mary, the apostles, martyrs, and all the saints is always made in the eucharistic prayer.[40] These blessed folk are understood to join with the church on earth in singing the praise of divine majesty. Saints are colleagues in the joy of praising God, rounding out each limited earthly assembly by their variety and numbers, being from every tribe and tongue and people and nation and time. Furthermore, Christian tradition has believed that in *imitatio Christi*, who lives to make intercession for those who are drawing near (Heb. 7:25), saints pray for the church on earth: "We rejoice for them, they pray for us" (Augustine). Their intercession for sisters and brothers still on the way rises to God in and with the prayer of Christ. In

---

38. See Yves Congar, *Tradition and Traditions: An Historical and Theological Essay*, trans. M. Naseby and T. Rainborough (New York: Macmillan, 1967), 450–51. Congar holds that the saints have a special authority as bearers of the tradition.

39. Leonardo Boff, *The Maternal Face of God*; Edward Schillebeeckx, *Mary, Mother of the Redemption*, trans. N. D. Smith (New York: Sheed and Ward, 1964), 101–28; Andrew Greeley, *The Mary Myth: On the Femininity of God* (New York: Seabury, 1977); Yves Congar, *I Believe in the Holy Spirit*, trans. David Smith (New York: Seabury, 1983), 1:159–66; Elisabeth Schüssler Fiorenza, "Feminist Spirituality, Christian Identity, and Catholic Vision," in Carol Christ and Judith Plaskow, eds., *Womenspirit Rising* (San Francisco: Harper and Row, 1979), 136–48; Elizabeth Johnson, "Mary and the Female Face of God," *Theological Studies* 50 (1989): 500–526.

40. Louis Bouyer, *Theology and Spirituality of the Eucharistic Prayer*, trans. Charles Quinn (Notre Dame, Ind.: Notre Dame University Press, 1968), 227–43.

the midst of the suffering of the world, such celebrations of common praise of God and expressions of mutual care signal that spirits refuse to be crushed and hope refuses to be killed.

HONORING SAINTS AND MARY

In public eucharistic liturgy the church venerates the memory of Mary and the saints every day, and celebrates the story of their lives on special feast days throughout the year. Insofar as individual believers participate in the liturgical life of the church, they are de facto involved in honoring the saints; nor would it do to denounce or dissociate oneself from this public veneration. However, there is no obligation on an individual person to incorporate any practices of veneration into private prayer, though such devotion is officially encouraged as good and useful. In matters of spirituality each person is led by the Spirit in diverse ways, and has freedom to follow personal conscience on the way to God. In the history of the church neither conciliar nor papal teaching, nor canon law old or new, nor the opinion of theologians has ever made private veneration of the saints an obligatory matter.

This leaves a wide field for creativity. Corresponding roughly to the above-mentioned ecclesial functions of the saints, certain basic devotional acts are characteristic of the tradition. First and foremost is giving praise and thanks to God who has so gifted people that the victory of grace shines through in their lives. Saints are also venerated by following their example, not in a slavish way but by creatively appropriating their paths in the circumstances of a different time and place. Allowing present-day faith to be inspired and encouraged by the companionship of the saints likewise honors them. Being conscious of joining with them in that "most noble" expression of solidarity during common liturgical worship of God (LG 50) is yet another form of veneration. When done within a rightly ordered faith, each of these actions serves to enliven the following of Christ. All are ecumenically viable.

An ecumenical problem arises over the Catholic practice of invocation, or asking saints for their prayers or even direct favors.[41] Thinkers of the Reformation tradition have traditionally judged this

---

41. For discussion of this and other ecumenical issues, see Joseph Burgess, et al., eds., *The One Mediator, the Saints, and Mary—Lutherans and Catholics in Dialogue*, vol. 8 (Minneapolis: Augsburg Fortress Press, 1991); the common statement and background papers contain a wealth of material. See also Georg Kretschmar and René Laurentin, "The Cult of the Saints," in George Forell and James McCue, eds., *Confessing One Faith* (Minneapolis: Augsburg, 1982), 262–85; and *Liturgy* 5, no. 2 (1985): 5–112—this whole issue analyzes saints from an ecumenical viewpoint.

practice to be a distortion of the gospel, for by it believers seem to transfer to the saints the trust that they should place in the sole mediator, Jesus Christ. While abuses have at times been rampant, involving even superstitious beliefs, abuse does not necessarily render a practice totally illegitimate. In the Catholic perspective it is possible to ask for the saints' prayers if the participatory nature of Christ's mediation and the community model of interrelation among believers are kept fully in view, that is, if the saints are understood to be praying in and with Christ (LG 62).[42] Then it becomes clear that saints in heaven are not situated as intermediaries between believers and Jesus Christ, but are companions with believers in Christ. Calling on a saint in heaven to pray for us is a precise categorical expression of solidarity in Jesus Christ, through the ages and across various modes of human existence. It is not necessarily an act trying to supplement what seems insufficiently given by Christ, but an act of openness to God in community with those whom Jesus Christ has redeemed. Similar to what is done among the living, persons definitively with Christ are asked to remember before God their sisters and brothers who are still on the way. Thus the bond of solidarity is activated, and pilgrims are strengthened in the following of Jesus.

Since Marian devotion has been a notable characteristic of the Catholic tradition, a special set of guidelines was issued by Paul VI to direct its development in the postconciliar church (*Marialis Cultus* 25–37). The honoring of Mary should be set within a rightly ordered faith. Theologically, this means that her veneration should make clear the trinitarian structure of belief, giving full expression to the one God who creates and governs the world, to Jesus Christ the one Redeemer, and to the Holy Spirit who alone sanctifies. The connection between Mary and the church, ancient but newly emphasized by the Second Vatican Council, should likewise be in evidence. Practically, devotion is to be shaped by attentiveness to four other concerns. It should be biblical, rooted in the great themes of salvation history; liturgical, shaped by the seasons and feasts of the year; ecumenical, sensitive to any expression that would give rise to misunderstanding, especially regarding the centrality of Christ; and anthropological, attuned to cultural realities of time and place, among which today is the emergence of women as equal to men in all fields of public endeavor. Taken together, these norms insure

---

42. The prayer of the saints is but a sharing in the one unique source who is Jesus Christ; see Karl Rahner and J. B. Metz, *The Courage to Pray*, trans. Sarah O'Brien Twohig (New York: Crossroad, 1980); Elizabeth Johnson, "May We Invoke the Saints?" *Theology Today* 44 (1987): 32–52.

that honoring the memory of Mary, as well as other saints, remains coherent with the vital structure of Christian belief.

In the postconciliar church a fair number of traditional practices of veneration have diminished in importance. There is need for creativity on the part of the people and pastors of the church in doing for this age what forebears in the faith did for theirs, namely, renew inherited practices of devotion and shape new ones suitable to the temperament of the times. While biblical prayer vigils, reflective reading of Scripture, preaching, litanies, pilgrimage, and personal meditation have all been adapted in renewed ways to honoring Mary and the saints, none seems to have developed universal appeal. There is room for creative experimentation here.

Apparitions of Christ or the saints, but more usually of Mary, are also part of the devotional picture. There is no definitive church teaching about what actually happens during an apparition, and theologians interpret the phenomenon in various ways. Such an occurrence is a manifestation of the charismatic element in the church, a freely given moment in which the Spirit of God inspires the imagination of a person to receive a message from heaven.[43] Or again, it may be interpreted as a hermeneutic of the nearness of God to someone who is outside the normal official channels of access to the holy, such as the poor, the young, the uneducated, and rural women.[44] In any event, such happenings are considered by the church to be a matter of private, not public, revelation. As with other devotional matters, church approval does not bind consciences to believe in the apparition or its historicity; rather, it indicates that the practices and prayers associated with the happening are in accord with the gospel, and that participating in them will not lead one astray. As the U.S. Catholic bishops explain in their pastoral letter on Mary:

> Even when a private revelation has spread to the entire world, as in the case of Our Lady of Lourdes, and has been recognized in the liturgical calendar, the Church does not make mandatory the acceptance either of the original story or of particular forms of piety springing from it. With the Vatican Council we remind true lovers of Our Lady of the danger of superficial sentiment and vain credulity. Our faith does not seek new gospels, but leads us to know the excellence of the Mother of God and moves us to a filial love toward our Mother and to the imitation of her virtues.[45]

---

43. Karl Rahner, *Visions and Prophecies*, trans. E. Henkey and R. Strachan (New York: Herder and Herder, 1963).

44. Schillebeeckx, *Mary, Mother of the Redemption*, 131–75.

45. U.S. Catholic Bishops, *Behold Your Mother: Woman of Faith*, in *Catholic Mind* 72 (1974): 26–64; no. 100.

CONCLUSION

In the present checkered situation a number of issues remain theologically unresolved. Ecumenically there is continuing difficulty over the practice of invocation, the two modern Marian dogmas, and the relative importance of Scripture and tradition, the phenomenon of Mary and the saints being largely a development of tradition. Superstitious practices that render the saints rivals of Christ do persist and present a pastoral challenge. Questions are pressed about the adequacy of the process of canonization that through its criteria and its demand for money and time continuously favors clergy over lay people, men over women, Europeans over non-Europeans; the same criticism is raised with regard to the liturgical calendar. In the midst of these difficulties, the Catholic tradition of Mary and the saints is a great resource for developing habits of the heart that cherish community, greatly needed in contemporary Western culture that so emphasizes the isolated individual. Sharing with the living dead in the Spirit of Christ expands consciousness as we acknowledge the graced existence of believers other than ourselves and receive benefit in company with them on the road of discipleship. The basic theological and liturgical intuition that has carried this tradition knows that Jesus Christ is never alone but is surrounded by a whole range of friends, living and dead. A theology of the saints and Mary may be summed up in the beautiful preface for the Feast of All Saints:

> Around your throne the saints, our brothers and sisters,
> sing your praise forever.
> Their glory fills us with joy,
> and their communion with us in your church
> gives us inspiration and strength
> as we hasten on our pilgrimage of faith, eager to meet them.
> With their great company and all the angels
> we praise your glory as we cry out with one voice:
> Holy, holy, holy...

FOR FURTHER READING

SAINTS

Brown, Peter. *The Cult of the Saints: Its Rise and Function in Latin Christianity.* London: SCM Press, 1981.

An enlightening study using the method of social history, which links the emergence of the cult of the saints to the cultural context of late antiquity.

Burgess, Joseph, et al., eds. *The One Mediator, the Saints, and Mary—Lutherans and Catholics in Dialogue.* Vol. 8. Minneapolis: Augsburg Fortress Press, 1991.

The common statement of this ecumenical dialogue, including points of continuing divergence and convergence, and supported by extensive background studies in Scripture, history, church teaching, and theology.

Cunningham, Lawrence. *The Meaning of Saints.* San Francisco: Harper and Row, 1980.

A systematic presentation replete with historical insight; focuses on the significance of saints as exemplars.

Liturgy 5, no. 2 (1985): 5–112.

An issue of this journal dealing with liturgical and devotional aspects of veneration of saints; written from an ecumenical perspective.

Perham, Michael. *The Communion of Saints.* London: SPCK, 1980.

A theological study particularly rich in patristic references as well as discussion of later developments in the Anglican tradition.

Rahner, Karl. "The Church of the Saints." In *Theological Investigations.* Baltimore: Helicon Press, 1967, 3:91–104.

A synopsis of his theological position and his reasons for holding it.

Sherry, Patrick. *Spirit, Saints, Immortality.* Albany: State University of New York Press, 1984.

A philosophical study that connects these three elements in a foundational way.

MARY

Brennan, Walter. *The Sacred Memory of Mary.* New York: Paulist, 1988.

A brief, thoughtful work that analyzes biblical and devotional material with the help of the category of living memory (anamnesis).

Brown, Raymond, et al., eds. *Mary in the New Testament.* Philadelphia: Fortress Press; and New York: Paulist, 1978.

An important ecumenical scripture study that uses historical-critical methods to deal with every New Testament verse concerning Mary.

Donnelly, Doris, ed. *Mary, Woman of Nazareth: Biblical and Theological Perspectives.* New York: Paulist, 1989.

A collection that probes the significance of Mary from contemporary perspectives; following an assessment of the Second Vatican Council's teaching, it includes essays on popular belief, justice, and evangelization in the Americas in addition to treatments from political and feminist theology and from scriptural, historical-critical, and symbolic points of view.

Gebara, Ivone, and Maria Clara Bingemer. *Mary: Mother of God, Mother of the Poor.* Trans. Phillip Berryman. Maryknoll, N.Y.: Orbis Books, 1989.

A study of Marian doctrine and devotion in the Latin American context; written from a liberation and feminist theological point of view.

Graef, Hilda. *Mary: A History of Doctrine and Devotion.* 2 vols. 1963. Reprint. Westminster, Md.: Christian Classics, 1985.

A compendium of historical data that traces the rise of Marian beliefs through theologians, prayers, and church teachings.

Jegen, Carol F., ed. *Mary according to Women.* Kansas City: Leaven Press, 1985.

Interpretations of traditional aspects of Catholic belief and veneration in the light of the experience of women.

Küng, Hans, and Jürgen Moltmann, eds. *Mary in the Churches.* Entire issue of *Concilium* 168. New York: Seabury, 1983.

Succinct studies of biblical material, followed by ecumenical discussion and a probing of new directions.

Rahner, Karl. *Mary, Mother of the Lord.* Trans. W. J. O'Hara. New York: Herder and Herder, 1963.

A series of meditations undergirded by his theological approach, which links Mary to the mystery of grace in communion with all human beings.

9

SACRAMENTS

SACRAMENTS

9.1

Sacraments in General

9.1

Sacraments in General

Regis A. Duffy

LIFE OF THE CHURCH—
SOURCE OF SACRAMENTAL DEFINITIONS

To speak of "sacraments" in a general way is to deprive them of their normal setting, the liturgical life of the church. The value of such an approach, however, is to describe the shared characteristics of all sacramental actions and thus indirectly note the unique purpose of individual sacraments. *Liturgy* is a more encompassing term than *sacrament* and refers to the whole range of actions and words of praise and thanksgiving that the church gives to God. Sacraments are highly focused action-words within this larger liturgical context.

183

A theological methodology for addressing the sacraments understood within the liturgy of the church is suggested in the fifth-century classic axiom, "The law of praying establishes the law of believing" (Denzinger-Schönmetzer, *Enchiridion Symbolorum* [hereafter DS], 246).[1] In its most fundamental meaning this axiom sums up how God's unearned redemptive action and the church's prayerful and grateful response have provided essential teaching moments in the life of the community. When this axiom is applied to sacraments, it indicates how the church's self-understanding as expressed in sacramental action and articulated in doctrinal statements has been developed and deepened. (The actual celebration of the eucharist, for example, gradually clarified the redemptive meaning of Christ's death for us.) The contemporary corollary is that God continues to teach the church through its sacramental practice.

In the recent theological discussion of how liturgy is a source for theology, this axiom has received renewed attention. The Eastern church, when true to its classical heritage, assigns the starting point of theology to the faith experience of the church, founded on the "epiphany" of the very events that the liturgy celebrates. Thus, the church itself is defined in terms of its liturgy as "the witness and the participant of the saving *event* of Christ, of the new life in the Holy Spirit, of the presence in 'this world' of the Kingdom to come."[2] In the Western traditions, the question is usually phrased in more systematic terms, but the concern is the same: Does one find theological formulations confirmed in liturgical tradition, or rather is not liturgy as symbolic language a necessary prelude to the second order of theological reflection?[3]

This same discussion might be rephrased in terms of the relation of theory and praxis in theological discourse. Several models of theological reflection can be proposed according to the primacy

---

1. "Legem credendi statuat lex supplicandi." The more familiar form as cited by Pius XII (DS 3792) is "lex orandi lex credendi." I concur with Paul De Clerck's assertion that the axiom does not simply refer to liturgical texts but to their testing point, the Word of God (see his "'Lex orandi, lex credendi': Sens originel et avatars historiques d'un adage equivoque," *Questions Liturgiques* 59 [1978]: 193–212), but I begin from the nature of justification (to be discussed in the section on the sacraments of initiation).

2. Alexander Schmemann, a particularly eloquent exponent of this tradition, in "Liturgy and Theology," *The Greek Orthodox Theological Review* 17 (1972): 86–100, here 91.

3. See the discussion occasioned by Geoffrey Wainwright's *Doxology: The Praise of God in Worship, Doctrine, and Life* (New York: Oxford University Press, 1980), with responses by David Power, "Doxology: The Praise of God in Worship, Doctrine, and Life," *Worship* 51 (1981): 61–69; Aidan Kavanagh, *On Liturgical Theology* (New York: Pueblo, 1984), 91–95, 123–50; and Catherine LaCugna, "Can Liturgy Ever Again Become a Source for Theology?" *Studia Liturgica* 19 (1989): 1–13.

they give to theory or praxis.[4] In view of what has already been said about the *lex orandi* as a source of theology, sacrament is a praxis in search of a theory. In a critical correlational model applied to sacrament, religious experience is the source of an authentic and shared Christian praxis that is symbolized in worship and that engenders a critical and clarifying theology. One test of such a theology is its ability to illuminate and critique its praxial source as well as being engaged by it.

Any definition of *sacrament*, then, must reflect this gradual ecclesial awareness of God's purposeful action among us. Some dimensions of this awareness would be: (1) the gratuitous and enabling character of God's offer of salvation as proclaimed by the gospel Word; (2) the ecclesial context within which sacrament is celebrated; (3) sacramental healing and strengthening as directed both to the effective mission of the church and to the individual's redemptive need; (4) the trinitarian dimension of all sacrament; (5) the paschal mystery; (6) the action of the Holy Spirit as crucial; and (7) the eschatological thrust of all sacrament.

A sacrament, then, is a presence-filled event in which God gratuitously enables us to welcome the message of salvation, to enter more deeply into the paschal mystery, and to receive gratefully that transforming and healing power that gathers us as the community of God's Son so as to announce the reign of God in the power of the Spirit. In the history of the church's sacramental praxis and theory, some dimensions of the definition of sacrament have usually been highlighted or obscured, reflecting the life of the church in a certain epoch and situation.

GOD'S LIFE AND ACTION—
SOURCE OF SACRAMENTAL EVENT

As a general rule, sacramental praxis and theology accurately reflect the operational and theoretical ideas held by the community and individuals about God's life as Trinity, and the corresponding ideas about Christ and the Holy Spirit. Recently there has been a call for a reexamination of the trinitarian basis of sacramental life.[5] Without attempting even to survey some of the sacramental corollaries of any

---

4. Matthew Lamb, "The Theory-Praxis Relationship," *Catholic Theological Society of America, Proceedings* 31 (1976): 149–78.

5. Lothar Lies, "Trinitätsvergessenheit Gegenwärtiger Sakramententheologie," *Zeitschrift für katholische Theologie* 105 (1983): 415–29; Edward Kilmartin, *Christian Liturgy. I. Theology* (Kansas City: Sheed and Ward, 1988), 98–179.

particular trinitarian theology, it is important to note that Christian worship uniquely symbolizes God's inner life, self-communication, and redemptive purposes: "A commonplace of contemporary trinitarian theology is the priority it grants to the narrative and symbolic discourse of Christian worship and proclamation over the leaner, conceptual discourse of theological theory itself."[6] (The sign of the cross in the name of the Trinity in all sacramental celebrations, e.g., symbolizes much more than can be conceptualized.) In brief, communal and individual sacramental experience cannot be separated from the self-communicating presence of God.[7] But the very nature of God's presence is such that sacrament is rooted in an experience of the mystery of God.

God's offer of salvation, as celebrated and appropriated in the sacraments, is concretized in the work of Jesus and the Holy Spirit. Athanasius captures the complementary nature of this work: The Word became flesh so that we might receive the Holy Spirit—God became a bearer of flesh so that we might become bearers of the Spirit.[8] In turn, reflection on the New Testament witness to the relation of the Spirit and the redemptive mission of Jesus enriches our understanding of the relational unity of the three in God.[9] Scripture scholars have long noted the systematic implications of the brief triadic patterns in the Pauline and Johannine writings.[10] Moreover, the explicit trinitarian expressions in the baptismal formulas of Matthew 28:19 and Didache 7:1–3 certainly reflect an early Christian awareness of trinitarian belief.[11]

The Trinity, as the doxological tenor of the New Testament indicates, refers to the dynamic unity and clearly differentiated self-

---

6. Edmund Dobbin, "Trinity," in Joseph Komonchak, Mary Collins, and Dermot Lane, eds., *The New Dictionary of Theology* (Wilmington, Del.: Glazier, 1987), 1046.

7. As Dobbin notes, a characteristic of much contemporary trinitarian theology is to avoid a separation of the immanent from the economic Trinity (ibid., 1058).

8. Athanasius *De incarn.* 8 (*Patrologia Graeca*, ed. Migne [hereafter PG], 26, 996C), as cited in Robert Hotz, *Sakramente im Wechselspiel zwischen Ost und West* (Zurich: Benziger, 1979), 223.

9. Kilmartin, e.g., develops a closely argued parallel between the processional and bestowal models of trinitarian theology and the "descending" (Logos) and "ascending" (Spirit) christologies of the New Testament (*Christian Liturgy*, 100–179, esp. 109).

10. Raymond Brown, *The Gospel according to John XIII–XXI* (Garden City, N.Y.: Doubleday, 1970), 642–43; Hans Conzelmann, *I Corinthians* (Philadelphia: Fortress Press, 1975), 207.

11. For the connections between the two citations, see Jean-Paul Audet, *La Didache: Instruction des Apôtres* (Paris: Gabalda, 1958), 361–65. Since the seminal work of Fritzleo Lentzen-Deis on the "deute-vision" (meaning-vision) in the New Testament accounts of Jesus' baptism, any triadic or trinitarian implications have to be more carefully nuanced; see his *Die Taufe Jesu nach den Synoptikern: Literarkritische und gattungsgeschichtliche Untersuchungen* (Frankfurt-am-Main: J. Knecht, 1970).

communication and self-revelation of God's aware love. Within this perspective, it is easier to appreciate the true nature of the justifying work of Christ that the sacramental event symbolizes and to retrieve the unique role of the Spirit in realizing the reign of God and in being the essential ground for all prayer to God (Rom. 8).

A systematic theology of sacrament, then, must take seriously the connection between the mystery of the economic Trinity and its symbolization in liturgy.[12] This systematic starting point provides a better appreciation of Christ as the basic sacrament and of the epicletic or Spirit-endowed character of all sacramental activity.

CHRIST AND THE SPIRIT
IN THE SACRAMENTAL EVENT

When we speak of Christ as the symbol and sacrament of God's presence, we are drawing out the implications of the trinitarian belief.[13] To clarify this truth within its New Testament context, two complementary christologies must be recognized. Logos ("descending") christology begins with the redemptive task of Jesus and the ensuing mission of the Holy Spirit. Spirit ("ascending") christology emphasizes the sanctification of the humanity of Jesus "created by the Godhead as such," that humanity having been elevated "to union with the Word who assumes it."[14] If we respect the message of both christologies, the action of the Spirit clarifies our understanding of Christ as the basic sacrament of God's presence.

When the Second Vatican Council speaks of "the sublime sacrament of the whole Church" (*Sacrosanctum Concilium* [hereafter SC] 5), it assumes that the Spirit in some way connects Christ and the church.[15] Since the council, however, there has been a retrieval and development of the theology of the Holy Spirit that has permitted us to value more deeply this connection. If the role of the Spirit in sanctifying the humanity of Jesus is recognized, then the similar

---

12. Kilmartin, *Christian Liturgy*, 101–2.

13. Francis Schüssler Fiorenza, *Foundational Theology: Jesus and the Church* (New York: Crossroad, 1984), 95.

14. Kilmartin, *Christian Liturgy*, 161–62; also 214–15. As Kilmartin notes, traditional Scholastic theology does not accord a personal mission to the Spirit in the economy of salvation (ibid., 162).

15. Fiorenza, *Foundational Theology*, 103. As Fiorenza indicates, this is the position of Walter Kasper (but for reasons somewhat different from those of Kilmartin). Two other theologians' differing justifications for this same position (Hans Küng, Edward Schillebeeckx) are also given (103–6).

task of anointing the church for the mission of Christ is more easily appreciated.

Once again, the best source for measuring the import of Spirit christology is the liturgy itself. Neville Clark, in fact, has argued that those communities that had a clear epiclesis (calling down of the Spirit in a sacramental action) in their eucharist were more open to an ascending christology (once again, *lex orandi lex credendi*).[16] The epiclesis in any sacramental action reflects the Pauline teaching of the Spirit grounding the prayer of the worshiping community (Rom. 8:26-27) and the patristic conviction that "whatever the Holy Spirit has touched is hallowed and changed."[17]

Sacramental theology derives a basic principle from the classic epicletic patterns of the eucharistic prayers in which the celebrant pleads for the coming of the Spirit over the community as well as the gifts that they may become the body of Christ. That principle, understood as a corollary of Spirit christology, can be expressed in this way: The Spirit sanctifies in every sacramental action so that the gathered church may more truly be the body of Christ and thus do the work of Christ. To assess the power of such sanctification and transformation in the sacramental event a strong Spirit christology is necessary.

THE CHURCH AS SACRAMENT

Once Christ is seen as the "primal sacramental word of God," Karl Rahner's description of the church as "the abiding presence of that primal sacramental word of definitive grace, . . . the truly fundamental sacrament, the well-spring of the sacraments" rings true.[18] The immediate sacramental corollary can be expressed in a Pauline paraphrase: as Christ, so the church. As Christ is anointed for redemptive service, so is his church. The mission of Christ is the mission of the church.

A practical test of this truth is how the institution of the sacraments is explained. Over the centuries, this question has been addressed in several ways. Probably the oldest explanation of sacra-

---

16. Neville Clark, "Spirit Christology in the Light of Eucharistic Theology," *Heythrop Journal* 23 (1982): 270–84. He cites some excellent examples in which christological controversies reflect eucharistic theologies. See also Edward Kilmartin, "The Active Role of Christ and the Holy Spirit in the Sanctification of the Eucharistic Elements," *Theological Studies* 45 (1984): 225–53.

17. Cyril of Jerusalem *Mystagogical Catechesis* 7.

18. Karl Rahner, *The Church and the Sacraments* (New York: Herder and Herder, 1963), 18.

mental institution begins with the understanding of sacrament as the "mystery of God" (*musterion*). This mystery is experienced in the whole work of redemption. The privileged symbol of this redemptive mystery expressed sacramentally is the blood and water pouring from the opened side of Christ on the cross (John 19:34). John Chrysostom and Augustine, as many of the church fathers, saw the source of the eucharist and initiation in this scene.[19] The advantage of this approach is to root the sacramental existence and purpose within the total mystery of redemption.

With the early Scholastic period, the question of institution assumed new importance and a different direction. The question of the number of sacraments is a specific corollary to the question of institution. A survey of the eleventh and early twelfth centuries shows a bewildering variety of positions on the question with the symbolic value of numbers playing some role.[20]

Wendelin Knoch has suggested three stages in the clarification of the question during the early medieval period.[21] First, other celebrations were considered "sacraments" if they met the criteria evidenced in baptism and eucharist. Second, institution was examined within the context of christology since the sacraments of the church must be those of Christ.[22] The so-called major sacraments (baptism and eucharist) are grounded in the very redemptive life and death of Christ himself while penance and orders are sacraments of "God the legislator," marriage is the sacrament of "God the creator," and "extreme unction" and confirmation are "apostolic sacraments."[23] The third stage recognized the self-awareness of the church as directly connected with salvation history. The unity of the church of Christ gives redemptive context for the multiplicity of sacraments. As Knoch points out, it was during this period that the church was freeing itself from secular control and reestablishing an ecclesiology in which a unified sacramental system was crucial. In the mid–twelfth century Peter Lombard specified seven sacraments in his influential *Sentences*,[24] and he defined them according to whether they are a remedy against sin and give grace (e.g., bap-

---

19. Josef Finkenzeller, *Die Lehre von den Sakramenten im allgemeinen: Von der Schrift bis zur Scholastik* (Freiburg: Herder, 1980), 22–23.

20. Ibid., 72–74.

21. Wendelin Knoch, *Die Einsetzung der Sakramente durch Christus: Eine Untersuchung der Frühscholastik von Anselm von Laon bis zu Wilhelm von Auxerre* (Müntser: Aschendorff, 1983), 411–14.

22. Ibid., 296.

23. Ibid., 415.

24. Peter Lombard *Sentences* IV d.2c.1.

tism), or simply a remedy (e.g., marriage), or support us in virtue and grace (e.g., eucharist and orders).[25]

Because Peter Lombard's *Sentences* provided the basic text for most theologians' commentaries in the high and late medieval periods, the sevenfold numbering of the sacraments was a given, though the reasoning for this may not follow Lombard's explanation. Bonaventure, for example, retrieved the classical notion of sacraments as "medicine" and then distinguished therapeutic approaches.[26] Thomas Aquinas, on the other hand, developed an analogy between the natural life with its stages from birth to death and its supernatural counterpart.[27] Thomas also taught that all sacraments are directly rooted in Christ, though specific sacramental actions and words are found in the apostolic tradition that the church passes on.[28]

The long history of this discussion might be summarized as either a search for continuity with the historical Jesus or with the risen Lord in his church.[29] In the sessions at Trent in the sixteenth century the problem of tracing every sacrament to the direct historical institution by Jesus was acknowledged. In a more developmental approach, certain sacraments (e.g., baptism, eucharist, ordination, penance) are regarded as expressing the sacramental nature of the church and, therefore, are described as divinely instituted by Christ.[30] A contemporary hermeneutical approach would insist that divine institution takes its meaning from the normative New Testament description of the relation between Jesus and the church.[31] Within this perspective, the overall redemptive purposes of Christ continue to shape the concrete sacramental actions of the church.

The more pressing theological question, then, is *not how but why* Jesus can be said to be the source of the sacramental life of the church. As suggested above, sacramental healing and strengthening cannot be separated from the effective mission of the church to the whole world: "The fundamental mission of the Church is that, having accepted a share in the life of the Trinitarian God, it proclaims the new reality it experiences in this life and invites all of humanity

---

25. Finkenzeller, *Die Lehre*, 123.

26. Bonaventure *Sent.* IV d. 2, a. 1, q. 3, concl. See Finkenzeller, *Die Lehre*, 162–63.

27. Thomas Aquinas *Summa Theologiae* III, q. 65, a. 1 c. See Finkenzeller, *Die Lehre*, 165–66.

28. Thomas Aquinas *Summa Theologiae* III, q. 64, a. 2 c. See Finkenzeller, *Die Lehre*, 175–76.

29. For an overview of theological positions, see Alexandre Ganoczy, *An Introduction to Catholic Sacramental Theology* (New York: Paulist, 1984), 43–50.

30. But, as Fiorenza points out, this approach has substituted "irreversibility" for "permanency" and thus causes other problems (*Foundational Theology*, 166–68).

31. Ibid., 168–70.

to join in the experience."[32] This larger viewpoint provides a basis for recognizing the ecclesial as well as the personal dimensions of every sacrament and for discussing the number of the sacraments.

When the Council of Trent named seven sacraments as having been instituted by Christ (DS 1601), it approved a theological consensus that was comparatively recent.[33] The question of the number of sacraments, as such, did not occupy the attention of theologians to any extent until well after the time of Augustine. In the eleventh and twelfth centuries theologians seemed to sometimes be using symbolic numbers in their lists of the sacraments.[34] As noted above, Thomas Aquinas's argument that the seven sacraments reflect the stages of life eventually gained theological favor. With the Second Vatican Council's retrieval of the church as sacrament, the seven sacraments are better contextualized as "representative of the deepest concentration of the sacramentality latent in all church activity."[35] That sacramentality, shaped by the mission of Christ, lends new depth to our appreciation of each sacrament.

FOUR STAGES IN THE UNDERSTANDING OF SACRAMENT

One approach in attempting to trace the historical evolution of "sacrament" is to ask how influential symbolic thinking was in the sacramental definitions of an epoch. Symbolic thinking is characterized by a profound respect for God's mystery and a grateful wonder for our access to participation in that mystery. Symbolic thinking is concerned more with the larger purposes of God's mystery as revealed in Christ than with the impossible task of explaining how a mystery works. Four stages of the historical understanding of sacrament will be discussed: (1) the Augustinian synthesis; (2) the medieval synthesis; (3) the Reformation challenge; and (4) the contemporary retrieval. The overall historical direction of this understanding might be characterized as a movement from earlier symbolic thinking, to a medieval instrumental thinking, to a partial retrieval of the symbolic during the Reformation and Counter Reformation, to

---

32. John Coleman, "Mission of the Church and Justice," in James Provost, ed., *The Church as Mission* (Washington, D.C.: Canon Law Society, 1984), 132.

33. For earlier historical developments, see Knoch, *Die Einsetzung der Sakramente durch Christus*, and Finkenzeller, *Die Lehre*.

34. Finkenzeller, *Die Lehre*, 73; see also Michael Seybold, "Die Siebenzahl der Sakramente," *Münchener Theologische Zeitschrift* 27 (1976): 113–41, for his treatment of how Trent's discussions were influenced by the symbolic character of numbers.

35. Kilmartin, *Christian Liturgy*, 280.

a more thoroughgoing contemporary retrieval of the symbolic. Just as the socio-cultural context of New Testament texts has become a significant factor in recent interpretation, so must that same context be taken into account in assessing the historical evolution of sacrament.[36]

THE AUGUSTINIAN SYNTHESIS

The New Testament is more likely to speak of "mystery" where we would employ the general notion of sacrament. In Paul's writings "mystery" is dynamic saving work of God that is revealed in Christ and that has already touched the lives of those who believe (e.g., 1 Cor. 2:7-10; Col. 1:26-27).[37] On the other hand, the New Testament context for references to baptism and eucharist is the relevance of Jesus for the life of the church.[38] In its celebrations of baptism and eucharist, as noted above, the early church clarified its understanding of the redemptive meaning of the death and resurrection of Jesus. Paul's articulation of what it means to be "the body of Christ" cannot be separated from his own or his hearers' eucharistic experience. In brief, the New Testament church's sacramental celebrations always clarified the paschal mystery of Christ's dying and rising and enabled it to enter more readily into that mystery.

When at the beginning of the third century Tertullian wrote *On Baptism*, one of the first extant monographs on sacramental theology, he demonstrated a complex and rich understanding of sacrament that he developed in subsequent writings. Not only did he translate the biblical idea of "mystery" by *sacramentum* (probably already in use from the early African Latin translation of the Scriptures), but he also associated the term with the complementary notions of individual sacraments and the analogous military oath. Tertullian is the first in a distinguished line of North African theologians (the line includes Cyprian and Augustine) who gave a definitive shape to the sacramental theology of the Western church. The salient char-

---

36. See, e.g., Wayne Meeks, *The First Urban Christians: The Social World of the Apostle Paul* (New Haven: Yale University Press, 1983); John Bossy, *Christianity in the West 1400–1700* (Oxford: Oxford University Press, 1985).

37. See Finkenzeller, *Die Lehre*, 10–13; Leonardo Boff, *Die Kirche als Sakrament im Horizont der Welterfahrung* (Paderborn: Bonifacius, 1972), 49–82.

38. These statements are not a contradiction of Finkenzeller's axiom that when the New Testament uses "mystery" there is no reference to a specific sacrament (*Die Lehre*, 10), but an emphasis on the positive connections between mystery and sacrament. Other sources still useful for the historical development of sacrament are Louis Villette, *Foi et sacrement*, 2 vols. (Paris: Bloud and Gay, 1959–64), and J. de Ghellinck, *Pour l'histoire du mot "sacramentum" I. Les Antenicéens* (Louvain: Spicilegium Sacrum Lovaniense, 1924).

acteristics of this African theology are: (1) a strong ecclesiological concern; (2) an expectation of unwavering witness in the face of persecution; (3) a spiritual honesty in sacramental participation; and (4) a reflective orthodoxy as a response to heresy.

These characteristics are reflected in the practical sacramental concerns of Cyprian and, in turn, determined the emphasis of some of Augustine's sacramental thinking.[39] Augustine did not set out to develop a systematic theology of sacrament but to respond to the Donatist and Pelagian heresies and to deal with the difficult pastoral situation of the post-Constantinian church in the unique North African situation. Rather than cite his multiple sacramental definitions, their meaning should be contextualized within the ecclesial problems of his time.

When Augustine gave philosophical descriptions of sacrament, he usually noted that (1) physical realities serve as a doorway to spiritual ones and (2) that there must be some connection between the sign and what is signified.[40] Neo-Platonic thought with its strong dualism between the material and the spiritual and with its persistent preference for unseen realities rather than the deceptive flux of the seen had been a major factor in Augustine's intellectual formation. With his conversion came a marked awareness of the eschatological thrust of all time and creation. These two contradictory influences were the basis of a new synthesis of symbol in which "sign" is grounded in God's creation and has an eschatological task to perform.

Signs point to another reality and by their impact on our senses make us think of another reality. In addition to natural signs (e.g., smoke = fire), there are conventional signs (e.g., words) that effectively address our attention. When Augustine spoke of a sacrament as a "sacred sign" and "visible words," he presumed and also transcended this philosophical background. Unlike others signs, sacraments encompass God's mystery and its saving purposes. Sacramental "reality" (*res*) is, then, the paschal mystery dynamically bridging the distance between ourselves and God.

At this juncture, it is also important to remember that much of Augustine's writing on *sacramentum* as the external sign cannot be separated from his insistence (against the Donatists) about the perduring nature of that sign (a topic I will return to in the sections

---

39. See Walter Simonis, *Ecclesia Visibilis et Invisibilis: Untersuchungen zur Ekklesiologie und Sakramentenlehre in der afrikanischen Tradition von Cyprian bis Augustinus* (Frankfurt: J. Knecht, 1970).

40. Finkenzeller, *Die Lehre*, 39–43.

on initiation).[41] In response to his own question about the power of baptismal water to cleanse the heart, Augustine answered that such cleansing occurs because the enacted Word has not only been said but also believed.[42] With these connections firmly in place, Augustine made the crucial connections between the personal and ecclesial participation in sacrament.

When he then developed these insights in symbolic thinking, he could easily retain, e.g., the Pauline understanding of the body of Christ as both sacrament and church and urge his hearers "to be what they receive."[43] When Augustine responded to the one-sided Donatist emphasis on the necessity of ecclesial and ministerial holiness, he countered with (1) a notion of a sacramental community, unified by the Spirit in a responsive faith,[44] that anticipates an eschatological society of saints;[45] (2) a distinction between the "use" and "fruit" (_res_) of a sacrament: "The integrity of the sacrament is everywhere recognized, though it will not avail for the irrevocable remission of sins outside the unity of the Church";[46] and (3) an insistence on the perduring nature of certain sacraments that are not repeated.[47] Augustine's symbolic thinking was able to include the complexity of God's saving presence in Christ, the flawed but sacramental character of the ecclesial community, and the crucial distinction between a sacramental event and its fruitful, intentional appropriation. As we shall see, anything less than symbolic thinking cannot account for this complexity of sacrament.

---

41. See the important articles of Nicholas H. Haring, "Berengar's Definitions of Sacramentum and Their Influence on Mediaeval Sacramentology," _Medieval Studies_ 10 (1948): 109–46; idem, "The Augustinian Axiom: Nulli Sacramento Injuria Facienda Est," _Medieval Studies_ 16 (1954): 87–117.

42. Augustine _Tract. in Eu Joan_ 80.3 (as cited by Finkenzeller, _Die Lehre_, 43). Again, see Haring's demonstration of how the earlier medieval theologians were divided on Augustine's meaning of "Word" in this citation ("Berengar's Definitions," 118–21).

43. Augustine "Sermon 262."

44. This distinction allows Augustine to protect the objective and unearned nature of sacrament in a sinful church while recognizing that holiness, as the _res_ (reality), does demand a change of heart.

45. Yves Congar, _L'Église de Saint Augustin à l'époque moderne_ (Paris: Cerf, 1970), 16–17.

46. Augustine _On Baptism_ 4.2–2.

47. "And as the baptized person, if he depart from the unity of the church, does not thereby lose the sacrament of baptism, so also he who is ordained, if he depart from the unity of the church, does not lose the sacrament of conferring baptism. For neither sacrament may be wronged" (_On Baptism_ 1.2). Augustine's regular analogy for this truth is the military tattoo that provides an external, ineradicable identification of a soldier's oath to the emperor.

THE MEDIEVAL SYNTHESIS

The early medieval history of sacrament is complex and, at times, bewildering.[48] For our limited purposes, one crucial change must be noted. Augustine's sacramental theology allowed for the complexity of God's mystery and the redemptive results that were intended. One of the striking characteristics of the early medieval period is that Augustine's terminology was being used without his well-founded sense of symbol or his highly developed ecclesiology. This problem is seen in the eleventh-century debates of Berengar and his opponents on the eucharist.[49]

Berengar retrieved Augustine's notion of the visible reality (*sacramentum*) and the invisible fruit that it signifies (*res sacramenti*).[50] This distinction is easily applied to the water of baptism and its redemptive effect but becomes problematic when applied to the eucharist. Berengar could not seem to explain convincingly the connection between the bread/wine and the real presence of Christ because without symbolic thinking, there is a weakened link between the visible elements and the eucharistic presence.[51]

As a response to Berengar's inadequate explanations, his opponents introduced two important developments: (1) the Aristotelian category of "substance" in order to safeguard the real presence in the eucharist; and (2) the distinction *sacramentum et res* to specify the total symbolic reality (in the case of the eucharist, the real presence).[52] "Substance" is a different and less complete way of referring to reality than symbolic activity offers and, in the popular understanding, can too easily be reduced to a physical reality. *Sacramentum et res* becomes a necessary distinction only because for many people "symbol" (*in figura*) is not connected to reality (*veritas*), which is limited in their minds to the physical. Above all, in lieu of symbolic thinking, *there is an inevitable tendency to ask how a sacrament works rather than why a sacrament is given.* Perhaps the most telling sign of this underlying problem is the popular eucharistic piety of this period

---

48. See especially Damien Van Den Eynde, *Les définitions des sacrements pendant la première période de la théologie scolastique (1050–1240)* (Rome: Antonianum, 1950).

49. See Haring, "Berengar's Definitions."

50. Ironically, it is Berengar who will popularize the Augustinian definition of sacrament as the "visible form of invisible grace" (see Finkenzeller, *Die Lehre*, 72).

51. It should be noted that most of Berengar's contemporaries seem to have been influenced by the antisymbolic historical approach to the eucharist that the ninth-century theologian Paschasius had popularized; see Gary Macy, *The Theologies of the Eucharist in the Early Scholastic Period* (Oxford: Clarendon, 1984), 31–35.

52. Compare the oaths of 1059 and that of 1079 that Berengar was made to sign where the term is introduced into the text (ibid., 36–37).

that often substituted eucharistic miracle stories of doubtful value for sacramental participation.[53]

When Thomas Aquinas (d. 1274) dealt with the general idea of sacrament in his later work, he did not provide a developed ecclesiology as its context.[54] As a result, certain connections that are easily made in Augustine's sacramental theology are more difficult to make in that of Aquinas. While retaining the patristic notion of sacrament as "medicine,"[55] this classic analogy was altered in such a way that sacrament was now seen as an efficient cause of spiritual health. In explaining sacrament as "sign," Aquinas had four sets of traditional definitions of sacrament to deal with: those of Augustine, those of Isidore of Seville, those of the ninth century (Paschasius and Rabanus Maurus), and those of the twelfth century (Abelard, Alger of Liège, and Hugh of Saint Victor).[56]

In contrast to his earlier work, Aquinas gave priority to the Augustinian notion of sacrament as "sign" but still had to account for the efficaciousness of this sign. In contrast to the Franciscan school's explanation of sacrament as the occasion for its recipients to receive grace, Aquinas, drawing on a christological analogy, described sacrament as an instrumental cause dynamically effecting what it signifies and explained its makeup in Aristotelian terms of sensible things as matter and words as form. The sacramental intention of doing what the church intends must therefore be coupled with the specific form of a particular sacrament.[57]

Thomas Aquinas achieved a masterful and innovative synthesis of sacramental theology. Given the historical, theological, and pastoral situation of medieval Europe, he provided a sacramental theology that dealt with the absence of symbolic thinking by affording a different approach. For this very reason what is missing is all the more noticeable. The absence of an ecclesiology that would give "sacrament" its proper context has already been noted. The pervasive role of the Holy Spirit in sacramental action (the epicletic principle) plays

---

53. Another indication is that even the important definition of sacrament in the Augustinian tradition, that of Hugh of Saint Victor (d. 1141), has serious weaknesses (Haring, "Berengar's Definition," 126–27; Van Den Eynde, *Les définitions*, 34–36) even though Hugh provides a rather remarkable theological context (Kilmartin, *Christian Liturgy*, 264–65).

54. See Karl Rahner, "Introductory Observations on Thomas Aquinas' Theology of the Sacraments in General," *Theological Investigations* (New York: Seabury, 1976), 14:151–52.

55. Thomas Aquinas *Summa Theologiae* III, q. 60, a. 1.

56. See Louis-Marie Chauvet, *Symbole et sacrement* (Paris: Cerf, 1987), 18–25.

57. Thomas Aquinas *Summa Theologiae* III, q. 60, a. 2; III, q. 62; III, q. 60, a. 7; III, q. 60, a. 8 c.

no crucial part here.[58] The connection between the Word of God and sacrament is not mentioned. The role of the sacramental minister and recipient (*opus operans*), detached from a developed ecclesiology, is less than satisfying.[59] These remarks are not so much a criticism of the best of medieval sacramental theology as a commentary on the ecclesial situation of that period. The fact that these brilliant speculative sacramental systems had no lasting impact on the deteriorating medieval pastoral situation suggests both a warning and a challenge to contemporary sacramental theology.

In the ensuing three hundred years that mark the distance between the great medieval theologians like Thomas Aquinas and Bonaventure and the Reformation debates, the early medieval problem of the weakening of symbolic thinking reasserted itself time and again. A succinct way of viewing this problem is to note how the profession of faith that Berengar was made to sign in 1059 continued to plague sacramental theology until the Council of Trent in the sixteenth century. Although this profession deals specifically with the eucharist, it is this sacrament that tests the adequacy of any description of "sacrament in general." In the profession, Berengar was obliged to admit that after the consecration the bread and wine are the true body and blood of Christ, "and that these are sensibly handled and broken by the hands of priests and crushed by the teeth of the faithful, *not only sacramentally but really*" (DS 690; emphasis added). Jaroslav Pelikan has pointed out the irony that three prominent fourteenth-century theologians (John of Paris, William of Ockham, John Wycliffe) who did not accept transubstantiation as well as their opponents all appealed to Berengar's 1059 profession of faith.[60] This apparently confused understanding of what the profession required is possible only because the connection between symbol and reality had not been adequately solved by applying Aristotelian categories of matter and form, substance and accident, to the difficulties of sacramental theology.

THE REFORMATION CHALLENGE

The sixteenth century with its Reformation and Counter Reformation debates on sacrament is best summarized as a partial retrieval

58. See Daniel A. Tappeiner, "Sacramental Causality in Aquinas and Rahner—Some Critical Thoughts," *Scottish Journal of Theology* 28 (1975): 243–57.

59. For a different view, see Colman E. O'Neill, *Opus Operans, Opus Operatum: A Thomistic Interpretation of a Sacramental Formula* (Rome: Pont. Athenaeum "Angelicum," 1958).

60. Jaroslav Pelikan, *Reformation of Church and Dogma (1300–1700)*, vol. 4 of *The Christian Tradition* (Chicago: University of Chicago Press, 1984), 54–59.

and an occasional (unintended) distortion of the classical teaching of previous periods. In reading Luther, Calvin, and other reform-minded theologians it must be remembered that the late medieval sacramental praxis was as much in question as was sacramental theory. And indeed, the pastoral abuse of sacraments was the occasion of separate and prolonged discussions at the Council of Trent. Furthermore, the larger questions of justification and faith framed the arguments and counterarguments on sacrament. Some sacramental praxis, the Reformers argued, implicitly denied the gratuitous and initiating character of God's action in the work of salvation. In reaction to the causality theories of late Scholastic theology, the Reformers sought to dephilosophize sacramental categories and preferred the biblical categories of God's power-filled promise to those who believe.

Luther was usually concerned with specific sacraments, but when he did give a general definition it was usually Augustinian in inspiration: Because the Word comes to the element, it is a holy sign of God's promise.[61] Sacrament is an expression of the Word of God and derives its power from that fact. When looking at a particular sacrament, three elements are found: the sign, the significance, and a responsive faith that believes that God effects what is signified.[62] In the same vein, it is not a sacrament because it is performed but because it is believed. In reaction to what was considered a proliferation of sacraments, the Reformers insisted that the Word of God must specifically connect a sign with God's promise. Only baptism and eucharist met this criterion (though Luther then spoke of penance as associated with baptism).[63]

Calvin had a particularly rich covenantal and epicletic dimension to his sacramental teaching; according to that teaching, sacrament confirms the Word of God and the Spirit enlightens the faithful to both Word and sacrament.[64] Thus, the three blessings of God, he argued, are connected: God's Word teaches us, the sacraments confirm that Word, and the Holy Spirit enables us to welcome this enacted Word. In defining sacrament, Calvin wished to avoid what he regarded as the major error in the Scholastic theologians' definitions, i.e., that sacraments confer justification even without faith as long as no obstacle is present. In contrast, he said that Jesus Christ is the

---

61. For citations, see Ulrich Kühn, *Sakramente* (Guetersloh: G. Mohn, 1985), 69–71; Eberhard Jüngel and Karl Rahner, *Was ist ein Sakrament? Vorstösse zur Verständigung* (Freiburg: Herder, 1971), 13–15.

62. "Treatise on Baptism," in *A Compend of Luther's Theology*, ed. H. T. Kerr (Philadelphia: Westminster Press, 1966), 165–66.

63. Kühn, *Sakramente*, 67–69.

64. Ibid., 104–5.

"matter or substance of all the sacraments." For this reason, sacraments arouse and confirm faith, enable Christians to witness before the world, and seal the promises of God to us. But since it is God "who does all" in a sacramental action, it is a passive act in which we are recipients.[65]

In assessing the response of the Council of Trent not only the canons but also the discussions preceding them must be taken into account. Since the procedure of the sessions was principally restricted to a response to Reformers, there was no attempt to construct a positive theology of sacraments. Equally important, both the Franciscan and Dominican schools of theology, with their sometimes widely divergent sacramental positions, dominated many of these sessions. Finally, the Reformers' critique of sacramental praxis was also a concern of the council: The sessions on the use and abuse of particular sacraments are arguably some of the most illuminating sacramental discussions of Trent.

Since justification enables faith and its sacramental expression, the sessions on the "sacraments in general" were immediately preceded by those on justification (DS 1600). Throughout the discussion of individual sacraments, the importance of faith as "the door" to sacramental participation was reiterated. The summary canons on sacrament reasserted the unique character of the Christian sacraments, their efficacious and objective nature (technically *ex opere operato*, emphasizing God's unique and indestructible work), their sevenfold expression, their importance in the process of salvation, the need in a sacramental minister for a minimal ecclesial intention, and the existence of "character" in baptism, confirmation, and orders (DS 1601–13). Some of the elements that made the Second Vatican Council's liturgical teaching theologically suggestive and pastorally effective were also present in the sixteenth-century discussions: a scriptural and patristic revival, a pressing pastoral need for reform, and a potentially fruitful debate between some brilliant theologians. But the polemical context, with its powerfully intertwined political and institutional factors, made productive dialogue between the Reformers and the Roman church improbable.

The theological aftermath of these sixteenth-century debates was not especially productive, at least for sacramental theology. Aquinas's attempt to retain the symbolic dimension of sacrament within Aristotelian categories had been mostly deflected by the late medieval nominalism. As just noted, the polemical character

---

65. John Calvin, *Institutes of the Christian Religion*, IV.14; IV.16; IV.19; IV.20; IV.26.

of the Roman Catholic and Tridentine debates did not lend itself to a constructive retrieval and development of classic sacramental theology. In the end, some dimensions of symbol continued to be emphasized by both Roman and Protestant theologians to the exclusion of others, with the identical Augustinian insights on sacrament being cited to support quite different positions. Crucial connections between Word, faith, and sacrament that had been polemically broached were not clarified and developed. The pneumatological dimension of sacrament that had been raised in the Council of Florence (1439–45) and to which Calvin devoted so much attention remained undeveloped in post-Tridentine theologies. While the immediate post-Tridentine sacramental theologies of Melchior Cano, Francis Suarez, and Robert Bellarmine contained some brilliant insights, they did not ultimately lay the foundations for a new and constructive approach.[66]

The theological precursors of the twentieth-century retrieval of sacrament are to be found in nineteenth-century Germany. With the advent of romanticism in the early part of that century and its reassertion of the Absolute realized in nature, there came a renaissance in sacramental theology.[67] J. A. Möhler at the University of Tübingen is a representative figure. His *Symbolik* (1832) not only set up a dialogue in comparing the ecclesial and sacramental systems of the Roman Catholic and Protestant traditions, but also proposed the church as "a collective, organic self, with various ministries and charisms; its concrete, symbolic realizations of the Holy Spirit were the sacraments."[68] The work of J. M. Sailer and J. B. Hirscher also contained an ecclesial dimension in their discussions of the connection between sacrament and moral theology.[69] In the second part of the century, with a more conservative Neo-Scholastic turn, M. J. Scheeben and Herman Schell still framed their sacramental theology firmly within a trinitarian context.

Meanwhile, monastic centers were not only a center of liturgical scholarship but also ecclesial models of sacramental praxis. Dom Guéranger's liturgical leadership as well as his influential *Liturgical Year* provided a praxis of worship and sacrament that had far-

---

66. For a somewhat more positive assessment, see Villette, *Foi et sacrement*, 2:252–82.

67. I am indebted not only to an article by my colleague, Thomas F. O'Meara, "The Origins of the Liturgical Movement and German Romanticism," *Worship* 59 (1985): 326–42, but also to his personal clarifications on the period.

68. Personal communication of O'Meara. He also cites the work of F. A. Staudenmaier and J. Amberger in Munich and that of F. X. Schmid and others.

69. See Helmut Weber, *Sakrament und Sittlichkeit* (Regensburg: Pustet, 1966), 411–13.

reaching influence. The Abbey of Beuron and its "descendants," the abbeys of Maredsous, Mont-César, and Maria Laach, also galvanized both scholarly and pastoral efforts for a liturgical renewal in America and Europe.[70] In particular, Dom Idefons Herwegen's writings and initial work of Dom Odo Casel in the *Jahrbuch für Liturgiewissenschaft* (1921) ensured a forum for ongoing liturgical research. Casel's central notion was that of "mystery," understood as the revelation of God to humanity through Christ. The saving acts of Christ are realized in the worship of the church. While some of Casel's historical and theological developments of "mystery" are questionable, his major insights challenged sacramental thinking and creatively retrieved important patristic teaching.

Meanwhile, in *A Key to the Doctrine of the Eucharist*, Dom Anscar Vonier, another Benedictine, was also making important connections between sacramental principles and liturgical life. In a refreshing retrieval of Thomas's teaching on sacramental signification, Vonier argued for the ecclesial dimension of sacrament and for the notions of liturgy and banquet in speaking of eucharist. Though this seems commonplace now, a comparison of Vonier's work with the usual sacramental tracts of the manuals will confirm this theologian's unique contribution at the time.

THE CONTEMPORARY RETRIEVAL

The sacramental theology incorporated into the documents of the Second Vatican Council was pioneered not only by a number of gifted theologians but also by the liturgical renewal of the twentieth century. The liturgical movement provided a *praxis ecclesiology* (i.e., a renewed ecclesial awareness through liturgy) at the same time that it invited the whole community to assume a more active and aware role in liturgical celebrations. This *lex orandi* and the succession of encouraging papal documents from Pius X (motu proprio, *Tra le Sollecitudini*, 1903) to Pius XII (*Mystici Corporis*, 1943, and *Mediator Dei*, 1947) facilitated the eventual liturgical renewal mandated by the Second Vatican Council.

Among the many theologians whose work prepared for the sacramental theology of the Second Vatican Council, the contributions of Edward Schillebeeckx and Karl Rahner must be briefly recognized. Schillebeeckx, employing the existential model of encounter, proposed Jesus as the "norm and source of every encounter with

---

70. See R. W. Franklin, "Humanism and Transcendence in the Nineteenth Century Liturgical Movement," *Worship* 59 (1985): 342–53.

God."[71] But the phenomenological approach to such an encounter would emphasize its visibility and embodied character. Taking inspiration from Leo the Great's axiom that whatever was visible in Christ has passed into the sacraments, Schillebeeckx then described sacrament in terms of a reciprocity or a "general sacramentality of being for the other." Sacramental encounter implies an ongoing dialogue between God and ourselves that results in a relationship that is both ecclesial and personal.

Within a strongly conceived theology of embodiment and its corollary of visibility, Schillebeeckx defined sacraments as "the face of redemption turned visibly towards us, so that in them we are truly able to encounter the living Christ."[72] The visible and believing church provides the context in which Christ is symbolically manifested. For this reason, the church can be described as the sacrament of the risen Christ. Since this discipled community embodies the mystery of Easter and Pentecost, Schillebeeckx then retrieved the trinitarian dimension of all sacrament and the particular action of the Holy Spirit. His insistence on the sacraments as the symbolic activity of Christ in his church is balanced by his existential description of the individual's sacramental encounter with Christ. Drawing out the corollaries of sacramental reciprocity, Schillebeeckx then outlined a dynamic process of transformation by which he attempted to correct minimalist attitudes about sacramental reception. Although he creatively used the inspiration and language of personalism, Schillebeeckx also argued from a close reading of Thomas Aquinas's sacramental teaching. It would be difficult to overestimate the impact his insights had on the pastoral as well as the academic communities of the time.

Rahner began his academic career with a series of historical studies of the sacrament of penance.[73] But his contributions to sacramental theology can be appreciated only within his comprehensive systematic theology. Rahner's essay on symbol provides an important context for his general sacramental theology.[74] Just as Schillebeeckx used corporeity/visibility to develop his notion of symbol-sacrament, so Rahner based his notion of symbol in its ability to realize what is essential in a being. As human beings, it would be impossible for us

71. Edward Schillebeeckx, _Christ, the Sacrament of Encounter with God_ (New York: Sheed and Ward, 1963), 18; also 62. The book is a summary of Schillebeeckx's monumental _De sacramentele Heilseconomie_ of 1952.

72. Schillebeeckx, _Christ, the Sacrament_, 43–44; also 70.

73. See Karl Rahner, _Theological Investigations_, vol. 15 (New York: Crossroad, 1982).

74. Rahner, "The Theology of Symbol," in _Theological Investigations_ (Baltimore: Helicon, 1966), 4:221–52.

to actualize our specific human nature without symbolic acts that are self-revelatory. Thus, the human person, transcending her or his limits, is involved in an existence shaped by symbolic activity. Jesus in his humanity is the perfect and perennial symbol of God's redemptive love and action. The church in turn continues this symbolic presence in time and space. The sacraments as basic and expressive acts of the church realize God's saving work in Christ: "The sacraments make concrete and real, for the life of the individual, the symbolic reality of the Church as the primary sacrament and therefore constitute at once, in keeping with the nature of the Church, a symbolic reality."[75]

Rahner's earlier insights on the church as the fundamental sacrament were consistently developed in a number of ways. Rahner firmly situated sacrament within the Word of God: "Sacrament is understood as one quite specific word-event within a theology of the word."[76] Further, this Word is addressed not only to the individual Christian but also to the specific community that gathers in Christ's name. The Word as symbol is an event that is graced and "exhibitive," i.e., it realizes what it expresses. Commenting on the Second Vatican Council's understanding of the church as a "kind of sacrament" (*Lumen Gentium* [hereafter LG] 1), he beautifully described it as "the bearer of that eschatologically victorious word that creates salvation," and thus a sacramental sign can be called an effective sign.[77] Individuals' sacramental participation takes place against the background of a graced human life ("the liturgy of life")[78] and reflects the larger ecclesial tasks of the community: "A sacrament is present when an *essential* self-actualization of the church becomes effective in a concrete and decisive situation in some person's life."[79]

The work of Rahner, Schillebeeckx, Otto Semmelroth, and other Roman Catholic theologians provided an ecumenical opportunity for a nonpolemical sacramental dialogue. Within this extensive and rich exchange, two crucial points should be noted: the meaning of sacrament and the connection between Word and sacrament. In a published dialogue with Rahner on the question of the nature of sacrament, Eberhard Jüngel observed that while Roman Catholic sacramental definitions have become multidimensional, Lutheran theologians have more often been content to comment on Luther's use of Augustine's definition. As in the latter's definition, the nature

---

75. Ibid., 241.
76. Rahner, *Theological Investigations*, 14:138.
77. Ibid., 143–44.
78. Ibid., 166–70.
79. Karl Rahner, *Foundations of Christian Faith: An Introduction to the Idea of Christianity* (New York: Seabury, 1978), 419, emphasis added.

of sign and its relation to God's mystery are crucial. Jüngel then proceeded from the scriptural warrants to Christ as the sacrament of the church whose salvific action is experienced in his Word, welcomed in faith, and realized in the two events of ecclesial existence, baptism and the Lord's Supper.[80] In this approach, while there is not an ecumenical consensus, the christological context does allow for a new and more dynamic examination of the connection of sign to mystery.

In a related discussion, Gerhard Ebeling has summarized the classic Roman and Protestant positions on the relation of Word and sacrament.[81] After describing the thought of Rahner and Semmelroth on the subject as a "break-through," Ebeling suggested that a further Protestant contribution to the discussion might be to recall that "the Sacrament in its various aspects emphasizes in a unique way what is the nature of the Gospel as a Word-event," especially in its symbolization of mystery.[82] The specificity of a sacramental event is found in the basic situation in which the Word-event occurs.[83] On the other hand, it is the constant insistence of Protestant theologians on the encompassing nature of the Word and a response in faith (*solo verbo—sola fide*) that still challenges how integral these dimensions are in the Roman Catholic theology of sacrament. If sacrament is once again contextualized in its normal liturgical setting, then some of these ecumenical concerns are not only addressed but dynamically restated. This is perhaps why the work of Peter Brunner and other liturgical theologians has been recognized by Ebeling as important.[84]

Neither the Council of Trent in the sixteenth century nor the Second Vatican Council in the twentieth century set out to construct a sacramental theology as such. The agenda of Trent was determined by the polemical task of refuting the Reformers while the Second Vatican Council pursued the goals of pastoral renewal. The ecclesiological context for the Tridentine discussion of sacraments was an institutional one while the Second Vatican Council benefited

---

80. Jüngel and Rahner, *Was ist ein Sakrament?* 36–59.

81. Gerhard Ebeling, *The Word of God and Tradition* (Philadelphia: Fortress Press, 1968).

82. Ibid., 226–27.

83. In his study of Ebeling's sacramental thought, Michael Raske has shown how it converges here in some respects with Rahner's later thought; see Raske, *Sakrament, Glaube, Liebe: Gerhard Ebelings Sakramentsverständnis—eine Herausforderung an die katholische Theologie* (Essen: Ludgerus Verlag, 1973), esp. 53–90.

84. Notice, e.g., Brunner's connection of Word and sacrament in the case of the eucharist: "Without Christ's word, that 'last' supper would not be the Lord's Supper.... All that was said about the anamnesis-character of the Gospel's proclamation applies particularly to the words voiced in Holy Communion.... The act in Holy Communion which is not word but action linked to the word becomes proclamation" (*Worship in the Name of Jesus* [St. Louis: Concordia, 1968], 167).

from a scripturally and patristically renewed theology of church: "It is through the sacraments and the exercise of the virtues that the sacred nature and organic structure of the priestly community is brought into existence" (LG 11).[85]

Equally important for a contemporary notion of sacrament is the Second Vatican Council's description of the several modes of Christ's presence—in his church as well as its liturgical celebrations, in all the sacraments (especially the eucharist), and in his Word (SC 7).[86] This developed notion of "presence" represents, in effect, an important return to the "mystery" of God's redemptive presence in Christ and to the symbolic thinking that it presumes.

The theological discussion of the fruitful participation of the sacramental minister and recipient has been somewhat skewed since the Augustinian refutation of Pelagianism and Donatism. The Council of Florence in the fifteenth century succinctly repeated the classic teaching: Sacramental ministers must have the intention of "doing what the Church does" (DS 1312), and the sacraments confer grace on those who receive them worthily (DS 1310). Trent essentially repeated these formulations a century later.[87] The Second Vatican Council, reflecting the more recent papal encyclicals, challenged Christians to celebrate "knowingly, actively, fruitfully" (SC 11).

THE FUTURE OF SACRAMENT

During recent decades, systematic theology has retrieved the important connections between praxis (what is actually being done) and theory (what should be done). Ideally sacramental praxis and theory should be in a constant and mutually challenging dialogue. In this postconciliar period we have learned, for example, that ritual reform can be more easily mandated than a renewed ecclesial-sacramental awareness. Sacramental theology, if it is to be effective for the mission of the church, must take into account some unresolved issues, among which are: (1) the cultural context of evangelization and sacrament; (2) the role of the Holy Spirit and its ecumenical corollaries; and (3) symbolic competence in a postindustrial age and its corollary, the responsible reception of sacraments.

---

85. See Giuseppe Alberigo, "The Christian Situation after Vatican II," in Giuseppe Alberigo, Jean-Pierre Jossua, and Joseph Komonchak, eds., *The Reception of Vatican II* (Washington, D.C.: Catholic University Press, 1987), 16–18, esp. n. 53.

86. See Kilmartin's extensive commentary in *Christian Liturgy*, 303–51.

87. DS 1611 on ministerial intention and DS 1606 on worthy reception, though the latter canon is phrased negatively ("those not placing an obstacle") to refute directly a statement of Luther (see DS 1451).

1. Paul VI in his 1975 *Evangelii Nuntiandi* (EN) in effect contested some sacramental theories that ignored the current praxis situation. He argues that the test of a profoundly evangelized culture is that it engenders communities of gospel witness and sacramental honesty (EN 23). He writes: "The role of evangelization is precisely to educate people in the faith in such a way as to lead each individual Christian to live the sacraments as true sacraments of faith—and not to receive them passively or to undergo them" (EN 47.1).

Word and sacrament cannot be separated from the values and priorities of God's reign that prophetically question each cultural system and its values. Liberation theology, for example, has shaped its sacramental theology with such prophetic questions in mind. In the so-called basic ecclesial communities of Brazil and elsewhere, a shared sacramental awareness is the result of an evangelizing community constantly being evangelized.[88] First World countries, on the other hand, have a different and often more subtle set of cultural assumptions that do not submit easily to evangelical values.[89] A systematic theology of sacrament cannot ignore sacramental praxis or the effects of its cultural contexts.

2. As noted earlier, the importance of the Holy Spirit in the sacramental process continues to be revalued. In contrast to the current indicative sacramental formulas of the Western church, the pleading for the Holy Spirit in earlier liturgies emphasized the ecclesial nature of the sacrament and of its ministry. Edward Kilmartin has summed up this epicletic theology of sacrament: "The epicletic formulas highlight the divine origin of the efficacy of the sacraments.... The sacraments combine the community's self-offering to the Father through Christ in the Spirit, with a prayer for the sanctification of the subject in whose favor the celebration takes place (six sacraments) or for the assembled faithful (Eucharist)."[90]

The ecumenical corollaries of the epicletic principle are suggestive. If Christian communities, historically separated from the Roman church through no fault of their own, firmly desire to do

---

88. See Marcello Azevedo, *Basic Ecclesial Communities* (Washington, D.C.: Georgetown University Press, 1987), 215–21. For a more radical interpretation, see Jon Sobrino, *The True Church and the Poor* (Maryknoll, N.Y.: Orbis Books, 1984), 104–5.

89. See the forceful critique of American Catholic theology by Gregory Baum, "The Social Context of American Catholic Theology," *Catholic Theological Society of America, Proceedings* 41 (1986): 83–100, esp. 94–98.

90. Kilmartin, *Christian Liturgy*, 248–49; see also his "The Active Role of Christ and the Holy Spirit in the Sanctification of the Eucharistic Elements," *Theological Studies* 45 (1984): 225–53.

what Christ intended and call down the Holy Spirit in their sacramental celebrations, a legitimate sacramental question arises: Would this situation preclude a valid sacramental celebration?[91]

3. Symbolic competence is the complement to symbolic thinking. As defined above, symbolic thinking gratefully appreciates God's mystery in Christ. Symbolic competence is the ongoing willingness to enter more deeply into that mystery and appropriate its consequences. The classic Pauline terms for such competence (*koinonia/metexein* in 1 Corinthians) are translated into the liturgical idea of *participatio*.[92]

Symbolic competence, though enabled by God, does not bypass the larger socio-cultural situation or the individual psychological profile of communities and their individuals. If sacramental theology is to deal more adequately with the complexity of symbolic competence, then an interdisciplinary methodology is necessary.[93] The human sciences as well as the philosophical disciplines continue to uncover the resources and problems of human symbolic activity. Two influential examples of such interdisciplinary dialogue in sacramental theology are the work of Paul Ricoeur in symbol and narrative[94] and that of Jürgen Habermas in praxis and communicative competence.[95]

Finally, in a retrieval of some of the earliest prophetic warnings about honest worship, sacramental theology has once more begun to develop the connections between fruitful communal and personal reception of the sacraments and questions of peace and social justice.

---

91. Some early statements of this epicletic approach were Jean-Marie Tillard, "L'Eucharistie et le Saint-Esprit," *Nouvelle Revue Théologique* 90 (1968): 363–87; Paul Lebeau, "Vatican II and the Hope of an Ecumenical Eucharist," *One in Christ* 5 (1969): 379–404. See the pertinent sections in the Windsor and Canterbury statements in *Documents on Anglican–Roman Catholic Relations* (Washington, D.C.: USCC, 1976), 63, 79.

92. See Martin Herz, *Sacrum Commercium: Eine Begriffsgeschichtliche Studie zur Theologie der Römischen Liturgiesprache* (Munich: K. Zink, 1958), 168–69, 202–3, 262–64, 311–12.

93. In particular, I would cite the seven-volume interdisciplinary study of the individual sacraments, Bernard Lee, ed., *Alternative Futures for Worship* (Collegeville, Minn.: Liturgical Press, 1987); David N. Power, *Unsearchable Riches: The Symbolic Nature of Liturgy* (New York: Pueblo, 1984); B. R. Brinkman, "On Sacramental Man," *Heythrop Journal* 13 (1972): 371–401; 14 (1973): 5–34, 162–89, 280–306; Regis Duffy, *Real Presence: Worship, Sacraments, and Commitment* (San Francisco: Harper and Row, 1982); and Louis-Marie Chauvet, *Du symbolique au symbole: Essai sur les sacrements* (Paris: Cerf, 1979).

94. See, e.g., Power, *Unsearchable Riches*, and his "Unripe Grapes: The Critical Function of Liturgical Theology," *Worship* 52 (1978): 386–99. For a critique of the use of Ricoeur in sacramental theology, see Stephen Happel, "Worship as a Grammar of Social Transformation," *Catholic Theological Society of America, Proceedings* 42 (1987): 60–87.

95. See, e.g., Duffy, *Real Presence*, 13–18.

Since each sacrament in its special way announces the reign of God coming toward us, it also enables sacramental participants to work for peace and justice, the proleptic marks of God's reign already begun among us.[96]

FOR FURTHER READING

Casel, Odo. *The Mystery of Christian Worship*. Westminster, Md.: Newman, 1962.

Casel's basic positions on the actualization of God's mystery as the core of the liturgical-sacramental event.

Chauvet, Louis-Marie. *Du symbolique au symbole*. Paris: Cerf, 1979.

An interdisciplinary (particularly structuralist) study of sacraments.

Chauvet, Louis-Marie. *Symbole et sacrement*. Paris: Cerf, 1987.

An original reexamination of sacramental theory that affords many insights.

Cooke, Bernard. *The Distancing of God: The Ambiguity of Symbol in History and Theology*. Minneapolis: Fortress Press, 1990.

A comprehensive interdisciplinary study of how the symbols of God's presence have been muted.

Duffy, Regis. *Real Presence: Worship, Sacraments, and Commitment*. San Francisco: Harper and Row, 1982.

An interdisciplinary approach that focuses on the relation between commitment and sacramental action.

Duffy, Regis, ed. *General Introduction*. Vol. 1 of *Alternative Futures for Worship*. Collegeville, Minn.: Liturgical Press, 1987.

An interdisciplinary collection of three articles that explores sacramental competence.

Finkenzeller, Josef. *Die Lehre von den Sakramenten im allgemeinen*. Freiburg: Herder, 1980.

One of the most competent histories of "sacrament"; spans the period from Augustine to the late Scholastics.

---

96. For a powerful statement of these connections, see the letter of the U.S. Catholic Bishops, *Economic Justice for All* (Washington, D.C.: USCC, 1986), nos. 325–38, esp. 325.

Ganoczy, Alexandre. *An Introduction to Catholic Sacramental Theology*. New York: Paulist, 1984.

A succinct but thorough introductory text.

Jüngel, Eberhard, and Karl Rahner. *Was ist ein Sakrament?* Freiburg: Herder, 1971.

An ecumenically important discussion of sacrament by two eminent theologians.

Hotz, Robert. *Sakrament im Wechselspiel zwischen Ost und West*. Zurich: Benziger, 1979.

One of the better treatments of Orthodox sacramental theology in dialogue with the Western traditions.

Kilmartin, Edward. *Christian Liturgy. I. Theology*. Kansas City: Sheed and Ward, 1988.

An important restatement of sacramental theory from a liturgical viewpoint.

Kühn, Ulrich. *Sakramente*. Guetersloh: G. Mohn, 1985.

A very competent compendium of Protestant sacramental theology up to 1985.

Leeming, Bernard. *Principles of Sacramental Theology*. 2d ed. Westminster, Md.: Newman, 1960.

One of the best of the preconciliar "manual theology" approaches to sacramental theory.

Power, David. *Unsearchable Riches: The Symbolic Nature of Liturgy*. New York: Pueblo, 1984.

A creative use of Ricoeur and others to probe the symbolic dimensions of sacramental action.

Rahner, Karl. *The Church and the Sacraments*. New York: Herder and Herder, 1963.

A landmark work that reestablished the ecclesial dimensions of sacrament.

Rahner, Karl. *Foundations of Christian Faith*. New York: Seabury, 1978.

Situates Rahner's sacramental theology within his total systematic thought.

Rahner, Karl. *Theological Investigations*. Vol. 4: Baltimore: Helicon, 1966. Vol. 14: New York: Seabury, 1976.

Multivolume work that offers a thorough representation of Rahner's thought, volumes 4 and 14 being particularly important.

Schillebeeckx, Edward. *Christ, the Sacrament of Encounter with God.* New York: Sheed and Ward, 1963.

Another benchmark in sacramental theology employing a personalist approach.

Schneider, Theodor. *Zeichen der Nähe Gottes: Grundriss der Sakramententheologie.* Mainz: M. Grünewald, 1987.

An excellent summary of contemporary sacramental theology with sections on each of the sacraments.

Semmelroth, Otto. *Church and Sacraments.* Notre Dame, Ind.: Fides, 1965.

An influential work in retrieving the ecclesial dimensions of sacrament.

9.2

Baptism and Confirmation

9.2

Baptism and Confirmation

Regis A. Duffy

A theology of initiation is inseparably linked to a theology of church. This axiom is true from both a theoretical and practical viewpoint and can be verified historically. This classic principle has been phrased in a more dynamic way in the *Rite of Christian Initiation of Adults:* "The initiation of catechumens is a gradual process that takes place *within the community of faithful.* By joining the catechumens in reflecting on the value of the paschal mystery and by renewing their own conversion, *the faithful provide an example* that will help the catechumens to obey the Holy Spirit more generously."[1]

The church constantly clarifies its own identity in the "doing" of the gospel and thus clarifies its sense of mission.[2] As it struggles to live, proclaim, and minister the meaning of Jesus for the peoples of a given historical epoch and its many cultural situations, the church

---

1. National Council of Catholic Bishops (NCCB), Introduction, *Rite of Christian Initiation of Adults* (Chicago: Liturgy Training Publications, 1988), no. 4, p. 3, my emphasis.
2. See Francis Schüssler Fiorenza, *Foundational Theology* (New York: Crossroad, 1984), 195–245, esp. 236–38.

is involved in a conversion process of interaction in which candidates and the baptized witness to what God is doing among them. Initiation, then, implies a process of ecclesial awareness as the church is continually renewed to do the work of the gospel and its candidates are enabled to enter into the paschal mystery of dying and rising with Christ.

THE CATECHUMENAL PARADIGM

From the second through the fifth centuries, the Eastern and Western church employed a catechumenal process of gradual incorporation into the community that provided a model of conversion and challenged those already initiated.[3] Within this process, the sacraments of baptism, confirmation, and eucharist formed a unified sacramental experience that usually culminated a long period of gospel formation.[4] There are several important characteristics readily apparent in this classical catechumenal model: (1) there is a clear connection between faith and sacrament; (2) the catechumen is mature enough to ask for initiation in faith; (3) the local ecclesial community has the responsibility of spelling out the practical commitments implied by conversion; (4) the catechumenal process actively involves the whole community in various ways; (5) the definitive character of this conversion, celebrated in the rites of initiation, is such that the church only reluctantly allows reconciliation of the baptized sinner once afterwards; (6) the local church's self-awareness and mission are reflected in the way that it prepares its catechumens; (7) the unified nature of the sacraments of initiation is evident; and (8) the paschal mystery is central to the initiation process.

Although the postconciliar restoration of the catechumenate is an important pastoral event, its theological implications are equally important.[5] The process not only provides a historical answer as to how the church in the first centuries understood initiation but sup-

---

3. For short but accurate historical accounts, see Michel Dujarier, *A History of the Catechumenate* (New York: Sadlier, 1978), and his *Made Not Born* (Notre Dame, Ind.: University of Notre Dame Press, 1976), 32–49. For a more complete account, see Georg Kretschmar, "Die Geschichte des Taufgottesdienstes in der alten Kirche," *Leitourgia* 5 (1970), 59–136.

4. The term *initiation*, as used in this article, comprises our present sacraments of baptism and confirmation in their original unified ritual expression while *sacraments of initiation* includes the eucharist.

5. The Congregation for Divine Worship permitted a provisional use of the *Rite of Christian Initiation of Adults* in 1972. A new edition was approved by the National Conference of Catholic Bishops (U.S.A.) in 1988.

ports the theological axiom cited above: as one's theology of church, so one's theology of initiation.

In attempting to present a comprehensive theology of initiation, five broad areas will be discussed: (1) the theological implications of the Pauline teaching on sin, justification, and baptism; (2) the gift of the Spirit in Luke-Acts; (3) some of the major historical developments of the rites and theology of initiation; (4) Augustine's teachings on sacramental character; and (5) the contemporary retrieval of initiation theology.

PAULINE CONNECTIONS

The New Testament is not interested so much in presenting a theology of baptism as in reminding Christians of its context, a theology of redemption. The gospel accounts of the baptism of Jesus in the Jordan are replete with Old Testament images and a "meaning-vision" to explain the role of Jesus as Savior.[6] In addition, Paul often treats questions of redemption, faith, and sacrament in view of the practical ethical and ecclesial results that should be expected. He sees very clearly that if the death of Jesus and its implications are not appreciated, then what is celebrated in baptism will be misunderstood. (The Galatian and Corinthian communities are cases in point.)

In response to the question Why baptism?, the general answer of the New Testament is that "your sins may be forgiven; then you will receive the gift of the Holy Spirit" (Acts 2:38). But Paul begins with a different question, Why a crucified Lord? In attempting to deal with the question, the apostle reviews the original human situation and finds that it was an impossible one. Before there was even a Law to break, there was sin and its result, a flawed human situation (Rom. 5:12-14) that one scripture scholar has described as "the massive disorientation of a whole society which expresses itself in a false-value system."[7] The observance of the Law only underscored and aggravated the problem: We could do nothing to change our unredeemed situation (Rom. 3:19-20).[8]

The one glimmer of hope in the Old Testament is Abraham, who was justified because he believed, not because he observed the Law.

---

6. See the seminal work of Fritzleo Lentzen-Deis, *Die Taufe Jesu nach den Synoptikern: Literarkritische und gattungsgeschichtliche Untersuchungen* (Frankfurt: J. Knecht, 1970).

7. Jerome Murphy-O'Connor, *Becoming Human Together: The Pastoral Anthropology of St. Paul* (Wilmington, Del.: Glazier, 1982), 98.

8. See ibid., 89–105.

This is a key comparison for the solution that Paul proposes briefly in his Letter to the Galatians and fully develops in his Letter to the Romans. As Abraham was challenged to believe in God's promise, Paul argues, so those who believe in Christ "who died for us godless people" are also justified in God's sight (Rom. 5:1-6).

Paul has carefully set the scene for his answer to the question Why a crucified Lord? In stark contrast to the radical human disobedience, Jesus is obedient even to death on a cross for our sake. Paul acknowledges the earlier theologies of redemption in the Christian communities with their sacrificial and atonement language but brings a penetrating insight to the question: Through Christ's crucified obedience "all shall become just" (Rom. 5:19).[9] The apostle sums up the total redemptive event and its effect on us: "Jesus... was handed over to death for our sins and raised up for our justification" (Rom. 4:25).[10] This "justice" transforms our impossible situation of disobedience. Through God's gracious gift in Christ, we too, as imitators of God's Son, are enabled to give the "obedience of faith," i.e., our grateful "yes" to God (2 Cor. 1:19).[11]

Paul, as a good teacher, has carefully prepared his review of baptism in chapter six of Romans by his insights in chapter five on the connection between Christ's death and our justification. The meaning of initiation is captured in a series of striking images—"baptism into his death... crucified with him... died with Christ" (Rom. 6:3-8).[12] These images describe the relationship of the baptized with Christ as a crucified Savior. Or, as Bornkamm expresses it, the baptismal event and the Christ-event are identical.[13] Given the radical value that Paul places on Jesus' self-gift on the cross, he then expects a radical change of life style and attitude in the baptized (Rom. 6:12-14).

Another dimension of this same relationship is revealed in the phrase "baptized into Christ Jesus" (Rom. 6:3). This prepositional phrase has an intriguing use in the pre-Pauline and Pauline tradi-

---

9. See Karl Kertelge in *Der Tod Jesu: Deutungen im Neuen Testament* (Freiburg: Herder, 1976), 114–36; Ulrich Wilckens, *Der Brief an der Römer* (Zürich: Benziger, 1978), 1:239–43.

10. Wilckens, *Der Brief an der Römer*, 1:278–79.

11. I have drawn out some of the sacramental implications of the current biblical retrieval of justification in "Justification and Sacrament," *Journal of Ecumenical Studies* 16 (1979): 672–90.

12. For the background of baptism as immersion in the sea of death, see J. Ysebaert, *Greek Baptismal Terminology: Its Origins and Early Development* (Nijmegen: Dekker and Van De Vegt, 1962), 53–56.

13. Günther Bornkamm, *Early Christian Experience* (New York: Harper and Row, 1969), 75.

tion to indicate not only a personal but an ecclesial relationship.[14] Through baptism the Christian stands in a unique and personal bond with the Lord Jesus. Precisely because of this bond, Paul can identify himself entirely with Christ (Gal. 2:19-20). Another equally important result is ecclesial unity: "All are one in Christ Jesus" (Gal. 3:28). Paul's insistence on such redemptive unity that recognizes neither gender nor social nor ethnic divisions is grounded in this baptismal reality.

For Paul, then, the initiation event is a process of total identification—as Christ, so we (Rom. 6:4). Baptism is the entrance into the paschal mystery of dying and rising with Christ. But the apostle is equally clear that we are baptized into the body of Christ (1 Cor. 12:12-14, 27). The redemptive unity already imperfectly present in the body of Christ is for Paul a powerful explanation and irrefutable proof of the paschal mystery and its effect on us (Col. 1:15-28). Furthermore, it can certainly be argued that Paul regards the Christian moral life as a living out of this paschal mystery that our baptism celebrates (2 Cor. 4:10).

From a theological viewpoint, Paul achieves an amazing integration of (1) the problem of sin, (2) the connection of redemption, justification, and initiation as actualized by the paschal mystery, (3) the ecclesial dimension of baptism, and (4) the Christian moral life as ongoing baptismal commitment. Each Christian era has to be measured in both its theology and pastoral praxis by these same Pauline criteria.[15]

THE GIFT OF THE SPIRIT

The historical reasons for the eventual separation of initiation into the sacraments of baptism and confirmation will be touched on in the next section. Theologically the gift of the Holy Spirit is an essential part of the whole initiation experience. As indicated in the section on sacraments in general, the trinitarian and pneumatological dimensions are a crucial context for the meaning of sacrament. Given my specific purpose, I must limit my remarks to three major emphases of the New Testament tradition on the role of the Spirit in initiation: (1) the Spirit of God as inseparable from our sanctifi-

14. Udo Schnelle, *Gerechtigkeit und Christusgegenwart: Vorpaulinische und paulinische Tauftheologie* (Göttingen: Vandenhoeck and Ruprecht, 1983), 109–22.

15. For a discussion of the apparent ignorance of the second-century fathers of the church about the Pauline baptismal teaching, see André Benoit, *Le baptême chrétien au second siècle: La théologie des pères* (Paris: Presses Universitaires, 1953).

cation and justification; (2) the gift of the Spirit as necessary for the conversion that precedes and accompanies initiation; (3) the "mark" of the Spirit and its meaning.

When Paul reminds the Corinthians that they were "washed... consecrated...justified in the name of our Lord Jesus Christ and in the Spirit of our God" (1 Cor. 6:11), he is repeating an older baptismal teaching, reflecting an Old Testament connection between sanctification and the Spirit.[16] The radical conversion experience of Christians, summed up in this line, is easily missed if we forget the context of the chapter. Paul is dealing with Christians suing one another in court and other ethical issues. In recalling their initiation instruction, the apostle questions why they do not see the far-reaching effects of this transforming experience. The passage, then, places initiation within the larger experience of conversion that God initiates through the Spirit and in the active response of faith.[17] As noted in the earlier section on sacraments in general, Paul later continues this same line of thought when he bases the efficaciousness of the community's prayer and worship on that same Spirit who alone knows the redemptive need of the community (Rom. 8:26-27).

The Acts of the Apostles presents another dimension of the Spirit's role: the enabler of conversion that must precede and accompany initiation. In the Pentecost scene of Luke-Acts the theme is announced, to be followed later by several variations: "What Jordan was to Jesus, Pentecost was to the disciples. As Jesus entered the new age and covenant by being baptized in the Spirit at Jordan, so the disciples followed him in like manner at Pentecost."[18] The disciples had struggled with the meaning of the death and resurrection of Jesus, now verified in the Pentecost experience, and became convinced of the urgent need to proclaim this paschal mystery to the world. The writer of Acts offers Pentecost as the paradigm for a community, initiated and anointed as Christ for service. As the subsequent preaching of Peter indicates, conversion and baptism imply an acceptance of Jesus who has ushered in the new age with its decisive gift of the Spirit.

But once this theme has been stated, Luke-Acts develops a series of variations that clarify how the Spirit may be welcomed or

---

16. George Montague, *The Holy Spirit: Growth of a Biblical Tradition* (New York: Paulist, 1976), 139–40; Hans Conzelmann, *I Corinthians* (Philadelphia: Fortress Press, 1975), 107. James Dunn, *Baptism in the Holy Spirit* (London: SCM, 1970), 120–23.

17. See Dunn's typical objections here (*Baptism in the Holy Spirit*); see also G. Beasely-Murray, *Baptism in the New Testament* (Grand Rapids, Mich.: W. B. Eerdmans, 1962), 162–67.

18. Dunn, *Baptism in the Holy Spirit*, 40; see also idem, *Jesus and the Spirit* (Philadelphia: Westminster Press, 1975), 146–58.

obstructed.[19] In the story of Simon and the Samaritans, all are baptized but do not immediately receive the Spirit (Acts 8:14-26). This scene is in sharp contrast to the conversion of Cornelius (Acts 10–11) where the Spirit is given before water baptism. Finally, there is the account of "disciples" who had not even heard of the Spirit (Acts 19). Although there are special factors that might explain the "entrance" of the Spirit in each story, the unifying thread is the nature of true conversion and the role of the Spirit in that process.[20] In Acts 8, for example, the Samaritans eventually receive the Spirit, in contrast to Simon, because their conversion is authentic.

The various accounts of baptism in Luke-Acts, then, do not deny the efficacy of water baptism but rather insist on the power of the Spirit that enables the conversion celebrated in initiation to be authentic and continuing. Furthermore, the Pentecost scene constantly reminds us of the larger issue behind baptism and the gift of the Spirit: We are initiated and anointed to serve the reign of God.

Finally, when Paul wants to remind initiated Christians of what the gift of the Spirit ultimately means, he employs several terms among which *arrabon* (i.e., "a first or down payment") is quite suggestive: "It is he [God] who has anointed us and has sealed us, thereby depositing the first payment, the Spirit, in our hearts" (2 Cor. 1:21-22; also 5:5). The apostle has transposed the commercial term into an eschatological one: The Spirit is even now our guarantee of God's future.[21] As seen above, the larger context of God's work in us (justification, conversion, initiation) highlights the continuing meaning of the Spirit for the Christian: The Spirit is God's promise to complete what has been begun in us.

THE EVOLUTION OF INITIATION

As might be expected, the larger concerns of the church are usually reflected in the preparation it gives its candidates. Until the official toleration of the church in the early fourth century, the periodically persecuted Christian communities were preoccupied with

19. I follow Dunn's arguments for the connections between these accounts in Luke-Acts (*Baptism in the Holy Spirit*).
20. Some exegetes (e.g., Beasely-Murray, Lampe) would explain the Samaritan story by citing the special problem Samaritans' entrance into the Judeo-Christian community presented. But even if this is true, it does not dismiss Dunn's arguments about the underlying conversion theme.
21. Montague, *The Holy Spirit*, 186–87; see also C. K. Barrett, *The Second Epistle to the Corinthians* (New York: Harper and Row, 1973), 80–81.

proclaiming and living the gospel in such a way that if the occasion demanded, the candidates and initiated could also die for it. In the New Testament churches the "handing on" of essential teachings of Jesus as well as practical moral formation were already in evidence.

But only in the second century do we discover the beginnings of a systematic preparation for initiation into the Christian way, called the catechumenate. The third-century Hippolytus, e.g., in his *Apostolic Tradition*, describes a demanding system, normally lasting three years, of evangelization, moral formation and commitment, and gradual insertion of the candidates into the liturgical life of the community. After a final period of examination and intense prayer and fasting, the catechumens were initiated with the oil of exorcism, the profession of faith, water baptism by immersion, a postbaptismal imposition of hands, and anointing by the bishop.

The catechumenal process presumed that candidates had enough maturity to choose freely to live the gospel and to ask in faith for initiation. The question of whether the early church baptized infants has provoked a great deal of scholarly debate.[22] Although there seems to have been a varied praxis of infant baptism into the third century, Hippolytus mentions the initiation of children (infants?). In known cases such as this, the reason seems to have been family solidarity, and not a question of later concerns about original sin.[23]

By the beginning of the fifth century, Augustine, in his anti-Pelagian insistence on the necessity of grace, was using the actual practice of infant baptism as a theological argument to prove original sin antecedent to any personal sin.[24] Ironically, the ninth-century theologian Wallafrid Strabo does not seem to have realized that he was reversing Augustine's argument when he then argued the necessity of infant baptism since there was original sin.[25]

At this point, several converging factors in the Western church should be noted: (1) with the increasing number of candidates, both adult and infant, in the fourth century, there was a trend not to re-

22. See especially Kurt Aland, *Did the Early Church Baptize Infants?* (Philadelphia: Westminster Press, 1960), and Joachim Jeremias, *Infant Baptism in the First Four Centuries of the Church* (Philadelphia: Westminster Press, 1960).

23. See Robert M. Grant, "Development of the Christian Catechumenate," in *Made, Not Born* (Notre Dame, Ind.: University of Notre Dame Press, 1976), 35–36.

24. See, e.g., Augustine "On the Merits and Remission of Sins, and on the Baptism of Infants" 1.20–24, in *Nicene and Post-Nicene Fathers*, ed. Philip Schaff (Grand Rapids, Mich.: W. B. Eerdmans, 1971), 5:22–24. Actually there are a number of changes in Augustine's positions; see Louis Villette, *Foi et sacrement*, 2 vols. (Paris: Bloud and Gay, 1959–64), 1:300–326.

25. Wallafrid Strabo *De Rebus Ecclesiasticis* XXVI, C.

serve initiation to the feasts of Easter and Pentecost (thus the bishop might not always be present); (2) with the increasing severity of canonical penance (to be discussed in the next section), there was a tendency to enroll male infants in the catechumenate and to delay their initiation; (3) after Augustine's victory over the Pelagians, there probably was an increasing practice of baptizing infants as soon as possible (again, with the possibility of the bishop not being present); (4) in the Western church, with the letter of Innocent I to Decentius in 416, the bishop was canonized as the ordinary minister of the final anointing of initiation (even though, in the Gallican rites, the priest was the ordinary minister until the early Middle Ages);[26] (5) the emergency ("clinical") baptism of catechumens was eventually extended to infants in danger of death with the same proviso that if there were a subsequent recovery, the bishop would "complete" the initiation rites by laying on hands;[27] (6) with the large influx of converts in the fourth century, the catechumenal process was not always able to prepare candidates in the same demanding fashion; (7) the necessity of additional rural churches made the presence of the bishop at the numerous initiation celebrations impossible;[28] and (8) the dismissal rite (the "missa") in which the neophyte came under the hand of the bishop (without any epicletic prayer) may have been at the origin of confirmation.[29] All of these factors would seem to contribute to the gradual separation of the last part of initiation, associated specifically with the gift of the Holy Spirit, into the present sacrament of confirmation.[30]

This historical overview summarizes a gradual disintegration of the unified rites of initiation in the Western church. There are several important theological corollaries that must be drawn. First, the ecclesial dimension of the sacrament had become mute, if not lost. Baptism was received for the forgiveness of sin, but the importance of incorporation into the body of Christ was gradually eclipsed. As this one-dimensional theology became predominant, the teaching of Augustine on "character" in initiation became distorted and the role of the Holy Spirit in the whole process of conversion and initiation was obscured.

---

26. J. D. C. Fisher, *Christian Initiation: Baptism in the Medieval West* (London: SPCK, 1965), 52–58.

27. The precedent for catechumens is given in canon 38, Council of Elvira (305), in E. C. Whitaker, ed., *Documents of the Baptismal Liturgy*, rev. ed. (London: SPCK, 1970), 222–23.

28. For a description of this problem, see Fisher, *Christian Initiation*, 72–73.

29. This is the closely argued liturgical textual position of Aidan Kavanagh; see his *Confirmation: Origins and Reform* (New York: Pueblo, 1988).

30. Ibid., 134–40.

SACRAMENTAL CHARACTER

In opposing the Donatist distortion of the holiness necessary for sacramental ministry and reception, Augustine creatively developed the notion of how and why certain sacraments (initiation and the ordained ministries) possess an objective value independent of the attitudes of both the sacramental minister and recipient. Unfortunately, Augustine's brilliant insight became obfuscated by the medieval and post-Tridentine discussions on "character."[31]

Actually Augustine employs not only the term *character* but other military terms (*nota, signum, signaculum*), all of which refer to the external identification branded conspicuously on the soldier's body to ensure fidelity to the emperor.[32] From this military analogy he draws several characteristics that are applicable to the sacramental situation: (1) the purpose of the mark is not to reward good conduct but to ensure fidelity to the "emperor"; (2) the external and irremovable mark points to the gift that cannot be lost;[33] and (3) this latter factor points to the ultimate glory or shame of the bearer.

In a typical citation, Augustine uses the analogy to counter the Donatist position:

> We recognize in heretics that baptism which belongs not to the heretics but to Christ.... For the sacraments indeed are holy, even in such men as these, and shall be of force in them to greater condemnation, because they handle and partake of them unworthily.... *What we fear, therefore, to destroy, is not yours, but Christ's; and it is holy of itself, even in sacrilegious hands.*[34]

In this approach, Augustine accomplishes several tasks: (1) he situates all sacramental action in the unique and gratuitous action of Christ; (2) he makes an important distinction between the ritual action of the sacrament (*sacramentum*) and the effects or grace of the sacrament (*effectus, usus*)—a distinction that an earlier North African, Saint Cyprian, failed to make; (3) he establishes a theological balance between the power of the trinitarian name in the sacramental event (initiated/ordained in the name of the Trinity) and the question of

---

31. The seminal article remains that of Nicholas M. Haring, "St. Augustine's Use of the Word 'Character,'" *Medieval Studies* 14 (1952): 79–97.

32. A related meaning for character is the branding of sheep to indicate ownership, and Augustine occasionally uses this meaning.

33. Augustine *On Baptism* 1.1.2.

34. Augustine *Contra litteras Petiliani* 2.c.109.247, in *Nicene and Post-Nicene Fathers*, ed. Philip Schaff (reprint; Grand Rapids, Mich.: Eerdmans, 1979), 6:595, my emphasis.

the individual's worthy reception and celebration of the sacrament;[35] (4) in one sense, his arguments are theological conclusions drawn from the liturgical praxis of not repeating certain sacraments; and (5) there is an important ecclesial context to this whole discussion.

Expressed more simply, Augustine was able to suggest a theologically satisfying answer to the question of how God might offer the sacramental experience to a sinful church and its members in a way that respected both the ultimately victorious nature of the gift and the flawed but free will of the recipients. But only portions of Augustine's teaching on character remained influential in the next five hundred years.[36] As a result, theologians' arguments about heretical or schismatic use of initiation (and orders) did not benefit from Augustine's development of character.[37] Thomas Aquinas insightfully retrieved some of the ecclesial dimension of Augustine's teaching in arguing that character prepared the person to participate in liturgical worship.[38] As Rahner comments on this insight of Aquinas: "Character in fact imparts a quite specific place and function to its subject in the *visible* Church as a worshipping community."[39]

In the larger medieval discussion, the trend was to interiorize character so that its original external quality was lost and to reinterpret it within very different concerns than those of Augustine.[40] The late Scholastic disputes over the nature of character are reflected in the minimal statements of Trent about character as a "certain spiritual and indelible sign" associated with the three sacraments (Denzinger-Schönmetzer, *Enchiridion Symbolorum* [hereafter DS], 1609).

In the contemporary retrieval of character, three classical elements are important: (1) the decisive *identification* of the sacramental recipient as linked to Christ for better or worse; (2) the prominent *ecclesial context* of the three sacraments linked to character (Rahner);

---

35. Haring, in particular, demonstrated the importance of the trinitarian formula in the later development of Augustine's teaching on "character" (see "St. Augustine's Use," 89).

36. See Josef Finkenzeller, *Die Lehre von den Sakramenten im allgemeinen: Von der Schrift bis zur Scholastik* (Freiburg: Herder, 1980), 74–77.

37. Ibid., 111–13. The central point of the twelfth-century theologians' teaching on character seems to be that sacraments that confer character cannot be repeated (ibid., 117–18).

38. Thomas Aquinas *Summa Theologiae* III, q. 63, a. 4, ad 1.

39. Karl Rahner, "Introductory Observations on Thomas Aquinas' Theology of the Sacraments in General," *Theological Investigations* (New York: Seabury, 1976), 14:157, my emphasis.

40. Not only do the Franciscan and Dominican schools continue to differ on the nature of character through the high Scholastic period but some late Scholastic theologians, such as Gabriel Biel, call into question the very idea; see Finkenzeller, *Die Lehre*, 209–10.

and (3) God's victorious purpose realized in a flawed church and its members. Character, then, should not be separated from the liturgical praise offered God in Christ by his church or from the mission to witness to the gospel that constantly renews the whole body of Christ. In contrast to the medieval discussion of character in ontological terms, current theological concerns might pursue the question somewhat differently: If God's decisive action in these sacraments is such that they need not be repeated, what ecclesial and personal responsibility is implied?[41]

THE CONTEMPORARY RETRIEVAL

INFANT BAPTISM—REFORMATION AND
CONTEMPORARY DEBATES

One of the most contested issues of the sixteenth-century debates on baptism was the question of infant baptism.[42] In addition to the Reformers' general concern about what they viewed as an instrumental notion of sacramental efficaciousness that prescinded from justification and faith, two specific considerations were at the root of these debates. First, since sacramental participation presumes personal faith, how can infant baptism be justified? Second, is infant baptism justified by the Augustinian teaching on original sin? These discussions were further aggravated by the Anabaptist movement, which relied on the early positions of Zwingli and others concerning the necessity of personal faith for reception of baptism.

Luther went through several stages in his position on infant baptism, moving from an Augustinian position, to an insistence on the Word and command of God as validating the practice, to a belief in infant faith. In fact, infants ideally offer less opposition to the power of God than adults. Luther insists on the saving power of God that is truly present in sacramental baptism. But it is not the faith of the parents or the church that is operative here, but rather the infant faith enabled by the sacrament. Luther evokes Christ blessing the children and promising them the kingdom. That same Christ is present

---

41. For a somewhat different approach, see Eliseo Ruffini, "Character as a Concrete Visible Element of the Sacrament in Relation to the Church," in Edward Schillebeeckx and Boniface Willems, eds., *The Sacraments in General* (entire issue of *Concilium* 31 [New York: Paulist, 1968], 101–14).

42. For the commentaries of the Reformers on the various ritual expressions of infant baptism, see the invaluable article of Bruno Jordahn, "Der Taufgottesdienst im Mittelalter bis zur Gegenwart," *Leitourgia* 5 (1970): 349–482.

in baptism.[43] Ultimately for Luther, God's boundless and gratuitous love provides the theological explanation for infant baptism. With baptism the infant is brought into a believing church where Word and sacrament are rightly proclaimed and celebrated.[44]

John Calvin was also forced to take issue with the Anabaptists to the extent that he added an appendix to the 1539 edition of his *Institutes of the Christian Religion.*[45] Consistent with the epicletic dimension of his sacramental teaching, he maintained the work of the Spirit already nurtures the beginnings of faith and repentance in infants. The gift of adoption has already brought them into the family of Christ long before the waters of baptism touch them. These convictions were grounded in the nature of justification. Since baptism is a sign of covenant, infants receiving this sacrament also partake of the covenant promise and community. Further, Paul's teaching that the infants of believers are already sanctified (1 Cor. 7:14) reflects the covenant promise made to Abraham's offspring (Gen. 17:7).[46]

The three Tridentine canons dealing with infant baptism principally address "believer's baptism" (i.e., baptism of those who are capable of and actually do make an act of faith) and reassert: (1) the legitimacy of early baptism, and (2) that baptized infants are to be counted among the faithful (DS 1625–27). In an earlier session, the council had already reiterated the connection between infant baptism and original sin (DS 1514). The missed opportunity at this point on the Roman and the Reformers' side was to reconsider (1) how justification is connected to the ecclesial community, and (2) how justification engenders a dynamic response in faith on the part of the believing community as well as its individual members (questions that contemporary biblical scholarship has reexamined with great insight).[47]

The proof that this question of infant baptism was not fully resolved was its reappearance from different quarters in the twentieth century. Joachim Jeremias devoted a good deal of his early writing to the subject of infant baptism in the early church as a positive and widespread practice. His equally distinguished colleague Kurt Aland,

43. Lorenz Groenvik, *Die Taufe in der Theologie Martin Luthers* (Göttingen: Vandenhoeck and Ruprecht, 1968), 154–72, esp. 166–67.

44. Georg Scharffenoth, "Taufe und Kirchengliedschaft in der Theologie Luthers und in den Kirchenordnungen der Reformation," in C. Lienemann-Perrin, ed., *Taufe und Kirchenzugehörigkeit* (Munich: Kaiser, 1983), 192–245.

45. John Calvin, *Institutes of the Christian Religion*, IV, 16:1–30.

46. See L. G. M. Alting von Geusau, *Die Lehre von der Kindertaufe bei Calvin* (Mainz: Grünewald, 1963).

47. See John Reumann, *Righteousness in the New Testament* (Philadelphia: Fortress Press, 1982); Regis Duffy, "Justification and Sacrament," *Journal of Ecumenical Studies* 16 (1979): 672–90.

using basically the same sources, argued to the opposite conclusion. But it was the work of Karl Barth and his son Markus that reopened the question of infant baptism for mid–twentieth-century theology. Karl Barth begins with a classical statement of baptism as union with Christ and partnership in the covenant. But Barth will have no part with either the subjective position of Zwingli or the objective celebration of the Roman church. It is Jesus Christ who freely acts within and without sacramental boundaries. Barth, taking his inspiration from Calvin, proposes baptism as a cognitive act (as opposed to a causative act). Baptism without a willing and ready recipient is "a wound in the body of the Church.... How long is she prepared to be guilty of the occasioning of this wounding and weakening through the baptismal practice which is, from this standpoint, arbitrary and despotic?"[48] Ultimately, Barth draws strong ecclesiological corollaries from his position: Believers' baptism evokes a gathered community that freely hears and welcomes the gift of Christ.[49]

Barth's position aroused a storm of debate. Two of his most eminent opponents were Oscar Cullmann, his colleague at the University of Basel, and Heinrich Schlier. Cullmann argues from Romans 6:1-11 that Christ's justifying death and resurrection form one salvific event that is received as forgiveness of sins and the gift of the Spirit by all Christians. He makes much of the passive baptismal verb forms in the New Testament (e.g., "You were baptized" in 1 Cor. 1:13) to show that the effects of baptism are independent of the decision of faith.[50] Therefore, infant baptism is justified. Schlier's line of argumentation is different although he too begins with Romans 6:1-11. Baptism as the instrument of salvation works _ex opere operato_. He grants that faith is necessary for adults who receive baptism, but since infants are incapable of this act and yet in need of the sacrament, the act of God is the ultimate explanation for the efficacy of infant baptism.[51]

In this rapid overview of infant baptism, it should be obvious that some of the crucial questions of sacramental theology are concretized: the nature of justification and its expression in baptism; the connection of Word and sacrament to the belief of the gathered community and of the individual recipient. To assess the current ecumenical progress on these issues, we have only to turn to a benchmark in such dialogues, the 1982 "Lima Document" of the World

48. Karl Barth, _The Teaching of the Church Regarding Baptism_ (London: SCM, 1948), 40f.

49. For an extended discussion of Karl and Markus Barth's positions, see Dale Moody, _Baptism: Foundation for Christian Unity_ (Philadelphia: Westminster Press, 1967), 57–71.

50. Oscar Cullmann, _Baptism in the New Testament_ (London: SCM, 1950).

51. Heinrich Schlier, _Die Zeit der Kirche_ (Freiburg: Herder, 1955), 107–29.

Council of Churches.[52] After reaffirming the scriptural warrants for baptism in its personal, ecclesial, and eschatological dimensions, the document acknowledges the two forms that the sacrament has taken historically: believer's baptism and infant baptism. In both cases the initiative of God in Christ is asserted as the crucial unifying belief. In both cases the sacrament is celebrated within a believing community whose conviction about the continuing nature of Christian faith and commitment precludes any instrumental understanding of the sacrament.[53]

INITIATION IN THE POSTCONCILIAR CHURCH

Although the Second Vatican Council basically retrieved the classical tradition on initiation, it represented a major advance over the limited canonical and Scholastic treatments of much preconciliar "manual" theology. This retrieved tradition of initiation might be summarized as follows: Initiation is (1) entrance into the paschal mystery (*Lumen Gentium* [LG] 7); (2) incorporation into a priestly and liturgical community (LG 11); (3) the bond of unity and a source of potentially full unity among the divided Christian communities (*Unitatis Redintegratio* 22); (4) a call to witness as a priestly, apostolic, and holy people (*Apostolicam Actuositatem* [AA] 11, 2, 3); and (5) a process of fairly lengthy formation into Christian life as well as doctrine (AA 14).

This conciliar retrieval was concretized in the catechumenal process, restored to the worldwide church in 1972. The catechumenate proceeds in four periods: (1) the precatechumenate of initial evangelization; (2) the catechumenate in which there is continued evangelization and catechesis; (3) the period of immediate preparation for and reception of the sacraments of initiation; and (4) the postinitiation catechesis and more active participation in the mission of the community. In proposing this process as the normal formation for the sacraments of initiation for adults, the church also reasserted a classical perspective on initiation: (1) while infant baptism is the usual pastoral praxis, the theological norm remains the person capable of asking for these sacraments in faith; (2) baptism, confirmation, and eucharist are united as initiating sacraments; (3) the ecclesial community is important in the whole process of initiation; and (4) conversion

---

52. *Baptism, Eucharist and Ministry*, Faith and Order Paper No. 111 (Geneva: WCC, 1982).
53. See the articles of Günter Wagner and Louis Mudge in Max Thurian, ed., *Ecumenical Perspectives on Baptism, Eucharist and Ministry*, Faith and Order Paper No. 116 (Geneva: WCC, 1983), 12–45.

is a gradual process. As is stated in the *Rite of Christian Initiation of Adults:* "The initiation of catechumens is a gradual process that takes place within the community of the faithful. By joining the catechumens in reflecting on the value of the paschal mystery and by renewing their own conversion the faithful provide an example that will help the catechumens to obey the Holy Spirit more generously."[54]

Prescinding from a discussion of the historical debates of the sixteenth century and their aftermath, the contemporary ecumenical discussion of sacraments in general and initiation in particular has gradually evolved into a fairly broad consensus based on the scriptural retrieval of justification.[55] The seminal work of biblical scholars has facilitated ecumenical discussions of how God's initial and gratuitous action grounds our liturgical and sacramental response of praise and thanksgiving as a Christian community.[56] This growing consensus is caught in the so-called "Lima Document" of 1982: "Churches are increasingly recognizing one another's baptism as the one baptism into Christ when Jesus Christ has been confessed as Lord by the candidate.... Mutual recognition of baptism is acknowledged as an important sign and means of expressing baptismal unity given in Christ."[57]

FOR FURTHER READING

Austin, Gerard. *The Rite of Confirmation: Anointing with the Spirit.* New York: Pueblo, 1985.

A succinct treatment of current approaches to the sacrament.

Bradshaw, Paul, ed. *Essays in Early Eastern Initiation.* Bramcote, Eng.: Grove, 1988.

Three essays that examine the early liturgical complexities of initiation's development in the Eastern church.

Duffy, Regis. *On Becoming Catholic: The Challenge of Christian Initiation.* San Francisco: Harper and Row, 1984.

Takes the catechumenal process as a paradigm for a theology of initiation.

---

54. NCCB, Introduction, *Rite of Christian Initiation of Adults*, no. 4, p. 3.
55. See Reumann, *Righteousness in the New Testament*.
56. See Duffy, "Justification and Sacrament," 672–90.
57. *Baptism, Eucharist and Ministry*, Faith and Order Paper No. 111, no. 15, p. 6.

Duggan, Robert, ed. *Conversion and Catechumenate*. New York: Paulist, 1984.
A collection of articles on the connections between conversion and the initiation process.

Dujarier, Michel. *A History of the Catechumenate: The First Six Centuries*. New York: Sadlier, 1978.
A brief but useful overview of key historical catechumenal developments.

Dujarier, Michel. *The Rites of Christian Initiation: Historical and Pastoral Reflections*. New York: Sadlier, 1979.
A pastorally informed precis of the theology of initiation.

Fischer, J. D. C. *Christian Initiation: Baptism in the Medieval West*. London: SPCK, 1970.
An examination of the ritual development of the sacrament.

Johnson, Lawrence, ed. *Initiation and Conversion*. Collegeville, Minn.: Liturgical Press, 1985.
Papers presented on this crucial theme at the 1984 convention of the Federation of Diocesan Liturgical Commissions.

Kavanagh, Aidan. *Confirmation: Origins and Reform*. New York: Pueblo, 1988.
A fascinating and closely argued thesis about the origins of confirmation with some interesting pastoral corollaries.

Kavanagh, Aidan. *The Shape of Baptism*. New York: Pueblo, 1978.
An articulate and challenging approach to the sacrament.

Müller, Karl, and Walter Blankenburg, eds. *Der Taufgottesdienst*. Entire issue of *Leitourgia* 5 (1970).
One of the most comprehensive treatments of initiation, with articles by G. Kretschmar, B. Jordahn, and E. Schlink. Kretschmar's historical analysis is exceptional and thorough.

National Council of Catholic Bishops. *Rite of Christian Initiation of Adults*. Chicago: Liturgy Training Publications, 1988.
The final version of the *RCIA* that became mandatory in the United States on July 1, 1988.

Osborne, Kenan. *The Christian Sacraments of Initiation*. New York: Paulist, 1987.
A summary of baptism, confirmation, and eucharist as parts of the initiation process.

Searle, Mark, ed. *Baptism and Confirmation.* Vol. 2 of *Alternative Futures for Worship.* Collegeville, Minn.: Liturgical Press, 1987.

An excellent interdisciplinary approach.

Thurian, Max, and Geoffrey Wainwright, eds. *Baptism and Eucharist: Ecumenical Convergence in Celebration.* Grand Rapids, Mich.: Eerdmans, 1983.

An important set of articles that broadens the usual ecumenical discussion of the subject.

Whitaker, E. C. *The Baptismal Liturgy.* London: SPCK, 1981.

A competent liturgical analysis.

Whitaker, E. C., ed. *Documents of the Baptismal Liturgy.* Rev. ed. London: SPCK, 1970.

A useful collection of key liturgical texts of initiation.

World Council of Churches. *Baptism, Eucharist and Ministry.* Faith and Order Paper No. 111. Geneva: WCC, 1982.

Crucial ecumenical consensus statements from the meeting at Lima.

Yarnold, Edward. *The Awe-inspiring Rites of Initiation.* Middlegreen, Eng.: St. Paul, 1971.

An examination of the baptismal homilies of Cyril of Jerusalem, Ambrose, John Chrysostom, and Theodore of Mopsuestia.

SACRAMENTS

9.3

Penance

9.3

Penance

Regis A. Duffy

As a general thesis it can be argued that the praxis and theology of penance and reconciliation in a given epoch accurately reflect the praxis and theology of initiation of that same period. In turn, anointing has usually mirrored the prevailing penance and reconciliation of its time. (Although the term *penance* will normally be used in this section as indicative of the ongoing nature of conversion of the initiated community and its individuals, the term *reconciliation* particularly recalls the ecclesial dimension of that same conversion.)

The suggestive biblical image of God, and eventually of Christ, as the *medicus* (the doctor) focuses the complementary dimensions of penance. The *medicus* attends to the wounds of sin and heals. Often enough, there is an eschatological dimension to this healing. Origen speaks of the church as Christ's room of healing,[1] while Augustine frequently alludes to Christ as doctor.[2] But this rich symbol has been understood quite differently in various historical periods. To appre-

---

1. Origen *Homily 8 on Leviticus*.
2. See George Dumeige, "Médecin (Le Christ)," in *Dictionnaire de la Spiritualité*, 10:891–901; Rudolf Arbesmann, "The Concept of 'Christus Medicus' in St. Augustine," *Traditio* 10 (1954): 1–28.

233

ciate this complex development of a systematic theology of penance, this article will briefly examine four periods: (1) the canonical period (up to ca. sixth century); (2) the Irish tax period and its medieval aftermath; (3) the Reformation and Tridentine period; and (4) the contemporary retrieval. Along the way I also include a section of theological observations.

THE THEOLOGY OF CANONICAL PENANCE

Although the systematic catechumenal formation of candidates for initiation probably did not exist before the second century, concern for the perseverance in conversion of both candidates and baptized is already in evidence in the New Testament writings. This initial conversion is summarized in the early kerygma of "penance for the remission of sins" (Luke 24:47). But the early communities had no easy task in forging a theology of reconciliation that could also deal with the gradual lessening of eschatological intensity and with the need to witness as a sinless messianic community.

A general pastoral strategy of the early first-century communities might be described in three terms: compassion, correction, and challenge. Mutual correction and forgiveness form part of the fabric of community life (Matt. 5:23-24; James 5:16). But this compassion for sinners is balanced by a keen awareness of how their actions impede the life and mission of the community. If the serious sinner will not be corrected, then some form of excommunication seems to be necessary (e.g., 1 Cor. 5:3-5; 1 Tim. 1:19-20). The "binding and loosing" passages of Matthew 16 and 18 and the "forgiveness of sin" passage in John 20 address not only the issue of whose reign, Satan's or Christ's, one is under but also the connections between being reconciled with the community and with God. Rahner sums it up: "It is the authority to allow readmission into the church which has meaning before God and which delivers man from the damning power of the devil."[3]

If compassion was to be realistic and correction effective, a challenge to ongoing conversion was also necessary. The striking references about the impossibility of repenting again (Heb. 6:4-6) and the blasphemy against the Holy Spirit (Mark 3:29; Luke 12:10) seem not to refer to any irremissible sins within the community but should be read as both a challenge and warning about an obstinacy to God that

---

3. Karl Rahner, "The History of Penance," in *Theological Investigations* (New York: Crossroad, 1982), 15:7.

contradicts baptismal commitments.[4] The transition from the penitential teaching of the late New Testament churches to its application in the second- and third-century churches was not to be an easy one.

In the period of canonical penance (broadly speaking, up to the early Middle Ages), the ecclesial concerns of the first-century churches are developed to meet the changing situations of each epoch. Several theological principles emerge from these developments. First, there is an integrated notion of church, initiation, and the need for continuing communal and personal conversion. For contemporary Christians it is sometimes difficult to appreciate how much the early churches regarded the initiation commitments made by adult converts as definitive. This initial and gratuitous forgiveness of sins was often referred to by the Greek term *aphesis* to distinguish it from the postbaptismal need to continue in the way of conversion (*metanoia*). (The Shepherd of Hermas already refers to the distinction in the [early?] second century.)[5] The proclamation of the good news of salvation had also been an invitation to participate in a community that symbolized this salvation. And however rudimentary the initial catechetical formation may have been, moral teaching included both the communal and personal dimensions of sin.

The initial hesitation about the treatment of seriously sinful Christians reflects a keen awareness of what the church must be rather than doubts about its responsibility to "bind and loose." As Rahner has correctly pointed out, "There is a clear awareness of the *sacramental nature* of church penance, insofar as the necessity of public church penance is stressed, reconciliation with the official church is considered necessary for salvation, even for martyrs, and the renewed bestowal of the Holy Spirit is ascribed to the rite of reconciliation and not to subjective penance."[6]

The early North African church of Tertullian and Cyprian exemplifies these connections between church, initiation, and penance. Tertullian speaks to catechumens of a "penitence which is undertaken but once and permanently preserved" but then reluctantly admits that God has permitted the door of forgiveness "closed and locked by the bar of Baptism, still to stand somewhat open."[7] This parallel treatment of initiation and penance continues as he describes the public ecclesial character of this second chance: "When you

---

4. For a more cautious view, see James Dallen, *The Reconciling Community: The Rite of Penance* (New York: Pueblo, 1986), 15–16.
5. Rahner, *Theological Investigations*, 15:77.
6. Ibid., 11.
7. Tertullian *On Penitence* 6, 7, in *Treatises on Penance*, trans. William Le Saint (Westminster, Md.: Newman, 1959), pp. 23, 29.

stretch forth your hands to the knees of your brethren, you are in touch with Christ. . . . When they shed tears for you, it is Christ who suffers."[8]

Second, the church is seen as possessing the Holy Spirit. Since it is the same Spirit who imparts the forgiveness and seal of baptism and who restores the penitent Christian to communion with God and the community, the church uniquely mediates this gift of the Spirit. Whether it is a question of the sacramental practice of heretics and schismatics or of lapsed Christians within the community, the assumption is that the Holy Spirit resides within the one church. (When this truth is pushed too far, then the controversy between Stephen and Cyprian on the valid and fruitful ministry of sacraments is inevitable.)[9] This active role of the Spirit is the context for the penitential ministries of the bishop and the community.

For Cyprian the bishop's task in receiving Christians into penance with its exclusion from the eucharist and their eventual reconciliation by imposition of hands and renewed eucharistic participation rests on the Spirit. For there is no "peace" (*pax*) or reconciliation with the church that does not communicate the Holy Spirit anew.[10] The community also had to participate in this penitential process, not as onlookers, but as suffering members of the same body. Just as catechumens were supported by the liturgical prayer and social encouragement of the whole community, so penitents were to benefit from this same ecclesial ministry.[11]

Third, as a result of both catechumenal and penitential concerns, the social, ecclesial, and personal dimensions of sin are gradually clarified. Or, more precisely, there is concern for sinners within the community and their impact on the community rather than analysis of sin per se. Several general remarks that summarize the major developments on this question can be made. In contrast to the rigorism of the older Tertullian, the church in God's name is able to forgive all sins. But not all sins are submitted to the church. Daily sins should be remitted through the sinner's own penance, works of charity, prayer, and participation in the eucharist. (As Rahner has noted, there is a somewhat semi-Pelagian emphasis in Cyprian on this point.)[12]

Serious sin, in this period, is not construed so much from an examination of the sinful act in itself but from its consequences:

---

8. Ibid., 10, p. 33.
9. See Rahner, *Theological Investigations*, 15:159–61.
10. Ibid., 296–99.
11. For a description of these gradual liturgical developments, see Dallen, *The Reconciling Community*, 65–73; see also Wolfgang Lentzen-Deis, *Busse als Bekenntnisvollzug* (Freiburg: Herder, 1969), 19–40.
12. Rahner, *Theological Investigations*, 15:172–73.

the necessary intervention of the church on behalf of those who by the loss of baptismal grace have separated themselves from the unity of the community and the eucharist. Although these sins are sometimes popularly reduced to apostasy, murder, and fornication, a survey of the actual praxis of the different churches of the period shows bewildering and sometimes contradictory lists of such sins, including sins of thought as well as action.[13] What differentiates this approach most from its subsequent development in the medieval period is the emphatic ecclesial context in which serious sinners are viewed as impairing the unity of the body of Christ; this view explains why it is necessary for such sinners to abstain from the eucharistic body of Christ. The lack of uniformity in lists of the "crimes" of sinners is probably more attributable to the different pastoral situations of the churches than to an undeveloped theology of sin.

Fourth, in canonical penance, conversion is implicitly treated as a lifelong process. In actual practice, canonical penance in the West was received only once in a lifetime and often enough some penitential aspects remained long after the sinner had been reconciled to the community. Christians who were not guilty of sins that required public penance or who lacked the courage to submit themselves to the process had a living model of conversion before their eyes in the penitential groups who were separated from and eventually brought back into the liturgical assembly by the bishop. This liturgical action centered on reconciliation rather than absolution.

It was in the liturgical context indeed that the penitential process implicitly taught an important doctrinal truth (another example of *lex orandi lex credendi*): Not only are there sinners within the church but there is a sinful church. Rahner develops this dimension: "But if she [the Church] is something real, and if her members are sinners and as sinners remain members, then she herself is sinful. . . . The Church is a sinful Church. . . . The Church can be sinful in her actions."[14] But our sin contributes to this very situation of the church. The church gathered in liturgical assembly becomes aware once more of the need for a shared repentance and conversion as well as for the healing of its individual members.

---

13. See Dallen, *The Reconciling Community*, 59–61; Herbert Vorgrimler, *Busse und Krankensalbung* (Freiburg: Herder, 1978), 70–73, esp. n. 410.

14. Rahner, "The Church of Sinners," in *Theological Investigations* (New York: Crossroad, 1982), 6:253–70, here 264–65; see also idem, "The Sinful Church in the Decrees of Vatican II," *Theological Investigations*, 6:270–94.

IRISH TAX PENANCE

During the late fifth and early sixth centuries when the practice of canonical penance on the continent was becoming impossibly rigorous, a new and quite different form of penance was developing in Ireland. Although the precise origins of Irish tax or tariff penance, as it is generally called, are not certain, no one disputes the generally monastic church of Ireland as the inspiration for this practice. The influence of pre-Christian Celtic law, customs, and clan systems probably also played a formative role. As in Eastern monasticism, monks were accustomed to discussing their spiritual life and its failings with another monk or with their abbot, who in turn would suggest a penance and then pray that God might forgive them.[15] The monastic chapter of faults provided a somewhat similar communal process. Since canonical penance never seems to have taken hold in Ireland, the monks ministered in the same way to the lay people who came to them.

In its evolved form, the penitent gave a detailed list of sins and their number. The spiritual counselor (eventually, the priest) then assigned a penance and gave absolution. The penance for each sin was systematically detailed in a unique body of literature, the Irish penitentials. Because the final calculated penance might be impossible to perform, certain substitutions were eventually allowed (e.g., having a Mass said or having another fast in one's place).

Even this cursory description suggests that this new penitential practice was quite different from that of canonical penance. Irish tax penance was repeatable while canonical penance in the West generally was not. The new penance tended to emphasize individualism while the older penance also had a strong ecclesial component. The Irish practice actually centered on a short-term view of conversion, moving from one absolution to another, while canonical penance encouraged a long-term view of conversion with its continuing penitential life style even after reconciliation.[16] Irish penance removed penitential reconciliation from the liturgical setting of Lent and Easter that canonical penance had employed.

---

15. Dallen makes the point, however, that Eastern monasticism eventually added a communal and liturgical dimension to this individual confession while Irish penance did not (*The Reconciling Community*, 104–5).

16. Dallen has argued that not only was there no ritual of reconciliation but there was probably no absolution in this period of Irish penance (*The Reconciling Community*, 109–11, esp. n. 15). There was not the later indicative form of absolution (that was not generally used until the thirteenth century), but I would suggest that the deprecative form of absolution, which seems to have some roots in monastic practice, might certainly have been used at this period.

By the end of the sixth century Irish missionaries were bringing their tariff penance to the continent. Although the new practice became popular, bishops seem to have regarded it as an innovation threatening the almost moribund canonical penance. Despite this initial setback, the new form of penance continued to gain in popularity, prompting a compromise in which canonical sins were submitted to canonical penance and other sins to private confession. Penitential books continued to proliferate on the continent and eventually evolved into the medieval manuals of confessors.

During the eleventh and especially the twelfth centuries there was a productive theological investigation of penance.[17] A major result of this discussion was a fairly general consensus that the contrition of the penitent was the operative factor in the forgiveness of sins. But the penitent must have the desire to go to confession and to do acts of penance. While most theologians assigned some importance to the absolution of the confessor since he is the minister of God, the acts of the penitent were considered the pivotal issue.

THE REFORMATION-TRIDENTINE DEBATES

To draw the lines of the sixteenth-century theological debates on the sacrament of penance, one could do no better than cite a brief statement of one of the conciliar theologians at Trent: "Penance is truly a sacrament, instituted by Christ, which cannot be received without sorrow and detestation of sins and an oral confession in which all sins and their circumstances must be confessed; only priests to whom alone this power has been given can absolve these sins."[18] The four elements of this understanding of penance are: (1) dominical institution, (2) necessary contrition, (3) integral confession, and (4) priestly power.

Although Luther never advocated the abolition of penance and Calvin proposed a pastoral alternative, the sacrament was problematic not only because of its historical abuses (which were discussed in separate sessions at Trent) but also because of its theological assumptions. Luther in his debates with Cajetan had consistently maintained that it is not the sacrament but faith in the sacrament that justifies the sinner. Trent's response was to reassert the objective nature of the sacraments against what it considered Luther's position: faith

---

17. See Paul Anciaux, *La théologie du sacrement de pénitence au XIIe siècle* (Louvain: Nauwelaerts, 1949).

18. *Concilium Tridentium* 7:311, my translation.

alone in God's promise (Denzinger-Schönmetzer, *Enchiridion Symbolorum* [hereafter DS], 1608). In examining the discussions of these canons, Harry McSorley has made a strong case that there was no clear dogmatic position on the question before the council. Some of the leading theologians, like Cardinal Seripando, noted that Luther's position could be interpreted as agreeing with a similar position held by Augustine.[19]

As for contrition, Luther had argued that the penitent cannot be forced to repentance by the obligation to confess: "A contrite heart is of great importance, but only in one who is terrified by an ardent belief in God's promise and warning.... In this way faith depresses conscience only to raise it up again, to comfort and to keep it contrite."[20] Luther castigated a repentance that hated the sentence for sin but not the sin itself. Trent inherited the Scholastic distinction between contrition (sorrow for sin motivated by the love of God) and attrition (whose motivation was less the love of God than fear of punishment, etc.); varying interpretations of the distinction were offered—ranging from discussions of stages of conversion (based on Thomas Aquinas) to discussions of psychological motivation (an interpretation based on Scotus). Given the Scotist and Thomist persuasions at Trent, the conciliar teaching is a broad one: True sorrow for sin and the desire for amendment reconcile the penitent even before the reception of the sacrament while attrition disposes the penitent within the sacramental celebration (DS 1676–78).[21]

Two of Luther's propositions condemned by Leo X in 1520 dealt with the confession of sins. Those propositions are contained in the following statement: "By no means presume to confess venial sins, and for that matter not even all mortal sins, because it is impossible for you to recall all mortal sins. Accordingly, only manifest mortal sins were confessed in the primitive Church. When we sincerely desire to confess everything, we desire in effect to leave nothing for God's mercy to forgive" (DS 1458–59).[22] Luther's reference to the "primitive Church" gives the clue to the underlying problem: Are

───────────────

19. Harry McSorley, "Luther and Trent on Faith Needed for the Sacrament of Penance," in Edward Schillebeeckx, ed., *Sacramental Reconciliation* (entire issue of *Concilium* 61 [New York: Herder and Herder, 1971], 89–98).

20. Martin Luther, *The Babylonian Captivity of the Church*, in Paul Palmer, ed., *Sacraments and Forgiveness* (Westminster, Md.: Newman, 1959), 227. See also Thomas Tentler, *Sin and Confession on the Eve of the Reformation* (Princeton: Princeton University Press, 1977), 353–55.

21. For the post-Tridentine positions of Baius and the Jansenists, see Dallen, *The Reconciling Community*, 197 n. 15.

22. Translation of Palmer, *Sacraments and Forgiveness*, 229.

we speaking of the confession of sins in the tradition of canonical or Irish tax penance? The metaphor that spans the two practices is that of *medicus* (doctor). As noted above, the soteriological image of Christ as *medicus* describes the healing of the wounds of sin. This image was used regularly by patristic writers in their discussions of penance and reconciliation. With the advent of tax penance and its emphasis on specific penances for specific sins, a new dimension was added to the original use of the metaphor: The patient must tell the doctor the symptoms before the proper medicine is prescribed.[23] This extension of the metaphor then was juridically applied to the confession of sins: The species and number of all serious sins must be confessed in order that the priest may give the proper penance.[24] The priest in this development is both doctor and judge, as the Roman Ritual of Paul V (no. 78) states. But if all the Tridentine discussions are carefully read, it is apparent that integrity of confession is a means to an end: conversion.[25] Although neither Luther nor Calvin accepted the juridical notion of confession, they certainly accepted the pastoral need for ongoing conversion.

Another missed opportunity of the sixteenth-century debates was the Reformers' concentration on the public and ecclesial dimensions of canonical penance and Trent's emphasis on the heritage of Irish tax penance. The attempt to deal with both the personal and ecclesial dimensions of penance and reconciliation would have to await the reforms of the Second Vatican Council. In the meantime, penance as a form of spirituality gained new momentum in the post-Tridentine church, especially as a preparation for more frequent communion. The Jansenist insistence on perfect contrition, delayed absolution, and abstention from communion as a form of mortification resonated with some approaches to spirituality in more orthodox quarters.[26] These aberrations only delayed a retrieval of penance as ongoing conversion within a theology of initiation.

---

23. For example, *Concilium Tridentium* 6:403.

24. For example, *Concilium Tridentium* 7:348, and the specific canon (DS 1707).

25. See esp. the articles of Carl Peter, "Auricular Confession and the Council of Trent," *The Jurist* 28 (1968): 280–97; "Renewal of Penance and the Problem of God," *Theological Studies* 30 (1969): 489–97; "Integral Confession and the Council of Trent," in *Sacramental Reconciliation*, 99–109.

26. See Catherine Dooley, "Development of the Practice of Devotional Confession," *Questions Liturgiques* 64 (1983): 89–117.

SOME THEOLOGICAL OBSERVATIONS

Much of the theology of penance that was taught up to the Second Vatican Council derived from the seminal discussions of the thirteenth and fourteenth centuries. The Irish development of private penance and Scholastic categories of matter and form were subsumed into a highly articulated theology that regards the acts of the penitent (contrition, confession, satisfaction) as the matter, and the absolution of the priest as the form of the sacrament. Historically the acts of the penitent had traditionally been considered the decisive factor in forgiveness. In the century and a half before Thomas Aquinas's time, the importance of absolution had also been theologically established. Aquinas harmonized these developments in his "matter and form" solution. Some comments on this solution must be made.

Contrition, understood as a profound sorrow for having offended a loving God coupled with the firm purpose of sinning no more, is the necessary first step even before confession. As Rahner points out, this is the oldest and most classical element of the teaching. But the genius of Aquinas's solution is that the penitent "is not only the passive recipient of this grace but is the one who, together with the priest, actively celebrates the sacred *mysterium* itself, which is the sacramental cause of grace which he receives."[27] If the penitent lacks this profound sorrow and yet turns away from sin, then the sacrament will transform this attrition into contrition and will thus enable the penitent to welcome the healing grace of God. Once again, Rahner sees the ecclesial dimension of penance in the very fact that sinners bring their perhaps imperfect dispositions and their request for forgiveness to the public forum of confession that "creates a reality in the dimension of the Church which... becomes the sign of the effective presence of God's forgiving grace."[28]

The integral confession of serious sins in their number and kind did not receive much theological comment since it had long been the practice in Irish penance. But with this demand for integrity came a shift in emphasis in the role of the confessor from that of *medicus* (doctor) to that of *judex* (judge).[29] Absolution summed up the end

---

27. Karl Rahner, "Forgotten Truths Concerning the Sacrament of Penance," in *Theological Investigations* (New York: Crossroad, 1982), 2:135–74, here 159.

28. Ibid.

29. Although the confessor is constantly spoken of as "doctor" at the Council of Trent, the title is used to reinforce his role as "judge": As the sick must first show their wounds to the doctor to be healed, so the sinner must reveal the species and number of serious sins to the confessor if there is to be any cure; see, e.g., *Concilium Tridentium* 6:403. In the canons of the council, absolution will be defended as a judi-

result of these titles: the forgiveness that is sacramentally signified in the words of absolution is actually given.[30] Somewhat later John Duns Scotus pushed this position much farther when he maintained that priestly absolution effectively cleanses the sinner, thus reducing the acts of the penitent to a prelude to absolution.[31]

The period between these teachings of the high Middle Ages and the sixteenth-century Reformation debates remains a warning to church historians and theologians alike that the socio-historical contexts of sacramental praxis cannot be ignored even in systematic theology.[32] Although the dogmatic sessions of Trent legitimated the theology just described (DS 1667–93; 1701–15), the dismal praxis situation was also trenchantly noted in the sessions on the abuses of the sacrament.[33] The council did attempt a reform of the sacrament, but some of the crucial dimensions of the earlier tradition of canonical penance were not retrieved. The best critique of this period is perhaps to be found in the directions of the Second Vatican Council and in the postconciliar pastoral efforts to renew penance and reconciliation.

THE CONTEMPORARY RETRIEVAL: A RENEWED PENANCE AND RECONCILIATION?

When the Second Vatican Council called for the reform of the rites of penance, there was every hope that the more comprehensive conciliar notions of conversion, sin in the world, church, sacrament, and mission would facilitate the renewal of penance and reconciliation (*Sacrosanctum Concilium* [SC] 72).[34] This hope was reinforced by the classical conciliar summary of the sacrament: "Those who approach the sacrament of penance obtain from God's mercy pardon for having offended him and at the same time reconciliation with the Church which they have wounded by their sins and which by

---

cial act; such a defense was made against the Reformers (DS 1709). For a discussion of this judicial analogy at Trent, see Anton Ziegenaus, *Umkehr—Versöhnung—Friede* (Freiburg: Herder, 1975), 200–209.

30. Thomas Aquinas *Summa Theologiae* III, q. 84, ad 5.

31. For a detailed examination of this shift in the medieval manuals of confessors, see Tentler, *Sin and Confession*, 263–301.

32. For an excellent example of a contextualized description of confession in this period, see John Bossy, *Christianity in the West 1400–1700* (Oxford: Oxford University Press, 1985), 35–56, 132–33.

33. See, e.g., *Concilium Tridentium* 6:403–7, 580–93.

34. For a detailed description of the conciliar and postconciliar discussions of the sacrament, see Dallen, *The Reconciling Community*, 205–49.

charity, example, and prayer seeks their conversion" (*Lumen Gentium* [LG] 11). When the new rite of penance appeared in 1974, it seemed to be a realistic pastoral implementation of the council's call for reform. In addition to a reformed rite of individual confession, there was also the possibility of a communal celebration with individual confession and absolution, and a third rite with general confession and absolution. To understand the subsequent overall decline of the praxis of the sacrament, some observations on the conciliar theology of penance and reconciliation must first be made.

First, there is a reemphasis on the ecclesial context of sin, penance, and, therefore, reconciliation. The new rite describes the church as a community in need of cleansing because of the sinners in its midst.[35] At the same time, the opposite possibility is noted: Just as Christians sometimes collude in sin, so they can help each other to do penance and share in the work of peace and justice in this world.[36] Therefore, a privatized notion of penance has been replaced by one of reconciliation with the community that first received us into the new life of initiation. Just as initiation takes place in the midst of the church, so too penance and reconciliation. But the ensuing debates over general absolution and the related problem of public celebrations of penance indicate that this is a theological truth that was theologically retrieved but practically ignored.

In 1922, B. F. Xiberta had defended the thesis that reconciliation of sinners is not simply with God through the mediation of the church but is also with the church. Bernhard Poschmann in turn vigorously supported this classical thesis in his own works on penance. But even by the time Rahner wrote "Forgotten Truths Concerning Penance," this understanding of reconciliation was far from being accepted.[37] To reestablish the ecclesial dimension of penance, he returned to the notion of initiation that includes meeting "the holy God of grace as a member of the Church."[38] But if the church is to be truly holy and fulfill its mission credibly, then the baptized must share in its upbuilding by a Spirit-filled life. In sinning, the baptized offend against the church's Spirit and its mission.

The underlying problem here is that a limited institutional notion of church can only theoretically acknowledge such an ecclesial notion of penance. But it is the penitential praxis of each historical epoch that accurately reflects the operational ecclesiology in vogue. In his Corinthian teaching Paul frames his teaching on Spirit, sacra-

---

35. "Rite of Penance," in *The Rites* (New York: Pueblo, 1990), vol. 1, no. 4.
36. Ibid., vol. 1, no. 5.
37. Rahner, *Theological Investigations*, 2:135–74.
38. Ibid., 137.

ment, and sin in the community by a firm theology of the body of Christ. The actual unity of this body witnesses to the power of God's salvation in Christ while actual disunity calls into question the church's sacramental and moral praxis as well as its theological understanding of "the way." Rahner correctly noted that his own analysis of Matthew 16 and 18 placed the question of ecclesial reconciliation on firmer ground than the historical approaches of Xiberta and Poschmann.[39] The notion of "binding and loosing" clearly shows that excommunication from the community was the normal sacramental penance in the early church and that grave sin was whatever removed the baptized from full participation in that body of Christ.[40] In this perspective, Rahner argued, not only the acts of the penitent but also the absolution belong to the sacramental sign because this latter action contextualizes the full meaning of the penitential event.[41]

This ecclesial approach does not downplay the personal dimension of sin but rather correctly re-situates it within God's larger purposes of salvation. As Rahner pointed out, the Pauline lists of sins that exclude from the reign of God correspond to his lists of sins for which the community must expel the sinner from its midst.[42] Further, it is the eschatological and the juridical consequences of serious sin (rather than the loss of grace) that are presented in the New Testament teaching.[43] These references help us to relocate the theology of sin within the ecclesial tasks of the community to proclaim the reign of God in Christ and its practical social as well as moral consequences. The failure of the postconciliar penitential rites, in particular its public celebration, reveals a privatized notion of sin on the part of many Christians that is rooted in a truncated notion of the baptismal vocation and its relation to the mission of the Christian community.

Sacramental penance is always both a test and explication of conversion. The classical definitions of conversion as sorrow for sin and determination to lead a new life are found throughout postconciliar documents. Since conversion, however, also implies a comprehensive notion of the sin from which we turn, to what extent does contemporary theology deal with social or structural sin as well as personal sin? The new rite does mention the "social dimension of grace and

39. Rahner, *Theological Investigations*, 15:19; see *Theological Investigations*, 2:140–49; *Theological Investigations* (New York: Seabury, 1977), 10:134–37.
40. Rahner, *Theological Investigations*, 10:136.
41. Rahner, *Theological Investigations*, 2:155.
42. Ibid., 143.
43. Rahner, *Theological Investigations*, 15:26–35.

sin whose effect is that in some way the actions of individuals affect the whole Body of the Church."[44] The question was advanced when the International Theological Commission insisted that conversion has social presuppositions as well as consequences and that personal acts do have a social dimension.[45]

The practical consequences of an adequate notion of conversion and sin, however, cannot be restricted to the acts of the individual penitent. If the sacrament is seen as an isolated moment in which these notions are examined apart from the wider life of the church, then inevitable muting of this essential teaching occurs. The very questions that the Synod of Bishops was asked to consider in preparation for discussing the sacrament are indicators of the contexts of conversion and sin: "Is your church truly an agent of reconciliation in your region?... What causes increase or diminish the sense of sin in your local church?... Are there in your region situations of disorientation which have their origin in history and which now have an influence in the church?"[46]

These observations in turn point to a dislocation between the theology of initiation and that of penance. If initiation is presented or celebrated as an isolated salvific act with ecclesial corollaries, then the theology of penance will inevitably correspond to this prior theology and praxis. If initiation teaches and celebrates God's gracious salvation concretized in the work of the Spirit that brings us into the community of the paschal mystery, then the need for penance is judged by the ways in which individuals (or a particular community) can separate themselves from the work of this same Spirit. Within such a theology, the notion of sin immediately retrieves the wider scope of God's Word while absolution is appreciated as an ecclesial action that is intimately united with God's avowed purpose for a "new creation" in Christ.

But as the International Theological Commission correctly remarked, the Word and ministry of reconciliation must be effectively dynamic if the church is to be a sacramental sign of reconciliation.[47] This Word and ministry proclaim the initial reconciliation of initiation and then invite the baptized to a renewed initiation commitment: "According to its innermost nature it [penance] is a comple-

---

44. "Rite of Penance," vol. 1, no. 25c.

45. International Theological Commission, "Reconciliation and Penance," *Irish Theological Quarterly* 51 (1985): 172; see also the outlines prepared for the 1983 Synod of Bishops, "Reconciliation and Penance in the Mission of the Church," *Origins* 11 (1982): 566–80, here 569.

46. Ibid., 569.

47. International Theological Commission, "Reconciliation and Penance," 169–92, here 176.

ment of baptism."[48] But this axiom brings us back to our initial contention: as the praxis of initiation, so that of penance. The original doctrine of the complementarity of initiation and penance derived from the actual praxis of the church communities (*lex orandi lex credendi*). To simply restate the doctrine while assuming such a supporting praxis is not necessarily a clarifying theological statement. To legislate communal celebrations of penance is not necessarily to retrieve the ecclesial dimension of the sacrament.[49]

Further, evangelization celebrated liturgically in penance as the Word of God clarifies our redemptive situation and enables our continuing response to God's call for conversion and mission: "A sacramental celebration remains incomplete and ineffective without a prior, preparatory evangelization; evangelization in turn remains incomplete unless it leads naturally into sacramental celebration."[50] Just as the catechumenal model relies on a continual evangelization to prepare candidates to receive God's justifying grace and sacraments, so the penitential model constantly refers to God's illuminating presence in the Word proclaimed liturgically. To avoid the temptations of a privatized morality or self-centered devotionalism, the proclamation and sharing of this Word dynamically present the priorities of the reign of God and its practical corollaries. Once more, to assume that evangelization has been accomplished because the ritual of the liturgy of the Word has been performed is to misunderstand the relation between Word and sacrament.

Finally, the classical medicinal or healing dimension of penance is a guide for understanding any juridical descriptions of the sacrament. If integrity of confession, for example, is understood solely in a juridical way, then the ultimate purpose of conversion may be forgotten. If the question of general absolution is discussed only from a juridical analogy, then the historical ways in which the church has compassionately chosen to exercise some latitude may be ignored.[51]

As the other Christian communities have retrieved a more encompassing notion of corporate worship, they have also reexamined their classical traditions of penance and reconciliation. Although certain dimensions of penance (e.g., the notion of satisfaction for sin)

---

48. Ibid., 178.

49. In the communal celebration with individual confession and absolution, there is in fact an uneasy juxtaposition of canonical and Irish elements (with their different ecclesiologies) without any integration of them.

50. Letter of Cardinal Villot in the name of Paul VI to the Latin American Episcopal Council (in *Documents on the Liturgy 1963–1979: Conciliar, Papal, and Curial Texts* [Collegeville, Minn.: The Liturgical Press, 1982], no. 581).

51. See, e.g., Dallen, *The Reconciling Community*, 125–29, 141, 376–81; Ziegenaus, *Umkehr*, 236–50.

might be problematic, there is a growing trend to celebrate penance in some communal form. In these traditions, penance would be considered a liturgical prayer or a form of pastoral care rather than a sacrament in the strict sense.[52]

FOR FURTHER READING

Anciaux, Paul. *La théologie du sacrement de pénitence au XIIe siècle*. Louvain: Nauwelaerts, 1949.

Anciaux's classic survey of the critical twelfth-century theological debates on penance.

Dallen, James. *The Reconciling Community: The Rite of Penance*. New York: Pueblo, 1986.

An excellent historical and theological presentation of the sacrament.

Favazza, Joseph. *The Order of Penitents*. Collegeville, Minn.: Liturgical Press, 1988.

A historical study of the penitential order in the early church with some pastoral applications to our contemporary situation.

Fink, Peter, ed. *Reconciliation*. Vol. 4 of *Alternative Futures for Worship*. Collegeville, Minn.: Liturgical Press, 1987.

An interdisciplinary approach to the sacrament.

Grotz, Joseph. *Die Entwicklung des Bussstufenwesens in der vornicänischen Kirche*. Freiburg: Herder, 1955.

A major work that radically challenged traditional historical interpretations since Poschmann and, as Rahner noted, has yet to be seriously debated.

Gula, Richard. *To Walk Together: The Sacrament of Reconciliation*. New York: Paulist, 1984.

Particularly helpful in discussing the moral implications of conversion and reconciliation.

Henchal, Michael, ed. *Repentance and Reconciliation in the Church*. Collegeville, Minn.: Liturgical Press, 1987.

Four papers presented to the 1986 convention of the Federation of Diocesan Liturgical Commissions.

---

52. See R. Underwood, "The Authority to Forgive Sins: Reclaiming Absolution for Pastoral Care," *Quarterly Review* 8 (1988): 23–41.

Kennedy, Robert, ed. *Reconciliation: The Continuing Agenda.* Collegeville, Minn.: Liturgical Press, 1987.

A particularly helpful collection of pertinent articles.

Lentzen-Deis, Wolfgang. *Busse als Bekenntnisvollzug.* Freiburg: Herder, 1969.

An important study of the penitential liturgies in the old Roman pontificals.

Poschmann, Bernhard. *Paenitentia Secunda: Die kirchliche Busse im ältesten Christentum bis Cyprian und Origenes.* Bonn: Hanstein, 1940.

A classic historical treatment of the crucial early penitential praxis.

Poschmann, Bernhard. *Penance and the Anointing of the Sick.* New York: Herder and Herder, 1964.

A competent summary by one of the great historians of the sacrament.

Rahner, Karl. *Theological Investigations.* Vol. 2: New York: Crossroad, 1982. Vol. 3: New York: Crossroad, 1982. Vol. 6: New York: Crossroad, 1982. Vol. 10: New York: Seabury, 1977. Vol. 15: New York: Crossroad, 1982.

Penetrating theological insights in the articles on penance in volumes 2, 3, 6, 10, as well as in Rahner's early historical studies of the sacrament in volume 15.

Schillebeeckx, Edward, ed. *Sacramental Reconciliation.* Entire issue of *Concilium* 61. New York: Herder and Herder, 1971.

Particularly good collection of articles that are still relevant.

Tentler, Thomas. *Sin and Confession on the Eve of the Reformation.* Princeton: Princeton University Press, 1977.

A study of the medieval manuals of confessors and the penitential praxis they disclose.

Ziegenaus, Anton. *Umkehr—Versöhnung—Friede.* Freiburg: Herder, 1975.

A penetrating discussion of the sacrament from the viewpoint of a responsible praxis within the community.

9.4

Anointing of the Sick

9.4

Anointing of the Sick

Regis A. Duffy

The perennial image of Christ as physician provides the theological context for this brief analysis of the sacrament of the anointing of the sick: "When the Church cares for the sick, it serves Christ himself in the suffering members of his Mystical Body. When it follows the example of the Lord Jesus, who 'went about doing good and healing all' (Acts 10:38), the Church obeys his command to care for the sick (Mark 16:18)."[1]

HISTORICAL OVERVIEW

The historical development of anointing of the sick may be briefly summarized in three periods. Up to the eighth century the sick who were not in canonical penance were anointed with oil blessed by the bishop so that the prayer of the church might restore them to health.[2] While not always explicitly mentioned in the liturgical prayers of this period, the general wholeness of the person and the

---

1. Decree *Infirmis cum Ecclesia* (in *Documents on the Liturgy 1963–1979: Conciliar, Papal, and Curial Texts* [Collegeville, Minn.: The Liturgical Press, 1982], no. 3320).

2. See Charles Gusmer, *And You Visited Me: Sacramental Ministry to the Sick and Dying* (New York: Pueblo, 1984), 11–21; Antoine Chavasse, "Prières pour les malades et onction sacramentelle," in *L'Église en Prière* (Paris: Desclée, 1965), 596–612, here 597–602; see also the latter's magisterial work, *Étude sur l'onction des infirmes dans l'Église latine du IIIe au XIe siècle* (Lyons: Sacre Coeur, 1942).

forgiveness of sins formed the background of the sacrament. The minister of the anointing could be either a priest, a layperson, or the sick person.

The second historical stage began in the early Middle Ages when canonical penance was almost extinct and deathbed repentance was a common event. An ambiguous juxtaposition of deathbed penance and anointing gave a different emphasis to the sacrament as preparation for death. At the same time, anointing began to be restricted to priests.[3] With this change came the new description of the anointing as "extreme unction" and the eventual insistence that it should be given only at the moment of death.

Since this sacrament shared with baptism and penance the same effect of remitting sins, medieval theologians had to attach some additional special purpose. The general medieval consensus on this unique effect of anointing (despite differences between the Franciscan and Dominican schools on the subject) might be summarized as a "tidying up" of whatever remnants of sin might remain in preparation for the glory of heaven.[4] This restricted theological viewpoint prevailed until the Second Vatican Council's reform of the sacrament, which initiated the third stage of its development.

THEOLOGICAL REFLECTIONS

The *lex orandi* provided by the conciliar reform of the sacrament prompts several theological reflections. First, the anointing of the sick is rooted in the conviction that the God who creates is also the God who heals and redeems. Expressed differently, our creation in God's image and our "new creation" in Christ sketch God's redemptive plan. But within a creation not yet fully transformed, suffering and death must be experienced not as punishment, but as part of our dying and rising with Christ.[5] In contrast to a purely philosophical approach to the power of evil and suffering in human existence, the gospel message proclaims God's victorious purpose as seen in the very sufferings and death of Christ as validated in his resurrection.

---

3. Chavasse calls this the third type of early medieval ritual (end of tenth century); see his "Prières," 602–3.

4. Herbert Vorgrimler, *Busse und Krankensalbung* (Freiburg: Herder, 1978), 222–25.

5. See *Pastoral Care of the Sick: Rites of Anointing and Viaticum*, nos. 1, 2, 5 (in *Documents on the Liturgy 1963–1979*, nos. 3321–22, 3325). For an interdisciplinary approach to the sacrament, see Peter Fink, ed., *Anointing of the Sick*, vol. 7 of *Alternative Futures for Worship* (Collegeville, Minn.: Liturgical Press, 1987).

For his own communities, Paul draws a continual lesson from the sufferings of Christ. The Christ who was both weak and strong (2 Cor. 13:4) is the model for the Christian. In his later writing Paul invites his readers to participate in suffering with Christ, so that they may be glorified with him (Rom. 8:16-19). Once more, this teaching stands in stark contrast to the Stoic doctrine on suffering or the pagan cults to the god-doctor Aesculapius. In effect, it provides a transforming motivation for valuing both health and sickness within God's perspective as made visible in Christ.

Second, the anointing of the sick is a privileged liturgical expression of the ecclesial care and mission of the community. The scriptural passage that is usually cited to justify anointing is James 5:14-15, in which the writer reminds his readers of an already existing custom in his church. When there are sick in the Christian community, the leaders anoint them with oil and pray for them. The promised effects are their being "raised up" and having their sins forgiven.[6] Behind this pastoral care of the sick is an implicit theology that God always touches the whole person in healing and that the community in doing this ministry imitates Christ. (The scriptural connection of physical healing and forgiveness exemplifies this conviction.) This ministry of the local community to the sick is liturgically concretized when the sick are brought the eucharist directly from the Sunday celebration by deputed members and when anointing is celebrated communally.[7]

Theology also provides a word of caution for this ministry. The sick are not healed for their private purposes but to fulfill their role within the larger mission of the church to the world.[8] The Second Vatican Council urges the sick to show their concern for the whole people of God "by associating themselves freely with the passion and death of Christ" (*Lumen Gentium* 11). In contrast to an individualistic concept of sacrament, the Christian's strengthening in the life of Christ cannot be separated from the work of Christ. Even the Christian's sickness should provide a witness to the transforming effect of the paschal mystery in human life.

Finally, the calling down of the Holy Spirit, with the forgiveness of sins proper to anointing, enriches our understanding and experience

---

6. Vorgrimler (*Busse*, 217) argues against any causal understanding of anointing and forgiveness. In addition to James 5, Mark 6:12 is also cited as a reference to the early anointing of the sick in the communities.

7. *Pastoral Care*, nos. 32–33 (in *Documents on the Liturgy 1963–1979*, nos. 3353–54).

8. *Pastoral Care*, no. 3 (in *Documents on the Liturgy 1963–1979*, no. 3323); see also Regis Duffy, *A Roman Catholic Theology of Pastoral Care* (Philadelphia: Fortress Press, 1983), 94–104.

of the forgiveness first extended in the initiating sacraments and then in penance and reconciliation. All adult sacramental participation presupposes a faith that is the first fruit of God's justifying work in us. In the sacramental ministry of the church, this faith is proclaimed in a privileged symbolic act. But these sacramentally expressed acts of faith always implicitly are a plea for God's continuing and enabling healing. The sacramental form of the anointing captures this plea: "Through this holy anointing may the Lord in His love and mercy help you with the grace of the Holy Spirit. May the Lord who frees you from sin save you and raise you up."[9]

Erik Erickson has suggested that the final task of the human person before death is integrity, literally "making a whole" of our lives. Sickness and death are to be counted among the ultimate limit-experiences from which we will either wring new meaning for our lives or put in jeopardy the search for such integrity. Within the Christian perspective, since Christ is the Alpha and Omega, the beginning and the end (as the Easter liturgy beautifully phrases it), both integrity and limit-experience are radically transformed. For two thousand years members of the Christian communities have pondered the meaning of the paschal mystery so that their own lives and deaths might have meaning. All the Christian traditions, whether they counted anointing of the sick among the sacraments or not, have shaped ministries and liturgies to help Christians profit from such experiences. For ultimately, eschatology is not a theological notion but an experience shaped by the praxis of our lives and their limitations.

FOR FURTHER READING

Duffy, Regis. *A Roman Catholic Theology of Pastoral Care*. Philadelphia: Fortress Press, 1983.

Stresses that the ministry of the sick has conversion as its ultimate goal.

Fink, Peter, ed. *Anointing of the Sick*. Vol. 7 of *Alternative Futures for Worship*. Collegeville, Minn.: Liturgical Press, 1987.

An interdisciplinary approach that emphasizes the familial and ecclesial contexts of the sacrament.

---

9. *Pastoral Care*, no. 3 (in *Documents on the Liturgy 1963–1979*, no. 6).

Gusmer, Charles. *And You Visited Me: Sacramental Ministry to the Sick and Dying.* New York: Pueblo, 1984.

Contextualizes the liturgical rite within the historical and theological developments with great insight.

Knauber, Adolf. *Pastoral Theology of the Anointing of the Sick.* Collegeville, Minn.: Liturgical Press, 1975.

A competent pastoral analysis of the sacrament.

Rahner, Karl. *The Anointing of the Sick.* Denville, N.J.: Dimension, 1970.

Rahner's pastoral reflections on the sacrament.

Rahner, Karl. *On the Theology of Death.* New York: Herder and Herder, 1961.

Illuminates the Christian connections between sickness and the cross, though Rahner's overall theme is death.

Triacca, Achille, ed. *Temple of the Holy Spirit: Sickness and Death of the Christian in the Liturgy.* New York: Pueblo, 1983.

A particularly wide-ranging and insightful group of papers given at the Saint-Serge Conference in Paris in 1974.

SACRAMENTS

9.5

Eucharist

9.5

Eucharist

David N. Power

INTRODUCTION

Eucharistic doctrine and theology, to whatever age they belong, always occur in the context of eucharistic practice. They reflect it, guide it, consolidate it, or at times try to correct and change it. The eucharistic teaching and theology of recent decades need to be placed in the contexts of the liturgical movement and of ecu-

261

menical convergence. The first encouraged a participation of all the faithful in eucharistic celebration and hence recovery of the rite as ecclesial sacrament, or sacrament of Christ's Body. The second took account of the celebration of the Lord's Supper in the Reformation tradition and of the riches of Eastern churches. This left room for a doctrine and a theology that could overcome some of the opposition bred from polemics, giving more attention to a tradition rooted in the Scriptures and unfolded through twenty centuries of plurality in unity.

ROMAN CATHOLIC TEACHING

As regards the eucharist, the major components of official Roman Catholic teaching in recent decades are to be found in four documents. These are the Constitution on the Sacred Liturgy of the Second Vatican Council;[1] *Mysterium Fidei,* an encyclical letter of Pope Paul VI of 1965;[2] the instruction *Eucharisticum Mysterium* (hereafter EM) of the Sacred Congregation of Rites in 1967;[3] and the Holy Thursday letter *Dominicae Cenae* of Pope John Paul II of 1980.[4] The first and third of these documents put teaching in the context of liturgical practice, thus emphasizing that doctrine is ordered to practice. The second and fourth documents integrate new insights into a more typical Roman Catholic perspective, as established by the Council of Trent.

Though it does not have the same authoritative standing as the conciliar and papal documents, the 1967 instruction of the Sacred Congregation of Rites can be taken as an apt summary of major doctrinal points, placed in the context of norms governing liturgical ritual and practice. The principal points of doctrine are found in section 3 of the document. First, it gives the three headings under which all eucharistic teaching may be summarized: the sacramental sacrifice that perpetuates the sacrifice of the cross, the memorial of the death and resurrection of Jesus Christ, and the sacred banquet

1. Second Vatican Council, Constitution on the Sacred Liturgy, in Austin Flannery, ed. and trans., *Vatican Council II: The Conciliar and Post Conciliar Documents* (New York: Costello Publishing Company, 1977), chaps. 1 and 2.

2. Paul VI, *Mysterium Fidei, Litterae Encyclicae de Doctrina et Cultu ss. Eucharistiae,* in *Acta Apostolicae Sedis* 57 (1965): 753–74. English translation in *The Pope Speaks* 10 (1965): 309–26.

3. Sacred Congregation of Rites, *Eucharisticum Mysterium,* in *Acta Apostolicae Sedis* 59 (1967): 539–73. English translation in Flannery, ed., *Vatican Council II,* 100–136.

4. John Paul II, *Dominicae Cenae, Epistula de ss. Eucharistiae Mysterio et Cultu,* in *Acta Apostolicae Sedis* 72 (1980): 113–48. English translation in *The Pope Speaks* 25 (1980): 139–64. Though a letter is not a very solemn form of magisterial teaching, for the moment at least this one has had considerable impact on the present situation.

in which the new covenant is renewed in the church in anticipation of the final coming of the Lord.

Along with these three principal points, the instruction recalls that the eucharist is the action both of Christ and of the church, an action in which all the faithful take part according to the ministry and order of each. It also repeats the teaching of the Second Vatican Council on the various modes of Christ's presence, namely, in the body of the faithful who gather in his name, in the Word that is proclaimed, in the ordained minister who presides, and in the species of bread and wine (EM 9).[5] Of this last or substantial presence, the point is made that it cannot be properly considered outside the context of the other forms of presence, even though it is to be taken as the mode of presence par excellence. To uphold the importance of this substantial presence both in doctrine and in practice, the instruction points out that the celebration of the Mass is complemented by other forms of eucharistic devotion that center on the reserved sacrament. At the same time, it encourages a practice and doctrine that can overcome past polemics when it asks for proper consideration of the celebration of the Lord's Supper in other churches (EM 8).

In his 1965 encyclical, Pope Paul VI was anxious both to open the door to contemporary explanations of eucharistic presence and to retain the Tridentine teaching on real presence and transubstantiation. The practical difficulty in the popularization of the Tridentine teaching was that it concentrated attention almost exclusively on the consecrated and reserved species and did not place the eucharistic presence of Christ in the context of celebration and eucharistic action. As a result it encouraged adoration and devotion but not communion and active participation in the ritual memorial. In order to offer a teaching that would encourage the latter, some theologians took their examples and analogies from a phenomenology of rite and symbol and addressed their teaching primarily to an engaged participation in Word, prayer, and table communion within the gathering of the Christian community.[6] Thus such words as *transignification* and *transfinalization* became popular in the 1950s and 1960s. Pope Paul allowed for the usefulness of such explanations but insisted that it was impossible to bypass the medieval and Tridentine teaching on substantial presence and transubstantiation. What he asked for in

---

5. The listing here differs somewhat from that given in the Constitution on the Liturgy, no. 7, which mentions first the priest who offers, then the species, then the Word, and finally presence in the assembly which gathers.

6. For a survey of the literature of this period, see Joseph M. Powers, *Eucharistic Theology* (New York: Seabury Press, 1967), 111–79.

contemporary theology was an integration of the old and the new, not a replacement of one by the other.

Not far into his pontificate, Pope John Paul II developed a practice of addressing a letter for Holy Thursday of each year to the bishops and priests of the Roman Catholic church. In the postconciliar context of the church in which all the faithful assumed a more active part in ministry, John Paul wanted to continue to emphasize the irreplaceable role of the ordained in forms of ministry, but especially in sacrament. In 1980 this letter treated of the mystery and worship of the eucharist. While it repeated and developed the position of the Second Vatican Council on the ecclesial nature of the mystery and on the participation of all the faithful, it singled out the doctrine of the Sacrifice of the Mass, particularly the Tridentine formulation of this doctrine, and the role of the priest in celebrating this sacrifice in the person of Christ.[7]

ECUMENICAL DIALOGUE AND CONVERGENCE

In the meantime, under the sponsorship of the Vatican Secretariat for Christian Unity, there have been innumerable ecumenical dialogues on the doctrine and practice of the eucharist at both the international and national level.[8] Those between the Eastern churches and the Roman Catholic church have resulted in documents that relate the mystery of the eucharist to the mystery of the Trinity, with singular attention to the doctrine and action of the Holy Spirit.[9] Those between the Roman Catholic church and Reformation churches have tried to find a path beyond the sixteenth-century impasse on questions of presence, sacrifice, and ordained ministry.[10] In these latter dialogues, the principal appeal has been to a recovery of the notion and reality of memorial and of the sacramental relation of the eucharist to the cross, so that it has become a broadly acceptable practice to speak or write of the Mass, Lord's Supper, Liturgy, or Eucharist as the sacramental memorial of the cross or the pasch of Christ, or even of the sacrificial memorial or the memorial of the sacrifice. Whatever doctrinal convergence has developed, and what-

---

7. For a commentary on the letter, see Edward J. Kilmartin, _Church, Eucharist and Priesthood_ (New York: Paulist Press, 1981).

8. See Hardins Meyer and Lukas Vischer, eds., _Growth in Agreement: Reports and Agreed Statements of Ecumenical Conversations on a World Level_ (New York: Paulist Press; and Geneva: World Council of Churches, 1984).

9. See Joint International Commission for Roman Catholic/Orthodox Theological Dialogue, "The Church, the Eucharist and the Trinity," _Origins_ 12 (1982): 157–60.

10. Meyer and Vischer, eds., _Growth in Agreement_, has several examples.

ever official reserve or popular opposition it still encounters, it has been greatly helped by a simultaneous convergence in the forms of celebration that has resulted from a historically unparalleled effort of liturgical renewal in the majority of churches, a renewal based on a broad knowledge of early, medieval, and Reformed rites and practice and at the same time attentive to the potential of contemporary cultural forms.[11]

THEOLOGY

Theological reflection today receives its challenge from the above liturgical, doctrinal, and ecumenical developments. On the one hand, it is possible to speak of a legitimate plurality in unity, both practical and doctrinal. On the other hand, it is impossible to overlook a certain conflict of interpretations. A mode of theology is needed that takes both these factors into account. Some dialectic between apparently opposing positions is possible, as with the East-West positions on the eucharistic epiclesis and on the matter appropriate to eucharistic celebration. It is also necessary to be attentive to the distortions that can creep into belief, theology, and practice as a result of bias, naive realism, or power structures that have inevitable effects on ritual and devotion.[12] Here we can account for some very materialistic conceptions of real presence and equally for some undernourished reductions of eucharistic presence to subjective piety. We can also account for a theology of priestly power that virtually excluded the faithful from an active role in celebration. Beyond such critical awareness, it is well to place and retrieve all teaching and practice in historical and cultural perspective. Most important of all, perhaps, it is necessary to recover the language of symbol, ritual, and poesis as key to celebration and as origin of all theological reflection. In other words, a theology of the eucharist has to be a theology of eucharistic celebration. With these principles in mind, we can see how current theology appropriates biblical origins, early church developments, medieval synthesis, and sixteenth-century polemic, as well as the insight into the language and forms of ritual celebration that is provided today by the human sciences, hermeneutics, and aesthetics.

---

11. For a collection of recent liturgical texts from different churches and countries, see Max Thurian and Geoffrey Wainwright, eds., *Baptism and Eucharist: Ecumenical Convergence in Celebration* (Geneva: World Council of Churches; and Grand Rapids, Mich.: Eerdmans, 1983), 136–209.

12. See Nathan Mitchell, *Cult and Controversy: The Worship of the Eucharist outside Mass* (New York: Pueblo Publishing Co., 1982), 66–195.

SCRIPTURAL FOUNDATIONS
OF EUCHARISTIC THEOLOGY

Christian theology has always given much attention to the New Testament accounts of the Last Supper, found in the Synoptic Gospels and in Paul's First Letter to the Corinthians.[13] This is still the case, but methods of scriptural interpretation have changed the focus. Because of the broad use of the historical-critical method, for some years much effort was put into a historical reconstruction of the final meal of Jesus with his disciples, into a recovery of Jesus' own intentions in celebrating the meal, and into a retrieval of his exact words, or *ipsissima verba*. Simultaneously, biblists tried to recover the rituals of the early church in New Testament times from these accounts and other texts. These investigations have not been without their fruits, though it has become apparent that it is unlikely that the final meal of Jesus was in fact a Paschal Seder as it is also apparent that the early churches did not have one uniform eucharistic practice. These very results of historical reconstruction have prompted scholars to recognize that authentic tradition is as much perspective as it is fact and that it is best recovered by reading the scriptural texts as literature. What is to be passed on is as much the meaning of the Lord's Supper expressed in literary form as it is a distinct and easily distinguishable rite.

TWO TRADITIONS

The narratives of Jesus' final meal are thus read in a fresh setting. Important to this setting is the constatation that in the early church there were two different traditions regarding the Last Supper, one a cultic tradition and the other a testamentary tradition.[14] The former presented the Last Supper as the charter story for the celebration of the Lord's Supper and existed in two forms, namely the Markan and the Antiochene (Paul and Luke). The second, found principally in John 13 to 17, presented it as a farewell meal at which Jesus asked

---

13. In English the important works available on the scriptural foundations of eucharistic theology are: Xavier Léon-Dufour, *Sharing the Eucharistic Bread: The Witness of the New Testament*, trans. Matthew O'Connell (New York: Paulist Press, 1987); Jean Delorme et al., *The Eucharist in the New Testament: A Symposium*, trans. E. M. Stewart (Baltimore: Helicon, 1964); Joachim Jeremias, *The Eucharistic Words of Jesus*, trans. Norman Perrin (Philadelphia: Fortress Press, 1978); Edward J. Kilmartin, *The Eucharist in the Primitive Church* (Englewood Cliffs, N.J.: Prentice Hall, 1965); Edward Schweizer, *The Lord's Supper according to the New Testament*, trans. James Davis (Philadelphia: Fortress Press, 1968).

14. Léon-Dufour, *Sharing*, 82–101.

to be remembered by his disciples for his service to them, exemplified in the washing of the feet, and gave them the commandment to love each other as he had loved them. The fulfillment of this command and the promises associated with it were the guarantee of the presence of Christ among the disciples in the agape that they practiced among themselves in the power of the Spirit. The testamentary tradition as recounted in John makes no mention of the meal ritual or its memorial command. However, the cultic and testamentary traditions are brought together in Luke's Gospel. After the sharing of bread and cup, completed by the memorial command, Luke recounts a kind of farewell discourse in which Jesus exhorts his followers to act toward one another as servants, an exhortation that applies as much to the one presiding at table as to the one serving (Luke 22:24-27). When cultic and testamentary traditions are thus combined they give a richer understanding of the eucharist and of its sacramental role in the life of the church. The promise of Jesus to remain with the church is realized both in the sacramental memorial and in the fulfillment of the love command in daily life through the power of the Spirit, the one being incomplete without the other.

SUPPER NARRATIVES

As far as the meal form of the eucharist is concerned, historical reconstruction offered two findings that at first appear to be negative.[15] For one thing, it is quite likely that the meal of Jesus with the disciples was not a Paschal Seder, despite the paschal references of the Synoptic accounts. Second, we learn from Saint Paul that at a relatively early date the ritual of bread and wine was separated from the full meal that early Christians were wont to take together. However, rather than weakening the ritual of the Lord's Supper, these findings help to make it clearer. In the first place, the paschal interpretation does not depend on the actual order of the Last Supper but has to do with how Jesus is to be remembered, and it is attached specifically to the blessings and sharing of bread and wine rather than to the full order of the meal. Second, the action in bread and wine does not forfeit its relationship to meal sharing and other acts of communion by being detached from a fuller meal setting. It actually gains a heightened significance by reason of its more formal ritualization, since in a commemorative and eschatological way it conjures up more than its own immediate context. Its reference, in other words, is greater than its ostensive context.

---

15. On the Supper narratives, see ibid., 102–79.

The actions and words of Jesus in blessing and sharing the bread and wine have to be interpreted in their fuller context and not merely by a semantic analysis of the individual sentences. From both context and actual words, one notes the importance of the references to the Pasch, the exodus covenant and blood, and the Suffering Servant of Yahweh. These are historical master images evoked by the narrative by means of which the prophetic and symbolic actions and words of Jesus are fitted into the dispensation of salvation. What is done at the Supper thus appears as the fulfillment of past figures and events and as the eschatological anticipation of the fullness of God's rule. Jesus himself is the one by whose death these figures are realized and the end-time inaugurated. By reason of these historical images, the meaning of the actual words "this is my body" and "this is my blood" (in whatever redaction they occur) is clarified. They signify the double self-gift of Jesus, the one whereby he gives himself to the Father for humankind and the other whereby he gives himself to the disciples at the Supper table as a means of sharing in the first-fruits. Of themselves and in their context, the words offer neither a clear concept of sacrifice nor a clear concept of presence, but all later theories are elaborated by way of reference back to these symbolic images. It is one of theology's tasks to ask what theories and concepts may serve to mediate the truth and meaning of the Supper to other generations and cultures, but in doing this it has to respect the richness of meaning found in the symbols and metaphors of the narratives.

MEMORIAL

One of the greatest helps that biblical interpretation has given to contemporary doctrine and ecumenical reconciliation is its setting of the memorial command in the fuller context of Hebrew memorial.[16] This makes it easier to read the command of Jesus to do this as his memorial as a ritual or liturgical command that embraces the entire eucharistic action, inclusive of proclamation, blessing, and ritual communion in the elements. It also allows the reader to understand the meaning of this memorial against the background of Old Testament memorial rites and prayers. While Christian writers are wont, naturally enough, to compare the Last Supper and the eucharist with

---

16. On memorial, see Fritz Chenderlin, *"Do This as My Memorial": The Semantic and Conceptual Background and Value of Anamnesis in 1 Corinthians 11:24–25* (Rome: Biblical Institute Press, 1982); Brevard S. Childs, *Memory and Tradition in Israel* (London: SCM Press, 1962); Max Thurian, *The Eucharistic Memorial*, 2 vols., trans. James Davies (Richmond, Va.: John Knox Press, 1960, 1961).

the meaning and rites of the Paschal Seder, it is incorrect to focus attention too stringently or exclusively on this comparison. All Old Testament, intertestamental, and Jewish liturgies, both public and domestic, have a memorial character. There is also a memorial character to proclamation and to prayer, with special attention given to the prayer of the Psalms and to the varied traditions of *berakah* and *todah*.[17] Paradoxically, while studies on Hebrew memorial have helped enrich understanding of the New Testament memorial command, they have resulted in a pluriform rather than in a uniform understanding of what it is to keep memory. Certain things, however, do seem clear enough, and it is well to take note of these.

First, as the Jewish people continue to look back to the foundational events of the Pasch and the covenant, so do Christians look back to the foundational event of Jesus' death and resurrection. A foundational event is one in which God enters into human history in such a way as to bring salvation and to change its course. It is a guarantee of continuing divine beneficence and opens out to the promise and hope of final salvation from sin and death. In the memorial ritual, not only do the people keep memory but they also plead that God will remember them in light of what the original divine intervention not only accomplished but promised.[18] In sharing as it were in the foundational event through the keeping of memorial, the people share in what it has given and in what it promises for the future. To establish the historical connection of the present with past and future, the memorial service has to include story, proclamation, blessing (comprehensive of praise, thanksgiving, intercession, and at times lament), and ritual action, chief among which is table ritual. Further, in Hebrew ritual, the persuasion that Yahweh is present among the people when they keep memorial can be expressed in the evocation of the figure of the angel. In the New Testament eucharistic ritual, it is guaranteed that the mediator, Jesus Christ, is himself present through the gift of the Spirit and in the symbolic action and elements. The Letter to the Hebrews elaborates on the original persuasion that believers enjoy communion in the benefits of Christ's death by typifying Christian life and prayer as a share in the heavenly liturgy that the eternal High Priest continues to offer to the Father.[19] It did not take much for Christians in the postapostolic period to apply this in a particular way to the eucharist. Rather,

---

17. For the Psalms, see Claus Westermann, *Praise and Lament in the Psalms*, trans. Keith R. Crim and Richard N. Soulen (Atlanta: John Knox Press, 1981).

18. See Jeremias, *The Eucharistic Words*, 237–55.

19. See James Swetnam, *Jesus and Isaac: A Study of the Epistle to the Hebrews in the Light of the Akedah* (Rome: Biblical Institute Press, 1981).

however, than finding this in the memorial command itself, it is more correct to see it as one of the elaborations on its meaning that time made possible. There is much indeed in the rhetoric and theology of memorial, both past and present, that cannot be identified with the meaning of the scripture text but that has to be seen as an attempt to draw out this meaning in a way that is persuasive and helpful to other generations and cultures.

OTHER TEXTS

Besides the Last Supper narratives, there are many other scriptural texts that foster a better appreciation of the eucharist.[20] An examination of the meaning of the "breaking of the bread" in the Book of Acts has yielded no entirely conclusive results, but it does serve to put the eucharist in the context of a gathering in which Word, prayer, food, and possessions were shared. Paul's interpretation of the Lord's Supper within this kind of gathering brings out its relation to the motifs of communion or *koinonia* and service or *diakonia*.[21] It also underlines its proclamatory and eschatological characteristics and the moral implications of participation in the ritual. The generally recognized ambiguity of the discourse found in John 6 points to faith in the Word of God made flesh as the foundation for faith in the eucharist. Finally, the composition of the stories of the multiplication of loaves in such a way as to reflect the ritual of the Supper brings out the value of the latter as eschatological sign and redemptive promise. These various features of the New Testament evidence facilitate a praxis-oriented understanding of the eucharist whereby it is seen in relation to the church's mission in the service of God's kingdom and to the church's aspirations to truth and justice for all peoples, in the memory and hope of Jesus Christ.

CONCLUSION

The current theological retrieval of the New Testament evidence on the Lord's Supper or eucharist can be summarized in the following points. That retrieval obeys the invitation into a world of symbols, textual and figurative, whose appropriation situates the eucharistic

---

20. These are treated in Léon-Dufour, *Sharing.*
21. See Jerome Murphy-O'Connor, "Eucharist and Community in First Corinthians," *Worship* 50 (1976): 370–85; 51 (1977): 56–69; Gerd Theissen, "Social Integration and Sacramental Activity: An Analysis of 1 Corinthians 11:17–34," in his *The Social Setting of Pauline Christianity: Essays on Corinth,* trans. J. H. Schutz (Philadelphia: Fortress Press, 1982), 145–74.

celebration in the context of the history that has its center in the pasch of Christ and unfolds in the memory of that event. By a better appreciation of what constitutes ritual memorial it serves the renewal of celebration and the possibility of placing this ritual at the center of the entire life of the church, in its configuration as eschatological people, service, proclamation, and mission. Finally, it offers this historical and memorial setting as the context within which to reconsider the doctrines of sacrifice, presence, and priesthood as they emerged and were disputed in later centuries.

EARLY CHRISTIAN CENTURIES

The early Christian centuries are important to eucharistic theology not only for the writers who treat of the eucharist in a variety of contexts but even more fundamentally for the way in which eucharistic liturgy and prayer developed. Indeed, the various forms of the anaphora or eucharistic prayer have become an important source of a theology that is liturgical rather than conceptual.

CHRISTIAN WRITERS

It is next to impossible to give an adequate account of writings on the eucharistic sacrament.[22] The literature is homiletic, catechetical, mystagogical, and epistolary rather than tractarian. For the most part, authors explain the eucharistic symbols and the figures of the eucharist in the Old Testament, such as the sacrifice of Melchizedek, the paschal lamb, and the manna. In some cases, as in the letters of Ignatius of Antioch, a reflection on the eucharist and on the celebration of the eucharist is the most basic form of early ecclesiology.[23] If mention of the eucharist occurs in a more tractarian form of literature, it is in connection with the doctrine of the incarnation, for the eucharist confirms the incarnation and the incarnation the eucharist.[24]

---

22. For a collection of texts, see Daniel J. Sheerin, ed., *The Eucharist*, Message of the Fathers, no. 7 (Wilmington, Del.: Michael Glazier, 1986); Adalbert Hamman, ed., *The Mass: Ancient Liturgies and Patristic Texts*, trans. Thomas Halton (Staten Island, N.Y.: Alba Publishing House, 1967).

23. See Raymond Johanny, "Ignatius of Antioch," in Willy Rordorf et al., *The Eucharist of Early Christians*, trans. Matthew O'Connell (New York: Pueblo Publishing Co., 1978), 48–70.

24. See Adalbert Hamman, "Irenaeus of Lyons," in Sheerin, ed., *The Eucharist*, 86–98.

An attempt to coordinate the findings of a study of this literature would have to center on church, memorial, sacrifice, and nourishment, and on the use made of Old Testament figures in explaining the sacrament. It is the first three features of eucharistic belief that are particularly important to contemporary theology.

The relation of the eucharist to the church is of paramount importance. It is the sacrament of the Body of Christ. It is the gathering on the Lord's Day of the assembly of the faithful, with its diversity of ministries, its proclamation of the Word, its memorial thanksgiving, and its communion at the table of Christ's body and blood. Many practical rulings derive from and maintain this conception. The ruling of the one assembly, under the presidency of the one bishop, at the one altar preserved both unity and orthodoxy.[25] Mitigations of the rule were not intended to take from its importance.[26]

Contemporary theology also gives considerable attention to the ways in which the eucharist was kept as a memorial. The reading of the Scriptures was ordered with this in mind. The many forms of the eucharistic prayer manifest a fundamental unity of structure and image that brings the memory of Christ's redemption to voice within the larger memory of all God's creative and salvific deeds, and in obedience to the memorial command given at the Last Supper. Catechesis and homily show the same intent and purpose in their elaborate comment on both scriptural and sacramental figures or signs, in their constant exhortation to the imitation of Christ's passion, as well as in their repeated promise of an eternal share in his glory. Within this parenetic context, martyrdom receives special mention.[27] It is the most awesome configuration to the death and resurrection that the church celebrates in the eucharist, a perception that led to the devotion to the tombs of the martyrs and the celebration of the eucharist in their honor.

Beyond these practical manifestations of keeping memory, it has to be admitted that Christian thought about memorial shows some ambiguity in its more philosophical moments.[28] This is not unimportant, given the current ecumenical convergence around the idea of keeping memory. In many cases, Hellenistic speculation had as much

---

25. See Hervé-Marie Legrand, "The Presidency of the Eucharist according to the Ancient Tradition," *Worship* 53 (1979): 413–38.

26. For more on this, see Robert Taft, "The Frequency of the Eucharist throughout History," in Mary Collins and David Power, eds., *Can We Always Celebrate the Eucharist?* (entire issue of *Concilium* 152 [New York: Seabury, 1982]: 13–24).

27. See the essays on Ignatius and Irenaeus in Sheerin, ed., *The Eucharist.*

28. Literature in English is not abundant, but see F. N. C. Hicks, *The Fulness of Sacrifice*, 3d ed. (London: SPCK, 1946); Odo Casel, *The Mystery of Christian Worship*, trans. B. Neunheuser (Westminster, Md.: Newman, 1962).

influence as Hebrew precedent. Elaborations on Old Testament types of the mysteries, on their antitypical fulfillment in Jesus Christ, on their imitation in the eucharist, and on their consummation in glory often betray Neo-Platonic conceptions of an ordered and participated reality. This is especially the case when Christ is evoked not only as Redeemer but as the Word of God in whom the whole ordered reality of creation and redemption is divinely conceived in eternity. There are times when writers comment upon the liturgy as a recollection of the earthly and past realities of the passion, death, and rising from the dead in the abiding hope of final beatitude, and times when they stand in awe before the ritual participation in the heavenly liturgy that the glorious High Priest continues to render to God in the company of angels and saints.

Perhaps it is in commentary on scriptural figures, such as the paschal lamb or the manna, or on sacramental signs, that one notes more clearly an evolution in thought about representation. The earliest writers (as the earliest prayers) saw representation primarily in historical and eschatological terms. The events remembered brought salvation and promise and could be recalled in that way. The past lived on in the church of the redeemed, and people looked forward to possessing the full reality of what was promised and guaranteed in the future kingdom. By the fourth century, the scriptural types and the sacramental signs appear to have been endowed with a greater reality and were taken to be representations and realizations in iconic form of those events that they reflected.[29] Hence, either the historic events of Christ's pasch or the heavenly liturgy to which he ascended could be said to be enacted in the eucharist, just as the Old Testament figures could be taken to be an anticipated if veiled representation of the truth of Christ and of the Christian sacrament.

Though the salvific deeds of Christ are remembered in a variety of images, the imagery of sacrifice is increasingly applied to this ecclesial memorial action.[30] This use of imagery seems to have had its origins in the use of cultic terms to speak of the Christian life, it being the redeemed people in their following of Christ who constitute the true worship of the gospel order. In the polemic about religion with both Jews and Gentiles, the great prayer of thanksgiving that culminated in the table action of communion is said to be the only

---

29. See Robert Daly, *Christian Sacrifice: The Judeo-Christian Background before Origen*, Studies in Christian Antiquity, no. 18 (Washington, D.C.: The Catholic University of America Press, 1978), 498–508; and Kenneth Stevenson, *Eucharist and Offering* (New York: Pueblo Publishing Co., 1986).

30. See Maurice Jourjon, "Justin," in Sheerin, ed., *The Eucharist*, 71–85.

sacrifice that Christians need to and can offer.[31] Such worship is of course offered in and with Christ, so that when the imagery of priesthood and sacrifice was simultaneously used to speak of Christ's death and risen life it was almost a matter of course to say that the sacrifice of the church is a sacramental participation in Christ's sacrifice, whether this latter was thought of as the sacrifice of his death or the priestly worship that the risen Christ offers in heaven to the Father. Since the sacrifice of a worthy life of grace, the thanksgiving sacrifice of the church's prayer, the sacrifice of obedience offered by Christ in death, and the sacrifice of praise offered by him in heaven were all so obviously interrelated as fullness and participation, there could be none of the polemics over the sacrificial interpretation of the eucharist that occurred in later times and that is only now being mitigated.

The participation of Christians in the mysteries of Christ and in his worship, as well as the hope of their participation in his glory, could not be conceived except in connection with the nourishment that they received at the table of his body and blood. It is because the command of Christ to keep his memory is obeyed in the prayer of blessing over the bread and wine that these are transformed into his body and blood. There is considerable accent on the fact that the elements are the flesh and blood of the risen Lord, now endowed with incorruptibility and immortality. Hence for Christians, this is nourishment for freedom from sin and death, the firstfruits of eternal life in the glory of Christ. At times the cosmic significance of the table is derived from the notion of firstfruits as it applies to the bread and wine and to the resurrection of the body of Christ as firstfruits of creation's redemption.[32] Since the table is the common table to which all Christians are invited, there is considerable reflection given to it as the sacrament of ecclesial love and unity, and indeed to the identification of Christians with Christ in the one sacrament of the one body.[33] Because of this communion in grace, the elements represent not only Jesus Christ but the faithful themselves.

Despite the variety of these early writings, their unsystematic style, and their often occasional character, the unity of the church's eucharistic vision that unfolds is impressive. In the eucharist, the entire Christian mystery is ever present, celebrated and realized anew in the church. There the people are gathered as the redeemed and

31. See Hamman, "Irenaeus," 86–98.

32. Augustine *Sermons* 227, 272, in Hamman, ed., *The Mass*, 204–8.

33. See Hans-Joachim Schulz, *The Byzantine Liturgy: Symbolic Structure and Faith Expression*, trans. Matthew O'Connell (New York: Pueblo Publishing Co., 1986), 154–59.

eschatological people, in the orthodoxy of the one faith, and in the unity of the one ordered assembly. There Christ is present in the power of the Spirit, in the sacramental action, and in the elements of heavenly nourishment. There his pasch is remembered, and the worship of the church is gathered into his worship of the Father, as a living sacrifice of praise. There the martyrs are revered and venerated as the ideal of full sacramental and eschatological participation in the death and resurrection of the Savior. There Christians are instructed in the one mystery of the pasch, their life is renewed at the table, and they are fortified in their discipleship, in the renewed expectation of a final and unending share in Christ's glory.

THE EUCHARISTIC PRAYER

No account of early Christian perspectives on the eucharist would be complete without some reference to the anaphora or eucharistic prayer traditions.[34] These present one of the richest sources for a contemporary theology of this sacrament that grasps at once both its essential unity and its cultural pluriformity. Scholarly debates on the origin and form of the prayer are by no means settled. Some relation to Jewish blessing is acknowledged, but beyond this general agreement opinions differ. There is clearly much to be learned from comparing the Christian prayer with Jewish table prayer, especially with the *birkat-ha-mazon* or prayer of blessing that concluded a meal. It is impossible, however, to restrict the comparison to this prayer as though the Christian anaphora grew out of it in orderly fashion. Some writers have looked as well at other prayers, for example, the eighteen benedictions of the synagogue service. In recent years, considerable attention has been given to a fuller blessing tradition as represented in the genre of prayer referred to as the *todah*, which includes all prayers, whatever the occasion, offered in remembrance of the saving deeds of God.[35] Finally, one has to make room for the changes in the nature of blessing introduced by Christian communities, not only in content but also in form.

34. The most exhaustive study of the eucharistic prayer is that of Louis Bouyer, *Eucharist: The Theology and Spirituality of the Eucharistic Prayer*, trans. C. U. Quinn (Notre Dame, Ind.: Notre Dame University Press, 1968). For a survey of recent studies on its genesis, see Enrico Mazza, *The Eucharistic Prayers of the Roman Rite*, trans. Matthew O'Connell (New York: Pueblo Publishing Co., 1986), 1–29; Thomas Talley, "The Literary Structure of the Eucharistic Prayer," *Worship* 58 (1984): 404–20. For a collection of texts in English translation, see R. C. D. Jasper and G. J. Cuming, *Prayers of the Eucharist: Early and Reformed*, 3d ed. (New York: Pueblo Publishing Co., 1987).

35. The study to which all refer is Cesare Giraudo, *La Struttura Letteraria della Preghiera Eucaristica. Saggio Sulla genesi letteraria di una forma. Toda veterotestamentaria, Beraka giudaica, Anafora cristiana* (Rome: Biblical Institute Press, 1981).

With all of these precautions, it is still possible to speak of a theology that is rooted in the form and content of the anaphora. It is the central and community form for keeping memory of the mysteries of Christ, the core around which the very identity of the church is built. Thus it is important to note that it is the prayer of the people, proclaimed by the one who presides, raised up in the power of the Spirit, and that it is both thanksgiving and intercession. To use a later language, this prayer of the church is the form through which Christ and Christ's pasch are sacramentally present in the community. The recitation of the Last Supper or institution narrative containing the words of Jesus over the bread and cup may possibly not have been included in the earliest prayers, though it was not long before it gained a permanent and necessary place in the prayer.[36] Its meaning, however, derives not simply from its repetition but from its position in the prayer, along with the invocation of the Spirit. In that context, it represents the apostolic faith of the church, its intention to fulfill the commandment of Christ in praise and sacrament, in the power of the Spirit that from his glory he poured forth on believers. It also represents the persuasion that it is this very obedience, as well as the promise contained in the command, that gives the sacramental action its power to represent anew the paschal mystery and to nourish the faithful for eternal glory. While we are now accustomed to prayers that include sanctus, anamnesis, epiclesis, and offering, it is helpful to remember that these are but elaborations on a fundamental form that is thanksgiving and intercession rendered in commemoration of the Lord's pasch and its victory over sin and death. In light too of disputes about the relation of the sacrament to the sacrifice of Christ's death, it is helpful to note that sacrifice was only one among the images used to express the meaning of what the prayer recalled. The very earliest prayers known to us indeed are more wont to perceive in Jesus, God's servant, the very wisdom of God,[37] or to recall the death, the descent into hell, and the resurrection in the imagery of a conflict between Christ and the evil powers that besiege humanity, especially sin and death.[38] It is also helpful to note that it was its very nature as memorial thanksgiving and intercession that occasioned the liturgical action to be called a sacrifice, and that it was its eucharistic form that guaranteed its sacramental

---

36. This question was raised by Louis Ligier, "The Origins of the Eucharistic Prayer," *Studia Liturgica* 9 (1973): 161–85.

37. See the text from the Didache in Jasper and Cuming, *Prayers of the Eucharist*, 23f.

38. See the texts of Hippolytus and Addai and Mari, in Jasper and Cuming, *Prayers of the Eucharist*, 35, 42–44.

efficacy in representing the mysteries of Christ in the liturgy of the church.

THE MEDIEVAL SACRAMENT

While Scholastic theology in its greatest accomplishment is a wondrously systematic and synthetic explanation of the priestly liturgy celebrated in the cathedrals, monasteries, and chapels of the medieval West, it remains something of a puzzle how the move was made from the actively participated in local assembly of early centuries to the priestly offering of the Middle Ages.[39] At any rate, one cannot properly read a work like the *Summa* of Saint Thomas without having in mind the kind of liturgical action that he set out to explain.

Already in the great ecclesiastical writers of earlier centuries, such as John Chrysostom or Augustine, even in the midst of their perorations on the sacrament of the Body, one notes the traces of disintegration. The people needed to be exhorted to frequent and regular communion and to a responsibility for the celebration. Some of the writers, like Chrysostom or Leo the Great, are themselves responsible for fostering a hieratic view of liturgy and of its ordained ministers. The liturgies of Rome and Constantinople endeavored to reach a peak of splendor as some earthly realization of the heavenly court in ways that influenced celebration across the whole of Christianity. It is the opinion of some that the failure to continue to adopt the people's language in the liturgies of the West, once the first transition from Greek to Latin had been made, was the greatest force in separating the liturgy from the people and the people from the liturgy so that it became a priestly and clerical enactment done for and on behalf of the people rather than together with them.[40] Language is indeed both a means of communication and a barrier. When access to the action through language was not possible, the people continued to have access to the visible, and the devotion to the consecrated and reserved species became the primary eucharistic reality for the populace at large, all the way from kings to peasants.

One could appeal to other influences as well, such as the hoary sinfulness of a virtually uninitiated baptismal throng whose deeds cried out for penance and propitiation, and who were at least helped to feel that way by monks and clergy. The priestly role of offering sacrifice for sins in the name and person of Christ took on

---

39. On the medieval sacrament, see Powers, *Eucharistic Theology*, 22–30; Mitchell, *Cult and Controversy*, 66–195.

40. Mitchell, *Cult and Controversy*, 118, 380–418.

greater importance in such a climate, and this replaced the great sacrifice of thanksgiving offered together with Christ by the assembled faithful.[41]

Scholastic eucharistic theology[42] is a theology of and for the priest rather than a theology for the baptized. At the center is the priest who in the person of Christ and of the church consecrates, confers grace, and offers sacrifice, parallel with his priestly role of forgiving sins through sacramental absolution. Since devotion centers around the consecrated species, much time is given to explaining the real presence of Christ and the manner in which this comes about through the words of the priest, which are in fact the words of Christ himself, whose power the priest has received. That symbolic thought that could locate the figured in the figure was on the wane, even if allegorical fantasies were not, so that categories adopted from Aristotelian thought were used to explain the difference between presence in truth and presence in figure. With the controversy surrounding Berengar of Tours,[43] the axiom *aut in figura aut in veritate* had become popular and replaced that mode of thought that could see the *veritas* in the *figura* not as the result of some supplementary action but precisely because it was a figure. Thus the real presence came to be explained, with much refinement that often eluded the people and the preacher, as substantial presence, and the means of this becoming present was explained as substantial change or transubstantiation. The thought of Thomas Aquinas on the real presence deserves a more wholesome consideration and respect than it often gets nowadays, but it cannot be denied that it was developed in a context that paid but scant attention to the presence of Christ and his mysteries in the liturgical action itself. Its great achievement in its time was that it prevented a reduction of presence to the purely figurative and allegorical, while at the same time it avoided the Charybdis of fleshly realism expressed in many a story of bleeding hosts and visions of the Christ child. Once Thomas has removed all possibility of presence through locomotion, corruption, generation, or copresence of the body with the bread, one is indeed left with the act of faith that the Christ who suffered and was crucified and is now enjoying glory in heaven is present in this sacramental form to which nothing else in human ken can be compared, and that he is there for the sake

---

41. There are several theories on the reasons for the multiplication of Masses. For one theory and an overview of the literature, see Angelus Häussling, "Motives for Frequency of Eucharist," in Mary Collins and David Power, eds., *Can We Always Celebrate the Eucharist?* 25–30.

42. Thomas Aquinas is of course the outstanding exemplar (see *Summa Theologiae* III, qq. 73–83).

43. Mitchell, *Cult and Controversy*, 137–63, summarizes these controversies.

of the faithful, not only to be worshiped but to be eaten by them for the forgiveness of sins, for grace, and for glory.

The Reformation controversies of the sixteenth century were about both practice and doctrine as these are essentially interconnected.[44] As far as practice was concerned, the Reformers objected to the concentration on the priestly acts of consecration and sacrifice and to the replacement of communion by the veneration of the species. They wanted the Lord's Supper restored as a sacrament, accessible in both kinds to all the faithful, and they would not brook the language of sacrifice when this was associated with propitiation. For them, the once and for all sacrifice was that of Christ and the cross, and the purpose of the sacrament was to make its mercy and forgiveness available to the communicants. Hence they expurgated the Mass of all language of sacrifice other than that of thanksgiving and self-offering.[45] This, however, was not a retrieval of the early Christian understanding of sacrifice since the Reformers saw this metaphorical sacrifice not as essential but as accessory to the Lord's Supper, whose only essence was the offer of the sacrament of the body and blood to the faithful and communion in the sacrament. For defenders of the Catholic faith, this undid the whole Catholic system of devotion and worship and stood as a denial of the essential doctrines of substantial presence, transubstantiation, and propitiatory sacrifice offered by the priest for the living and the dead. It takes many volumes to discuss anew the exact doctrinal and theological positions of both Catholic apologists and Reformers. Whatever is said about these, it has to be said that the situation was one of impasse and led to the defensive definitions of the Council of Trent that were concerned with both faith and practice and that established the medieval eucharist as the core Catholic practice for four more centuries, even though the postconciliar reforms did purge it of many of its more impious and superstitious abuses.[46] In the Decree on the Sacrament of the Eucharist, the Council of Trent defined real presence and the change of the bread and wine into the body and blood of Christ that this presence demands (see Denzinger-Schönmetzer, *Enchiridion Symbolorum* [hereafter DS], 1651–53). The term *transubstantiation* was not said to be a necessary part of the defi-

---

44. For a summary, see Alasdair I. C. Heron, *Table and Tradition: Toward an Ecumenical Understanding of the Eucharist* (Philadelphia: Westminster Press, 1983), 108–45.

45. For an English translation of the liturgies of the principal Reformers, see Bard Thompson, ed., *Liturgies of the Western Church* (New York: Collins World, 1975), 95–307.

46. See Josef Jungmann, *The Mass of the Roman Rite* (New York: Benziger, 1951), 1:134–35.

nition. Instead, the council simply said that it was a most suitable way in which to express the change that takes place in the elements. In the Decree on the Sacrifice of the Mass (DS 1738–59),[47] the council abjured any idea of mere metaphorical sacrifice and sternly defined the propitiatory character of the sacrifice as offered by the ordained priest. One can certainly find language in the conciliar teachings that shows a healthy sense of the sacramental and representational relation of the Mass to the cross, as one can also find encouragement of more frequent communion by the faithful, though not under both kinds, which could have smacked too much of Protestant persuasion (DS 1747, 1760). There is however no getting away from the fact that Trent favored a priestly conception of eucharistic doctrine and practice and did nothing to overcome the clericalization of liturgy that was so much a part of the medieval heritage.

The mistake of later centuries, encouraged by the Catechism of the Council of Trent, was to take the Tridentine decrees as the authentic and full teaching of the Christian faith on the eucharist rather than as the historically determined, apologetic, and defensive documents that they actually were. Without setting themselves up as judges of history, Catholics today can face their own critical issues only through a better understanding of what took place in the sixteenth century and of the reasons why the Council of Trent chose to define certain articles of the mystery of the eucharist as essential to the faith and practice of the time.

CONTEMPORARY ROMAN CATHOLIC THEOLOGY

Some idea of the major interests of the contemporary theology of the eucharist found in Roman Catholic writers has already been given in the introduction to this essay. For one thing, it is done in an ecumenical context with the purpose of finding ways to appreciate the contribution of Reformation and Orthodox thought to the Western churches. It is also more historically and culturally conscious, attentive to past context and to the possibilities of eucharistic celebration and understanding in African and Asian cultures.[48] Most important of all, eucharistic theology often adopts a liturgical starting point. It is then presented as reflection on celebration and a contribution to its

---

47. For a study of this decree, see David N. Power, *The Sacrifice We Offer: The Tridentine Dogma and Its Reinterpretation* (New York: Crossroad, 1987).

48. This is not much developed here, but see the examples in Thurian and Wainwright, eds., *Baptism and Eucharist*, 186–209.

advancement. Consequently, it has a critical edge, being attentive to what has in the past distorted the tradition and to what in the present impedes a full and authentic celebration. Since it is concerned with celebration, it has to integrate the insights of the human sciences and of the arts into symbol and ritual. At the same time, because eucharistic theology belongs in tradition, it is engaged in retrieving its biblical and early Christian past and in reckoning with the Catholic emphasis on presence, transubstantiation, and priestly sacrifice. This essay has concentrated mostly on the work of retrieval since this is the necessary groundwork for the other tasks.

All of this is as much agenda as it is accomplished fact. Indeed, it is next to impossible to find a Roman Catholic systematic theology of the eucharist that incorporates this agenda fully and represents a system that could be compared with the Scholastic or post-Tridentine system. Nonetheless, a schematic and ordered summary is attempted here, by way at least of a guideline to reflection and practice.

The core perception of this proffered synthesis is that the eucharist or Lord's Supper is the sacrament of the church as the living eschatological sign of God's salvific rule, proclaimed and promised in the death and resurrection of Jesus Christ. This perception is elaborated upon from a liturgical starting point as a reflection on that action by which the church comes to be in the representation of Christ's mysteries through Word, prayer, and ritual. All the components of the action have to be taken into account: the gathering in the Spirit, the recall of God's saving acts in the proclamation of the Word, the great commemorative prayer of thanksgiving and intercession, and the communion in Christ's body and blood.[49]

Cultural and anthropological studies remind us that a people finds its identity in story and rebuilds its hope in times of crisis from the recall and retelling of this story. The eucharist is liturgically built around the narrative of Christ's passion and death, to which it relates a host of other stories, those concerning Jesus himself, those taken from the Old Testament, and those about the nascent church. Narrative is complemented by other genres of texts, especially prophetic, sapiential, and parenetic, which makes it possible to integrate what is narrated into a community basis for vision and action. The liturgy of the Word is not simply preparatory to memorial but is integral to it.

Rather than using a proclamation/response schema to explain the traditional two parts of the Mass, it is better to use a schema of

---

49. See David N. Power, *Unsearchable Riches: The Symbolic Nature of Liturgy* (New York: Pueblo Publishing Co., 1984), 108–43.

flow. The great thanksgiving prayer flows from the narrative and serves to bring it in an action-orienting way into the life of the church. From one point of view one can say that people respond to story, but when story is viewed as that which forges identity, one has to ask what are the means by which it becomes a constitutive part of their lives and of their vision. The eucharistic prayer is couched in a nonbiblical idiom, even when it adopts scriptural story and imagery. Though studies on the eucharistic prayer ought to have made people aware of cultural diversity, its cultural rooting is not sufficiently respected in contemporary liturgical developments. Perhaps this is because the theological necessity of this rooting is not appreciated. The anaphora is actually a reinterpretation of the scriptural story in cultural context and idiom and in prayerful form. It is what can be called an appropriation by a people of their Christian tradition, worked into the fabric of their dominant perceptions and attitudes.[50] That these attitudes are expressed in the form of thanksgiving and intercession reflects the ways in which people see God's power active in their lives and history. The possible developments in the genre itself probably need deeper consideration, attentive to the ways in which people today in face of contemporary history might express their sense of configuration to Christ and of a divinely saving power in the life of humankind. It is on this account that some thought has been given recently to an inclusion of lamentation in the memorial prayer, though one can hardly say that this suggestion has received widespread and popular acclaim.[51]

The table ritual is associated with story and prayer. To truly appreciate this ritual as the communion in hope in Christ's body and blood, reflection is needed on what it signifies of the community that gathers.[52] Before it symbolizes Christ's presence, before it is changed by the transforming prayer, the table signifies and represents the people. Even after the prayer when it represents Christ and his self-gift, it continues to represent the people, now caught up in the fullness of their being in Christ. The significance of bread and wine and of the common table in themselves is important to an understanding of the

---

50. See David N. Power, "The Song of the Lord in an Alien Land," in Herman Schmidt and David Power, eds., *Politics and Liturgy* (entire issue of *Concilium* 92 [New York: Herder and Herder, 1974]: 85–106).

51. See David N. Power, "The Eucharistic Prayer: Another Look," in Frank C. Senn, ed., *New Eucharistic Prayers: An Ecumenical Study* (New York: Paulist Press, 1987), 239–57.

52. See Philippe Rouillard, "From Human Meal to Christian Eucharist," *Worship* 52 (1978): 425–39; 53 (1979): 40–56; Enrique Dussel, "The Bread of the Eucharistic Celebration as a Sign of Justice in the Community," in Schmidt and Power, eds., *Politics and Liturgy*, 56–65.

presence of Christ in these elements. They represent fundamental human needs and desires. They represent the work that is done to bring them to the table. They represent humanity's communion with the whole of creation and with its cycles of production and reproduction. The breaking of bread and sharing of a common cup are ritual actions brought into many a human situation to express both a necessary mutual dependency and a common hope. When the bread and wine are transformed into the body and blood of Christ, they lose none of this significance but carry it with them into the reality of communion in Christ, renewed in the life-giving and eschatological power of the Spirit. The thanksgiving and the intercession that the community renders to the Father in the life of the Spirit and in the appropriation of Christ's memory come now to center on this table, where human lives and human hopes are transformed. The vision of faith, love, and hope already expressed in the prayer is made more concrete, as is the sense of Christ's continuing presence in the church and in human history. The reconciliation and the justice of God's rule are embodied in the symbols that represent Christ and with and in him a transformed humanity and a transformed creation. From such action, the church emerges in the concreteness of time and place as the sign of the promise, the eschatological sacrament of what has been accomplished and promised in the pasch of Christ, the pattern of its agapic praxis suggested to it by the very sacrament that it celebrates.[53]

If this is the vision of the eucharist that comes from a study of Scripture and tradition, related to the concreteness of human culture and history, theology has to develop several of its tasks from this center. It needs to be critical of what impedes such a celebration. Even while it acknowledges many of the fruits of medieval devotion and practice, it cannot but see the human elements that impeded a more authentic development. Whatever historical explanations can be justly offered, it must be seen that a cultic theology that identifies the eucharistic action with the priest is an impediment to an ecclesial theology that fosters a celebration of the church as an eschatological people. It must also be seen that a theology of real presence that removes contact with the sacrament from all the senses but the visual is a long way from the communion of the Supper room and from the command that Christ gave to the disciples to keep his memory. Similarly, it needs to be recognized that an excess of the language of propitiation prevents a retrieval of the sacrifice of thanksgiving

---

53. See Tissa Balasuriya, *The Eucharist and Human Liberation* (Maryknoll, N.Y.: Orbis Books, 1979).

as the core expression of what minister and community pronounce over the table. Finally, a theological explanation of the elements of bread and wine that withholds their power to represent people, their history, their culture, and their aspirations is a long way from the truth of the incarnation.[54]

It is in this context that Roman Catholic theology has to incorporate that which is permanently valid in the doctrines of real presence, substantial change, sacrifice, and priesthood. Substantial presence and substantial change are not to be reduced to purely anthropological or phenomenological categories. They can be better appreciated for what they say of Christ's presence if the starting point is the resurrection and the Spirit that assures the presence of the risen Lord in the church. After the memorial thanksgiving over them, the bread and wine are indeed no mere material substances. They belong in the world of communion with the risen Lord and thus assume a new reality whereby he is present in the midst of his faithful. Since our theology can hardly account for the transformation of the humanity of Christ through the resurrection in the Spirit, there is still much to be learned from the ascetically developed theology of Thomas Aquinas that insists that all distracting images be removed before any positive explanation is offered. It is because we do believe that the humanity of Christ has been transformed in the Spirit through his death and resurrection as the firstfruits of all creation that we believe that he is present in the sacrament, but what accounting is there for the nature of this change except in the imagery of faith and hope? Important to a just retrieval of the doctrine of substantial change are the belief in this transformation and the hope that it carries with it. It is for this very reason that all talk of the presence in the elements and of their change is put in the context of the promise and guarantee of the Spirit given to the believing community. The presence in the elements is related to the presence in the community itself, in the Word and in the prayer, as has been indicated by the conciliar and postconciliar documents of the universal Vatican synod.[55]

As for the Tridentine definition that the Mass is a sacrifice in no purely metaphorical sense but that it is propitiatory for the living and the dead, many problems have already been overcome through certain results of ecumenical dialogue. First, there is the common recognition that the eucharist can be spoken of as sacrifice only in sacramental relation to the sacrifice of the cross, of which it is the

---

54. This gives rise to discussion about the nature of the eucharistic elements in different cultural settings.

55. See Peter Fink, "Perceiving the Presence of Christ," *Worship* 58 (1984): 17–28.

representation. Historical studies[56] have made it clear enough that this language was already used at Trent but that in the circumstances of the time it was not enough to overcome oppositions between Catholic and Protestant interests and beliefs. Second, the primary offering of the Mass is the offering of Christ himself to the Father, and as communion gift to the church. The offering of the church is a communion in Christ's self-offering and has no validity aside from its inclusion in that offering. There is no unanimous agreement among Catholics as to whether it is appropriate to say that the church offers Christ by way of expressing its will to be taken up into his offering and its confidence in Christ's acceptance by God for the sins of the world.[57] Beyond these clarifications of the dogma, headway has to be made by way of overcoming the apparent opposition between a sacrifice of thanksgiving and a sacrifice for sin. Much that has already been explained in this essay serves in that direction, for the study of the eucharistic prayer makes it clear that it is through the memorial prayer of thanksgiving and intercession that the pasch of Christ is represented and becomes efficacious for the community gathered in his name and in the Spirit. It has also become clear that the prayer is a prayer over bread and wine and leads normally to the communion table.

Communion is the ordinary rather than an extraordinary way to participate in the sacrament and in its fruits, while at the same time communion at the table cannot be separated from participation in the memorial prayer. This helps to get beyond the seeming conflict between the Protestant position that forgiveness of sins is given to the believer through communion and the Catholic position that the Mass may be offered by the priest for the sins of the living and the dead. The intercessory power of Christ's priestly prayer with which the church is in communion and the gracious efficacy of the sacrament stand together rather than in opposition. On the other hand, the distinctive note of Catholic belief, embodied in the dogma, that there is an abiding and salutary communion in Christ between the living and all the dead (not only the saints) and that this is given expression in the prayer of the church in the Mass, is worthy of retention. Practices of Mass-offerings may well need to be revised, if they are not already under revision, so as to do away with a note of superstition and certain connotations of priestly power. This does not however mean forgetting the fundamental tenet of the communion

---

56. Power, *The Sacrifice We Offer*, 69–76, 96–116.

57. This is the explanation adopted by the Catholic party to the Lutheran/Roman Catholic dialogue. See Lutheran/Roman Catholic Dialogue, *The Eucharist* (Geneva: The Lutheran World Federation, 1980), 20.

between the living and the dead that lies behind the remembrance of the dead in the Mass.[58]

These few remarks must suffice to show how the importance of the doctrines on real presence and sacrifice stands out more fully and clearly when they are put in the context of a theology of the eucharist as the sacrament of God's eschatological people that receives its life and mission from the living presence of Christ in its midst, through the power of the Spirit. As explained, this theology is explored through a reflection on the order of the eucharist, which includes in one integral memorial rite the narrative of the pasch, the thanksgiving prayer, and the communion table. This reflection provides the needed context for the Catholic dogmas and their reappropriation. As for the role of the priest, that is dealt with in the essay on orders.

CONCLUSION

In the introduction to this essay on current Roman Catholic theology of the eucharist, the threefold context of liturgical renewal, ecumenical convergence, and doctrinal concern was noted. It was stated that much of theology's work at present is a retrieval of the whole of tradition in that context. There followed a presentation of current biblical studies on the Lord's Supper or eucharist. After that, material was culled from early Christian centuries, with specific mention of the theological import of the anaphora or eucharistic prayer. This led up to a consideration of the particularities of the medieval sacrament and its consolidation at the Council of Trent. The essay concluded with the outline of a contemporary perspective, rooted in the recovery of the eucharist as sacrament of Christ's body and of its proper liturgical form. This provided the context in which persisting doctrinal concerns can be considered and reappropriated.

---

58. Power, _The Sacrifice We Offer_, 158–60.

FOR FURTHER READING

Bouyer, Louis. *Eucharist: The Theology and Spirituality of the Eucharistic Prayer.* Trans. Charles Underhill Quinn. Notre Dame, Ind.: University of Notre Dame Press, 1968.

A careful study of the origin and development of eucharistic prayers in different traditions; an important book for the reference to the eucharistic prayer as theological source.

Léon-Dufour, Xavier. *Sharing the Eucharistic Bread: The Witness of the New Testament.* Trans. Matthew O'Connell. New York: Paulist Press, 1987.

The best available study of the New Testament data by a Roman Catholic scholar; comprehensive, up-to-date on exegetical studies, and satisfyingly theological.

Mazza, Enrico. *The Eucharistic Prayers of the Roman Rite.* Trans. Matthew O'Connell. New York: Pueblo Publishing Co., 1986.

A theological study of the current prayers of the Roman Sacramentary, done with due attention to theological and liturgical concerns by an author well known for his studies on the liturgy.

Mitchell, Nathan. *Cult and Controversy: The Worship of the Eucharist outside Mass.* New York: Pueblo Publishing Co., 1982.

The first part studies the development of this cult and relates it to theological and spiritual interests as they emerged in the first millennium. The second part is a pastoral and theological commentary on present directives and practices in the Roman Rite.

Power, David N. *The Sacrifice We Offer: The Tridentine Dogma and Its Reinterpretation.* Edinburgh: T and T Clark; New York: Crossroad, 1987.

A study of the doctrine of Trent on the sacrifice of the Mass, based on an examination of the acts of the council looked at in the context of current ecumenical dialogues in which the Roman church is engaged.

Rordorf, Willy, et al. *The Eucharist of Early Christians.* Trans. Matthew O'Connell. New York: Pueblo Publishing Co., 1978.

A clear and readable set of articles presenting the eucharistic practice and thought of pre-Nicene church orders and writers such as Ignatius of Antioch, Irenaeus of Lyons, Cyprian of Carthage, and Origen and Clement of Alexandria. Important for a knowledge of early eucharistic theology.

Schillebeeckx, Edward. *The Eucharist.* New York: Sheed and Ward, 1968.

An important study of the classical theology of transubstantiation and of the doctrine of the Council of Trent, in relation to the issues raised by *Mysterium Fidei*, an encyclical letter of Pope Paul VI.

Seasoltz, Kevin, ed. *Living Bread, Saving Cup: Readings on the Eucharist.* Rev. ed. New York: Pueblo Publishing Co., 1987.

A collection of essays that appeared originally in *Worship* and that address many of the current exegetical, liturgical, and theological questions important to eucharistic theology.

SACRAMENTS

9.6

Order

9.6

Order

David N. Power

INTRODUCTION

The current context for the theology of the sacrament of order in the Roman Catholic church is set by the teachings of the Second Vatican Council and by the developments in the ecclesial life that belong to its aftermath. These include improved relations with other churches and a large participation of the faithful in the ministry.

Since the high Middle Ages the sacrament of order had been defined primarily in terms of priesthood and the offering of the eucharistic sacrifice. Ordination to the priesthood was practically identified with ordination to the presbyterate, or second rank of the hierarchy, so that it was even a common opinion that the episcopacy was not a sacrament but a jurisdiction of divine institution.[1] In its Constitution on the Church (*Lumen Gentium* [hereafter LG]), after considerable debate the Second Vatican Council declared the sacramental nature of the episcopacy. It also taught that ordination

---

1. The most ample work in English to date is that of Bernard Cooke, *Ministry to Word and Sacraments: History and Theology* (Philadelphia: Fortress Press, 1976).

meant ordination to the threefold ministry of Word, sacrament, and pastoral care, thus going beyond the idea that it was connected only with the ministry of sacrament or liturgical priesthood (LG 21, 26). It also asked for the restoration of that much neglected order, the diaconate, which for centuries was nothing more than a step toward priesthood. To implement this the council laid down the conditions for the restoration of the diaconate as a life-long ministry (LG 29). Thus the council formulated the teaching that the sacrament of order includes the tripartite ministry of bishop, presbyter, and deacon, and that ordination to each one of these is ordination to the ministry of Word, sacrament, and pastoral care. This was a return to the vision and practice of early Christian centuries and marked a separation from the prevailing medieval and post-Tridentine perspectives. Both in the Constitution on the Church and in other documents, the council gave further specifications about the precise nature of the ministry of each of these orders (see the Decree on the Pastoral Office of Bishops and the Decree on the Ministry and Life of Priests).

All of this teaching on the sacrament of order was given in the context of a renewed ecclesiology and a renewed appreciation of baptism as a full induction into the life of the church. As is well known, the council spoke of the church as the people of God and of its participation in the threefold office of Christ as prophet, priest, and king. It then spoke of the part that each and all of the baptized have in this threefold activity, through responsibility for the transmission of Christian faith, for the church's liturgical life, and for the apostolate, in one or other of its many forms (LG chap. 4; Decree on the Apostolate of the Laity). In the aftermath of the council the more active part that the baptized had already begun to take in the ministerial life of the church increased a hundredfold all over the world, so that people have come to dub this period as one of an explosion of ministries. Naturally this has affected both the exercise and the conception of the ordained ministry. There has been considerable debate over the use of the word *ministry*, as some would prefer to give it a restricted usage and employ it only for activities marked off by official designation, but in general it is given much the same employment and meaning as the word *charism*, or gift of service, in the Pauline letters.[2] Consequently, it proves useful to note the distinction between ministry and order. This recognizes that some participation in the church's ministry is a normal part of all adult

---

2. See the discussion in Thomas O'Meara, *Theology of Ministry* (New York: Paulist Press, 1983), 134–75.

Christian life but that the order of the church, necessary to its existence, marks off the part of each and assigns specific sacramental and leadership roles to those who receive the sacramental laying on of hands. It is inadequate simply to list the offices and actions for which bishop, presbyter (or priest), and deacon are respectively ordained. It behoves theological reflection to explain the precise purpose and character of ordination, or of the sacrament of order. To do this, sacramental theologians and ecclesiologists look back to the origins and later developments of ministry in order to sort out issues pertinent to its future. As they do this, theologians in the Roman Catholic church find themselves necessarily in dialogue with theologians of other churches who are faced with similar questions and who are looking for a unified approach to order that will foster ecumenical reconciliation and unity. Because of past dissensions, in its own way this ecumenical interaction draws attention to the relation between the common priesthood of the baptized and ministerial priesthood and to the meaning of the tripartite division within the one pastoral ministry.[3]

NEW TESTAMENT ORIGINS

It is part of the traditional teaching of the Roman Catholic church that the origins of its hierarchical ministry are to be found in the New Testament and more specifically in the dispositions of Jesus himself.[4] When accused by the Reformers in the sixteenth century of having distorted the evangelical reality of the church and of its ministry, the church responded through the Council of Trent that the episcopacy as then instituted was the proper realization of the ministry to which Christ had commissioned the apostles.[5] This was in substance repeated at the Second Vatican Council (LG 18). Neither Trent nor

---

3. To date, the high point of these discussions is Faith and Order Paper No. 111 of the Faith and Order Commission of the World Council of Churches, *Baptism, Eucharist and Ministry* (Geneva: World Council of Churches, 1982), and the response to it. See nos. 19–31 of the section on ministry.

4. See Cooke, *Ministry*, 33–57. Also, Raymond Brown, *Priest and Bishop: Biblical Reflections* (New York: Paulist Press, 1970); Jean Delorme, ed., *Le ministère et les ministères selon le Nouveau Testament* (Paris: Le Seuil, 1974); Andre Lemaire, "Ministries in the New Testament: Recent Research," *Biblical Theology Bulletin* 3 (1973): 133–66; Edward Schillebeeckx, *The Church with a Human Face: A New and Expanded Theology of Ministry* (New York: Crossroad, 1985); John H. Schulz, *Paul and the Anatomy of Apostolic Authority* (Cambridge: Cambridge University Press, 1975); Edward Schweizer, *Church Order in the New Testament* (London: SCM, 1961).

5. Council of Trent, Decree on the Sacrament of Order (in Denzinger-Schönmetzer, *Enchiridion Symbolorum* [hereafter DS], 1767–69, 1777).

Vatican II wished to say that the tripartite ministry of bishop, presbyter, and deacon in its exact form could be traced back to the New Testament, but they did wish to maintain a factual and legitimate continuity with the origins of the church in the community of Jesus' followers, or in other words with the apostolic church.

Historical and form criticism make it clear that one should not look to the New Testament for a clearly focused institution, and that it is not possible to trace an exact linear history of the origins of ministry and its ordering. The task is rather to see what understanding of ministry that is expressed in the New Testament needs to be constantly kept alive in the church, granted that this will always be in a form shaped by history and proper to any given place and time, as the Holy Spirit guides the community in its life and mission.

First among the New Testament factors important to ministry is the relation between ministry, church, and kingdom of God. The church as community of belief and discipleship is the historical manifestation of God's rule in the world as it reached its prophetic fulfillment in the death and resurrection of Jesus Christ and in the Spirit-filled community of his followers.[6] It always exists in relation to the kingdom and as sign of that kingdom for all humankind. It exists not for and of itself, but in service to the kingdom of God. Its ministry is the ministry of an apostolic community. That is to say, it builds up the community in itself as a community of apostolic witness, and it must promote both the inner life of the church and its ways of proclaiming the gospel. The word, power, and service of Jesus are the paradigm for all ministry. The twelve who ate and drank with Jesus, who listened to his teaching and who witnessed to his death and resurrection, are the fountainhead of the church's life and ministry, though they cannot be said to represent its definitive institutional form.[7]

In the communities of the apostolic era, we need to distinguish between the ministries that we find active in them and the order that governed their lives. There are several lists of charisms and services in the churches, but none that is exhaustive. The general impression is that ministry is wide-ranging, that it comes from the power of the Spirit, and that it goes with membership in the community rather than being the result of any particular commission. The New Testament vocabulary is more often that of charisms and service. Charism stands for a gift received from the Holy Spirit for the service (*diakonia*) of the church and of the gospel. The one criterion

---

6. Schillebeeckx, *The Church*, 13–39.

7. See Sean Freyne, *The Twelve: Disciples and Apostles* (London: Sheed and Ward, 1967).

of authenticity is that ministry contribute to the common good of the life of faith and the witness of the truth abroad. Theologians are wont to classify the ministries for the sake of comprehension.[8] This can help provided the tentative and provisional nature of the classification is recognized. Thus one can distinguish between ministries of Word, inner service, and worship, and within the ministries of Word between the apostolic or kerygmatic, the prophetic and the didactic. Of the ministries of worship, little is said, but one may distinguish between the use of the many different gifts that enliven worship and the presidency, without however having any clear signals as to who presided or how this was done. At the center of worship was of course the Lord's Supper, with its reading of the Scriptures, its apostolic Word, its blessing prayer, and its table ritual in the body and blood of Christ. It is quite possible that presidency over this service and the proclamation of the blessing and memorial prayer (in essence a Word ministry) were at least at times done by different people.[9]

This of course already touches on the ordering of the community and on the ordering of relations between churches. One has to look at the way in which order is served within each community and at the way in which the communities are bound together as the one body of Christ. By and large, one can distinguish between the internal order of the church in Jerusalem, that of the Pauline churches, and that adumbrated in the later pastoral letters.[10] Each seems to have adopted a different model from cultural surroundings, and it is in the pastoral letters that concern for the transmission of faith and ministry looms larger.

Beyond that, one has to take note of the role that the original twelve, particularly Peter, and the apostle Paul played in proclaiming the Word and in binding the churches together in submission to the apostolic witness and the grace of the Spirit. The forging of the image of the apostle was important to development and historical continuity.[11] The word actually owes more to Paul than to the twelve. It is meant broadly speaking to express a witness to the resurrection of the Crucified One (a commission received from the risen Christ), the proclamation of this gospel, and a life of faithful witness that commands authority. It is a designation that covers Paul and the

---

8. See *New Catholic Encyclopedia*, s.v. "Ministry."

9. On presidency of the Eucharist in the early church, see Hervé-Marie Legrand, "The Presidency of the Eucharist according to the Ancient Tradition," *Worship* 53 (1979): 413–38.

10. See the summary of studies in O'Meara, *Theology*, 76–94. Also, Raymond Brown, "Episkope and Episkopos: The New Testament Evidence," *Theological Studies* 41 (1980): 322–38.

11. Schulz, *Paul*.

holy women of John's Gospel as much as Peter and the eleven, but that was then associated in a particular way with the twelve in order to express the origins of the church in the discipleship of Jesus' companions, in the witness of his deeds and teaching and of his death and resurrection, and in the mission to proclaim this gospel continually. That is the rather particular meaning that the church in subsequent centuries gave to the image of the twelve apostles and of a church founded on the apostles, while always recognizing that the proclamation of the original apostolic witness was in fact more complex than the image might suggest. Paul at least was always there to remind the church of this.

Apart from the development of the image of apostle and twelve apostles, the role of Peter and of Paul in regard to many churches is a reminder that besides the inner ordering of churches some broader ordering of churches in their mutual relations was required. They needed to be bound together in their common fidelity to Jesus Christ and in a life of communion and of witness to the power of God's kingdom, made manifest in the works of the Spirit. Though Peter and Paul are the chief figures in this regard, the Council of Jerusalem, the apostolic work of Barnabas and Silas, the leadership of Stephen and six others among the Hellenists, the discipline exercised by Timothy and Titus, and the itinerant mission of prophets all had a role to play. It is not however until the subapostolic period that any clear lines of a commonly accepted order begin to emerge.

EARLY CHRISTIAN CENTURIES

Looking to early Christian centuries, we need to be attentive to the development of church order and to the development of an ordination service.[12] Ministry in the service of the church and of its mission is more wide-ranging than that which is covered under these headings, though unfortunately it is true that all ministries tended to be absorbed in the course of time into the ordained ministry.

Ignatius of Antioch is an early witness of the appearance of the tripartite order of bishop, presbyterium, and deacons in the churches of Asia Minor. In the same period, however, other churches appear to have been governed by a presbyterium or college of presbyters. For Ignatius, the truly important significance of the one church under the pastoral care of the one bishop was that the church was

---

12. See Cooke, *Ministry*, 75–112. Also, H. von Campenhausen, *Ecclesiastical Authority and Spiritual Power in the Church of the First Three Centuries* (Stanford, Calif.: Stanford University Press, 1969); Schillebeeckx, *The Church*, 125–55.

maintained in its unity and in its apostolic faith by gathering for the eucharist under his presidency. Later on, this was likewise brought into evidence by writers such as Cyprian of Carthage. With the *Apostolic Tradition* of Hippolytus and the church orders associated with it, one could say that the image of the church had come into bold relief as one eucharistic communion, under the presidency of the one bishop, assisted in government by the presbyterium and in multiple services by deacons. It is in the context of eucharistic communion that ordination to the threefold ministry took place. By all accounts, the faithful had an active part in electing the bishop and some say in the choice of presbyters, though this probably varied. Though bishops from other churches presided at the ordination of a bishop, the service was a liturgy of the entire community, allowing one to say that the church ordained its bishop in the communion of all churches, as represented by those bishops who presided at the ceremony.

The central ritual action of the ordination service for bishop, presbyters, and deacons was the laying on of hands with a prayer of blessing, invoking the descent of the Holy Spirit.[13] The laying on of hands was of course a very common ritual action, used in many circumstances, but in appointment to ministry in the church it was marked off as specific to these three orders. People appointed to such orders as those of widow, reader, or cantor did not receive the laying on of hands. As far as the meaning of this ordination rite is concerned, there are shades of meaning that distinguish an Eastern from a Latin perspective. In Greek-speaking churches, *cheirotonia* meant primarily the invocation of the Spirit who blessed the candidate with those gifts of service that enabled him to perform a ministry for the church. In Latin-speaking churches, the word *ordinatio* took precedence over the image of laying on of hands and designated primarily the appointment to an order or office in the church.[14] With the poorly developed pneumatology of the Latin churches, the prayer of ordination often failed to include an invocation of the Spirit. This is important because it meant that in common understanding and theological reflection the notion of an institutional transmission of office and power prevailed over that of a response of the Spirit to the prayer of the church and an enabling for ministry through its gifts.

---

13. See W. H. Frere, "Early Ordination Services," *Journal of Theological Studies* 16 (1915): 323–69; Pierre-Marie Gy, "Ancient Ordination Prayers," in Wiebe Vos and Geoffrey Wainwright, eds., *Ordination Rites* (Rotterdam: Liturgical Ecumenical Center Trust, 1980), 70–93.

14. See Gy, "Ancient Ordination Prayers."

One of the factors that most strongly influenced the development of the theology of order was the change in the role of presbyters.[15] Their original office appears to have been to assist the bishop in the governance of the church and indeed to assure that this was done within each church in a collegiate way. In time, however, through varied kinds of development they became pastors and sacramental ministers in smaller communities that remained under the supervision of the bishop. This meant that their ordination was to pastoral care, sacramental ministry, and at least some teaching. Indeed, it paralleled in miniature the ministry of the bishop, so that the question of the distinction between these two orders was blurred. Simultaneously, the ministry of bishops was less and less connected with eucharistic communities and more and more devoted to communion between churches. One could say that this kind of ministry was devoted to keeping unity in the diocese, fidelity to the apostolic tradition through teaching in communion with other bishops, and the catholic communion of all churches with each other. Though it was once an important and even powerful ministry involving much church administration, the order of deacon was gradually reduced to the performance of liturgical ministry.[16] For disciplinary reasons, much connected with the requirements of celibacy, it even became nothing more than a steppingstone to ordination to the presbyterate.

THE MEDIEVAL HIERARCHY AND PRIESTHOOD

The influence of the thought of Dionysius the Areopagite, coupled with organizational developments, contributed much to a theology of order that accentuated hierarchy and priesthood.[17] Hierarchy, which etymologically means sacred power, represented a universal vision that portrayed creation as an ordered participation in supreme truth within which those possessing higher degrees of participation influenced those below them. This universal law of creation operated also within the church and within its ministry. The faithful were perceived as those who received the grace of God through the

---

15. See David N. Power, *Ministers of Christ and His Church* (London: Geoffrey Chapman, 1969), 52–88.

16. See John M. Barnett, *The Diaconate: A Full and Equal Order* (New York: Seabury, 1981), 1–131.

17. On the medieval hierarchy and priesthood, see Cooke, *Ministry*, 113–32; Schillebeeckx, *The Church*, 156–94. For Dionysius the Areopagite, see his *The Ecclesiastical Hierarchy*, trans. and annotated by Thomas L. Campbell (Washington, D.C.: University of America Press, 1981).

ministry of the ordained within an ordered church. The ordained themselves were ranked in the descending order of bishop, presbyter, and deacon, according to the degree of their participation in sacred power.

A variety of factual developments, including an increase of priests within monasteries and of clergy ordained exclusively to provide the landed with Mass and ritual, meant that presbyterate was increasingly seen as priesthood and the power to consecrate and offer the sacrifice of Christ's body and blood. This even became the definition of the sacrament of order, and the hierarchy or sacred power of the bishop was associated with his jurisdiction over the life of the diocese. In the ordered world of the high Middle Ages, represented by its Romanesque basilica or Gothic cathedral, and by the divinely constituted offices of prince and bishop, spiritual jurisdiction, the offering of the sacrifice of the Mass, and priestly absolution of sins were powerful and important mediations of divine grace. Ordination rites, with the accent on anointings and instruments of office, reflected this world and this concept of mediation.[18] Though the term had originally been used to underline that it was Christ who acted through the minister in the sacraments, the notion of the priest acting in the church *in persona Christi*, or representing Christ, became the focal point of the theology of order.

It was an order of things that to the sixteenth-century Reformers appeared to curtail the freedom of divine mercy and grace and to leave little room to the faith of the baptized.[19] It seemed to absorb the community of faith into a powerful and power-controlled institution, with little respect for the ministry of Word and sacramental gift and for the exercise of the royal priesthood of all believers. Much of the criticism, both practical and theological, was on target but the scene was obscured by polemics and reciprocal accusations. The very idea of hierarchy was spurned by the Reformers, and they professed but one divinely intended ministry of Word and sacrament, without internal distinction between bishop and presbyter. In response, the Council of Trent defined the power of the priest to consecrate and offer sacrifice, the institution of priesthood and hierarchy by Christ, and the divine origin of the episcopacy as it actually functioned in the church of the time, as well as the essential difference between the baptized and the ordained in their relation to Christ and to church.[20] Much pastoral reform followed in the wake of the Council of Trent, but for centuries there was little room for an integration of the just

---

18. See Power, *Ministers*, 87–98.
19. See Cooke, *Ministry*, 133–69.
20. Council of Trent, Decree on the Sacrament of Order (DS 1763–78).

insights of the Reformers or for modification in the actual ordering of ministry.

CONTEMPORARY ROMAN CATHOLIC THEOLOGY

As with much else, the major effort of the current theology of order and ministry is to retrieve important aspects of the history of ministry and to relate them to present circumstances and a diversity of cultures.[21]

In the first place, ministry as a gift of the Spirit and an ecclesial act is more fundamental and comprehensive than order. It includes a wide variety of activities done for the spiritual good of the church and for its mission in society. On the one hand, it is something in which all the baptized can participate and that requires both a recognition of diversity of gifts and a discernment of the presence of the Spirit. On the other hand, lest this diversity bespeak an excess of individualism and split communities, a greater consciousness of ministries has to be accompanied by a greater consciousness of the local church community as a eucharistic communion. The church in its universality and in its particularity in place and culture has a corporate mission. This mission is rooted in apostolic witness to the power of the Spirit of the risen Christ and is directed to the service of God's transforming and reconciling rule in the world. The needs of the faithful, spiritual and bodily, have to be taken care of within the church, while it is built up as a body that in corporate witness and action can serve its apostolic mission. It is through the eucharist, sacrament of Christ's body and communion table, and through the sacraments related to it as center, that all ecclesial activities converge. The community of discipleship is nurtured, bonded, and oriented to mutual service and apostolic mission through the gift of the Spirit that is bestowed in this celebration through Word and sacramental gift.

An understanding of the sacrament of order belongs in this context of reciprocal ministry, mission, and eucharist. Like all other sacraments, it is a sacrament of the church that signifies something essential to its being and vitality, even while it engages specific individuals in a particular form of ministry and responsibility. It is not

---

21. See works by Cooke, O'Meara, Schillebeeckx. Also, Bernard Cooke, "Fullness of Order: Theological Reflection," *Jurist* 41 (1981): 151–67; Jean Galot, *Theology of the Priesthood* (San Francisco: Ignatius Press, 1984); Edward Kilmartin, "Apostolic Office: Sacrament of Christ," *Theological Studies* 36 (1975): 243–64.

meant to bring about a monopoly of any ministry, either in sacrament, in teaching, or in pastoral care, either at the local or at the catholic level. It is rather an ordering of ministries within the one eucharistic fellowship and in the communion of churches. For the church as such, it represents the need for unity and the need for the service of Word, sacrament, and care if the church is to be faithful to its apostolic origins and to its apostolic mission. With ordering there goes a presidency, so that the ordained do indeed have some specific functions that are necessary to this ordering. Whereas for some centuries the accent was on the functions to which the minister was appointed, today the good of ministry is better retrieved if attention is paid to what the role of the ordained signifies for the entire church, as people of God and sacrament of Christ.

This is not to say that all theologians pursue these developments. Some continue to emphasize the particular call of the priest and take the essential difference between laity and priest as the key element in a theology of order.[22] Though the Second Vatican Council modified the traditional language of *in persona Christi* to *in persona Christi Capitis* (Decree on the Ministry and Life of Priests 2), these writers continue to underline the idea of the priest as representative of Christ in the community and particularly in the sacraments. Recognition of the service of the laity is subordinated to this, or is placed in another category, particularly that of apostolate in the world.[23]

As alternative to this hierarchical theology, from early church history it is possible to retrieve a vision of the sacrament of order as organic reality, with its own interior diversity. This diversity represents different aspects and needs of the life of the church. Present reflection needs to show how it is to be respected in shaping the future. Within individual churches, the role of the priest or presbyter carries much of the responsibility of the early episcopacy. The presbyter is the leading liturgical minister and the one who must attend to unity in the community and to the fidelity to the apostolic witness, as well as to the provision and encouragement of all those services that the church needs. The ministry of bishops is less tied to individual communities and is more directly in the service of the communion of communities, both within a diocese and within the universal church. The risk is that a bishop loses touch with the reality of eucharistic community and the episcopacy becomes an ad-

---

22. Thus Jean Galot, *Theology of the Priesthood*, and Bonaventure Kloppenburg, *The Priest: Living Instrument and Minister of Christ the Eternal Priest* (Chicago: Franciscan Herald Press, 1974).

23. This is done by developing no. 31 of the Constitution on the Church; no. 31 is on the secular character of the vocation of the laity.

ministration rather than a ministry. In this regard, much can be gained through a contemporary retrieval of collegiality in the diocesan church, a synodality that includes presbyters and faithful but that can be strongly fostered through the presbyterium. One purpose of the presbyters in the early church was that in matters vital to the church the presidency of the bishop would be tempered by collegial responsibility. In the circumstances of the present time, it might be wise for bishops to take on a more directly pastoral role in the presidency of a local church or parish, and to attend collegially with the presbyters to the unity of the diocese and to the fostering of multiple ministries and a synodal church that is inclusive of all the baptized.

The restoration of a permanent diaconate is of vital importance to the organic ordering of the church's ministry and to what is represented by the sacrament of order.[24] There is much hesitation and lack of clarity on this score in church teaching, in theology, and in practice.[25] Some tendencies seem to emphasize the role of the deacon in liturgy and in preaching. The risk is that the deacon become either a liturgical ornament or a substitute for priests in times of scarcity. One does better to see that the liturgical ministry of the deacon is in necessary conjunction with that which is specific to deacons in the common life of the church. In early centuries, the deacons were charged with the care of the poor and in connection with this with the administration of the community's patrimony and of its common funds. In the eucharist, they received the gifts of the people and administered the bread and wine to the bishop at the eucharistic table. This was an admirable and fitting sacramental expression of their broader responsibilities and service. A secular task, as it were, was integrated into the life of the church as a communion of charity through a sacramental action. This points to considerable possibilities for the restoration of the diaconate that are very pertinent to the mission of today's churches. There is a great emphasis on the church's service of the poor and on the witness that it needs to bear in society for the creation of a more just world. This is one side of the promotion of the involvement of all the baptized, but it can also contribute to the separation of people and clergy. The diaconate could serve, in keeping with its origins, as the bridge. The apt choices for the diaconate are persons mature in Christian life and in a spirit of service. They do not need to give up their secular occupations

---

24. Barnett, *Diaconate*, 133–60.

25. There is some lack of clarity on this score in no. 29 of the Constitution on the Church. On the one hand, the document seems to accentuate the function of the deacon in liturgy and preaching, and on the other hand his function in works of charity and administration. What is important is to show how these belong together.

but can guide the rest of the church in relating a Christian care for the poor to secular action. Their regular participation in the liturgy in receiving the gifts and in administering them outside the liturgy brings together the sacramental and the more specifically diaconal quality of church life. At the same time their wider concern with Christian witness in the life of society expresses the link between it and worship.

These are some of the main lines of contemporary thought on ministry and order. They imply of course a host of other questions that cannot be developed here because of editorial restrictions of allotted space but that cannot be dismissed as unimportant. Such questions include the developing role of women in ministry and its proper recognition, a critical approach to the choice, image, formation, and spirituality of priests and bishops, and of course the mutual recognition of ministries between the churches. Each of these is matter for a separate essay. The present essay may offer a framework within which such subjects can be creatively addressed.

FOR FURTHER READING

Cooke, Bernard. *Ministry to Word and Sacraments: History and Theology*. Philadelphia: Fortress Press, 1976.

A very comprehensive study of the development of ministry and of the sacrament of order from New Testament times to the present, taking account of literature in several languages.

Galot, Jean. *Theology of the Priesthood*. San Francisco: Ignatius Press, 1984.

A defense of the classical approach to ministerial priesthood done in the light of history and current magisterial teaching.

Mitchell, Nathan. *Mission and Ministry: History and Theology in the Sacrament of Order*. Wilmington, Del.: Michael Glazier, 1982.

Starts with roots in the Old Testament and traces the historical and theological development of priesthood and ministry to the present.

O'Meara, Thomas. *Theology of Ministry*. New York: Paulist Press, 1983.

Offers, in light of current issues, a survey of the development of forms of ministry in cultural context and addresses present questions about priestly and lay ministry.

Osborne, Kenneth B. *Priesthood: A History of the Ordained Ministry in the Roman Catholic Church.* New York: Paulist Press, 1988.

An overview of the history of the sacrament of order. After an initial presentation of New Testament and early church materials, it concentrates on priesthood in the Roman church. Because it introduces the reader to historical texts, it could be useful as a manual in course work.

Power, David N. *Ministers of Christ and His Church: A Theology of the Priesthood.* London: Geoffrey Chapman, 1969.

Takes its point of departure in the history of ordination rites in the Western churches and then looks at the development and theology of the sacrament of order, concluding with a discussion of the teaching of the Second Vatican Council.

Schillebeeckx, Edward. *The Church with a Human Face: A New and Expanded Theology of Ministry.* Trans. John Bowden. New York: Crossroad, 1985.

A revised and expanded version of an earlier work, adopting a critically hermeneutical approach to historical texts and developments. Important for addressing such current issues as the ministry of base Christian communities, lay preaching, and the ordination of women and married men.

SACRAMENTS

9.7

Marriage

9.7

Marriage

Francis Schüssler Fiorenza

Today marriage is a fragile institution. Societal changes have led to an increased rate of divorce. A growing number of couples decide to live together prior to or without a civil or church wedding. The number of families with a single parent as head of the household continues to grow. Violence within marriage, both the battering of wives and children and the sexual abuse of children, lead many to criticize the traditional patriarchal structure of marriage. Some persons see the very institution of marriage as challenged. "Is Marriage Obsolete?" was the provocative title of an article in *The Boston Globe*. The article described our society as "postmarital." It argued that the dominance of the single-parent family, the high rate of divorce, and the legal acknowledgment of survivorship and rights between unmarried persons are signs of the demise of marriage. Its author concluded: "By the third millennium marriage will be regarded as déclassé, a tacky arrangement practiced only by benighted and idolatrous monogamy freaks, an obscure and despised sect of something or other."[1] If this were to come to pass, people in the third millennium would obviously have no use for a theology of marriage as a sacrament and no sense for the religious significance of marriage.

Within the Roman Catholic church, exegetical and historical research has led Cardinal Joseph Ratzinger to offer a clear challenge to familiar ideas of marriage as a sacrament. Commenting on these traditional ideas, Ratzinger has asserted: "If one remains with the classic catechism, whereby a sacrament is an external sign, instituted by Christ, that signifies and effects inner grace, then these phrases say little; indeed they are in every respect questionable: neither has Jesus instituted marriage nor given it a specific external sign."[2] Moreover, Ratzinger continues, if the sacrament of marriage is understood as mechanically providing a couple with a grace that both makes their relation similar to the Christ-church relation and enables them to fulfill their tasks in the face of the reality of marriage, then the traditional teaching can "no longer be understood as a convincing, meaningful understanding of the notion of the sacrament."[3] In such cases, "the representative of systematic theology must appear, in more than one respect, as a hopeless dilettante."[4]

Such diverse challenges should impel us to examine carefully and critically the Roman Catholic tradition about marriage as a sacrament. A study of this tradition should take into account not only historical evidence about the long and diverse development

---

1. David B. Wilson, "Is Marriage Obsolete?" *The Boston Globe*, Sunday, August 6, 1989, sec. A.

2. Joseph Ratzinger, "Zur Theologie der Ehe," *Theologische Quartalschrift* 149 (1969): 53–74, here 54. See also Ratzinger's expositions of sacraments in general, *Die sakramentale Begründung christlicher Existenz* (Friesing: Kyrios Verlag, 1973), and *Zum Begriff des Sakraments*, Eichstätter Hochschulreden, vol. 13 (Munich: Minerva, 1979).

3. Ratzinger, "Zur Theologie der Ehe," 54.

4. Ibid., 53.

of the Christian understanding of marriage. It should also examine philosophical and social background theories that have been the underlying assumptions of this tradition. Moreover, it would need to explore our contemporary experience and social constructs as articulated within diverse religious and social groups. This task can be approached here only in a very limited fashion. In this brief treatment, I shall first examine biblical teaching, then Roman Catholic theological and church traditions, and finally contemporary systematic expositions.

BIBLICAL TEACHING ON MARRIAGE

The canonical Hebrew and Christian Scriptures contain many chapters and verses touching on marriage and issues related to married life. Nevertheless, it would be highly inappropriate to look to the Bible for a theology of marriage, as if the Bible contained a "theology *of* marriage." Too often the Bible is looked upon as a source book for various "theologies of," be it a theology of work, a theology of nature, or a theology of sex. The Bible does not offer such a comprehensive systematic or conceptual analysis of marriage. On the other hand, it would be equally inappropriate if we did not attend to some of the diverse views and images of marriage that are reflected in biblical texts, for they have decisively influenced Christian theology.

HEBREW SCRIPTURES

The Genesis accounts of the creation of the first human couple have influenced the interpretation of marriage in the West as much as the horizon of subsequent experience has influenced the interpretation of these verses. Historical-critical scholarship has shown, moreover, that the first chapters of Genesis contain two distinct accounts of the creation of the first couple: the Priestly account in Genesis 1 and the Yahwist account in Genesis 2 and 3.

The central verses of the Priestly tradition on the creation of humanity are Genesis 1:26-28: "Then God said, 'Let us make man ['*adam*] in our image, after our likeness. . . .' So God created ['*adam*] in his own image, in the image of God he created him; male and female he created them. And God blessed them, and God said to them, 'Be fruitful and multiply.'" This text describes the creation of human persons in the image of God as a creation of "the human" as male and female. The creation of the first couple takes place simultaneously. It is the human as both male and female that is created in the image of God and that represents God. This text is rather limited. "It says nothing about the image which relates 'adam to God nor about God as the referent.... It is not concerned with sexual roles, the status or relationship of the sexes to one another or marriage. It describes the biological pair, not a social partnership; male and female, not man and wife."[5]

The Yahwist account in chapters 2 and 3 of Genesis contains the story of Adam and Eve in the Garden of Eden. In this narrative account Adam is created first and Eve is created afterward, formed from Adam's side in order to be his helpmate (Gen. 2:18-25). These verses have puzzled scholars. Traditional rabbinic literature interpreted these verses to mean that God originally created an "androgynous person," and those who translated the passage into Greek expressed this meaning by writing "a male with female parts." A more recent interpretation, however, suggests that 'adam literally means "the earth creature." Consequently, the intent of the story is not so much to stress that God created a male being first as to emphasize that God created humankind.[6]

Throughout the history of Jewish and Christian literature, both biblical accounts have been diversely interpreted and the source of much philosophical and religious speculation.[7] Yet one must exercise a certain reserve in the appropriation and use of this material. The Genesis accounts do not contain an implicit theology of marriage that seeks to legislate for all time the meaning of male and female and their division into their proper roles. Rather the Genesis accounts function as mythic accounts of the origin of the world and of its inhabitants.

The Scriptures contain many verses and images about marriage. These have been the source of much poetic inspiration and theological reflection. Images of marriage and marital love can be found in the prophetic traditions, the Song of Songs, the story of Tobit, the Book of Proverbs, the Wisdom of the Son of Sirach, and Qoheleth. This literature is quite diverse in its conceptions and views. For example, the erotic imagery of the Song of Songs that so passionately exults in the beloved contrasts sharply with the skeptical advice of

---

5. Phyllis Bird, "'Male and Female He Created Them': Gen. 1:27b in the Context of the Priestly Account of Creation," _Harvard Theological Review_ 74 (1981): 129–59, here 155. Bird's analysis counters Karl Barth's influential analysis of the _imago_ passage; see Karl Barth, _Church Dogmatics_ (Edinburgh: T and T Clark, 1958), 3/1:183–206.

6. Phyllis Trible, _God and the Rhetoric of Sexuality_ (Philadelphia: Fortress Press, 1978).

7. See Elaine Pagels, _Adam, Eve, and the Serpent_ (New York: Random House, 1988).

the Son of Sirach that there is no wickedness or wrath on the earth greater than that of a woman (c. 25:13).

The diverse literary genres and the contrasting social attitudes in these texts alert us to what can still serve as a source of inspiration and what needs to be assessed within its limited historical context. The negative attitudes toward women are pervasive, from the prophetic use of the harlot imagery[8] to Sirach's attribution of the origin of sin to women (25:24). At the same time, the ideals of fidelity and love are present in these texts. The negative texts must be acknowledged for what they are. They reflect not God's views, but the views of God's people—a sinful and wandering people like other peoples. The negative texts should be compared with more positive texts, and they should not be elevated above their socially and historically conditioned status to an eternal divine teaching about the sacrament of marriage.

EARLY CHRISTIAN SCRIPTURES

The early Christian Scriptures, like the Hebrew Scriptures, contain a variety of statements about marriage in diverse contexts. Quite often certain of these statements—e.g., Jesus' statements about divorce, the adultery exception of Matthew, or the Pauline exception—are highlighted from a particular systematic perspective. These verses, however, should not be isolated, but should be understood and interpreted within the context of diverse biblical traditions.

Relativization of Marriage for the Sake of Discipleship

The earliest texts in the New Testament that refer to marriage stem from the early Christian missionary movements. These texts indicate a disruption and disturbance of traditional family structures: "Jesus said, 'Truly, I say to you, there is no one who has left house or brothers or sisters or mother or father or children or lands, for my sake and for the gospel, who will not receive a hundredfold" (Mark 10:29). Likewise: "Truly, I say to you, there is no man who has left house or wife or brothers or parents or children, for the sake of the kingdom of God, who will not receive manifold more in this time, and in the age to come, eternal life" (Luke 18:29).

---

8. See the critical analysis by T. Deborah Setel, "Prophets and Pornography: Female Sexual Imagery," in Letty M. Russell, ed., *Feminist Interpretation of the Bible* (Philadelphia: Westminster Press, 1985).

The early Christian missionary movement, often referred to as the "Jesus movement," provides the context of these verses.[9] The earliest disciples of Jesus did not at first establish local communities. Instead they became wandering charismatics—traveling apostles, prophets, and disciples who moved from place to place and who left everything behind. As wandering preachers, they were homeless; they lacked possessions; and they lacked a family. The disciples left these behind for the sake of their preaching and missionary activity. For the sake of preaching God's kingdom, they chose a life with neither family nor possessions.

Eschatological Vision and the Command against Divorce

Another tradition of texts about marriage concerns divorce and remarriage.[10] These texts are Mark 10:11-12, Matthew 5:31-32 and 19:3-9, Luke 16:18, and 1 Corinthians 7:10-11. These sayings against divorce belong to the oldest traditions in the New Testament. They are a part of the Jesus tradition. If any sayings can with some degree of historical certainty be attributed to the historical Jesus, then these statements would be among the prime candidates.[11]

Scholars offer diverse interpretations of these sayings. Some scripture scholars attempt to explain them away as allegorical. For example, Bruce Malina argues that when taken literally the statements make "as little sense as 'you are the salt of the earth.' "[12] Such an interpretation patently waters down the verses and substitutes personal conjecture for historical interpretation. Nothing in the text indicates metaphorical or allegorical language. In fact a literal interpretation of the texts conforms well to the historical situation within first-century Judaism.[13] During this period, Judaism permitted divorce but limited its conditions. Sectarian groups such as the Essenes, how-

---

9. For a social analysis of the Jesus movement, see Gerd Theissen, *Sociology of Early Christianity* (Philadelphia: Fortress Press, 1978).

10. For general Roman Catholic exegetical treatments, see Rudolf Pesch, *Freie Treue: Die Christen und die Ehescheidung* (Freiburg: Herder, 1971); Rudolf Schnackenburg, "Die Ehe nach der Weisungen Jesus und dem Verständnis der Urkirche," in Franz Henrich and Volker Eid, eds., *Ehe und Ehescheidung*, Münchener Akademie Schriften, vol. 59 (Munich: Kösel, 1972), 11–34.

11. Paul Hoffmann, "Jesus' Saying about Divorce and Its Interpretation in the New Testament Tradition," in Franz Böckle, ed., *The Future of Marriage as an Institution* (entire issue of *Concilium* 55 [New York: Herder and Herder, 1970]: 51–66).

12. Bruce Malina, *The New Testament World: Insights from Cultural Anthropology* (Atlanta: John Knox Press, 1981), 118–21.

13. Joseph Fitzmyer, "The Matthean Divorce Texts and Some New Palestinian Evidence," *Theological Studies* 37 (1976): 197–226; reprinted in *To Advance the Gospel* (New York: Crossroad, 1981), 79–111.

ever, rejected divorce outright. They had a distinct eschatological perspective on which they based their rejection of divorce.

Instead of explaining away these verses, some scholars point to their context and trajectory, especially to the debate in Palestine between the Hillel school, with its more lenient interpretation allowing divorce for the husband, and the Schammai school, which permitted divorce only for the most extreme cases. This perspective suggests that Jesus sides with the stricter interpretation and goes beyond it. Some exegetes suggest that Jesus' interpretation offers a protection for women, as Matthew 5:28 implies.[14]

Other scholars suggest that these Matthean verses should not be interpreted as a debate between two schools, but as a part of Jesus' radical eschatological vision. It is pointed out that in the Jesus traditions that predate the Gospels (these traditions being reflected in Mark 10:2-9 and 12:18-27), Jesus' eschatological vision critically challenges traditional patriarchal marriage. It interprets marriage structures not in relation to an order of creation, but in relation to an apocalyptic theology of the restoration of original creation. The eschatological being of men and women is not based on sexual difference, but on freedom from sexual differentiation.[15] Jesus' imperatives do not provide valid norms for the historically conditioned circumstances of his time, but show that God's coming kingdom has an eschatological character that transcends the limits of traditional moral interpretations.[16]

Some exegetes have observed that in view of its literary genre, argumentation, and textual quotations from the Greek version of Genesis, the controversial dialogue constituting the pericope Matthew 5:31-32 expresses not a Palestinian dispute, but a debate within a Jewish-Christian Hellenistic community.[17] Some argue, however, that this debate in the Hellenistic community presupposes as known a decision or statement going back to the historical Jesus.[18]

Since the "except for" (Matt. 5:31) clause has significantly influenced the systematic position concerning divorce, its interpreta-

---

14. See Dieter Luhrmann, "Eheverständnis und Eheseelsorge im Neuen Testament," in Günther Gassmann, ed., *Ehe, Institution im Wandel* (Hamburg: Lutherische Verlagshaus, 1979), 67–81.

15. See Elisabeth Schüssler Fiorenza, *In Memory of Her* (New York: Crossroad, 1983), 140–45.

16. Kurt Niederwimmer, *Askese und Mysterium: Über Ehe, Ehescheidung und Eheverzicht in den Anfängen des christlichen Glaubens*, Forschungen zur Religion und Literatur des Alten und Neuen Testaments, no. 113 (Göttingen: Vandenhoeck, 1975), 12–41.

17. See Pesch, *Freie Treue*, 10–60.

18. Rudolf Schnackenburg, *Die sittliche Botschaft des Neuen Testaments* (Freiburg: Herder, 1986), 1:148–53.

tion has been controverted. Among contemporary Roman Catholic exegetes two divergent interpretations have emerged about the meaning of *porneia* in the text. One suggests that *porneia* refers to illegitimate marriages between relatives that were impermissible for Jewish Christians and that pagan Christians were also to avoid (Acts 15:20, 29). According to this interpretation, the exception adds not so much an exception as a further restriction. Divorce is not allowed except for marriages that are really impermissible.[19] The other solution points out that *porneia* can also mean "adultery." This interpretation suggests that divorce is allowed when the marriage is already broken.[20]

In 1 Corinthians 7 (one of the most difficult chapters to interpret), Paul touches on several themes of marriage. In the first instance, he affirms the early Christian missionary ideal of the excellence of ascetic celibacy. Such a priority of asceticism over marriage was significant in the early Christian movement, so much so that, as recent exegetical research has shown, many in early Christianity viewed baptism and marriage as incompatible.[21] Though Paul acknowledges a priority of the unmarried state and recommends that the unmarried remain such, he does display a realism that acknowledges marriage. Paul does not so much develop a theology of marriage as concede the possibility of marriage as a practical necessity. Despite the examples of married couples as missionary apostles in the early Christian movement, such as his co-workers Prisca and Aquila, Paul argues that commitment to the work of mission favors asceticism over Christian marriage.[22]

In charging that neither husband nor wife should divorce one another Paul refers to a word from the Lord. Such reference to a word from Jesus is a rare instance in Paul's writings. Nevertheless, in spite of the authority of this word, Paul argues from experience for an exception. In the history of Christianity Paul's action has led to a broadening of the exception, and it has raised the issue of the power and responsibility of the community.

---

19. Jean Bonsirven, *Le Divorce dans le Nouveau Testament* (Paris: Desclée, 1948), and Joseph Fitzmyer, *To Advance*, 79–111.

20. Carlo Marruci, *Parole di Gesù sul divorzio* (Brescia: Morcelliana, 1982); Gerhard Schneider, "Jesu Wort über die Ehescheidung in der Überlieferung des Neuen Testaments," *Trierer theologische Zeitschrift* 80 (1971): 65–87. See also the works of Paul Hoffmann, Rudolf Pesch, and Rudolf Schnackenburg quoted above. In *Die sittliche Botschaft*, Schnackenburg retracts his earlier advocacy of the first interpretation.

21. Niederwimmer, *Askese und Mysterium*, 42–124. Niederwimmer shows the ascetic, christological, and eschatological basis for such a priority in early Christianity.

22. See Schüssler Fiorenza, *In Memory of Her*, 160–204.

Household Codes and Christian Marriage

The deutero-Pauline and the pastoral epistles contain a third tradition, the household codes, which were given that name because they were meant to regulate the behavior of the household. In contrast to the early Christian affirmation of asceticism and to the Pauline commendation of the unmarried state, these epistles affirm the importance of marriage and of family. Indeed, the pastoral epistles stipulate that bishops must be successful in marital and family life before their election to office; they must be married only once and have raised a solid family: "Now a bishop must be above reproach, the husband of one wife.... He must manage his own household well, keeping his children submissive and respectful in every way; for if a man does not know how to manage his own household, how can he care for God's church?" (1 Tim. 3:3-5).

Ephesians 5:21-33 contains a much more explicitly theological analysis of marriage. These verses have become the classic biblical reference for much theological reflection on marriage. The household codes in Ephesians deal not only with the relations between husbands and wives, but also with the proper relations in regard to children and slaves (6:1-9). The household codes provide three parallel orders of relation: husband and wife, parents and children, masters and slaves. The first member of each pair has the role of leadership and responsibility, whereas the second has the role of obedience. With regard to marriage, the husband as the head of the wife parallels Christ as the head of the church.

These household codes have been diversely interpreted. Some have viewed them as expressing a divinely ordered sphere of subordination.[23] Others underscore the element of Christ's love for the church with the concomitant demands of the husband's love for the wife. Recent scholarship on the New Testament has illumined the specific context and meaning of these texts. In the Greco-Roman world, the early Christians were considered disruptive of the sociocultural order. The earliest Christians were in fact called atheists because they did not participate in emperor worship. Moreover, insofar as Christian communities allowed a wife, child, or slave to convert and to join the community without the permission of the male head of the household, they were looked upon as disruptive of the patriarchal family order of the time.

The early Christian communities with their emphasis on equality of discipleship and their admittance of individual women or indi-

---

23. Most recently, Hans Urs von Balthasar, *Theologik* (Einseideln: Johannes Verlag, 1987), 3:317–18.

vidual slaves to the community seemed to bear out this charge. Consequently, the household codes, which are in the later books of the Christian Scriptures, represent in part an apologetic attempt to show that Christianity was not opposed to the Roman socio-cultural order. The texts, therefore, borrow from the Aristotelian philosophy current at that time, which was embodied in a set of codes that reinforced the patriarchal order. It is this apologetic context of the texts that should deter today's Christians from accepting the Roman social order of patriarchy in regard to wives, children, and slaves as a divinely ordained order.[24] Theological reflection and pastoral preaching, therefore, have to be alert to the socially conditioned background theories or assumptions in elaborating a theology of marriage for and in modern societies not based upon the Roman patriarchal order.

In assessing the theological appropriation of these verses from Ephesians, it is important to note that a specific translation has greatly influenced the understanding of these verses. Because the Greek word *mysterion* was translated in the Vulgate as *sacramentum*, Ephesians 5:32 has often been used as the basis for justifying the Scholastic doctrine of marriage as a sacrament. Some medieval theologians (for example, Peter Lombard) were aware of this translation problem. Moreover, Luther's polemic against the Roman Catholic teaching on marriage as a sacrament included this charge of mistranslation. As Walter Kasper has observed: "Most scholars are agreed now ... that the later idea of sacrament should not be presupposed"[25] when one reads this passage from Ephesians. A theological justification of marriage as a sacrament should not be based exclusively on this passage.

Not Really a Harmony

One cannot bring these diverse traditions into harmony with one another as theologians of previous generations did when they attempted to synthesize ideas from various early Christian Scriptures into unified systematic concepts within a biblical theology or a theology of the New Testament. There is not a biblical theology of marriage as a unified set of ideas and concepts. Instead one has to view the richness and diversity of the various early Christian traditions.

---

24. Elisabeth Schüssler Fiorenza, *Bread Not Stone* (Boston: Beacon Press, 1984). For a more popularly written version, see her "Marriage and Discipleship," *The Bible Today* 102 (April 1979): 2027–33.
25. Walter Kasper, *Theology of Christian Marriage* (New York: Crossroad, 1983), 30.

The traditions that I have highlighted are central to the early Christian Scriptures. These traditions have impacted Christian thought throughout the centuries and can serve to criticize a one-sided appropriation of any particular tradition. The eschatological horizon of the Jesus movement with its emphasis on asceticism relativizes marriage and family for the sake of radical discipleship. Its emphasis sharply contrasts with the deutero-Pauline praise of the standard of a respectable family. The commitment to Jesus in a radical discipleship of equals relativizes the emphasis on the Roman patriarchal order in the household codes. Yet there is also the eschatological ideal of marriage in relation to the original human creation that represents a hope and a vision beyond the frailty in marriages. The insight that relations among humans are meant to mirror the divine-human relation provides a challenge for theological reflection that Christian theology has taken up in various ways throughout the centuries.

MARRIAGE IN THE HISTORY OF ROMAN CATHOLIC THEOLOGY

The history of Christian theological views toward marriage displays diverse attitudes, and the development of the Roman Catholic understanding of marriage as a sacrament is a complex topic. Rather than present a historical survey, I shall merely highlight a few salient points from the history of theology: first, Augustine's understanding of the sacrament in marriage within the context of his influential treatment of the goods of marriage; second, the development of medieval conceptions of marriage; third, the affirmations of the Council of Trent; and fourth, recent official teachings of the Roman Catholic church regarding marriage.

AUGUSTINE: THE SACRAMENT IN MARRIAGE

Although many of the early Christian writers dealt with marriage, Augustine's views have most strongly influenced Western theology.[26] Augustine did not so much affirm marriage as one of the sacraments of the New Law; rather he affirmed that there is in all marriages, and not just Christian marriages, a sacrament. Augustine used the term

---

26. For a survey of the views on marriage in the ancient church, see Alfred Niebergall, *Ehe und Eheschliessung in der Bibel und in der Geschichte der alten Kirche* (Marburg: N. G. Elwert, 1985), 101–253.

sacrament in a general and a narrow sense.[27] In a very general sense, sacrament refers to visible words, things, and actions that are signs of what is invisible and transcendent. In a more narrow sense, sacrament refers specifically to the sacraments of the Catholic church, among which baptism and eucharist have a predominant role.

Augustine understands the sacrament in marriage in the broad rather than narrow sense, as is evident in his treatment of the goods of marriage—a specific teaching that has greatly influenced traditional Roman Catholic teaching about marriage. Though the words *goods* and to a lesser extent *blessings* or *benefits* are often used in the English translation of Augustine, the word *values* probably expresses more adequately Augustine's thought. In *The Good of Marriage*, Augustine taught that marriage has three values: fidelity, offspring, and sacrament.[28] Fidelity (*fides*) is the faithfulness in the mutual love that each spouse has for the other. Augustine interprets fidelity in relation to the sexual love and intercourse of the married couple. Yet he does so in a way that disallows the denigration of one partner or the other to a mere sexual object. In his view, even sexual relations open to procreation can be sinful if the partner is reduced to a mere object of libido. Fidelity relates to sexual love, but it entails more than a sexual commitment. Rather, it is a commitment of love and trust. Fidelity is the virtue that also supports the second value of marriage, offspring. This second value entails the acceptance of children in love, their nurturance in affection, and their upbringing in the Christian religion.

The third value of marriage is the sacrament of marriage. In chapter 18 of *The Good of Marriage* Augustine explains that the sacrament is found in first marriages. It primarily refers to the union of the spouses as an indissoluble bond. For these marriages are a visible sign, that is, they signify the image of the one society of the blessed in eternity. A Christian marriage signifies visibly on earth the future unity of the people of God in eternity. The union of the spouses, their visible covenant with one another, is a tangible sign of the unity of all people in eternity.

These three values show that Augustine does not view marriage simply as a bond between two individuals. Instead he understands marriage as a sign and sacrament. He describes its sacramentality within the framework of the distinction between the old and new

---

27. Charles Couturier " 'Sacramentum' et 'Mysterium' dans l'ouvre de Saint Augustin," in *Études Augustiniennes*, Théologie, vol. 28 (Paris: Aubier, 1953), 161–332.
28. Augustine *The Good of Marriage*, in Saint Augustine, *Treatises on Marriage and Other Subjects*, Fathers of the Church, vol. 15 (New York: Fathers of the Church, 1955), 9–51.

covenant. The marriages of the Hebrew patriarchs symbolized the future church that consisted of many nations and people, and this was signified by their polygamous marriage (*sacramentum pluralium nuptiarum*). The marriage of a bishop, as a marriage with one wife, differs from the marriage of the patriarchs. The one church from many nations already exists as a reality, even though it is not yet perfect. Therefore, the marriage of a bishop constitutes a sign of the radical unity and peace of the eschatological city (*sacramentum nuptiarum singularum*).[29] This vision of marriage as a sacrament underscores that marriage is a sign of societal peace and unity. It is not simply that the fidelity of two spouses aids in the continued nurturing of children, but also that the visible union of the couple signifies the eschatological unity of all people and nations.

Too often, contemporary theologians tend to neglect these positive elements within Augustine's theology and mention only what they perceive as the negative elements: for instance, his view of marriage as a remedy for concupiscence and his negative assessment of sexuality.[30] Augustine also taught that marriage "does not seem to be good only because of the procreation of children, but also because of the natural companionship between the sexes."[31] Moreover, as Augustine matured as a Christian, his belief in the incarnation led him to move further away from his early Manichean attitudes to a more positive assessment of human corporeality.[32]

MEDIEVAL THEOLOGY: MARRIAGE AS A SACRAMENT

A considerable development took place from Augustine's view of the sacrament of marriage as a visible sign of a transcendent unity of the people of God to the view of marriage as one of the seven sacraments. The incorporation of marriage into the rank of sacraments occurred during the medieval period between the eleventh and twelfth centuries. The context for this development was both doctrinal and liturgical. The doctrinal occasion was the spread of the Cathari or Albigenses, who were ascetics who viewed marriage as an evil. Their views prompted a theological response that affirmed the goodness of marriage and spurred the development of a theology

---

29. Ibid., chap. 18: "Just as the many wives of the ancient fathers signified our future churches of all races subject to one man-Christ, so our bishop, a man of one wife, signifies the unity of all nations subject to the one man-Christ."

30. Augustine often argues against several fronts. It is in his writings against the Manicheans that his most positive evaluations of marriage are made.

31. Augustine *The Good of Marriage* chap. 3.

32. See Margaret Miles, *Augustine on the Body* (Missoula, Mont.: Scholars Press, 1979).

of marriage as a sacrament. In fact, the first official explicit affirmations of marriage as a sacrament occur in statements condemning the Cathari. In 1184 the Council of Verona under Pope Lucius III anathematized the Cathari for their opinions about marriage. In 1208 Pope Innocent III required as a condition for return to Catholicism that the Waldenses subscribe to a profession of faith that accepted all the church's sacraments, including marriage. In 1274 the Second Council of Lyons proposed a similar requirement as a condition for reunion for the Byzantine emperor Michael Palaeologus.

Liturgical celebrations also influenced the development of the notion of marriage as a sacrament.[33] The church's liturgical practice of the wedding ceremony appropriated Roman and Teutonic traditions. Germanic, Frankish, and Lombardic laws emphasized the handing over of the bride, different from though not unlike the Roman custom of the handing over of the bride to the husband as the paterfamilias. As a result, people came to equate the blessing of marriage with the "handing over of the bride." A parallel was seen between the veiling and handing over of the bride and the veiling and handing over of the consecrated virgin, as a "bride of Christ," to the church. This analogy between the bride and the consecrated virgin was significant for the developing understanding of marriage as a sacrament. Whereas the virgin was consecrated directly to Christ, the bride was consecrated through the human relationship with her husband, the figure of Christ. The bride's visible relationship to the husband was a sign of her invisible relation to Christ. The text of Ephesians 5:21-32 influenced this development. Since the virgin was consecrated directly to Christ, this consecration was not viewed as a sacrament. Since the consecration to the husband was a visible sign of a more profound relation to Christ, marriage was a sacrament. Such a development and view went beyond Augustine's view of the mutual fidelity in marriage as a sign of the unity of the people of God.

The doctrine of marriage as a sacrament developed gradually within the medieval period. Moreover, theological speculation about marriage during the medieval period was quite diverse. Three distinct theories existed about what constituted the nature of marriage. Does the marriage bond derive primarily from the consent of the two partners, from the consummation through sexual intercourse, or from marriage's social function? The consent theory, also known as the French theory, was advocated by theologians in Paris. They argued that the essence of marriage was the free consent of the in-

---

33. For a discussion of this development, see Edward Schillebeeckx, _Marriage: Secular Reality and Saving Mystery_ (New York: Sheed and Ward, 1965), 302–43.

dividual couple. A marriage continued to be a full marriage even when sexual intercourse played no role, as in the example of Mary and Joseph. Procreation belonged to the task (*officium*) of marriage, but not its constitution. The second view, known as the *copula* theory, was advocated by canonists, especially in Italy. They argued that marriage was constituted by sexual intercourse and believed marital consent to sexual intercourse was the essential element of the marital relation. A third view argued that marriage was an institution that provided the social and human foundation for the bringing up of children.

Between proponents of the first two views there was a significant debate concerning the relation between mutual consent and the community of marriage.[34] Both agreed that mutual consent formed the basis of marriage, but they made a distinction between the contracted marriage (based on consent) and the ratified marriage (sealed through sexual consummation). Theologians such as Peter Lombard argued that the marriage bond was established by the mutual consent. It was this mutual consent that was the sacrament of the unity of Christ and the church. The canonists argued that a marriage, though valid due to mutual consent, could be dissolved if it was not consummated.

The influence of this debate, especially the Parisian emphasis on spousal consent, can be seen in Hugh of Saint Victor's theological treatment of marriage.[35] Hugh posited two sacraments of Christian marriage. The *sacramentum conjugi* consists of the love union between man and woman that signifies and images God's love for humans and the human love for God. The *sacramentum officii* is expressed in sexual intercourse that images the love of Christ and the church—a love in the flesh. The theological position that marriage requires consent led to an emphasis on love within marriage.[36] Richard of Saint Victor (d. 1173) gives a lyrical description of marital love in *Of*

---

34. For a description of the medieval controversies, see James A. Brundage, *Law, Sex, and Christian Society in Medieval Europe* (Chicago: University of Chicago Press, 1987).

35. See Hugh of Saint Victor *De Beatae Mariae Virginis Virginitate*, written between 1131 and 1141. His *De Institutione Sacramentorum* treats of marriage in book 2, 11: *De Sacramento Conjugii*. See Roy J. Defarrari, ed., *Hugh of St. Victor: On the Sacraments of the Christian Faith* (Cambridge: Medieval Academy of America, 1951). For a general treatment of diverse monastic views of marriage, see Jean Leclercq, *Monks on Marriage: A Twelfth-Century View* (New York: Seabury Press, 1982); for a broader historical survey see Georges Duby, *Medieval Marriage: Two Models from Twelfth-Century France* (Baltimore: John Hopkins Press, 1978).

36. Although medieval marriages were first of all social and economic relationships, one should not underestimate the importance of affective criteria in the choice of partners. See David Herlihy, "The Making of the Medieval Family: Symmetry, Structure and Sentiment," *Journal of Family History* 8 (1983): 116–30.

the Four Degrees of Passionate Love. His treatment gives a priority to human affection. "We know that among human affections conjugal love must take the first place, and therefore in wedded life that degree of love which generally dominates all other affections seems to be good. For the mutual affection of intimate love draws closer the bonds of peace between those who are pledged to each other, and make that indissoluble, life-long association pleasant and happy."[37]

The institution of the sacrament of marriage was viewed somewhat differently from that of the other sacraments. One could not simply affirm that Christ instituted the sacrament of marriage, since marriage existed before Christ, indeed was present even in paradise. Therefore, Scholastic theologians refer to stages in the institution of this sacrament. Anselm of Laon argued that marriage, in contrast to other sacraments, was instituted before the fall. Christ did not institute it, but confirmed it at the marriage in Cana. Three stages of institution are outlined in Thomas's *Summa Theologiae.* (Since Thomas died before completing the *Summa,* Reynaldo of Piperno completed the treatise on the sacraments by drawing on Thomas's earlier commentary on Peter Lombard's *Sentences,* where Thomas had basically followed Albert the Great.) These three moments of the institution of marriage are: the natural orientation prior to the fall, the healing institution of the Law of Moses after the fall, and finally, the institution of the New Law as a sign of union between Christ and the church.

Although it has been often noted that Thomas was much more negative in his assessment of women than Augustine due to the influence of Aristotle's biology,[38] he actually had a more positive view of human sexuality, as the debate about marriage in paradise showed. Some argued that in the Garden of Paradise prior to the fall, human procreation would have occurred without sexual intercourse. Against such a view Aquinas argued on the basis of the naturalness of human sexuality for procreation. It was not human sexuality, but "excessive concupiscence" that was absent.[39] Moreover, with a healthy realism, Thomas stressed the importance of friendship for marriage.

---

37. Richard of Saint Victor, *Selected Writings on Contemplation* (New York: Harper and Brothers, n.d.), 215.

38. See Kari Elisabeth Borresen, *Subordination and Equivalence: The Nature and Role of Woman in Augustine and Thomas Aquinas,* rev. ed. (Washington, D.C.: University Press of America, 1981).

39. Thomas Aquinas *Summa Theologiae* I, q. 98. For a defense of Thomas's view of human sexuality, see Otto Hermann Pesch, *Thomas von Aquin: Grenze und Grösse mittelalterlicher Theologie* (Mainz: Matthias-Grünewald, 1988), 254–56, and in regard to women, 20–227. See also Lisa Sowle Cahill, *Between the Sexes: Foundations for a Christian Ethics of Sexuality* (Philadelphia: Fortress Press, 1985), 105–22.

"The greater that friendship, the more solid and long-lasting it be. Now, there seems to be the greatest friendship between husband and wife, for they are united not only in the act of fleshly union, which produces a certain gentle association even among beasts, but also in the partnership of the whole range of domestic activity."[40]

Bonaventure distinguished among three types of sacraments. The common sacraments of the old and new covenant are marriage and penance. They exist from the wisdom of nature and are merely confirmed by Christ.[41] Baptism, eucharist, and ordination are partially prefigured in the Old Testament, but they flourish in the New Testament. Only these three are established in a proper sense by Christ. Beyond these, there are sacraments distinctive to the New Testament, confirmation and the anointing of the sick. They were established in the church by the Holy Spirit.

THE COUNCIL OF TRENT ON MARRIAGE

Prior to modern papal and conciliar teaching, two major councils were significant for the Roman Catholic church's teaching on marriage: the "Union" Council of Florence (1439–45) and the Council of Trent (1545–63). Whereas Florence was concerned with Eastern traditions, Trent affirmed both the sacramentality and the indissolubility of marriage in the context of Martin Luther's criticism of Roman Catholic teaching and practice.[42] The notion that marriage is indissoluble is evident in canon 7 (November 11, 1563): "Whoever says that the Church errs when it has taught and still teaches that, according to the evangelical and apostolic doctrine, because of the adultery of one spouse, the bond of marriage cannot be dissolved and that both, even the innocent party, who has not given cause for adultery, cannot contract another marriage while the other spouse is still alive... may he be excluded."[43]

---

40. Thomas Aquinas *Summa Contra Gentiles* 3.123.6 (trans. Vernon J. Bourke [New York: Image Books, 1956]).

41. Ratzinger, "Zur Theologie der Ehe," 59.

42. Martin Luther, "The Babylonian Captivity of the Church," in Theodore G. Tappert, ed., *Selected Writings of Martin Luther, 1517–1520*, vol. 1 (Philadelphia: Fortress Press, 1967); for the section on marriage, see 444–58. See also "A Sermon on the Estate of Marriage," in Timothy F. Lull, ed., *Martin Luther's Basic Theological Writings* (Minneapolis: Augsburg Fortress Press, 1989), 630–37, where Luther develops a complementary idea of marriage as an estate.

43. Denzinger-Schönmetzer, *Enchiridion Symbolorum* (hereafter DS), 1807; for literature on the Council of Trent, see Hubert Jedin, "Die Unauflöslichkeit der Ehe nach dem Konzil von Trient," in Klaus Reinhardt and Hubert Jedin, *Ehe–Sakrament in der Kirche des Herrn*, Ehe in Geschichte und Gegenwart, vol. 2 (Berlin: Morus, 1971), 61–135; Piet Fransen, "Divorce on the Ground of Adultery—The Council of

The Council of Trent made two basic affirmations about marriage. The first states that marriage is a sacrament and within the provenance of the church. Marriage is not simply a matter of private, personal, or individual decision, but concerns the community. Therefore, Trent required that Catholic marriages should take place in the presence of a priest. It, thereby, sought to curb the widespread practice of clandestine marriages. In addition Trent reaffirmed the church's teaching and practice, especially as it developed in the Western church, that prohibited divorce and remarriage for cases of adultery. The council maintained that this teaching and practice are "in accordance with" evangelical and apostolic doctrine. Scholars have maintained that the language used by the council pointed to obligatory teaching and practice, "not an ultimately obligatory dogma in the modern sense of the word."[44] It sought to underscore that the church's practice and teaching were in accordance with the New Testament. This affirmation was deliberately very nuanced. "In accordance with" is not the same as "identical with." In other words, "it is not simply the teaching of the Gospel."[45]

The decision of Trent, as Walter Kasper summarizes it, was limited. "The only intention was to come to a decision in the controversy that had been raging at the time between the Catholic Church and the Lutherans. Controversies within the Catholic Church itself were, however, left open. No previous decision of any kind was therefore made by the Council of Trent with regard to the pastoral problems of the twentieth century."[46]

RECENT OFFICIAL ROMAN CATHOLIC TEACHING

Within modern times, several statements on marriage provide the content of the Roman Catholic church's official teaching on the subject.[47] In *Arcanum Divinae Sapientiae*, published in 1880, Pope Leo XIII took issue with the trend toward seeing marriage as a purely secular event and as subject only to civil law. In contrast he ar-

---

Trent (1563)," in Böckle, ed., *The Future of Marriage as an Institution*, 89–100; Peter J. Huizing, "La dissolution du mariage depuis le Concile de Trente," *Revue de Droit Canonique* 21 (1971): 127–45.

44. Kasper, *Theology*, 61.

45. See Karl Lehmann, *Gegenwart des Glaubens* (Mainz: Matthias-Grünewald, 1974), 274–308, here 285. Lehmann relies on the interpretations of Piet Fransen (in Böckle, ed., *The Future of Marriage as an Institution*, 89–100) and Joseph Ratzinger, "Zur Frage nach der Unauflöslichkeit der Ehe," in Henrich and Eid, eds., *Ehe und Ehescheidung*, 35–56, esp. 49ff.

46. Kasper, *Theology*, 62.

47. See Benedictine Monks of Solesmes, eds., *Papal Teaching: Matrimony*, trans. Michael J. Byrnes (Boston: St. Paul's Editions, 1963).

gued for the sacramentality of marriage and the marital contract as a sign that imaged the relation between Christ and the church. Fifty years later in *Casti Connubii*, Pius XI took up many of the themes of Pope Leo's encyclical. He especially deplored the many abuses surrounding marriage. At the same time, he sought to further elaborate the religious meaning of marriage. In his view, "this mutual inward molding of husband and wife, this determined effort to perfect each other, can in a very real sense, as the Roman Catechism teaches us, be said to be the chief reason and purpose of marriage, provided marriage be looked at not in the restricted sense as instituted for the proper conception and education of the child, but more widely as the sharing of life as a whole and the mutual interchange and partnership thereof" (no. 24).[48] Pope Pius XII continued the basic teaching of his predecessor. In diverse talks to various groups, most notably his addresses to "Italian Catholic Obstetricians" and to "Italian Catholic Midwives," Pius XII sought to reaffirm the traditional papal teaching.[49] At the same time, he introduced some elements of the personalist philosophical approaches to marriage current at the time. These papal discourses provided the basic contours of Roman Catholic teaching prior to the Second Vatican Council.

The Second Vatican Council's constitution *Gaudium et Spes* (GS) made a decisive attempt to reflect theologically on marriage in the modern world. Though primarily concerned with the church in the modern world, this constitution deals also with marriage. It refers to marriage as an intimate community of love, a Christian vocation, a sacred bond and covenant, and a mutual gift of two persons. It is noticeable that the traditional language describing marriage as a contract is missing. Its main theological point was to rethink the question of whether procreation constitutes the primary, natural end and purpose of marriage. Its formulation was very careful: Though it speaks of children as the gift of marriage and of the orientation of marriage toward the procreation and nurture of children, it affirmed that "while not making the other ends of marriage of less value, the true conduct of marital love and the entire meaning of family life that comes from it have this goal, that the spouses be willing to co-work courageously with the love of the Creator and Savior" (GS 50).[50]

---

48. The English translation of the encyclical is in Benedictine Monks of Solesmes, eds., *Papal Teaching*, 219–21.

49. For a collection of Pius XII's discourses, see ibid., 301–506.

50. For an exposition of the teaching of *Gaudium et Spes* on marriage, see Joseph A. Selling, "A Closer Look at the Doctrine of Gaudium et Spes on Marriage and the Family," *Bijdragen* 43 (1982): 30–48, and idem, "Twenty Significant Points in the Theology of Marriage and Family Present in the Teaching of Gaudium et Spes," *Bijdragen* 43 (1982): 412–41.

Within Roman Catholic theology, contemporary reflections on many issues take as their starting point the documents of the Second Vatican Council. However, the situation differs in regard to marriage, and especially the issue of human sexuality. On June 23, 1964, Pope Paul VI removed the issue of the control of human fertility from the agenda of the Second Vatican Council. He expanded the Pontifical Study Commission, which Pope John XXIII had established, and instructed it to report directly to himself. The commission recommended a change in traditional teaching. Pope Paul VI rejected their concrete recommendation. His encyclical *Humanae Vitae* (1968) further developed the Roman Catholic understanding of marriage. In previous papal documents, the arguments against the limitation of birth were drawn from the end or purpose of marriage, namely, the procreation of children. Since the Second Vatican Council's statements broadened the understanding of the primary purpose of marriage, Pope Paul VI had to nuance the argumentation and gave it a more anthropological and personalist basis.

This argumentation has been echoed and further developed by Pope John Paul II's Apostolic Exhortation on the Family (*Consortium Socialis*) and in his Wednesday general audience talks on the "Theology of the Body."[51] To develop his understanding of sex and marriage John Paul II draws on phenomenology and personalist philosophy in order to explicate the importance of intersubjective bodily relations between the spouses. The human person is embodied as a sexual being with the task of integrating physical and spiritual acts. In the pope's view this integration requires that loving sexual unions be procreative.[52] In recent decades the issue of marriage has also been treated within the broader context of the nature and role of the family within modern society, as the documents of the bishops' synod and the International Theological Commission indicate.[53]

---

51. John Paul II's Apostolic Exhortation on the Family is published with commentaries in Michael J. Wrenn, ed., *Pope John Paul II and Family* (Chicago: Franciscan Herald Press, 1983). For the "Theology of the Body" series, see vol. 3 of *Reflections on Humanae Vitae: Conjugal Morality and Spirituality* (Boston: Daughters of St. Paul, 1983).

52. For a critical analysis and interpretation, see Lisa Sowle Cahill, "Community and Couple: Parameters of Marital Commitment in Catholic Tradition," in William P. Roberts, ed., *Commitment to Partnership: Explorations of the Theology of Marriage* (New York: Paulist Press, 1987), 81–101. For a different perspective that defends papal teaching, see Richard M. Hogan and John M. LeVoir, *Covenant of Love: Pope John Paul II on Sexuality, Marriage, and Family in the Modern World* (Garden City, N.Y.: Doubleday and Co., 1985).

53. Jan Grootaers and Joseph Selling, eds., *The 1980 Synod of Bishops "On the Role of the Family": An Exposition of the Event and an Analysis of Its Texts*, Bib-

MARRIAGE AS A SACRAMENT
IN CURRENT SYSTEMATIC THEOLOGY

Within contemporary theology, the sacrament of marriage has been the subject of many studies. Much of the writing on marriage within theological literature concerns moral, pastoral, and canonical issues. Nevertheless, several important directions for a clearer understanding of marriage have been elaborated within contemporary systematic theology. In the following, I shall briefly sketch some contemporary directions, then offer some of my own systematic reflections on the sacrament of marriage, and finally summarize some of the discussion surrounding two practical pastoral issues that result from the Catholic theological view of marriage.

THREE CONTEMPORARY DIRECTIONS

Approaches to a theology of marriage as a sacrament reflect the general theological emphases of their historical contexts. During the last decades, three distinct trends within Roman Catholic theology have affected these approaches to marriage: christocentrism, the salvation-historical view, and the anthropological-ecclesial view. Due to the influence of Karl Barth, a christocentric focus entered not only Protestant neo-orthodox theology, but also Roman Catholic theology. Roman Catholic "christocentrism," however, displays its own distinctive forms with an emphasis on the sacramental notion of the body of Christ. Likewise the salvation-historical approach, exemplified by Oscar Cullmann and influential in French theology, made an impact upon Roman Catholic theology in the 1950s and 1960s and has affected the analysis of the sacrament of marriage. In addition, Karl Rahner's development of the anthropological-ecclesial foundation of marriage as a sacrament has deeply influenced Roman Catholic thought on the subject.

Christocentric View of Marriage

The christocentric focus that flourished within Roman Catholic theology in the 1950s has its roots in the nineteenth century. It was especially applied by Matthias Scheeben (1835–88) to marriage.[54]

---

liotheca Ephemeridum theologicarum Lovaniensum, 64 (Louvain: University of Louvain Press, 1983); and International Theological Commission, "Propositions on the Doctrine of Christian Marriage," *Origins* (September 28, 1978): 235–39.

54. Matthias Scheeben, *The Mysteries of Christianity* (St. Louis: B. Herder, 1946), chap. 21.

Within French Roman Catholic theology, the notion of the body of Christ or the mystical body of Christ, as it was then understood, became the key metaphor used to interpret marriage as a sacrament.[55] Whereas the sacrament of baptism signals an incorporation of a person into the body of Christ, the sacrament of marriage entails a further incorporation within the body of Christ. As a result the Christian couple participates in a distinctive and special vocation.

Salvation-historical View of Marriage

Roman Catholic theology has always been aware that the understanding of marriage as a sacrament has changed and developed throughout the ages. Many theologians interpret these changes not just as changes in the theological understanding of marriage. Instead they argue that the nature and meaning of marriage itself have changed within the history of salvation. Such a view is present within medieval theology, as exemplified by Bonaventure's understanding of marriage. Within recent decades, theologians have sought to relate marriage to salvation history in the same way that they have related it to the evolving history of the world and to the history of religious experience.[56]

Edward Schillebeeckx has elaborated a theological interpretation of marriage as a sacrament with this basic thesis: "Marriage is a secular reality which has entered salvation."[57] The relation between secular reality and religious reality is not a static relation but has a history. Human thought changes and develops in the process of continually reflecting on historical experience. Marriage has significance as a reality of created life. However, the historical experience by God's people of God's covenant and the Christian experience of Jesus as paschal event also contribute to the understanding of the significance of marriage. Marriage is then no longer understood simply as a secular reality within creation, but it is understood also as a promise in the light of the experience of God's covenantal promise. Created reality is both affirmed and relativized in the light of the eschatological hope. Love within marriage is understood not only in relation to natural attraction, but also in relation to the historical

---

55. Gustav Martelet, "Mariage, amour et sacrement," *Nouvelle Revue Théologique* 85 (1953): 577–97; Henri Rondet, *Introduction à l'étude de la théologie du mariage* (Paris: Lethielleux, 1960).

56. Piet Schoonenberg, "Marriage in the Perspective of the History of Salvation," in his *God's World in the Making* (Techny, Ill.: Divine Word Publications, 1964), 106–34.

57. Schillebeeckx, *Marriage*, 384.

experience of Jesus' death and resurrection and the understanding of God and of love proclaimed by the gospel.

Anthropological-ecclesial View of Marriage

Karl Rahner contributes to the understanding of marriage as a sacrament by bringing together several key ideas of his theology: God's universal will for salvation, the fundamental unity of creation and salvation, the idea of a real symbol, and his understanding of the church as the basic sacrament.[58] For Rahner, God's love and gracious self-bestowal constitute the innermost dynamism of the world and of the history of humankind. It is God's gracious love that empowers us to love God and to love each other. Consequently, genuine love as a theological virtue is an event both of God's love for us and of our love for God.

The radical and real symbol of the unity of God's love for us and the human response of love is in the incarnate Christ. The church as a basic sacrament is real sign and symbol of God's love for humanity and the human love of God. In this context, marriage "is the sign of *that* love which is designed in God's sight to be the event of grace and a love that is open to all."[59] Moreover, marriage is a sacrament that concretizes and actualizes the church. For as Rahner expresses it: "The love that unites married spouses contributes to the unity of the Church herself because it is one of the ways in which the unifying love of the Church is made actual. It is just as much formative of the Church as sustained by the Church."[60]

TOWARD A THEOLOGY OF MARRIAGE AS A SACRAMENT

These three directions have greatly enriched our understanding of marriage as a sacrament. Nevertheless, recent advances in fundamental theology, christology, and ecclesiology lead beyond these contributions. Recent shifts within fundamental theology regarding the foundation of the church and within ecclesiology concerning the nature of the church have suggested a new understanding of the church as a sacrament. It has thus become necessary to bring the conception of the sacramentality of marriage into accord with these changes. In addition, traditional theological expositions of marriage

---

58. Karl Rahner, "Marriage as a Sacrament," in *Theological Investigations* (New York: Crossroad, 1973), 10:191–221. For his basic understanding of sacraments, see *The Church and the Sacraments* (New York: Herder and Herder, 1963).

59. Rahner, "Marriage as a Sacrament," 209.

60. Ibid., 212.

as a sacrament have, in some aspects, been based on patriarchal assumptions of marriage and family or have been shaped by outmoded social and anthropological assumptions about gender roles. It has become necessary to elaborate the meaning of the Roman Catholic vision and ideal of marriage in view of equalitarian assumptions about gender and marriage.

Marriage as Sacrament: The Community of the Spirit

Much of traditional theology focused on the text from Ephesians as the symbolic basis of the sacrament of marriage. Unfortunately, use of the image of the Christ-church relation as a model for the marital relation between husband and wife has certain shortcomings. In the image of the relation between Christ and the church, Christ is the one who rules, who saves, and who heals. The church is the one who is obedient and who needs healing and salvation. The application of such symbolism to the marriage relation between husband and wife places the husband in the role of ruler and savior and the wife in the role of sinner and subordinate.[61]

Even though the biblical verses emphasize that Christ's self-sacrificing love for the church should be paradigmatic for the husband's attitude and behavior, the symbolism still implies a superiority of the husband as the suffering redeemer in the marriage relation. Such imagery has as its background the prophetic tradition's description of the relation between God and Israel, with the images of a faithful God versus an unfaithful harlot. The image of the covenant relation between Christ and the church as the basic symbol of the marriage relation may stress God's fidelity, but may also unintentionally associate the husband with a faithful God and the wife with a fickle harlot. It also makes the husband superior to the wife and places her along with children and slaves in a subordinate obediential position.

In addition, the household codes' imagery as well as imperative of the superiority of the husband to the wife have had negative consequences within the history and practice of marriage. We have become increasingly sensitive to the prevalence of the problem of physical abuse of wives by husbands. But within the Christian tradition, such abuse was explicitly condoned and recommended in legislation with appeal to the household codes. Under the doctrine of "moderate correction," a husband was enjoined to beat or physically chastise

---

61. Whereas Rahner argues that the subordination of wife to husband depicted in Ephesians is time-conditioned in that it "belonged to *that period alone*" (ibid., 221), von Balthasar argues for its relevance (*Theologik*, 3:318).

his wife "moderately," as distinct from "excessively," as a loving correction for the good of her soul.[62]

For these reasons, which serve as retroductive warrants, I would like to suggest a fundamental shift in the underlying imagery of the relation between husband and wife in their relationship to God, Christ, and the church. As a part of my argument I would like to draw attention to an important shift in Roman Catholic systematic theology in the understanding of the church as a sacrament. Walter Kasper has argued for several good reasons that the church should be understood as the sacrament of the Spirit.[63] First, his proposal seeks to take into account the post-Easter emergence of the Christian community with its faith in the death and resurrection of Jesus. Kasper is following the Roman Catholic position elaborated by Eric Peterson, Heinrich Schlier, and Joseph Ratzinger concerning the origin and foundation of the church. In addition, the notion of the church as a sacrament of the Spirit takes into account the distinction between Christ and the church. If the church is viewed exclusively as the sacrament of Christ or as the continuation of the incarnate Christ, then the danger exists that the distinction between Christ and the church is neglected and the church is reduced to a "quasi-mythological hypostasis."[64] The metaphor of the church as the sacrament of the Spirit of Christ relates the church to Christ in a way that does not divinize the church. This metaphor allows one to understand the church as emerging in the post-Easter disciples. The church is the community of disciples that emerges under the impact of God's Spirit.

I suggest that an adequate theological understanding of the sacrament of marriage needs to take into account these developments in Roman Catholic theology concerning the foundation of the church and the sacramental nature of the church. If the church is understood primarily as the community of God's Spirit and as the

---

62. For example, Friar Cherubino of Ciena (ca. 1450–81) writes that if pleasant words do not work, "scold her sharply, bully, and terrify her. And if this still does not work...take up a stick and beat her soundly, for it is better to punish the body and correct the soul than to damage the soul and correct the body...." Quoted in William J. Hawser, *Differences in Relative Resources: Familial Power and Abuse* (Palo Alto, Calif.: Mayfield, 1982), 8. A customary law in thirteenth-century France stated: "It is licit for the man to beat his wife, without bringing about the death or disablement, when she refuses her husband anything." Quoted in Jean-Louis Flandrin, *Families in Former Times: Kinship, Household, and Sexuality* (New York: Cambridge University Press, 1979), 123. See also Edward Shorter, *A History of Women's Bodies* (New York: Basic Books, 1982).

63. Walter Kasper and Gerhard Sauter, *Kirche—Ort des Geistes* (Freiburg: Herder, 1976).

64. Walter Kasper, *Glaube und Geschichte* (Mainz: Matthias-Grünewald, 1970), 294.

sacrament of the Spirit, then marriage should be understood as a sign and symbol of the church precisely insofar as it is a sign of the community brought about by the Spirit of God and Christ. A marriage between two individuals is the beginning of a new community, a community of equal disciples and partners under the impact and power of the Spirit. The community of Christians arose after Jesus' death, in discipleship of Jesus, and in the proclamation of God's power in the face of death.[65]

To view marriage as both a symbol and an actual beginning of new community concurs with the insights of the recent salvation-historical approach that argues for a specific meaning of marriage within the Christian dispensation. Christians who view marriage in the light of faith see the meaning of marriage in relation to their experience, their Christian belief in Jesus, and their act of Christian discipleship. For Christians marriage has a specially Christian meaning. Marriage is not simply the new image of God's creative activity symbolized by the Adam and Eve narrative. Nor is marriage an image of the covenantal relation between God and Israel, as symbolized in the prophetic literature. Instead marriage is the symbol of a new community of life, one that images the origin of post-Easter, early Christian communities and one that anticipates the Christian eschatological hope of community. By stressing that the sacramental and symbolic function of marriage relates primarily to the church as the emergent post-Easter community of disciples rather than to the covenantal relation between Christ and the church, I seek to emphasize the fundamental equality of husband and wife in the role of forming a new community. Their equality in discipleship and in the formation of a new community of marriage and their hope for that community can symbolize the equality and hope of discipleship in the post-Easter Christian community.

Sacramental Vision and Roman Catholic Identity

When Roman Catholic theology affirms that marriage is a sacrament, it is not simply making a statement about the number of sacraments. Much more fundamentally it is bringing to expression the Roman Catholic vision of reality. We can distinguish two different cognitive and practical attitudes, in practice intermingled, in the way we relate to our world and society. One is instrumental or functional, the other

---

65. For an interpretation of the post-Easter emergence of the church in relation to the life-praxis of Jesus and of the earliest Christian proclamation of God's power in relation to Jesus, see Francis Schüssler Fiorenza, _Foundational Theology: Jesus and the Church_ (New York: Crossroad, 1984), 3–192.

symbolic or communicative. An instrumental attitude asks about how things function as instruments for some useful purpose. It asks: What utility or function does a particular institution have? A symbolic or communicative attitude is quite different. Its primary question focuses not on utility or function, but on meaning and value. What meaning does an action have? What ideal does an object symbolize? What do we want to communicate?

A similar distinction can be made with reference to C. S. Peirce's semiotic categories that enable us to place signs on a continuum according to their representational and communicative aspects. Some signs or complexes of signs are used referentially to convey information; others are used to communicate in a way that evokes participation. An engineer's model of the Brooklyn Bridge is referential and iconic, whereas a painter's picture is presentational and sensory.[66]

For Roman Catholic theology, then, the affirmation that marriage is a sacrament is an affirmation that marriage is not only instrumental or functional, but is also symbolic and communicative. Marriage is not merely an instrument by which various societies perpetuate themselves; nor is it simply a useful social arrangement by which the human race propagates itself. Instead marriage is also a symbol that communicates meaning, a meaning articulated in relation to a historical memory and a future hope. When Roman Catholic theology describes marriage as a sacrament, it is not so much giving a referential or iconic characterization of marriage, as it is seeking a presentational vision that should evoke one's participation in marriage in a specifically meaningful way.

Louis-Marie Chauvet, a French sacramental theologian, has applied the distinction between sign and symbol to the sacraments in general.[67] Arguing that the traditional doctrine of the sacraments has been based on the classical binary notion of sign, he suggests the appropriateness of the notion of symbol. Classically a sign refers to something else. For example, smoke is a sign of fire and grey hair is a sign of advanced age. The sign leads us to a new knowledge of something else. A symbol, however, introduces us to the cultural order to which it belongs. The sign of the cross, a religious habit, and a Bible are symbols of Christian identity. They

---

66. See Stanley Jeyariaja Tambiah, *Magic, Science and Religion and the Scope of Rationality* (New York: Cambridge University Press, 1990), 84–110.

67. Louis-Marie Chauvet, *Symbole et sacrement: Une relecture sacramentelle de l'existence chrétienne*, Cogitatio Fidei, vol. 144 (Paris: Éditions du Cerf, 1988). See also his earlier work, *Du symbolique au symbole: Essai sur les sacrements* (Paris: Éditions du Cerf, 1979).

do not primarily present new information or lead to new knowledge, as smoke leads us to suspect a fire. Instead they are visible ways in which we mediate our identity. The sign of the cross is more than a sign of something else; it is also a symbol of Christian identity.

It seems helpful in discussions about marriage to take up the distinction between sign and symbol and to ask how marriage is both a sign and a symbol. The liturgical celebration of the sacrament of marriage within the Christian community symbolizes the meaning that marriage has for Christians within the context of Christianity. Marriage takes place before a representative of the Christian community, the communities of two families and sets of friends come together, and the couple starts out beginning a new community. In many cases, and most appropriately, the celebration of marriage is linked with a eucharistic celebration by which the Christian community assembles and actualizes itself.

In my opinion, some theological treatments of marriage make romantic love the central notion of their thematizations. Such treatments can have several weaknesses. First, they overlook that for many centuries and in many areas, the romantic love of the partners for each other was not the personal and social condition of marriage.[68] Second, they sometimes apply an abstract ideal of love as self-gift to marriage without attending to the specific characteristics of love in marriage. Third, such an approach often leads to an intensification of expectations about marriage and the endurance of passion and romance that heightens the possibility for disappointment.[69]

If the meaning of marriage is seen primarily in relation to community rather than in relation to a romantic and individualistic ideal of love, then one is in a better position to understand the specific characteristics of both the marital community and the love that

---

68. Edward Shorter and Lawrence Stone argue that it was in the eighteenth century that a shift took place from marriages based on interest to those based on affection and romantic love. See Lawrence Stone, *Family, Sex, and Marriage in England: 1500–1800* (New York: Harper, 1977), and Edward Shorter, *The Making of the Modern Family* (New York: Basic Books, 1975). A nuanced correction of this view is offered by Herman R. Lantz, "Romantic Love in the Pre-modern Period: A Sociological Commentary," *Journal of Social History* 15 (1982): 349–70. Lantz points to the existence of romantic love further back in Western history, but sees its spread as a part of the process of modernization.

69. Compare Ernest W. Burgess, et al., *The Family: From Traditional to Companionship* (New York: Van Nostrand, 1971); Niklas Luhmann, *Love as Passion: The Codification of Intimacy* (London: Polity Press, 1986); George Levinger and Harold L. Raush, *Close Relationships: Perspectives on the Meaning of Intimacy* (Amherst: University of Massachusetts Press, 1977).

emerges in marriage, both the love of spouses for each other and the love of parents for their children and vice versa.

In a marriage commitment is primarily to a community. Obviously such a community has been differently understood. Traditionally marriage was viewed primarily as the continuation of the community of a particular family, whereas since the eighteenth century, marriage has been viewed as the beginning of a new community. What is important, however, in the stress on community and not simply on partnership or love, is that marriage entails a combination of personal and impersonal relations. It is not simply that the outside world is the world of the impersonal, whereas the family is the realm of the personal. (Often, one-sidedly understood, the public, outside world has been designated as the realm of the male, and the private, personal world has been designated as the domain of the female and family.) In my view, the commitment in marriage to community implies that the impersonal as well as the personal, the objective as well as the subjective, become the object of discourse and of life's energy. One develops a relationship not simply as an intimate relation to a private other, but rather as a community of intersecting relationships and interests.[70]

Love within marriage is often associated and equated with sexual attraction. Yet marital love entails not only desire, but also generosity and an ability to relate on diverse levels. As an eros, marital love includes passion and attraction. It grows from an initial attraction, pleasure, and happiness with one another to a full sexual passion and desire for one another. This passion and desire expand not only into a deeper passion but also into solidarity and commitment. Each spouse learns to respect the other as other and to encourage the other in his or her personal autonomy and hopes. The friendship that may bring the two together as an individual couple has to grow and develop to include others, has to broaden out to other tasks and to other communities. The more this broadening takes place, the more multiple the relationships, the more solid the foundation for the marriage. In the love of spouses for one another, all these elements are intermingled: friendship and passion, desire and generosity, communality and individuality, personal and communal interests. One does not pass from one to the other as if a stage of eros leads to a stage of agape, as if desire leads to solidarity, or friendship leads to love. Instead love, friendship, inclusion of others, and the inter-

---

70. For some recent literature, see Mark Cook and Glenn Wilson, eds., *Love and Attraction: An International Conference* (Oxford: Clarendon, 1979).

secting of diverse and common interests coexist, each strengthening one another.

Just as the love between two spouses involves an intermingling of love and sexual attraction that is both powerful and multifaceted, so too does there also emerge in marriage the ambiguity of the love of parents for children. It is a love that begins as love for children as one's very own offspring and yet as such must give way and become transformed to give birth to a love and support that encourage freedom, independence, and autonomy, especially from the parents. The love of children for parents, to whom they owe their very existence, is at first a very dependent love that must eventually grow into a form of independence.

All of this suggests a dialectic of commitment and love in marriage that expresses a continued transformation parallel to the experience of the beginning of the Christian community. The Christian experience of Jesus' life-praxis solidarity, his suffering and death, is combined with an experience of new life after Easter and an experience of new life and hope. Yet this hope is based also upon the previous experience and community with Jesus. The new community of the church understands itself at first also as part of the community of Israel. Similarly, the experience of a new community and love in marriage continually gives birth to a transformed love, desire, hope, friendship, and responsibility.

If we take marriage as a sign or symbol of the new community of Christians under the impact of the Spirit, then we can better understand ourselves as Christians in relation to historical remembrance and history. We can understand marriage not simply as a self-giving love, but as a sign or symbol of a community that understands itself in relation to time and history and that is committed to a faith that trusts in a reality of love, hope, and transcendence. This faith is not above history, but is intermingled with disappointment, death, and weakness. For the Christian faith, reality is ultimately grounded in a gracious God, and this God is both manifest and present in Jesus. A couple's public promises of love and commitment within the context of a Christian assembly both signify and symbolize the Christian hope and faith. Their promises signify and symbolize a trust and hope in the face of the common experience of the fragility of marriage.

Meaning and Purpose of Marriage

Roman Catholic theological treatments of the meaning and purpose of marriage have discussed the question of procreation versus mutual fulfillment as the end of marriage and the question of individual gender roles within marriage. Whereas traditionally the procreation of children was considered the primary purpose of marriage, more recently a more personalistic view has gained favor. In my opinion, some reactions against traditional conceptions of the purpose of marriage have either caricatured the traditional position or have themselves offered an overly narrow understanding of the goal and purpose of marriage.

Contemporary treatments of marriage often announce an important shift between traditional and modern Catholic views on the goal and purpose of marriage. They often describe this shift as a shift from procreation to life partnership as the goal of marriage. They increasingly emphasize that the goal and purpose of marriage consist of this life partnership. They often present the Roman Catholic tradition as having asserted that the primary and exclusive end of marriage is the reproduction of children. It is important, however, not to caricature the tradition. Indeed throughout the tradition many theologians affirmed procreation as the purpose of marriage and often took Genesis 1:28 ("Be fertile and multiply") as a key code and biblical foundation for the meaning of marriage. Nevertheless, such affirmations were never exclusive. The Roman Catechism (*Catechismus Romanus*) of the Council of Trent (1566) affirms that "nature itself by an instinct implanted in both sexes impels them to such companionship, and this is further encouraged by the hope of mutual assistance" (II, 8:13). Pius XI in the encyclical *Casti Connubii* distinguished between a narrow and broad sense of marriage. The former referred to the conception and education of the children, whereas the latter referred to "the mutual inward molding of husband and wife" and the "determined effort to perfect one another" as "chief reason and purpose" (no. 24).[71]

Many contemporary Catholic books on marriage view it primarily in the categories of interpersonal fulfillment, and the subject of marriage is seen as the individual couple. They argue against the traditional emphasis on procreation and children and they stress the interpersonal love, intimate sexual encounter, and mutual fulfillment of the couple as the meaning and purpose of marriage. Marriage is essentially a profound I-Thou relation between two individuals.[72]

---

71. See Benedictine Monks of Solesmes, eds., *Papal Teaching*; DS 2232.

72. Examples of the personalist direction are: Dietrich von Hildebrand, *Marriage* (London: Longman, Green and Co., 1942), and Herbert Doms, *The Meaning of Marriage* (London: Sheed and Ward, 1939). More recently, Theodore Mackin, *The Marital Sacrament* (New York: Paulist, 1989). Mackin polemicizes against the traditional understanding of marriage as a contract at a time when feminist theory is pointing to the importance of contracts within marriage to underscore the mutual responsibilities and obligations in regard to the common tasks that a couple face. See also Michael G.

Although this literature contains much of value, it may also risk replicating the individualism of much modern culture.[73] The very experience and phenomenon of marriage go counter, in my opinion, to this view of the married pair as an isolated individual couple. Moreover, insofar as such theologies of marriage make interpersonal affection and love the central component of marriage, they not only mirror the individualism of modern culture, but also, contrary to their very intention, contribute to the breakdown of marriages. For as one historian of divorce has noted, "The logical progress of this trend in modern Western society, where love is conceived as being the single most important consideration in the choice of spouse and in the relationship between husband and wife, is that the loss of sentiments of love on the part of one spouse toward the other (or mutually) is the more likely than ever to be perceived by them as indicative of the breakdown of their marriage."[74]

Rather, along with school and work, marriage socializes individuals beyond their intimate family into a new network of families and friends. Marriage is not just a life partnership, but the bringing together of families, groups of friends, and co-workers. Through children parents often come into greater contact with other families and with the community. Along with offspring comes the heightened responsibility that individuals bear not just for the next generation, but also for society as a whole, and for the earth on which the next generations are to live. Marriage as an encounter with another leads to the acceptance of responsibility for others. To define marriage primarily in terms of an interpersonal relation of two without recognizing the social and communal responsibilities that marriage entails is to offer a reductionistic view of marriage. The communal and social meaning of marriage needs to be explicated, especially in the face of an individualistic overemphasis on personal fulfillment.

The inclusion of this social and communal dimension helps insure an adequate understanding of the purpose of marriage. A theology of marriage must also steer the middle course between a romanticism of identity and a romanticism of difference. The romanticism of identity is present in writings that imagine some sort of mystical union takes place between two persons so that they become one. One

---

Lawler, *Secular Marriage, Christian Sacrament* (Mystic, Conn.: Twenty-Third Publications, 1985); Lenore J. Weitzman, *The Marriage Contract: Spouses, Lovers, and the Law* (New York: Free Press, 1981).

73. For a criticism of this individualism in relation to marriage, see Robert N. Bellah, et al., *Habits of the Heart: Individualism and Commitment in American Life* (New York: Harper and Row, 1985), 85–112.

74. Roderick Phillips, *Putting Asunder: A History of Divorce in Western Society* (New York: Cambridge University Press, 1988), 359.

popular Roman Catholic book on marriage divides the human person into three levels of being and action: the physical and biological (the animal level), the psychological (the level of human senses and emotions), and the spiritual (the religious level). The author concludes: "To become one biblical body, one whole person, a man and a women must become one on all three levels."[75] The author does not critically reflect on the connection between his advocacy of the imagery of the couple becoming one body and the mythic belief that at first an androgynous being was created and that marriage brings split sexes back into one body. Fortunately, the author concedes that a husband and wife need not agree about everything on all three levels. One should affirm instead that the goal of mutual perfection should encourage each partner not only to develop self-respect and individuality, but also to achieve autonomy and self-possession. Ideals such as partnership or common good are indeed fine ideals, yet they can become oppressive to individuals. One of the merits of feminist theology and theory has been to demonstrate that too often such ideals as partnership or the common good lead to a sacrifice of the woman's own personal development—a sacrifice often with negative consequence for the wife, but also for the personal maturity of each spouse as well as the marriage itself.

The other romanticism is the glorification of sexual difference. This type of thinking became fully developed first in the Romantic period when the differences between male and female were considered essential differences. The novelty of this development is often overlooked. It has been observed that two basic views of gender or the sexes dominate the last two millennia of Western thought: the one-sex and the two-sex theories.[76] According to the one-sex theory, which dominates classical learning up until the modern Enlightenment, woman is an imperfect version of man. Her anatomy, physiology, and psychic makeup reflect this inferiority. The two-sex theory, which became dominant in nineteenth-century Romanticism, argues that the body determines gender differences and that woman is the opposite of man. She has incommensurably different organs, functions, and feelings. If the one-sex theories were once accepted as reflecting the divine order of creation and were used in order to justify a subordinate position of women within marriage and the exclusion of women from ordination, today two-sex theories are often used in theological analyses of marriage and in the interpretation of the order of creation. Such views of male and female as complemen-

---

75. Lawler, *Secular Marriage*, 71.
76. Thomas Laqeur, *Making Sex: Body and Gender from the Greeks to Freud* (Cambridge: Harvard University Press, 1990).

tary poles have found popularity in pop-psychology and in a more nuanced fashion in Jungian psychoanalysis.

Within a theological analysis one must acknowledge the degree to which gender roles are social and historical constructions. The inadequacies of the one-sex theory have been widely discussed, but it is important to point out that the two-sex theory is also historically limited and appears increasingly inadequate to deal with gender roles in marriage and in the church. Theoretically, the two-sex theory has been criticized by feminist theologians.[77] Socially, it is inadequate for understanding the roles of male and female in the marriage of a dual-career couple, where both spouses bear mutual responsibility and equal time for the diverse tasks of parenting.

PASTORAL-PRACTICAL ISSUES

Two of the most controversial issues within contemporary Roman Catholic teaching on marriage are birth control and divorce. Papal teaching on the nature and purpose of marriage has consistently excluded "artificial means" of birth control. The Council of Trent unambiguously affirmed the indissolubility of sacramental marriage. These issues are usually treated within pastoral and moral theology. Since, however, these issues pertain to the nature and meaning of marriage, it is appropriate here to include a brief sketch of the *status quaestionis* within Roman Catholic theology concerning these issues today.

A sharply controversial topic in contemporary Roman Catholic teaching in regard to marriage is the ethical issue of birth control—an issue related to the meaning and purpose of marriage. Its full treatment can be adequately developed only within a theological discussion of moral and ethical norms. From a systematic theological point of view, a shift has occurred within recent official church teaching. The importance of responsible parenthood together with the significance of mutual love as a primary purpose of marriage have received increasing affirmation within official church teachings. In turn, many Roman Catholic theologians and many married Roman Catholics infer from the shift that responsible parenthood and mutual love would allow various methods of birth control. Many theologians concur with what Cardinal Ratzinger wrote some years ago: "It is clear that the orientation of marriage to 'the procreation of offspring' and the model of 'in accordance

---

77. I have been especially influenced by Elisabeth Schüssler's critique of Gertrude LeFort's advocacy of duality; see Elisabeth Schüssler, *Der Vergessene Partner* (Düsseldorf: Patmos, 1964).

with nature' that is closely connected with that view can no longer
in its traditional form be the standard for the ethics [of marriage]."[78]
At the same time, Ratzinger notes that the ideals of partnership
and mutual fulfillment do not suffice as ethical standards. He concludes his analysis of the ethics of marriage in the following way:
"We stand firm: One certainly no longer has an easily managed
norm that is established from physiology."[79] Instead he argues
that there is the responsibility before the totality of love, humanity, the future, the command of God, and the double mystery of
death and hope. All of this means that there is "no unambiguity.
These responsibilities can require the limitation of offspring, so that
this limitation is what is ethically demanded and the opposite is
immoral."[80]

Reflections similar to those of Ratzinger have led innumerable
theologians to argue that the Catholic church should change its traditional opposition to "artificial means of birth control."[81] At the
same time both Pope Paul VI and Pope John Paul II have consistently and unambiguously rejected that implication. When Pope
Paul VI issued *Humanae Vitae*, more than 450 North American
Roman Catholic theologians protested against this encyclical. Several episcopal conferences responded by recommending that the
faithful should indeed attend to papal teaching, but they also suggested that the faithful should form their own conscience; such
suggestions seemed to intimate cautiously the possibility of dissenting decision. Many theologians, such as Bernard Lonergan and Karl
Rahner, elaborated the foundations for dissent, whereas many ethi-
cists, such as Bernard Häring and Charles Curran, explicitly took
dissenting views.[82] At present a crisis exists in the Roman Catholic church. There continues to be an enormous gap between the
opinions of the majority of professional theologians and the princi-
pled practice of a majority of Roman Catholic married laity within
the modern industrialized West, on the one hand, and the unam-

---

78. Ratzinger, "Zur Theologie der Ehe, 70; my translation here and following.
79. Ibid., 71.
80. Ibid.
81. For an invaluable historical survey, see John Noonan, *Contraception*, 2d ed.
(Cambridge: Harvard University Press, 1988).
82. Karl Rahner, "On the Encyclical *'Humanae Vitae,'*" in *Theological Investigations*
(New York: Crossroad, 1974), 11:263–87. See also his "Magisterium and Theology," in
Theological Investigations (New York: Crossroad, 1983), 18:54–73. An important early
article on the philosophical presuppositions of the debate was Bernard Lonergan's
"Finality, Love, Marriage," in his *Collection* (New York: Herder and Herder, 1967),
16–53. See essays by diverse theologians in Charles E. Curran, ed., *Contraception:
Authority and Dissent* (New York: Herder and Herder, 1969).

biguous and legitimate official teaching of recent popes, on the other.[83]

Despite this split and the controversy about the means of birth control, a fundamental unity of vision exists within the Roman Catholic church about the meaning and purpose of marriage. Its vision of marriage as sacrament entails the responsibility of the individual couple not only for themselves, but also for the community and society at large. This responsibility is an essential element of sexuality. It extends from the sphere of the individual family to encompass the future of the community and society. This responsible love, as a sign and a promise, gives marriage a mission to be a sacrament of the presence and power of God's creative love on earth.

The other difficult question is divorce and remarriage. The indissolubility of marriage has remained the ideal of Roman Catholicism from its very beginning. Nevertheless the fact remains that marriages do fail and remarried couples wish to participate actively as Roman Catholics in the church's sacramental life. Thus a pastoral problem of some weight arises out of the tension between the ideal and the actual practice. Despite all good intentions and all good will marriages do break down.[84] Sometimes, the breakdown results from a failure of commitment and trust. At other times, the breakdown results from a set of conditions and events beyond individual responsibility. In some situations, the two should quite clearly never have gotten married and the eventual collapse of the marital relation was obvious. In some circumstances a physical separation is the best for the individuals concerned as well as for the children—though no cases exist where there is not hurt that affects all involved. Proclamation of the ideal of marriage as indissoluble remains an important reminder not only of one's commitments and what one hopes for, but also of the suffering and hurt one seeks to avoid.[85]

---

83. For a discussion of the reception of *Humanae Vitae*, see Joseph Komonchak, "*Humanae Vitae* and Its Reception: Ecclesiological Reflections," *Theological Studies* 39 (1978): 221–57.

84. For the causes of the breakdown of marriages as well as of divorce (two distinct issues), there is much recent literature. For a survey of recent research, see Gay C. Kitson and Helen J. Raschke, "Divorce Research: What We Know; What We Need to Know," *Journal of Divorce* 4 (1981): 1–37; George Levinger and Oliver C. Moles, eds., *Divorce and Separation: Contexts, Causes and Consequences* (New York: Basic Books, 1979); Stan L. Albrecht, et al., *Divorce and Remarriage: Problems, Adaptations and Adjustments* (Westport, Conn.: Greenwood Press, 1983); and Barbara Thornes and Jean Collard, *Who Divorces* (London: Routledge and Kegan Paul, 1979).

85. It should still be noted that despite the increase in the number of divorces in the West in the twentieth century, the majority of marriages do not end in divorce. Moreover, Robert H. Lauer and Jeanette C. Lauer ("Factors in Long-Term Mar-

In the face of the conflict between the religious ideal and the concrete practice, two pastoral solutions seem to have emerged in practice. One approach is canonical insofar as it involves the expanding of the canonical acknowledgment of the annulment of marriages. This has resulted in a de facto increase in annulments. The new Code of Canon Law expands the traditional grounds for nullity to include lack of understanding, lack of partnership and conjugal love, psychological immaturity, psychopathic and schizophrenic personality, and several other reasons.[86] In addition, an increased leniency in granting annulments has sought to deal in a practical and pastoral way with the breakdown of marriages. Yet in practical terms, this solution de facto renders children into bastards by declaring that a marriage was from the start null and void. Such an approach appears, in my opinion, to go against the spirit, if not the letter, of what was defined at the Council of Trent and affirmed in traditional Roman Catholic teaching. It is with considerable justification that unofficial Vatican statements have criticized the widespread use of this practice.

Another approach within contemporary Roman Catholic theology deals with the problem as a pastoral, practical issue. This approach is pastoral insofar as it highlights overlooked practices in the tradition of the church concerning second marriages. Three theologians now occupying episcopal offices, Walter Kasper, Karl Lehmann, and Cardinal Joseph Ratzinger, have defended this pastoral solution, though in different degrees. This approach points to more lenient practices in the first millennium of Christianity.[87] Origen and Basil mention that in cases where persons had become divorced because of adultery and then remarried, church leaders had allowed them to participate in the eucharist. Ambrosiaster and Augustine also made reference to this practice. In the beginning of the medieval period, several church synods and various penitential books permitted a second marriage even when the first partner was still alive. The Eastern church tolerated the possibility of second marriage, whereas the Western church as a result of Gratian's Decree established a stricter practice.

riages," *Journal of Family Issues* 7 [1986]: 382–90) have noted that in marriages lasting more than fifteen years, 83 percent of both partners consider themselves happily married.

86. As an example of such practical recommendations, see Joseph P. Zwack, *Annulment* (New York: Harper, 1983). For a study of marriage and the new code, see Ladislaus Orsy, *Marriage in Canon Law* (Wilmington, Del.: Glazier, 1986).

87. Henri Crouzel, *L'Église primitive face au divorce, du premier au cinquième siècle*, Théologie historique, vol. 13 (Paris: Beauchesne, 1971). For corrections and modifications of Crouzel's arguments, see Peter Stockmeier, "Scheidung und Wiederverheiratung im Neuen Testament," *Theologische Quartalschrift* 151 (1971): 28–38.

Diverse proposals have emerged from this historical data. Whereas some advocate that the Roman Catholic church should change its position and others advocate no change, the middle position takes a pastoral approach that still affirms the Council of Trent's teaching on marriage and yet suggests a change in pastoral practice.[88] Kasper writes:

> The Church should act in accordance with God's way of acting and for this reason, it should be possible to admit divorced persons who have remarried to the sacraments on three conditions: 1) when they are sorry for their guilt and have made amends for it as well as they can; 2) when everything humanly possible has been done to achieve reconciliation with the first partner; and 3) when the second marriage has become a morally binding union that cannot be dissolved without causing fresh injustice.[89]

Kasper's solution seeks to be faithful to traditional teaching as well as to pastoral practice. Personally, I would modify his formulation of the first condition. Obviously, there should be sorrow over a failed marriage and one should never consider oneself totally guiltless. Nevertheless, there are many situations where the failure of the first marriage results from situations and conditions for which an individual may not be primarily responsible. To admit this situation and to deal honestly with the issue of second marriages is not to reject what marriage is. To quote Karl Lehmann, "The toleration of a second marriage and the associated admission to the sacraments should in no way place in question the obligatory basic form of indissoluble marriage."[90]

One might even state that in face of the fragility of marriage, the celebration of the sacrament of marriage gives visible manifestation to the unconditionality of love as present in the conditions of human existence. The Roman Catholic church's affirmation of the indissolubility of marriage expresses the unconditionality of the commitment to a new community. It is the nature of solidarity, love, and commitment to be resolute, steadfast, and unreserved. To say that I am committed to you in solidarity on the condition that you stay healthy, wealthy, beautiful, and wise is absurd. Human commitment and solidarity have an unconditional, unreserved, transcending dimension. This dimension, which is symbolized in the sacrament of marriage, expresses the Christian faith in a transcendent hope and trust.

---

88. See Joseph Ratzinger, "Zur Frage nach der Unauflöslichkeit der Ehe," 35–56.
89. Kasper, *Theology*, 70.
90. Lehmann, *Gegenwart des Glaubens*, 292 (my translation).

Such an ideal is often frightening, for we know too often of our own fragility and weaknesses. We know that marriages too often break down. We know that love and commitment are not certainties upon which we can rely. The mutual commitment in marriage is as much a hope as a faith or trust. It parallels in many ways our faith in God—an experience not of certainty, but of hope. It is this hope that the Catholic church expresses through its teaching and through its celebration of marriage as a sacrament.

FOR FURTHER READING

Barth, Karl. *The Doctrine of Creation*. Vol. 3, pt. 4 of *Church Dogmatics*. Edinburgh: T and T Clark, 1961, 116–323.

An influential presentation by a major Protestant theologian. Barth develops the nature of marriage as a life partnership. See the reprint of part of this text in *On Marriage* (Philadelphia: Fortress Press, 1968).

Brundage, James A. *Law, Sex, and Christian Society in Medieval Europe*. Chicago: University of Chicago Press, 1987.

Detailed historical research on neglected aspects of medieval law and practice.

Cahill, Lisa. *Between the Sexes: Foundations for a Christian Ethics of Sexuality*. Philadelphia: Fortress Press, 1985.

An exposition of marriage that takes into account recent developments in biblical studies, gender studies, and anthropology. The work was written by a leading Roman Catholic ethicist.

Häring, Bernard. *Marriage in the Modern World*. Westminster, Md.: Newman Press, 1965.

Somewhat dated but still provides an invaluable treatment of marriage with an emphasis on moral, pastoral, and social issues. Häring is a leading Roman Catholic moral theologian.

Kasper, Walter. *Theology of Christian Marriage*. New York: Crossroad, 1983.

Offers a brief theology of marriage with special consideration to biblical and pastoral themes.

Kosnick, Anthony, et al. *Human Sexuality: New Directions in American Catholic Thought*. New York: Paulist, 1977.

A controversial study commissioned and "received" (that is accepted but not approved) by the Catholic Theological Society of America.

Lawler, Michael G. *Secular Marriage, Christian Sacrament.* Mystic, Conn.: Twenty-Third Publications, 1985.

Popular introduction to marriage with a strong personalist emphasis.

Mackin, Theodore. *The Marital Sacrament.* New York: Paulist, 1989.

A comprehensive historical survey of the theological understanding of marriage from biblical to contemporary writings. Excellent bibliographies. This volume updates and completes a trilogy of volumes on marriage, the others being *What is Marriage?* (1982) and *Divorce and Remarriage* (1984).

Phillips, Roderick. *Putting Asunder: A History of Divorce in Western Society.* New York: Cambridge University Press, 1988.

A comprehensive historical and sociological survey of divorce in the West that covers religious beliefs, legal regulations, and social practice.

Rahner, Karl. "Marriage as a Sacrament." In *Theological Investigations.* New York: Crossroad, 1973, 10:199–221.

Develops Rahner's fundamental notions of marriage as a sacrament with reference to his ecclesial understanding of the sacraments.

Roberts, William P., ed. *Commitment to Partnership: Explorations of the Theology of Marriage.* New York: Paulist Press, 1987.

A collection of essays by diverse authors. Offers distinct contemporary perspectives (exegetical, ethical, theological, and pastoral) on the nature of marriage.

Schillebeeckx, Edward. *Marriage: Secular Reality and Saving Mystery.* New York: Sheed and Ward, 1965.

Two volumes have been printed together in the American edition. The first volume deals with the biblical writings; the second with marriage in the history of theology. Although a promised third volume has not appeared, Schillebeeckx's systematic theology of the sacraments is applied here in a theology of marriage.

Whitehead, James, and Evelyn Whitehead. *Marrying Well: Stages on the Journey of Christian Marriage.* New York: Doubleday, 1984.

An important treatment of marriage that is highly recommended for counselors. Reflects on the relation between marriage and maturation.

Whitehead, James, and Evelyn Whitehead. *A Sense of Sexuality: Christian Love and Intimacy.* New York: Doubleday, 1989.

Well-written with a thorough development of the pastoral and psychological dimensions of sexuality. Deals with important topics that are often neglected in theological treatments, such as intimacy, pleasure, and sexual experience.

10

ESCHATOLOGY

10

ESCHATOLOGY

Monika K. Hellwig

INTRODUCTION

Eschatology is the systematic reflection on the content of our Christian hope. As corollary to this it also includes reflection on the risk of not attaining what our hope holds out to us. The word *eschata* in Greek means ends or outcomes, and the discussion of eschatology has traditionally been titled "the last things" (often "the four last things"). These were listed as death, judgment, hell, and heaven, though the discussion also included the questions of purgatory and limbo and the end of the world. In the renewal of Catholic theology pursuant to the Second Vatican Council, the church has come to view Christian eschatology in a different perspective from that taken in the manuals of Catholic dogmatic theology in use between the Council of Trent in the sixteenth century and the Second Vatican Council of the mid–twentieth century.

In our times the focus of eschatology is on the realization of the promised reign of God in all human experience and in all creation. All aspects of a Christian anthropology (see the chapter on sin and grace) are understood in the light of this goal of the fully realized reign of God. So are christology, ecclesiology, and the sacraments, because eschatology is concerned with the core content of the gospel or good news of Jesus Christ. The gospel holds promises both for the individual and for the whole human community. By focusing on the coming reign of God, contemporary eschatology places strong emphasis on the community dimension of our hope, and looks at the hope for the individual in the context of the community hope. Moreover, this focus on the reign of God also means that eschatology is not solely concerned with what lies beyond death and outside of history, though our Christian hope certainly has a transcendent dimension. This rediscovery of a practical and vital hope for the world in the history in which we are taking part, and for which we all share responsibility, is relatively new and to many devout Christians is still surprising.

In order to gain a thorough understanding of the Catholic tradition on eschatology, it is helpful to consider it in five steps: the hermeneutics or rules for interpretation of eschatological statements; the biblical and traditional symbols in which hope has been expressed; a systematic development of general eschatology or hope for the world; a systematic development of individual eschatology or hope for each person; and finally, the spirituality called forth by Christian hope.

THE HERMENEUTICS
OF ESCHATOLOGICAL STATEMENTS

The content of Christian hope, and before that of biblical hope, has been expressed in prayer, confession of faith, and catechesis in bold, concrete images such as a banquet (Luke 14:15-24), a wedding feast (Matt. 22:1-14; 25:1-13), a city without walls or a city of light that no longer needs the sun for illumination (Rev. 21), a society in which the barriers between people collapse, and so forth. There have also been more subtle expressions such as eternal rest (e.g., in the office for the dead and the responsory at evening prayer), everlasting beatitude (office of the dead, collects), and the beatific vision (literally, a gazing that makes one supremely happy [see 1 Cor. 13:12]). It is clear that such expressions are metaphors. They try to capture something of which we do not have direct experience by an analogy with situations of which we do have such experience. Metaphors have also been used to express the realization that it is possible for human freedom to be misdirected and fail to reach the promised goal. Thus we have biblical images of loss and damnation such as the outer darkness where there is weeping and gnashing of teeth (Matt. 22:13), the fires of gehenna (Matt. 5:22-29; Luke 16:19-31), and so forth.

Theological interpretation of these expressions is made more difficult by the fact that through considerable periods of history the metaphors were dealt with rather literally in visual arts, drama, and literature, as well as in preaching and catechesis. Yet interpretation is clearly necessary if the traditions of eschatology handed down through the ages are to be intelligible in our own times, playing their proper role in the shaping of Christian life and action. Moreover, interpretation has always been part of the process of passing on the tradition, though until recently those who engaged in the handing on were not quite as explicitly and critically aware of their own method and function.

Rules for the interpretation of eschatological statements and questions present special problems because we are not dealing with the understanding of past events or present situations and experiences. We are dealing with a future that has never yet been, and indeed with what might be called the absolute future that is radically different from anything that has ever been.[1] In the first place, therefore, any attempt to describe the content of Christian hope shares the limitations of other attempts to describe something that is in the future. We do not know the future in the same way in which we know the past and present. We do not know it in the same definitive concreteness, but by a kind of extrapolation from what we have already experienced. We have a high expectation that certain events will be repeated in much the same way, for instance tomorrow's dawn or next year's spring, or the general pattern of birth and growth, decline and death of generations of living beings. Where human freedom is concerned we can anticipate the future only rather cautiously, for instance, how an election will turn out, what children will become when they mature into adults, what an artist will produce when commissioned to design a monument.

---

1. The seminal text for contemporary Catholic thought on the interpretation of eschatological statements is that of Karl Rahner, "The Hermeneutics of Eschatological Assertions," in *Theological Investigations* (New York: Harper and Row, 1982), 4:323–54. The context and implications of this text are concisely explained by Peter C. Phan, *Eternity in Time: A Study of Karl Rahner's Eschatology* (Toronto: Associated University Presses, 1988), chaps. 2 and 3.

When we turn our attention to the absolute future, knowledge must necessarily be even more tentative. The fulfillment of the whole movement of history, or the resolution of a person's life and striving and development, eludes our comprehension though we can glimpse some of the possibilities. We can glimpse the possibilities because they correspond to our nature and the nature of the world in which we live together. There is an exigency and a promise in our freedom or creativity, and in the fact that we are conditioned in our possibilities by our situation in time and space and corporeality, and by our interdependence on one another, as well as our total dependence on God for existence and all its aspects. We are blessed with great possibilities and great yearnings which imply a promise in creation that they can be fulfilled. But these possibilities also imply an exigency upon us to cooperate in the fulfillment of what is promised. Even if we do not refer explicitly to revelation, but simply think about our human nature as we experience it, we find ourselves goal-directed, with a sense of purpose moving us forward in our individual lives and in the history of the human race. We move toward a future that is partly shaped by the demands and limitations of our present and partly shaped by the projection of future possibilities.

It may seem that this kind of reflection is irrelevant once we turn to revelation, because God who is all-knowing has communicated something of the divine foreknowledge of future outcomes to us. A careful reading of the Bible and tradition refutes this easy solution, however, because what is said about outcomes is subtle, suggestive, and expressed in analogies (1 Cor. 15:35-44; 1 John 3:2). Moreover, the analogies are necessarily culturally conditioned by the contexts in which they were first used, and they acquire additional meaning and connotations as they continue to be handed on and reflected upon in changing circumstances. A general pattern that emerges is the choice of actual experiences of personal and communal happiness as promissory events pointing to the open future, and of experiences of intense pain, deprivation, and frustration as warning events of possible final disaster.

BIBLICAL AND TRADITIONAL SYMBOLS OF HOPE

The Hebrew Scriptures offer us a long history of hope, though many texts may seem strange to our way of thinking because they are so resolutely concerned with specific events in history and so apparently unconcerned with a transcendent future beyond death and history (Pss. 79–84; Exod. 15:1-18; Isa. 51:8; 60:1-11). What they are concerned with is usually the rescue of the community of Israel from some present suffering or danger—from foreign occupation and domination, from famine due to the devastation of fields in war, and from similar concrete and immediate sufferings.

At a more subtle level there emerges the idea that there are several promissory events in the history of the people that speak to them of a final redemption and reconciliation in which ultimate fulfillment and well-being will be reached for all Israel.[2] Chief among these are the exodus from Egypt, the Sinai covenant, and (in retrospect) the creation. The Hebrew celebration of the Passover Seder has always looked back to the unexpected and wonderful liberation out of the political and economic slavery of Egypt, in order to look forward in expectation of a deeper realization of all that was implied in those earlier events. God sees the plight of the oppressed and forgotten, for all human lives have a purpose, and even the most abandoned are called to be the people of God. But the celebration of the Passover was linked to that of the giving of the Law on Sinai: God redeems by sharing the divine wisdom by which peoplehood and total human well-being become possible. Because such happiness is possible only by the Law of God, the giving of the Law and the binding of the people in covenant are the great redemptive gifts at work in the Chosen People for their own good and that of the nations. In further reflection on these historical moments, creation itself is seen as a liberation of the world and the people in it from chaos, meaninglessness, and darkness.

Couched in story form, these great themes are profound meditations on the meaning and purpose of human existence, and therefore on the goals of human life. They connect with the story of the Garden of Eden, with its suggestion of what went wrong in the world when human beings began to appropriate that central harmonizing control that is the divine prerogative. The connection becomes even clearer in the history of the Hebrews with the theme of the reign of God that is one day to be restored (1 Sam. 8; Isa. 24:21-23; 33:21-22; Zeph. 3:11-18; Obad. 20–21; Zech. 14:16-21). There is a long history, at first of charismatic leaders and later of dynasties of kings, but alongside of it runs the prophetic admonition

---

2. A very thorough study of biblical eschatology is that of Rudolf Schnackenburg, *God's Rule and Kingdom*, 2d ed. (New York: Herder, 1968). A concise biblical study that deals entirely with the New Testament and gives more attention to the outcomes for the individual is that of Hubert J. Richards, *Death and After* (Mystic, Conn.: Twenty-Third Publications, 1987).

that in the truth of things it is God who is King of Israel, and indeed of all the nations. For the poor and oppressed, and for all Israel during the long periods of foreign domination, the vindication by God, reclaiming the Kingship, was a wonderful, sustaining promise, though it was always understood that for those who oppressed the poor and the powerless and the faithful, the Day of the Lord was a threat (Amos 5:18-20; Isa. 2:11-15; 13:9-10; Zeph. 1:7-9; Mal. 3:1-5).

All of this expectation seems to have been this-worldly and concerned with those still living at the time of redemption. Only rather late in the history of ancient Israel, and in the compiling of its Scriptures, is concern expressed about what happens on the other side of death. It is only in the intertestamental period that an answer begins to shape itself in scribal traditions. When the day of deliverance comes, it will be as though God personally goes to seek out the faithful who have died, calling them by name to rouse them from the sleep of death, taking them by the hand to raise them from the couch of their tombs and to lead them into the rejoicing throng. This powerful imagery anticipates much in the Christian vision of the redemption. It is noteworthy that it still relates the salvation of the dead to this world and its history by having them brought back into it, though at the final moment of its glorious consummation under the divine reign.

There is another aspect of the intertestamental teaching that is most significant for understanding the teaching of Jesus. The question as to when the reign of God (the kingdom of heaven in the intertestamental language) could finally be expected was answered in an interesting way. There was a twofold response.[3] First, an array of apocalyptic imagery was offered to suggest that God had by no means lost control of creation and history, and would at the proper time triumphantly bring all things to their consummation in a resounding cosmic event. But second, for those who persisted in wanting to know more, there was the advice to live now as though God reigned and as though no other power had any control at all, for this is the way to "see" the reign of God coming in an intimate way. That is of course an answer of great subtlety, and it is picked up in the preaching of Jesus and of the apostles in the New Testament (e.g., Matt. 5:3-10; 13:10-11, 44-46; 2 Peter 1:3-11).

---

3. For details on the intertestamental teaching and its relation to biblical texts, see H. Kleinknecht et al., "Basileus," in Gerhard Kittel, ed., *Theological Dictionary of the New Testament* (Grand Rapids, Mich.: Eerdmans, 1964–76), 1:564–93. See also H. A. Guy, *The New Testament Doctrine of the "Last Things"* (New York: Oxford University Press, 1948), chap. 2.

For us as Christians it is the teaching of Jesus that has the highest authority, and therefore it is of supreme importance to try to understand correctly what the Gospels have to tell us about that teaching. We learn, particularly from the many parables of Matthew's Gospel, that the kingdom of heaven (literally the rule or reign of the skies) was the hope that Jesus held out to those who would listen. Nowhere in the New Testament does the early community of the followers of Jesus redefine what the reign of the heavens might mean. The exact phrase that Jesus is reported to have used does not appear in the Hebrew Scriptures, but it is well attested in the intertestamental literature. It is simply a circumlocution for the reign of God that is to be fully realized in human society and in all creation, giving ultimate happiness to all whom it encompasses.[4] Mark's Gospel uses the more direct phrase, kingdom of God (e.g., Mark 1:15).

In the parables of Jesus, the words "the kingdom of heaven is like..." never lead to a description of that kingdom. What they do lead to is an increased hope and an increased awareness of how one should look for the coming of the kingdom. Cumulatively, the parables suggest that the kingdom is surely coming because God is not defeated, that one should hope confidently in spite of all setbacks, that the kingdom is established incrementally, and that its growth is often invisible (Mark 4:26-29; Matt. 13:31-50; Luke 13:6-9, 18-30; 14:7-24). We learn elsewhere in the preaching of Jesus that the kingdom is already offered to the human community in the present; it is not some unreachably far off goal in distant time (Matt. 4:17; 10:7; 12:28; Mark 11:10; Luke 10:9-11; 17:20-21). The kingdom is among the listeners and within them; the gift that is already being offered in the present is contingent upon human acceptance (Luke 19:11-27). It is therefore useless to speculate upon the time of its coming, or to try to imagine exactly what the kingdom is like in concrete terms; it is enough to live now in total trust and total community with others in the conviction that God reigns, and that all else will follow.[5]

Nevertheless the element of urgency in the preaching of Jesus about the coming of the reign of God translates into the confrontations that bring Jesus to his early and dreadful death, and the theme of resurrection from the dead comes to the forefront of New Testament eschatology. The claim is introduced that by his death and resurrection Jesus has already in a seminal way brought about the reign of God in human society while, on the other hand, the full manifestation and enjoyment of that victory are still to come. Indeed,

---

4. See Kittel, ed., *Theological Dictionary*, 1:576–90.
5. Schnackenburg, *God's Rule and Kingdom*, 77–159.

the early community writes of the expectation of another coming of Jesus in glory, fulfilling all the prophecies as yet unfulfilled (1 Cor. 15:23; 1 Thess. 2:19; 3:13; 4:15-18; Col. 3:4). Entry into the community and communion of the risen Jesus offers a life of grace that will unfold into the ultimate joy of the fully realized reign of God. There is a certain urgency in preaching and evangelizing, so that the world may be ready for the consummation.

In all of this the individual is not forgotten. The community remembers that Jesus spoke, in parable and exhortation, of an outcome for the individual beyond death—Lazarus, who died at the rich man's gate, being gathered to Abraham's bosom (Luke 16:19-31); the repentant insurgent crucified with Jesus gaining entry into paradise that very day (Luke 23:39-43). Also recorded among the sayings of Jesus is the possibility of being cast into outer darkness (Matt. 22:11-14) or into the fires of gehenna (Matt. 5:30). In the argument between the Pharisees and the Sadducees over the resurrection of the dead to participate in the joy of God's reign, Jesus emphatically asserted the right of the people to this hope (Matt. 22:31-33).[6]

The Hebrew perception of the human person was that of a living body whose existence is necessarily corporeal. In the early centuries of Christian life, this perception came into confrontation with the Greek perception of a certain independence or transcendence of the human spirit—a problem that later Judaism also had to meet. In the Hebrew anthropology any personal existence beyond death would naturally be imagined as corporeal, and therefore as an awakening from death to resume a human life. In the Greek anthropology another possibility emerges—that of the continued life of the human spirit in a disembodied way. Both views are projections interpreting what we do not know by extrapolation from what we do know—our bodily life in the world and our introspective consciousness. In the eschatology developed in the course of Christian history, the two anthropologies produced a hybrid projection full of paradoxes. To the extent that people realized that they were dealing with metaphors and analogies this could be enriching. However, when the images were taken literally it could lead to confusion and the predominance of fear over hope—a distortion unfortunately well attested in our history.[7]

---

6. For a detailed listing of the New Testament texts, see Pierre Grelot and Raymond Deville, "Kingdom," in Xavier Léon-Dufour, ed., *Dictionary of Biblical Theology* (New York: Desclée, 1967), 254–58.

7. A well-annotated summary of the historical development of eschatological thought in Christian tradition is given by Peter Müller-Goldkuhle, "Post-Biblical

During the first three centuries when the church was still being persecuted sporadically but viciously, hope for the coming reign of God was not lost, but the heavenly realms began to acquire a simultaneous and other-worldly rather than a future-worldly existence. This simultaneity is not the same as that of the New Testament Johannine eschatology, where the gift of divine "eternal" life is already enjoyed by believers in some measure during their earthly lives (John 5:24-26; 1 John 3:2). In the visions and dreams of the martyrs, we find them passing through a gate into a beautiful garden (reminiscent of the Garden of Eden) in which they meet all their friends who have already died in the persecution. This simultaneity fits better into a Greek cosmology than a Hebrew one. Yet it corresponds to some of the imagery found in allegorical texts such as Job, and to the reported dying words of Jesus about being in paradise with him that very day (Luke 23:43).

After the Constantinian patronage and establishment of the church in the fourth century, a subtle change came about in the imagery of eschatology. The persecuting pagan empire had become the "reign of God on earth" through the emperor as "vicar of Christ." Participation in public Christian worship and public confession of faith were not only possible without risk of penalty, but became quite prestigious and even profitable. Consequently there was a certain assimilation of the expectation of the coming reign of God into the present achievement of a Christian empire. General eschatology gradually faded and was reduced eventually to an image of fear—the terrible day of judgment at the end of the world, when hidden sins will be revealed in a context of cataclysmic disasters, and terrible punishments, mainly of a physical type, will be inescapable. In the same context the imagery for individual outcomes gradually became more concrete and more the center of focus. This was compounded from the sixth century onward by a cultural hiatus in the transmission of the Christian tradition. With the decline of the ancient Mediterranean cultures, leadership in liturgy and theology for the Western church passed to the barbarian peoples, who became Christian without fully assimilating the stories, images, and symbolism of the tradition. This culture gap contributed to a tendency toward literal understanding of imagery originally intended as figurative. Out of this history emerged the well-known pattern of the "four last things." Death, judgment, hell, and heaven were further elaborated so that an individual and a general judgment were con-

Development in Eschatological Thought," in Edward Schillebeeckx and Boniface Willems, eds., *The Problem of Eschatology* (entire issue of *Concilium* 41 [New York: Paulist Press, 1969], 24–41).

sidered, paralleling individual death and the end of the world, while the fate of the disembodied soul had to be considered as well as the doctrine of resurrection. To this was added the possibility of temporal punishment in a kind of extraterrestrial time as an alternative to eternal punishment, to meet the problem of those who seemed to qualify neither for the happiness of heaven nor for eternal punishment. Definitions were extrapolated for this category under the name of "purgatory," and for the additional categories of the "limbo of the patriarchs" for those who died before Christ and the "limbo of children" who died unbaptized.[8] There is no doubt that the great medieval theologians were aware that they were dealing with analogous language, but the transmission in preaching and even in the manuals of dogmatic theology in use from shortly after the Council of Trent to the time of the Second Vatican Council tended to repeat the elaboration of the imagery without adequate acknowledgment of its figurative character and function. Even the official church teachings on eschatology, scanty as they were, did this.[9] In consequence of

8. A clear exposition of this traditional pattern can be found in J. P. Arendzen, *What Becomes of the Dead? A Study in Eschatology* (New York: Sheed and Ward, 1951).

9. The official teaching of the church may be traced by consulting the "Index systematicus," L 1–7, pp. 922–26, in H. Denzinger and A. Schönmetzer, eds., *Enchiridion Symbolorum, Definitionum et Declarationum de Rebus Fidei et Morum* (New York: Herder, 1965) (hereafter DS). A selective summary in translation is available in Josef Neuner and Heinrich Roos, eds., *The Teaching of the Catholic Church*, re-edited by Karl Rahner (New York: Alba House, 1967), chap. 11, 413–22. These official teachings up to the time of Vatican II dealt scarcely at all with general eschatology. The Synod of Constantinople in A.D. 543 rejected the idea of an assured final universal reconciliation of the wicked (known as *apokatastasis*), and insisted on the real risk of eternal damnation (DS 411). Moreover, the theory of a one thousand year reign on earth of the returning Christ (millenarianism) was steadily rejected by the ordinary teaching of the church. Beyond this the focus was on individual eschatology, where the main issues were as follows. The full flowering of grace beyond death is in "the vision and enjoyment of the divine essence intuitively and face to face" (DS 819, from the constitution *Benedictus Deus* of Pope Benedict XII in 1336). People may fail to attain this because they are unbaptized and still burdened with original sin when they die, in which case they suffer only the deprivation of the sight of God, but those who are burdened with actual (i.e., their own) sin suffer not only the deprivation but also positive torment (DS 780, from the letter of Pope Innocent III to the bishop of Arles in 1201). Those who die repentant of sin but without having expiated it adequately are detained in purgatory (DS 1580, from the Canons on Justification of the Council of Trent). Moreover, there are two judgments. The above-mentioned determinations happen at death, but at the end of time all souls resume their bodies and appear in person before Christ for the last or general judgment, and at this point their happiness or misery is experienced in its bodily aspect (DS 801, from the Fourth Lateran Council of 1215). This last point raises a question about the condition of souls between death and final judgment. In response to earlier sermons of Pope John XXII, who claimed that the souls of the blessed could not enjoy the fullness of the beatific vision until the general resurrection, Pope Benedict XII taught that they could enjoy this fullness immediately after death (DS 819, also from the constitution *Benedictus Deus* of 1336). Clearly these declarations of official teaching make assumptions about

this tendency to deal with the imagery literally, theology before the Second Vatican Council generally left eschatology brief and undeveloped, focusing on individual outcomes almost to the exclusion of general eschatology, and making the threats so much more concrete than the promises that the total effect expressed anxiety rather than hope.

This development accorded ill with the questions and the expectations of intelligibility aroused by the aftermath of the Enlightenment in modern believers. Purely arbitrary rewards and punishments beyond death, connected to the substance of human life in the world like an afterthought, seem to modern believers to be quite out of harmony with the God of Jesus Christ. A return to Scripture, and to the understanding expressed in patristic writings and the early liturgy of the church, has encouraged a renewed Christian reflection on the experiences of being human and on the experience of lives lived in the grace of the risen Christ. It has also encouraged a renewed focus on communal and this-worldly redemption, not to exclude but to balance the concern with what transcends death and human history in the world as we know it. The Second Vatican Council, in those few passages that deal with eschatology,[10] while asserting the traditional symbols, leaves them open to more thorough interpretation and to the inclusion of the communal and historical aspects. The same may be said for subsequent teaching of the ordinary magisterium of the church.[11]

---

the nature of time and about the human capacity for determining and understanding the judgments and dispositions of God. They take biblical and traditional imagery at face value. However, the central intent becomes clear in the further teaching that the faithful can help souls in purgatory by their prayers (DS 1867, Tridentine Profession of Faith of 1564), with the recent official observation, "The Church excludes every way of thinking or speaking that would render meaningless or unintelligible her prayers, her funeral rites, and the religious acts offered for the dead" (Sacred Congregation for the Doctrine of the Faith, "A Letter on Certain Questions concerning Eschatology," *Acta Apostolicae Sedis* 71/2 [1979]: 939–43).

10. *Lumen Gentium*, nos. 48–50, contains brief allusions to the consummation, using biblical imagery without any attempt to interpret it. *Sacrosanctum Concilium*, no. 8, does the same. *Gaudium et Spes*, no. 18, mentions the mystery of death and the confident hope of eternal life in communion with God. But one would look in vain to Vatican II for an explicit account of a renewed understanding of eschatology.

11. The main subsequent statement is that of the Sacred Congregation for the Doctrine of the Faith, "A Letter on Certain Questions concerning Eschatology." The gist of that instruction is the reaffirmation of: resurrection of the whole person of the dead (nos. 1, 2); the immortality of the human self or soul (no. 3); a distinct glorious manifestation of Christ in the future (nos. 4, 5); the assumption of Mary as anticipatory of the glorification of all the elect (no. 6); the happiness of the elect who will one day be with Christ; the eternal punishment of sinners having a repercussion on their whole being; and purification for the elect before they see God (no. 7). Although these sections reaffirm traditional imagery, it is important to note that the instruction also warns that we have no basis for a "proper picture of life after death," that literalism

GENERAL ESCHATOLOGY

If we are to take the teaching of Jesus himself as the criterion, then the comprehensive and dominant category for eschatology must be the reign of God. That category has two aspects: the rule of God as the governing principle in the lives and consciousness of individuals, and that same rule as the governing principle of all the relationships of creatures with one another. Clearly, the category also has two phases: the process and the consummation. While we cannot concretely describe the consummation or assign a specific future time to it, it is necessary for us to acknowledge a goal to which everything is destined and which it is possible to reach—a goal which in its broadest sense is even guaranteed by God.

The rule of God as the supreme and comprehensive governing principle in individual lives and consciousness is to be discussed in the following section. The communal and worldly aspect, which is concerned with the integrity and harmony of creation, has acquired new visibility and urgency in our times.[12] It has not always been fully acknowledged. A cataclysmic end of the world, such as was long envisaged in discussion of general eschatology, stressed a discontinuity between what is built up in history and what constitutes the kingdom of God of the end-time. A return to our biblical roots calls for a redressing of this imbalance. The point of stressing discontinuity was surely to emphasize salvation as the undeserved gift of God. But

---

is not to be encouraged any more than abandonment of the basic teachings, and that essential to Christian faith is a certain tension between fundamental continuity between a graced life and ultimate salvation—a continuity provided by the role of charity—and radical discontinuity because faith becomes vision.

12. This has particularly been so in the "liberation theologies" which have projected the content of Christian hope from two interrelated sources: the biblical narrative and imagery; and the discernment in mass suffering of the sinfulness of the world in need of redemption. For an introduction to this literature, see Claude Geffré and Gustavo Gutiérrez, eds., *The Mystical and Political Dimensions of the Faith* (entire issue of *Concilium* 96 [New York: Paulist Press, 1975]). It should be noted, however, that there is a sharp debate on the topic of the connection between political responsibility and eschatology. Joseph Cardinal Ratzinger (in *Eschatology* [Washington, D.C.: Catholic University of America Press, 1989], and elsewhere) has maintained that the notion of the reign of God must be kept radically separate from questions of political responsibility for developments in history. He takes issue not only with current developments in systematic theology that include a worldly-historical dimension in eschatology, but he claims that they are based on a false exegesis of the biblical term *reign of God.* He sees the New Testament equating the reign of God with the person of the risen Christ and with personal salvation reached only by death. For a differing understanding of the relationship of death and the reign of God, see Gisbert Greshake, "Endzeit und Geschichte," in G. Greshake and G. Lohfink, eds., *Naherwartung, Auferstehung, Unsterblichkeit* (Freiburg: Herder, 1975), 11–37. The matter is further dealt with in Herbert Vorgrimler, *Hoffnung auf Vollendung* (Freiburg: Herder, 1980).

the point of stressing a certain continuity as balance to this is to take seriously the teaching of Jesus that the kingdom of God is within us, among us, and at hand. It is not a gift that can be bestowed on the human community in spite of its resistance. The reign of God as the ruling principle of human society has to be received by human society.

In the earlier stages of Christian history this could not have quite the same political overtones that are found in the documents of the Second Vatican Council and in many theological and pastoral documents since then. The earliest Christians clearly understood that welcoming the breakthrough that Jesus had made in his death and resurrection required them to be a countercultural movement in a very specific way—by radical sharing of material resources (Acts 2:42-47; 4:32-37); by a style of leadership that was service rather than domination (John 13:6-17); by a very basic trust of divine providence and of one another (Matt. 6:25-34); by forgiveness and nonviolence (Rom. 12:1-21); by simplicity, total truthfulness, and a deep level of fellowship (1 Cor. 12:4-31); by a style of life permeated by prayer; by fearlessness; and so forth. The extension of this kind of life throughout the world by evangelization was to be the way to hasten the second coming of Christ in glory and the full realization of the kingdom of God. In the context of their time—without democratic organization of society, without universal literacy and mass media, without social and economic analysis of poverty and injustice, without access to social and political means of changing the structures of the larger society—what they were able to do was to change the structure of relationships and of distribution of material goods and opportunities within their own group of believers, and to welcome more and more outsiders to become members of their group. As we know from subsequent history, this was economic and political change working from the grassroots upward through the larger structures of society. What has happened in modern times, partly through the long impact of Christianity and partly through technical, social, and political developments in society, is that we have become empowered to act more directly to change the larger structures of our relationships with one another in history. That empowerment has brought with it a new eschatological exigency. To hope seriously for the coming reign of God means to reorder not only immediate individual relationships in justice, charity, and compassion, but also those larger structures or patterns of relationship among us that determine whether people live or starve, whether they can live humanly or are brutalized, whether they can participate in community or are excluded, whether their lives are an experience of the gracious goodness of the creator or are lived in torture and constant fear.[13]

Thus the reign of God as the promised goal of Christian life and hope necessarily has a this-worldly, public dimension. To welcome and hope for God's reign is not an abstraction; it means the expectation of a radical reordering under God's rule of our world with all that this implies in the way of responsibility for one another, without the exclusion of anyone and with the inclusion of future generations. Reshaping the world according to God's rule not only depends on voluntary human acceptance of the divine wisdom shared with us and human commitment to inclusive concern for one another, but it depends also, unavoidably, on a commitment to restructuring the present order, distorted as it is by the cumulative consequences of deeds of violence, greed, and domination. It would be simply inconsistent, knowing that we can act and that the reign of God is made accessible to us, to accept present injustice and oppression as the inevitable and enduring pattern of history, and to expect that in utter discontinuity with the relationships and structures built up in history there would suddenly be a day on which God would restore the divine rule, rewarding each for individual behavior without reference to the social responsibility that is the other side of social empowerment.

This is another way of acknowledging the reality of human freedom and the consequent risks of history. Our creaturely existence is one of freedom as well as one of interdependence. But that means that we are at risk not only of the misuse of our own freedom but also of the misuse of freedom by others. Likewise it means that the fullness of redemption cannot be offered to each in isolation. It is a matter of the salvation of the world rather than salvation of souls out of the world. What we are is largely constituted by relationships not only with God as creator and end but also with the fellow creatures of God. Thus it is clear that on the one hand ultimate salvation is continuous with all aspects of human development in history, including the political, economic, and social structures in which people affirm or deny the existence and rights of others, while on the other hand ultimate salvation transcends what we can grasp with the imagination or predict by calculation or extrapolate speculatively.

---

13. This realization, proposed and popularized in the mid–twentieth century by German Protestant theologians, mainly Jürgen Moltmann, was first assimilated into Catholic theological discussion by J. B. Metz in the development of his "political theology." The central thesis is well explained in Metz's "The Future in the Memory of Suffering," in J. B. Metz, ed., _New Questions on God_ (entire issue of _Concilium_ 76 [New York: Herder, 1972], 9–25). See also Edward Schillebeeckx, "The Interpretation of Eschatology," in Schillebeeckx and Willems, eds., _The Problem of Eschatology_, 42–56.

Nevertheless, the question of the "end of history" and of the nature of that general judgment that has been an integral part of the tradition includes the very important issue of how all the successive generations of the human race through the centuries are to be understood as participating in the communal destiny of the reign of God. A first part of the answer to this is necessarily that they participate by being part of the process that moves toward the goal, and therefore by enjoying the fruits of the process in partial and anticipatory ways. This is another way of expressing the "eschatological tension" to be found in the New Testament between the "already" of the resurrection of Jesus and consequent empowerment of the followers of Jesus on the one hand and the "not yet" of the second and glorious coming of the Lord on the other hand. But the other half of the answer concerning the participation of the generations who have passed in history is the doctrine of the general resurrection.

There is a sense in which the teaching of the general resurrection belongs to general rather than individual eschatology. The imagery of all the dead awakening and rising out of the earth simultaneously to take part in the final disentangling of the plot of human history is an imagery that insists on the essential interrelatedness and community of destiny of all human persons at all times and places. This sense of community of destiny and common responsibility for all that transpires in the history of the world seems to be a more important aspect of the interpretation of the doctrine than any attempt to determine the exact way in which such a resurrection might be possible.

INDIVIDUAL ESCHATOLOGY

Although in biblical and early Christian perspectives general eschatology, under the aspect of the coming reign of God, is the prior and more inclusive category, there is no doubt that for most of us the questions concerning individual eschatology seem more urgent. That may be in part due to the expectations aroused by the catechesis and preaching of recent centuries. However, it is certainly also an outcome of our present intensely individualistic culture. An intensely self-centered life is more obviously threatened by death than a life that is more pervasively conscious of community and more constantly focused outward on a common purpose.

Individual eschatology deals in the first place with the universal phenomenon of death—with the way it is experienced and with the influence it has in shaping life.[14] It is axiomatic in Christian thought that the way we experience death as frustration, disaster, and ultimate threat is due to sin and sinfulness. The story of the Garden of Eden plays on the idea of what it is that is truly life-giving, truly a reflection of the divine immortality, and what it is that condemns to death. The imagery of the story (with the tree at the center which is the exclusive prerogative of God) suggests that it is only when human beings try to place themselves at the center and to arrange the world around themselves according to their own demands and whims that contingency and vulnerability become terrifying. Death means a surrender of control over the world, over other people, and over one's own destiny. Death means crossing into the unknown. In an ideal human life perfect trust takes the terror out of death because it is the ultimate act of surrender to a gracious and welcoming divine providence. Likewise, in such an ideal life, full fellowship and dedication to the common good take the sense of frustration out of death because in such a case death is not the collapse and failure of everything the individual has striven to build up in the course of his or her lifetime. It is only when the focus has always been on self that death is the destruction of everything.

There is a sense, therefore, in which death itself is the judgment of the individual; death is the condemnation of all that embodies self-centeredness and selfishness, but it is the consummation of all that embodies love and generosity because it is such a radical going forth from the self. Death fulfills these functions not only at the moment when it happens; it really casts its influence over the whole of life by the fact that it is always imminent and its moment is not known beforehand. The fact of death as certain but of its timing as unpredictable asks for a certain humility and acknowledgment of dependence and contingency at all times, in all projects and relationships. The refusal of such acknowledgment, which is in effect the denial of death, establishes an inauthentic mode of living and of relating to others as well as to God. This is the disorientation and alienation of sin that affect all human beings in history to some extent, exception being made by Christian faith in the case of Jesus himself and in a relative way of Mary. The New Testament is full of allusions to Jesus' having saved us from death. Clearly, Jesus himself did die, and so did all his followers when their time came. What they were saved from was not biological death with its definitive demand for surrender. That is a constitutive element of being human.

---

14. Especially significant contributions to Catholic thought on the subject are: Karl Rahner, *On the Theology of Death* (New York: Seabury, 1973), and Ladislas Boros, *The Mystery of Death* (New York: Herder, 1965).

But they were saved from the overwhelming terror and frustration of death with its crippling effect on human freedom and community during life, and its condemnatory quality at the very moment of death (Heb. 2:14-15).

One of the ways in which death shapes human lives is simply by guaranteeing that they will end and that they are therefore a limited opportunity for human freedom and self-determination. If one were to expect one's life to go on indefinitely there would not be the same exigency to make something of it, to do something determinate with one's creativity and freedom. But the fact that the time of freedom and potential is coming to an end imposes a certain urgency and concreteness on the project of one's life. If we want to realize the potential of our freedom, we should order ourselves to our goals as human creatures in the historical world, for human freedom is not only a gift but an imperative, and that imperative is given in the context of human society and the relations with other human persons. The goal of our individual freedom, which the certainty of death urges upon us, is a self-gift to others in loving concern which is the ordinary mode of expressing the love of God. That is to say that death invites us toward an ecstatic way of living in the literal sense of the word *ecstatic*—being carried out of or beyond oneself. In such a perspective it is no longer necessary to list death and judgment separately as two items among the "last things," but it may be appropriate to point out that death seen as the judgment is not impersonal but is precisely the call and judgment of God for each person.

We are so used to hearing the list—death, judgment, hell, and heaven—that it may not be immediately apparent that in speaking of death we are dealing with something that is at least partially observable, while in speaking of heaven and hell we are dealing with metaphors for the unknown and unobservable. Heaven, in the literal sense, means the sky. Hell, in the literal sense translating *gehenna*, means a deep valley, perhaps a pit in that valley, where trash was burned in New Testament times, and where human sacrifices had been offered in earlier times. Moreover, although the terms *heaven* and *hell* are those now most commonly used to designate final salvation and final perdition, they are by no means the only images offered by our Scripture and tradition, as mentioned earlier in this chapter.

What Christian teaching asserts under the designation "heaven" is that the destiny intended by the creator for every human person is to find ultimate happiness and the final resolution for the quest of life in intimate and essentially indescribably personal communion with God, and in God with all creation. There has, of course, been much discussion about the kind of communion that constitutes such ulti-mate happiness for a human person. Earlier ages were content with the understanding that it consisted of being reunited with the risen Christ and with all the blessed, placing heavy emphasis on fellowship and harmony within God's creation. The medieval discussion envis-aged the entry into the state of the blessed by disembodied souls which would not be reunited with their risen bodies until the end of history and time. Medieval theologians were therefore inclined to focus on purely spiritual blessedness as the essential happiness of heaven. The overflow of that blessedness into the additional enjoy-ment of a risen body was considered only tangentially, and remained rather awkward. It gave rise to the question how anything could be added to the happiness of heaven that the souls enjoyed, because the happiness of heaven was intrinsically perfect. Moreover, the general resurrection demanded a conception of heaven as a place while the heaven of disembodied souls could simply be a state of being.[15]

More interestingly, the medieval discussion took in the question whether the essential happiness of heaven would be primarily in the intellect or in the will. Was it primarily a matter of being so to-tally dedicated to God in love that it constituted ultimate blissful ecstasy? Or was it primarily a matter of being rewarded by the "vi-sion" or knowledge of God as God really is (see 1 John 3:2)? The latter understanding, held by the school of Saint Thomas Aquinas, won predominance at least in the vocabulary used, and the term _be-atific vision_ came into common usage. Yet there is much to be said for the alternative, because it has always been axiomatic in Chris-tian theology that salvation is by charity, a theme that appears in the preaching of Jesus in the Gospels, in the letters of Paul, and most ex-plicitly and repetitively in the Johannine literature (1 Cor. 13; John 15:7-17; 1 John 4:17-21).

In fact, when we speculate about the nature of the happiness of heaven we are projecting what we know about our own humanity and its needs and longings. On the one hand we infer from our ex-perience of reality that there is a benign and purposeful creator of all that is, and that the power of the creator is not limited by ex-ternal factors because that creator is the one and only God, ground of all being, horizon of all possibilities. On the other hand we then conclude that such a benign and purposeful creator does not bring into existence beings who, by their very nature, are destined to ulti-mate frustration of the longing and potential which are part of their

---

15. For a more detailed treatment of the question of disembodied souls, see José-María González-Ruiz, "Should We De-mythologize the 'Separated Soul'?" in Schillebeeckx and Willems, eds., _The Problem of Eschatology_, 82–96.

creaturely makeup. This means that there must be fulfillment and happiness beyond what we can see, particularly for those whose lives among us never escape from oppression, persecution, humiliation, or simple grinding poverty and pain. The God of Jesus Christ cannot be imagined as less faithful or less good than the creatures which that God has brought forth, yet within the world and the history subject to our observation virtue is not always rewarded, nor are innocent sufferers always vindicated. That is our first reason for the assertion that beyond death, beyond history, beyond what we can observe, God fulfills the promises implicit in creation and in the history of salvation that is centered upon the person of Jesus.

There is a further and more elusive reason in human experience as interpreted by Christian faith. Human introspection, as experienced when Christian faith embraced categories of Greek anthropology, insists on the capacity of the human consciousness or soul to transcend particularities of space and time, to join the speculation of other minds that lived long ago and far away in other cultures, to rejoice in the happiness and weep for the sorrows of people whom it has never met, and to yearn for beauty and wisdom and goodness. In other words, there is a certain testimony from human introspection suggesting not only that human beings, transcending their corporeal circumstances, wish to live forever, but also that this can be rationally conceived as possible—some would even say, as necessary. In spite of many modern philosophical arguments to the contrary, Catholic teaching has steadily asserted such human spiritual survival, notwithstanding the paradoxical tension between the expectation of the immortality of the soul and the expectation of personal bodily resurrection.

What is of central importance, however, is not the particular projection by which the hope for the individual is expressed, but the assertion that God holds out hope of final happiness in divine intimacy to each human being in such a way that that promise and its fulfillment transcend all external threat or evil that can be brought to bear upon that person's being by outside forces. There is a certain unresolved paradox in this: On the one hand we assert the interdependence of human beings and the communal character of redemption, but on the other hand we assert the individual, personal care of God for each human being as finally overcoming what any other power can do to harm that person. And maintaining that paradox is critically important to Christian life and action in the world.

At the same time, there is evidently no intention in our tradition to suggest that people are safe from the harm they can do to themselves. On the contrary, the tenacity with which church teaching has held on to the doctrine of hell testifies to the deep conviction that everything in the outcome of a human life is really at stake in the way each person uses human freedom. As already mentioned, Jesus himself, according to the Gospels, preached the certainty of God's offer of the gift of salvation, but he also preached that the individual's reception of that gift was a matter of total human freedom. He used stark images of destruction and consuming suffering. He did not hesitate to use the image of fire burning. This image of fire predominated in the history of the church to such an extent that it seems to have taken over rather literally, and this is due no doubt to the effectiveness of the image as representing the threat of total and terrible destruction in a process of intense suffering.

The church, in insisting on the image of fire combined with the idea of permanence, seems to have been responding to the perennial temptation to postpone serious reflection on the choices of one's life and one's commitments, and to the temptation to suppose vaguely that things will all work out somehow. The false but insidious assumption that status and privilege in society can protect one indefinitely from full responsibility for one's action and inaction is perhaps a factor both in the dogged insistence on the terrible image of fire and in the tendency to press for a literal understanding of it. Fire is no respecter of persons.

When we look at the image and realize its important symbolic significance, another aspect of fire emerges, namely that fire is used for refining and purifying. In Scripture, fire is a symbol not only of suffering and destruction, but also of God and of the human encounter with God (Exod. 19:18; 24:17; Deut. 4:11-36; 5:4-26; Ps. 79; Ezek. 36:5). The ambivalence of the symbolism is important. The encounter with the living God refines, purifies, and transforms those who are open to conversion, but destroys those who persist in asserting the self as independent of God and of God's reign in the world of creatures. This ambivalence in the symbolism suggests an interpretation of hell as painful self-damnation and self-destruction in such many-faceted ways as a human existence offers. The question of whether this involves a particular state beyond death seems really to be the issue of a concluding reality beyond our observation. The question of eternity, and what that might mean in relation to self-destruction, can perhaps better be understood in terms of permanence as finality. In any case, a pastoral exigency in our times is to present the very real risk that human freedom can be used for self-destruction; that presentation must be made in such a way that it is intelligible rather than simply matter for ridicule.

As Protestant theology has constantly pointed out, the idea of purgatory is not found in the Scriptures.[16] It may have arisen spontaneously from two considerations: first, there is the biblical sense, already mentioned, of the ambivalence of the imagery of fire, and of its use to express the human encounter with God; second, there is the realization that few people seem to die with the project of their lives an integrated and completed whole for good or evil. It seems coherent to envisage the encounter with God in death in terms of a consuming fire which, if it does not destroy, will purify and transform. Again, the insistence of church teaching on the reality of purgatory plays an important function in underscoring the seriousness of all life's choices, relationships, attitudes, and actions, and the redemptive need to restore integrity. There seems to be no reason in the nature of the case or in the tradition for insisting that purgatory means in the literal sense an extension of quasi-time outside worldly time, extended beyond the moment of death. The possibility of the imagery of purgatory representing another aspect of death as the divine judgment, demanding a refocusing and reordering of all aspects of the person's expectations and relationships, seems strong, credible, and intelligible.

The question whether salvation is in fact open to all, or only to those who have in some way been exposed to the self-revelation of God through Jesus Christ, has long preoccupied Christian thinkers. It provided arguments that led to the formulation of the notion of limbo.[17] The term *limbo* was introduced by Saint Albert the Great in the thirteenth century to designate a state of deprivation of blissful union with God which was not otherwise a state of punishment or torment. This idea accommodated the unresolved question about good people before the time of Christ and of children dying unbaptized. Yet the overwhelming weight of our tradition asserts the universal salvific will of God as the context within which all such questions must be asked.

While all questions of final salvation in specific instances remain hidden in the mystery of divine providence, there is every reason to conclude that God does not damn or exclude anyone without that person's deliberate rejection of redemptive grace. This leads to the

---

16. For church teaching on the existence of purgatory, see DS 838, from a letter of Pope Innocent IV to the papal legate to the Greeks in 1254; DS 1066 and 1067, from a letter of Pope Clement VI concerning reunion of the Armenian church in 1351; DS 856, from the profession of faith of Michael Palaeologus, agreed upon at the Council of Lyons in 1274; and DS 1867, from the Tridentine profession of faith, 1564.

17. The history of the notion of limbo is traced in some detail in George J. Dyer, *Limbo: Unsettled Question* (New York: Sheed and Ward, 1964).

inference that saving grace reaches many or most of the people of the earth in ways hidden from our scrutiny, even while we maintain that such grace flows to them because of the difference that the event of Jesus Christ has made in history. The manner of the connection or relationship provides matter for speculation that is of great interest and importance for the wider ecumenism. However, the coherence of Christian eschatology simply calls for the recognition that such an inclusive possibility of salvation must exist.

CONCLUSION:
THE SPIRITUALITY OF CHRISTIAN HOPE

It is clear that our hope shapes our Christian spirituality. As Christians we do not believe that time is simply cyclic. On the contrary, we see all of human history moving toward a very definite goal—the reign of God fully extended in all creation through the reconciliation of individual human beings and of human society as a whole. That means that we cannot accept any actual situation in history as simply the will of God, but must at all times look at all human situations critically. And the criteria for our assessment are the vision of Jesus and the person of Jesus as interpreting what is truly human and what is consonant in human society with the will and reign of God.

This perspective on human society and history calls for an active or prophetic spirituality—one that engages the world in all its relationships and structures in order to bring those relationships and structures, and the values and expectations on which they rest, into correspondence with the demands of the reign of God in human society. Such a spirituality necessarily embraces all aspects of life, public as well as private, professional as well as familial, technical as well as personal, economic and political as well as cultural and aesthetic.

Such a spirituality is in sharp contrast to one that is passive not only toward God but also toward the evil in human situations. It has at times seemed as though obedience to the commandments of God and the church, combined with sacramental worship and private prayer and the practice of virtue in private life, constituted Christian spirituality and held high hope of salvation after death. In this view, the sinfulness of human society and its values and structures was to be recognized in order to avoid its contaminating one's individual life, and that was best done by not becoming too involved in public and conflictual issues. The attitude to evil was to try to remain unsullied by it, rather than to act to change it. This attitude was consonant with a privatized perception of the content of Christian hope, seen as individual salvation of the soul after death. However, this attitude also belonged to an era when Christendom seemed established as God's interim reign on earth and when there was as yet little knowledge or empowerment to change the larger structures of society directly.

Today we live at a time when all things conspire to draw us into a more far-reaching interpretation of the content of hope as Jesus preached it: the conversion of the world to the reign of God.

FOR FURTHER READING

Boros, Ladislas. *The Mystery of Death.* New York: Herder, 1965.

Experiential, philosophical, and theological reflections on the phenomenon of death, presented sequentially to build up a Christian interpretation.

Hayes, Zachary. *Visions of a Future: A Study of Christian Eschatology.* Wilmington, Del.: Michael Glazier, 1989.

Systematic, up-to-date treatment of the content of Christian hope, on a strong historical foundation.

Hellwig, Monika. *What Are They Saying about Death and Christian Hope?* New York: Paulist Press, 1978.

Brief, nontechnical account of contemporary theology of death and beyond, within the context of the official teaching of the Catholic church.

Moltmann, Jürgen. *The Theology of Hope.* New York: Harper and Row, 1967.

The original exposition of the perspective on the Christian gospel which considers it in the large socio-economic and political realm of human responsibility and creativity.

Mussner, Franz, et al. *Readings in Christian Eschatology.* Derby, N.Y.: Society of St. Paul, 1966.

Short, incisive essays by ten renowned European theologians on key issues in contemporary individual eschatology, written in nontechnical style and language.

Rahner, Karl. *On the Theology of Death.* New York: Seabury, 1973.

An elaboration of the implications of Rahner's anthropology for the interpretation of death as biological phenomenon, death as consequence of sin, and death in Christ; philosophical in style and vocabulary.

Ratzinger, Joseph. *Eschatology*. Washington, D.C.: Catholic University of America Press, 1989.

A more traditional interpretation by an influential contemporary theologian.

Richards, Hubert J. *Death and After: What Will Really Happen?* Mystic, Conn.: Twenty-Third Publications, 1987.

A succinct but very comprehensive discussion of New Testament eschatology, written in response to contemporary questions in a style accessible to any careful reader.

Schillebeeckx, Edward, and Boniface Willems, eds. *The Problem of Eschatology*. Entire issue of *Concilium* 41. New York: Paulist Press, 1969.

Essays by well-known authors applying contemporary questions about the future of the world to the traditional themes of Christian eschatology; in style and vocabulary accessible to any educated reader.

Schnackenburg, Rudolf. *God's Rule and Kingdom*. 2d ed. New York: Herder, 1968.

An extremely thorough study of the biblical foundations of Christian eschatology, focusing on the theme of the reign of God; written for any educated and attentive reader, using occasional Greek and Hebrew terms.

Van de Walle, A. R. *From Darkness to the Dawn*. Mystic, Conn.: Twenty-Third Publications, 1985.

A careful systematic elaboration of all the traditional elements of eschatology, based on Scripture, tradition, and contemporary experience, emphasizing practical implications.

INDEX